Oh My Goddess!

ああ女神さま

WRONG NUMBER

PUBLISHER
Mike Richardson

SERIES EDITORS
Peet Janes & Mike Hansen

COLLECTION EDITOR
Chris Warner

COLLECTION DESIGNER
Amy Arendts

ART DIRECTOR
Mark Cox

*English-language version produced by Studio Proteus
and Dark Horse Comics, Inc.*

OH MY GODDESS! Vol. I: Wrong Number

This volume collects issue one of the Dark Horse comic-book series *Oh My Goddess!* and stories from issues one through five of the Dark Horse comic-book series *Super Manga Blast!*

Published by
Dark Horse Comics, Inc.
10956 SE Main Street
Milwaukie, OR 97222

www.darkhorse.com

To find a comics shop in your area, call the Comic Shop
Locator Service toll-free at 1-888-266-4226

First edition: June 2002
ISBN: 1-56971-669-2

3 5 7 9 10 8 6 4
Printed in Canada

Oh My Goddess!

あぁ女神さま WRONG NUMBER

STORY AND ART BY
Kosuke Fujishima

TRANSLATION BY
Dana Lewis, Alan Gleason & Toren Smith

LETTERING AND TOUCH-UP BY
Susie Lee & PC Orz, Pat Duke & Radio Comix, Digital Chameleon, Jason Hvam, Chris Chalenor

DARK HORSE COMICS®

Kosuke Fujishima

Born in 1964, Kosuke Fujishima began his comics career just after graduating high school as an editor for comics news magazine, *Puff*. An interview he conducted with *Be Free!* creator Tatsuya Egawa led to becoming Egawa's assistant, which led to Fujishima's first professional panel work, a comics-style report on the making of the live-action *Be Free!* film. Fan mail he received for the piece inspired him to create *You're Under Arrest!* which was serialized in *Morning Party Extra* beginning in 1986.

In 1988, Fujishima created a four-panel gag cartoon that featured the *YUA!* characters praying to a goddess. Fujishima was so pleased with the way the goddess turned out that she became the basis for Belldandy and inspired the creation of the *Oh My Goddess!* series for *Afternoon* magazine, where it still runs today after more than a decade.

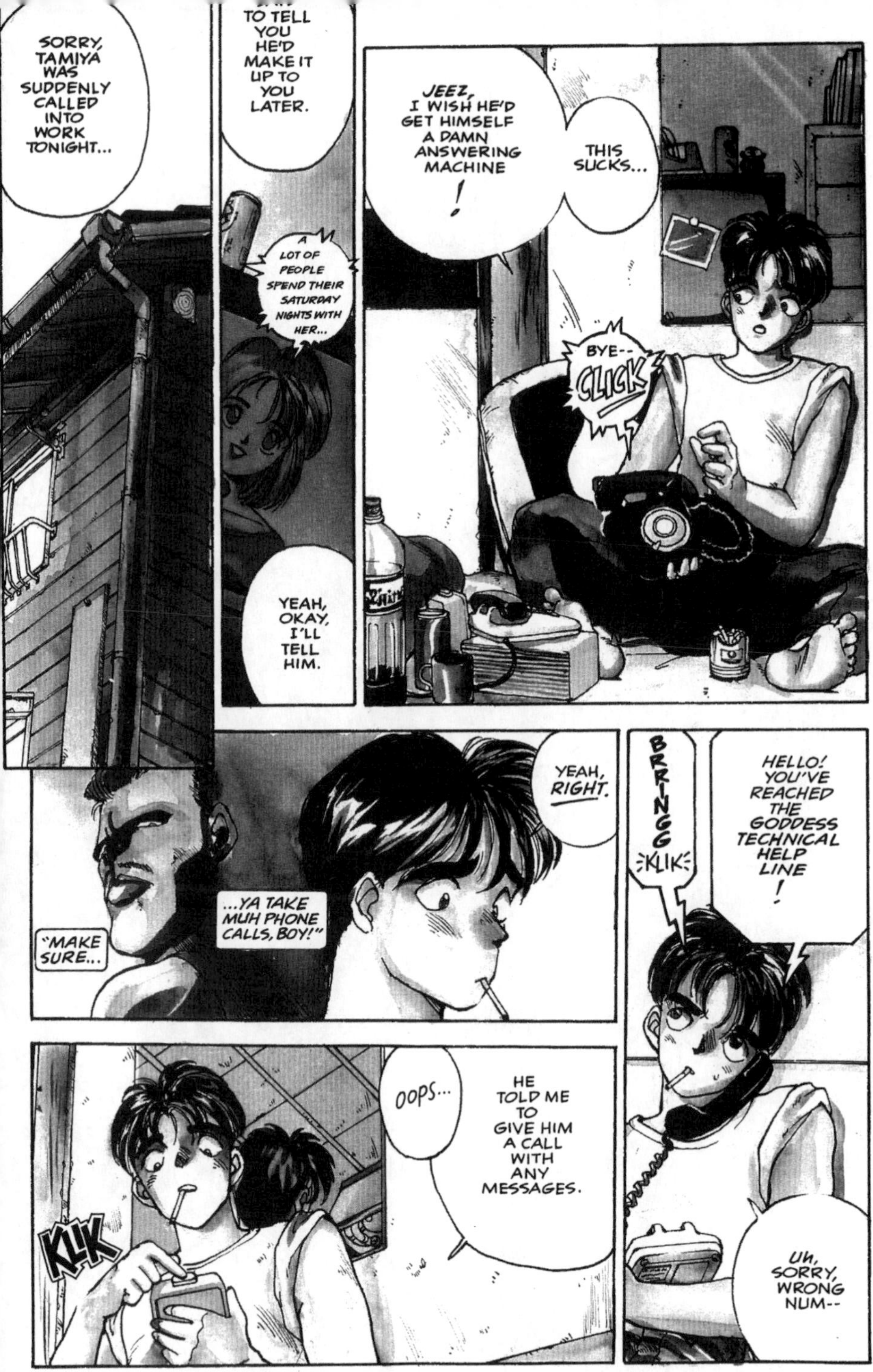
SORRY, TAMIYA WAS SUDDENLY CALLED INTO WORK TONIGHT...
TO TELL YOU HE'D MAKE IT UP TO YOU LATER.
A LOT OF PEOPLE SPEND THEIR SATURDAY NIGHTS WITH HER...
YEAH, OKAY, I'LL TELL HIM.
JEEZ, I WISH HE'D GET HIMSELF A DAMN ANSWERING MACHINE!
THIS SUCKS...
BYE--
CLICK
"MAKE SURE...
...YA TAKE MUH PHONE CALLS, BOY!"
YEAH, RIGHT.
OOPS...
HE TOLD ME TO GIVE HIM A CALL WITH ANY MESSAGES.
KLIK
BRRINGG
KLIK
HELLO! YOU'VE REACHED THE GODDESS TECHNICAL HELP LINE!
UH, SORRY, WRONG NUM--

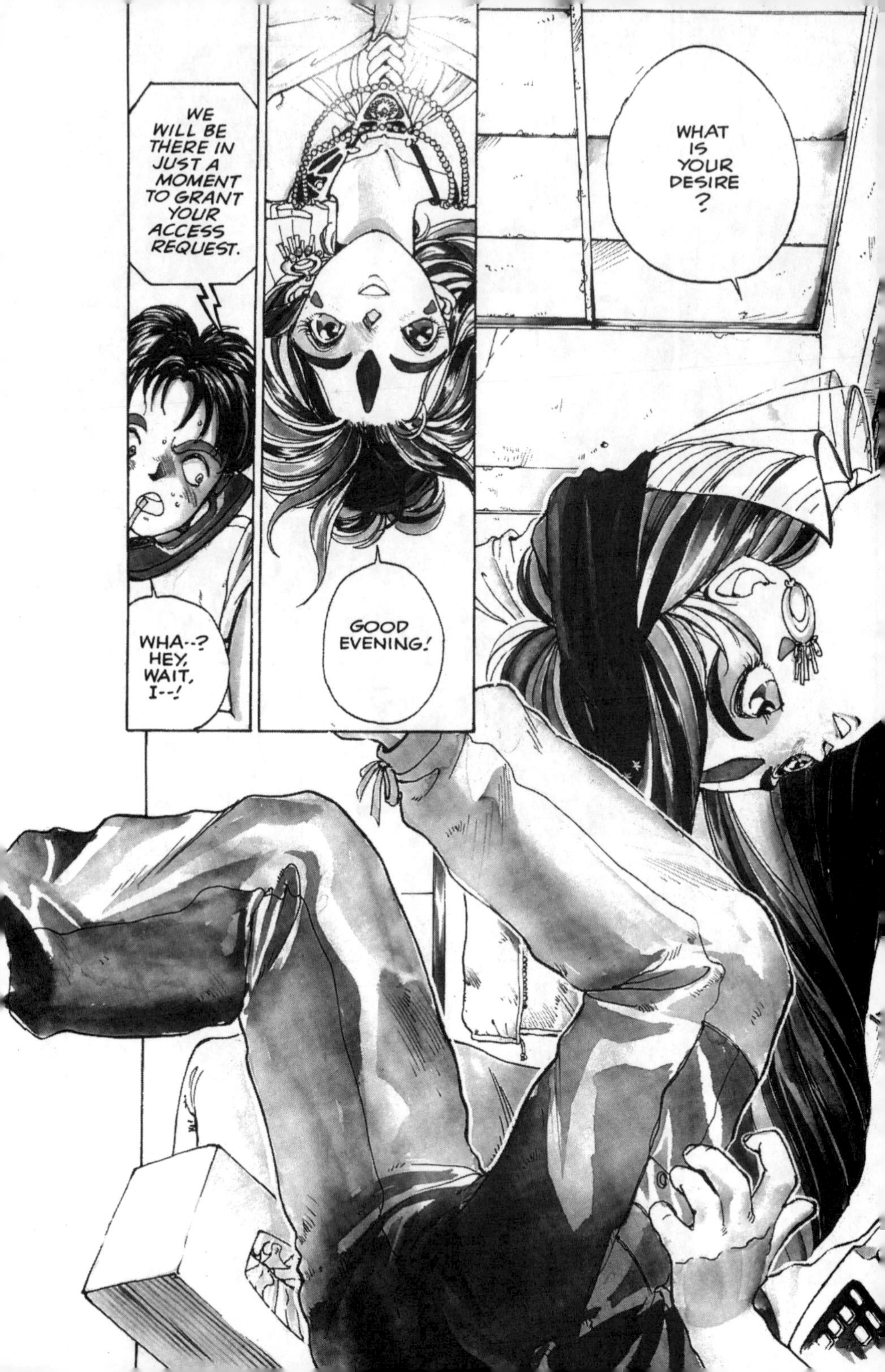
WE WILL BE THERE IN JUST A MOMENT TO GRANT YOUR ACCESS REQUEST.
WHA--? HEY, WAIT, I--!
GOOD EVENING!
WHAT IS YOUR DESIRE ?

WRONG NUMBER

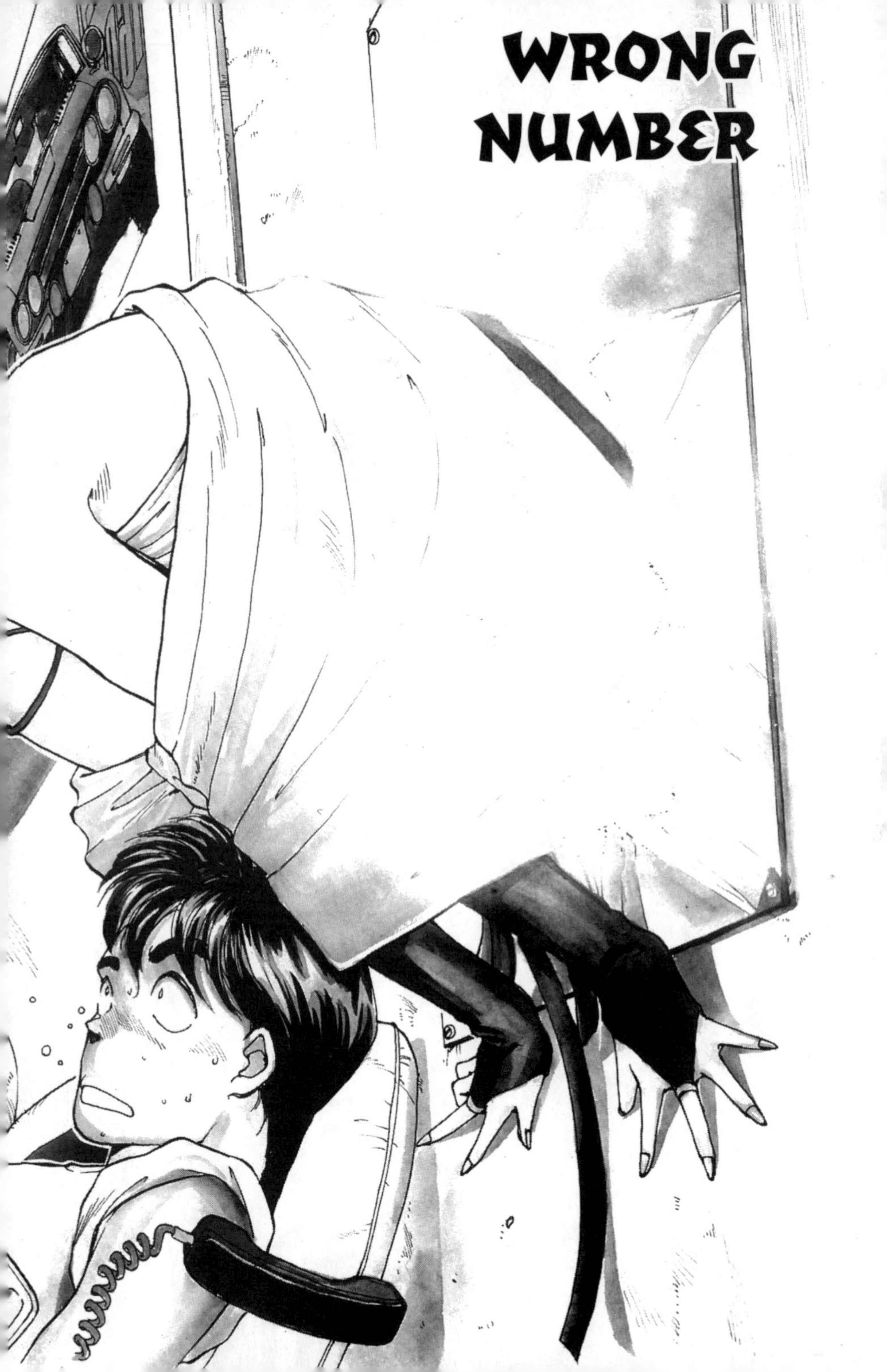

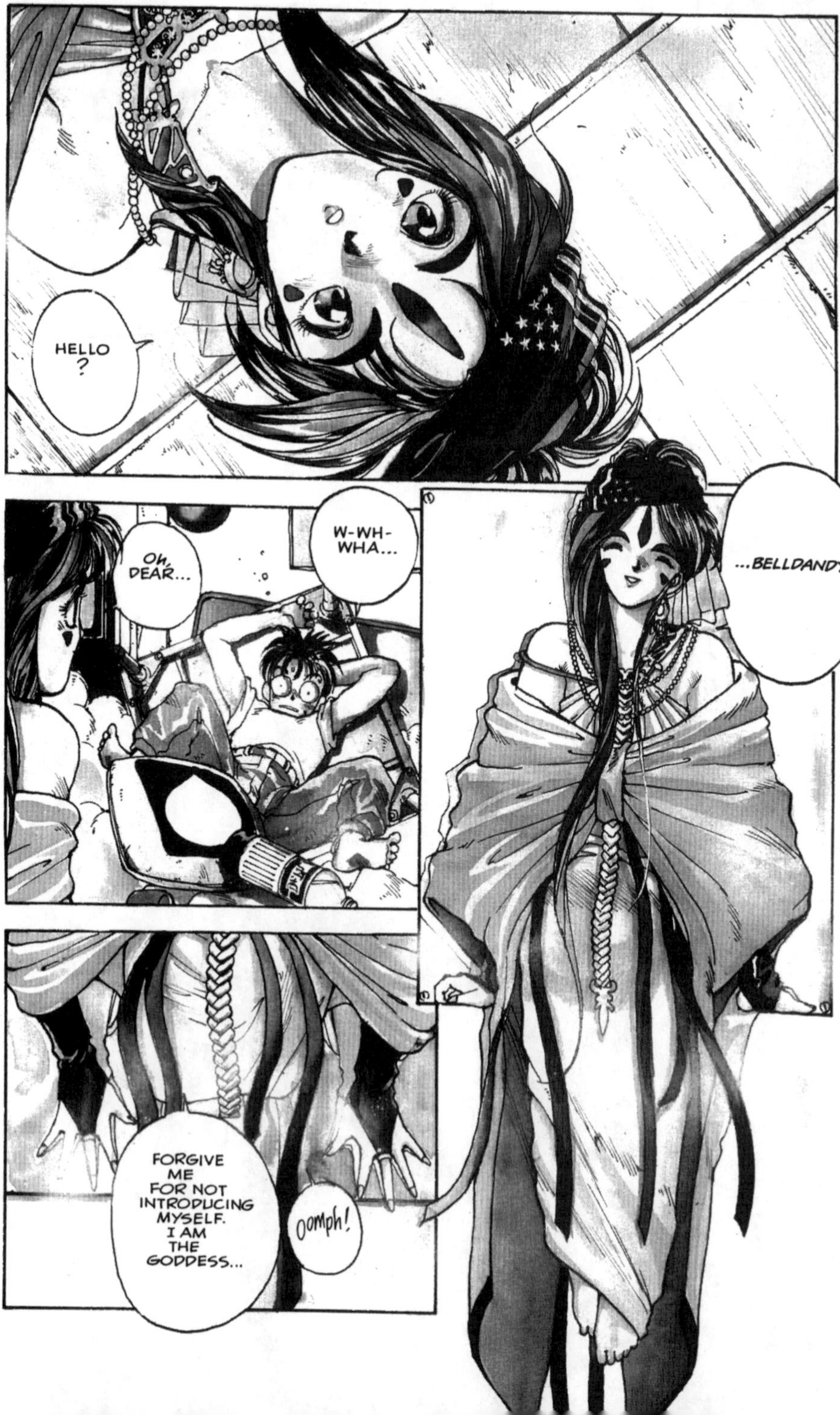
HELLO ?
Oh, DEAR...
W-WH-WHA...
...BELLDANDY.
FORGIVE ME FOR NOT INTRODUCING MYSELF. I AM THE GODDESS...
oomph!

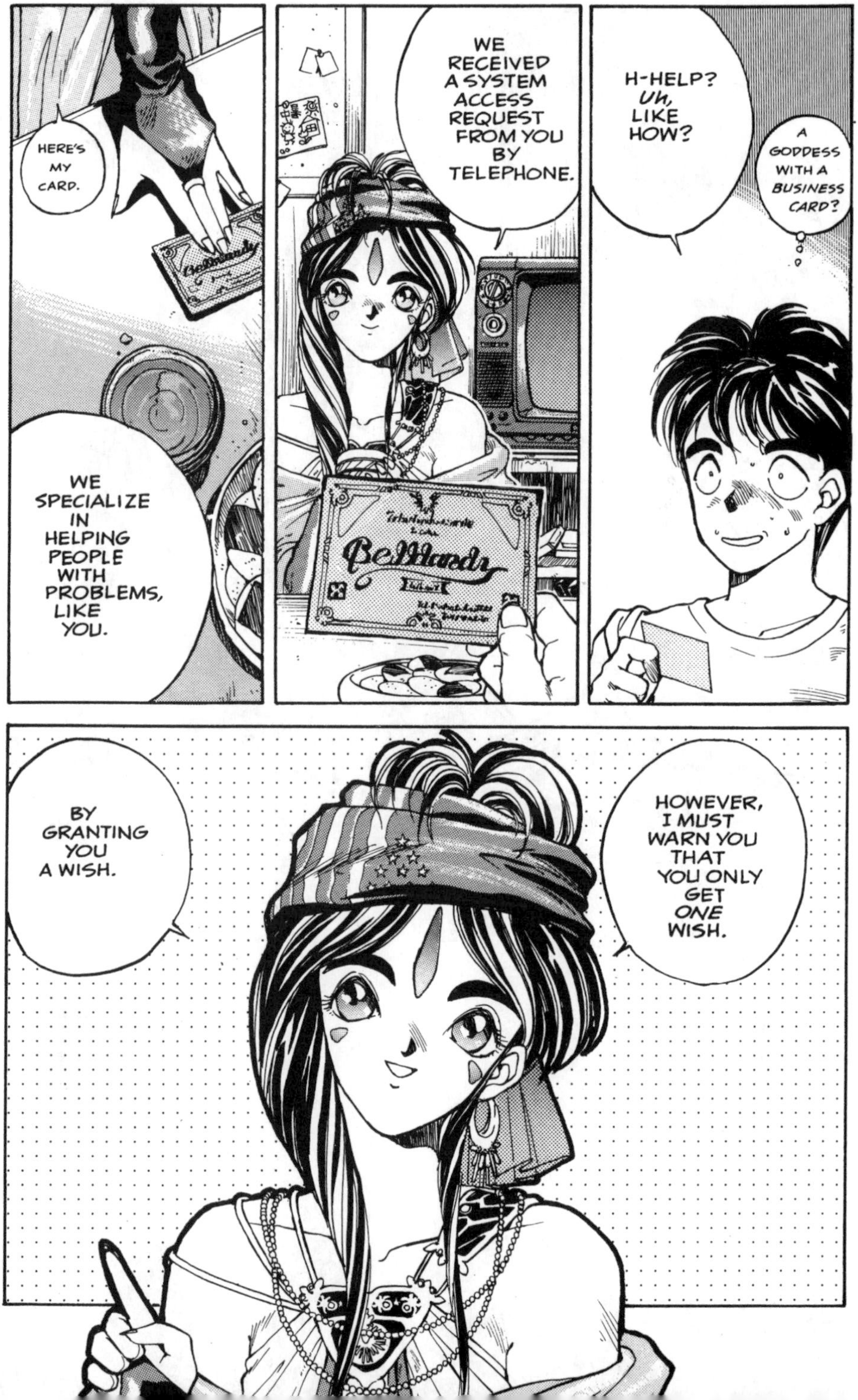
HERE'S MY CARD.
WE SPECIALIZE IN HELPING PEOPLE WITH PROBLEMS, LIKE YOU.
WE RECEIVED A SYSTEM ACCESS REQUEST FROM YOU BY TELEPHONE.
H-HELP? *Uh,* LIKE HOW?
A GODDESS WITH A *BUSINESS* CARD?
BY GRANTING YOU A WISH.
HOWEVER, I MUST WARN YOU THAT YOU ONLY GET *ONE* WISH.

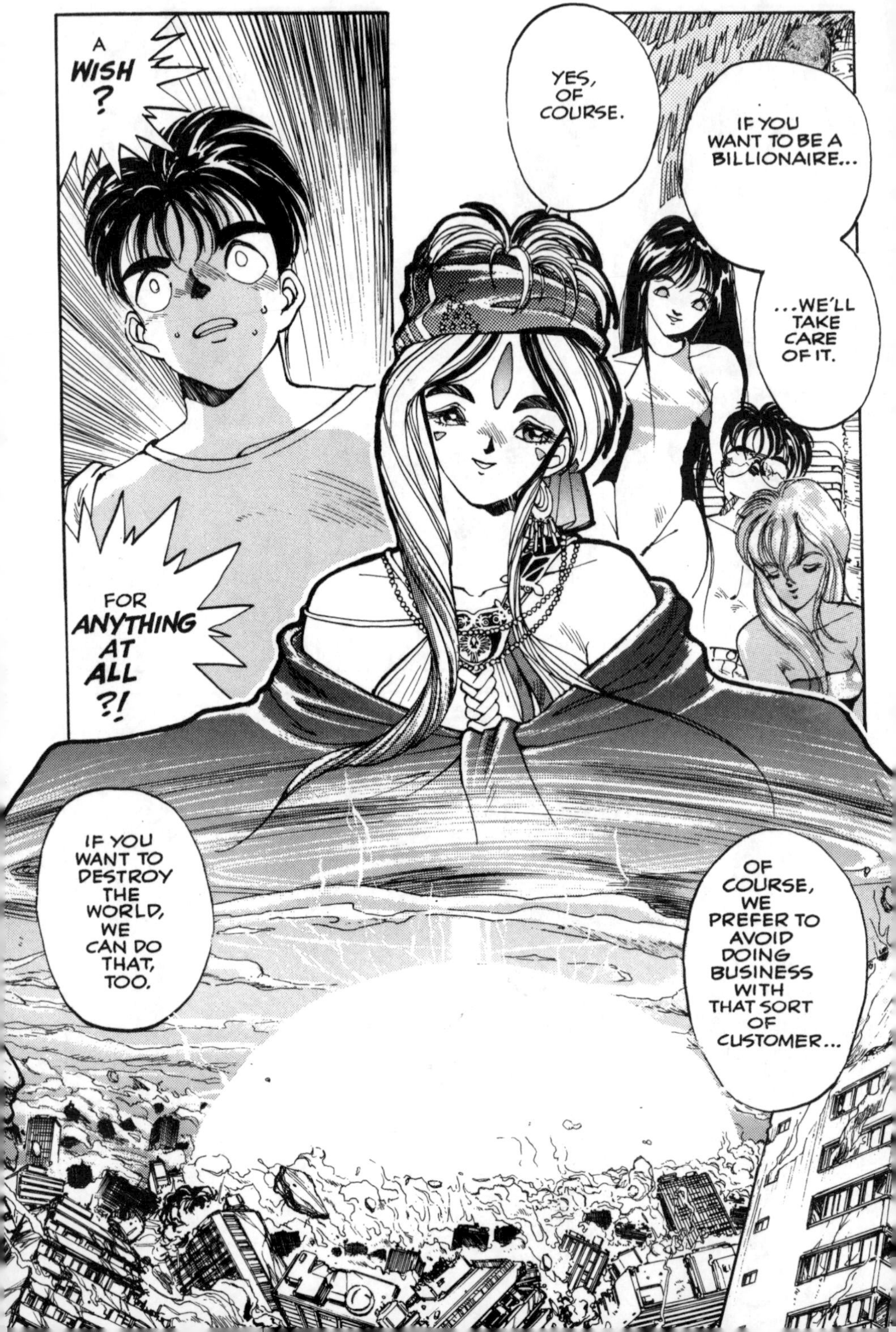
A WISH?
FOR ANYTHING AT ALL?!
YES, OF COURSE.
IF YOU WANT TO BE A BILLIONAIRE...
...WE'LL TAKE CARE OF IT.
IF YOU WANT TO DESTROY THE WORLD, WE CAN DO THAT, TOO.
OF COURSE, WE PREFER TO AVOID DOING BUSINESS WITH THAT SORT OF CUSTOMER...

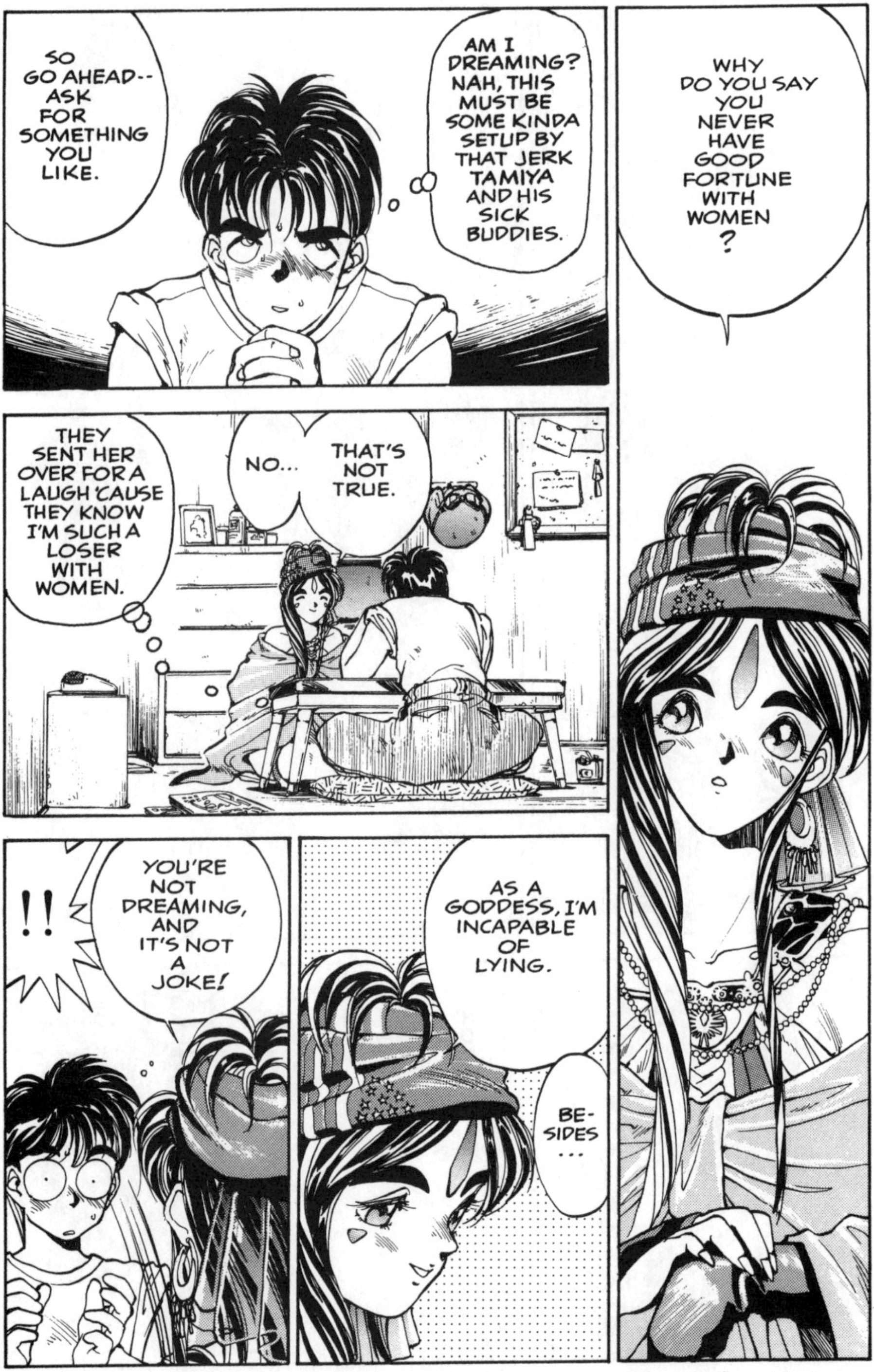
SO GO AHEAD-- ASK FOR SOMETHING YOU LIKE.
AM I DREAMING? NAH, THIS MUST BE SOME KINDA SETUP BY THAT JERK TAMIYA AND HIS SICK BUDDIES.
THEY SENT HER OVER FOR A LAUGH 'CAUSE THEY KNOW I'M SUCH A LOSER WITH WOMEN.
NO...
THAT'S NOT TRUE.
!!
YOU'RE NOT DREAMING, AND IT'S NOT A JOKE!
AS A GODDESS, I'M INCAPABLE OF LYING.
BE-SIDES...
WHY DO YOU SAY YOU NEVER HAVE GOOD FORTUNE WITH WOMEN?

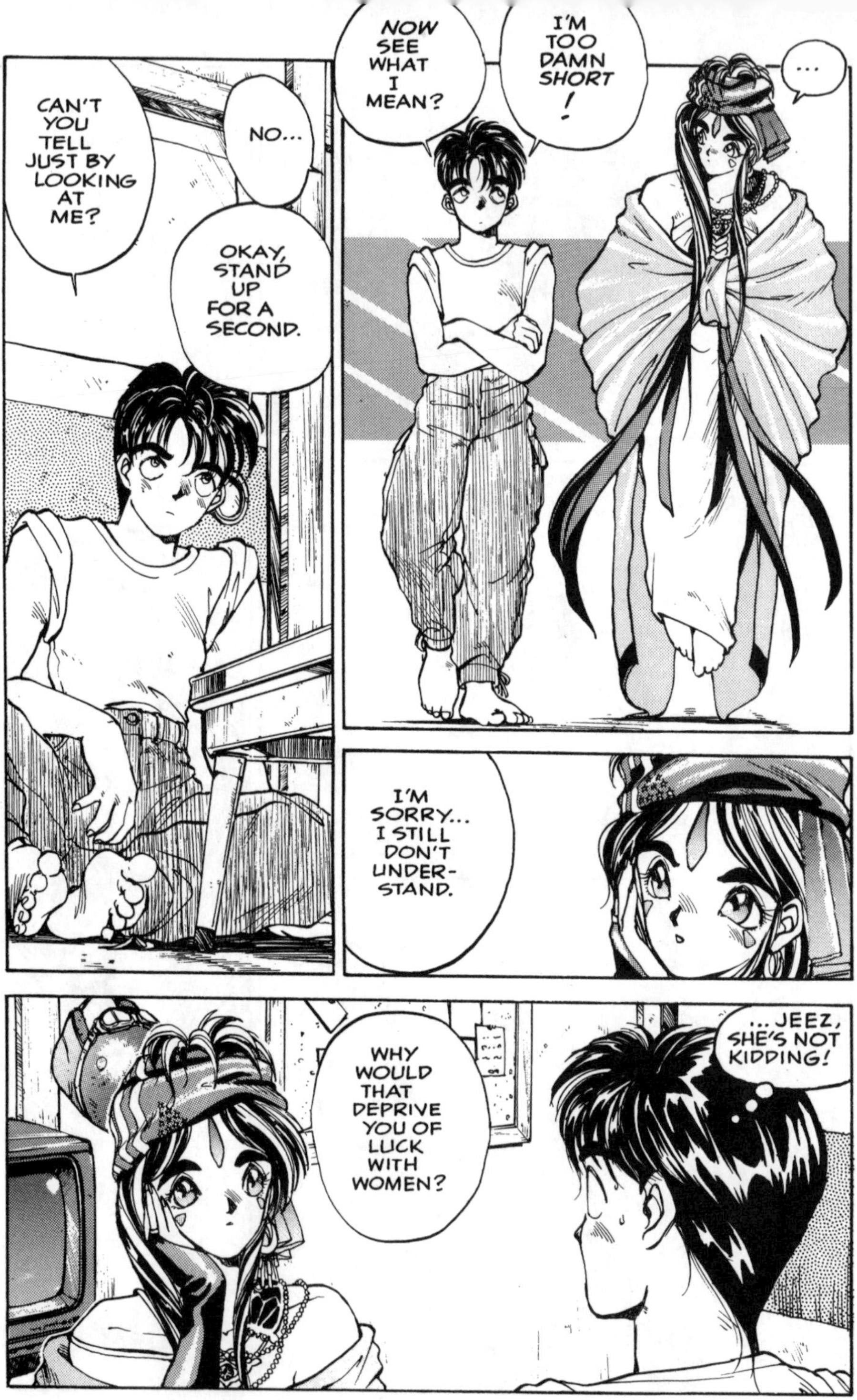
CAN'T YOU TELL JUST BY LOOKING AT ME?
NO...
OKAY, STAND UP FOR A SECOND.
NOW SEE WHAT I MEAN?
I'M TOO DAMN SHORT!
...
I'M SORRY... I STILL DON'T UNDER-STAND.
WHY WOULD THAT DEPRIVE YOU OF LUCK WITH WOMEN?
...JEEZ, SHE'S NOT KIDDING!

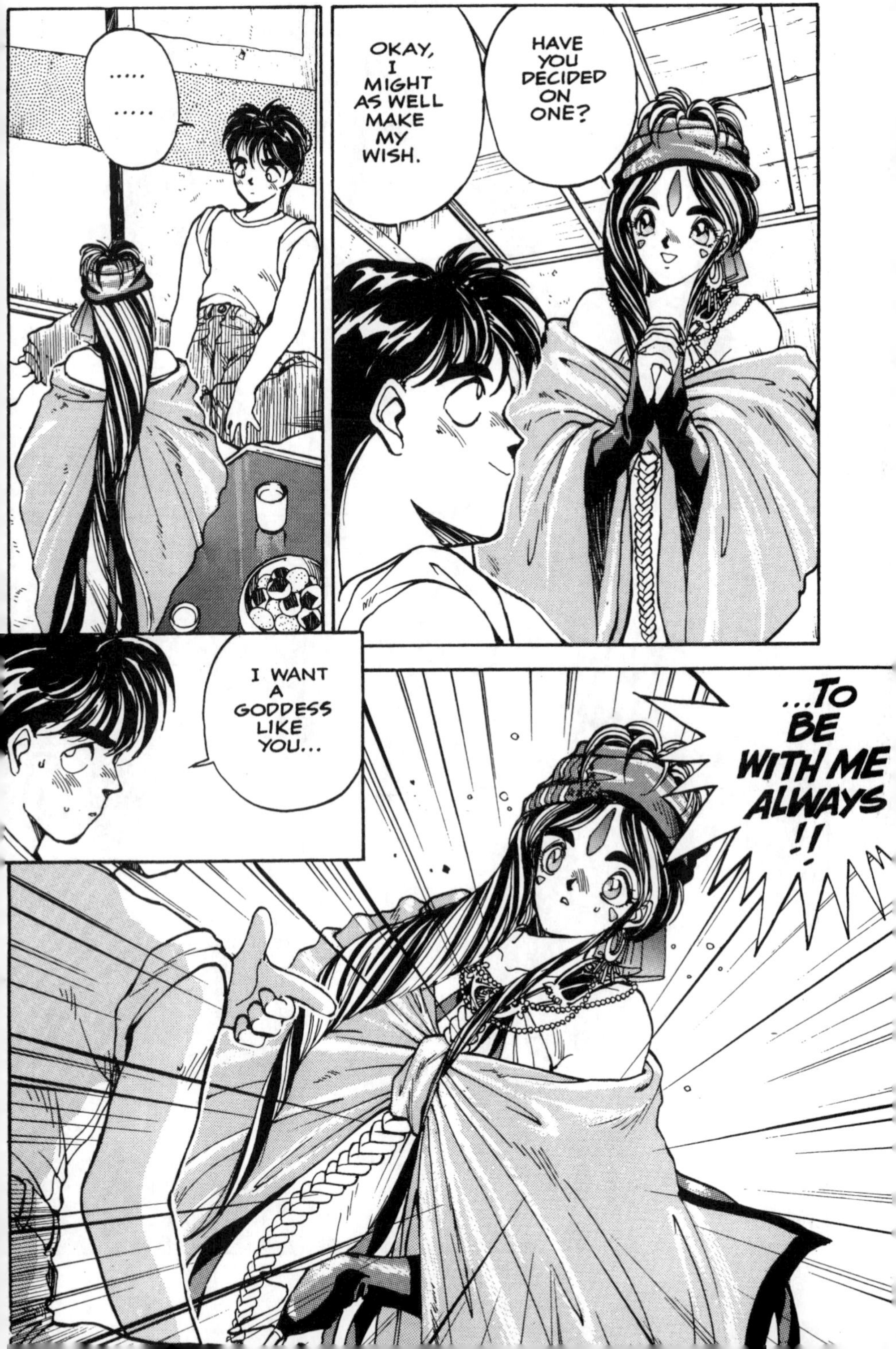
.....
.....
HAVE YOU DECIDED ON ONE?
OKAY, I MIGHT AS WELL MAKE MY WISH.
I WANT A GODDESS LIKE YOU...
...TO BE WITH ME ALWAYS!!

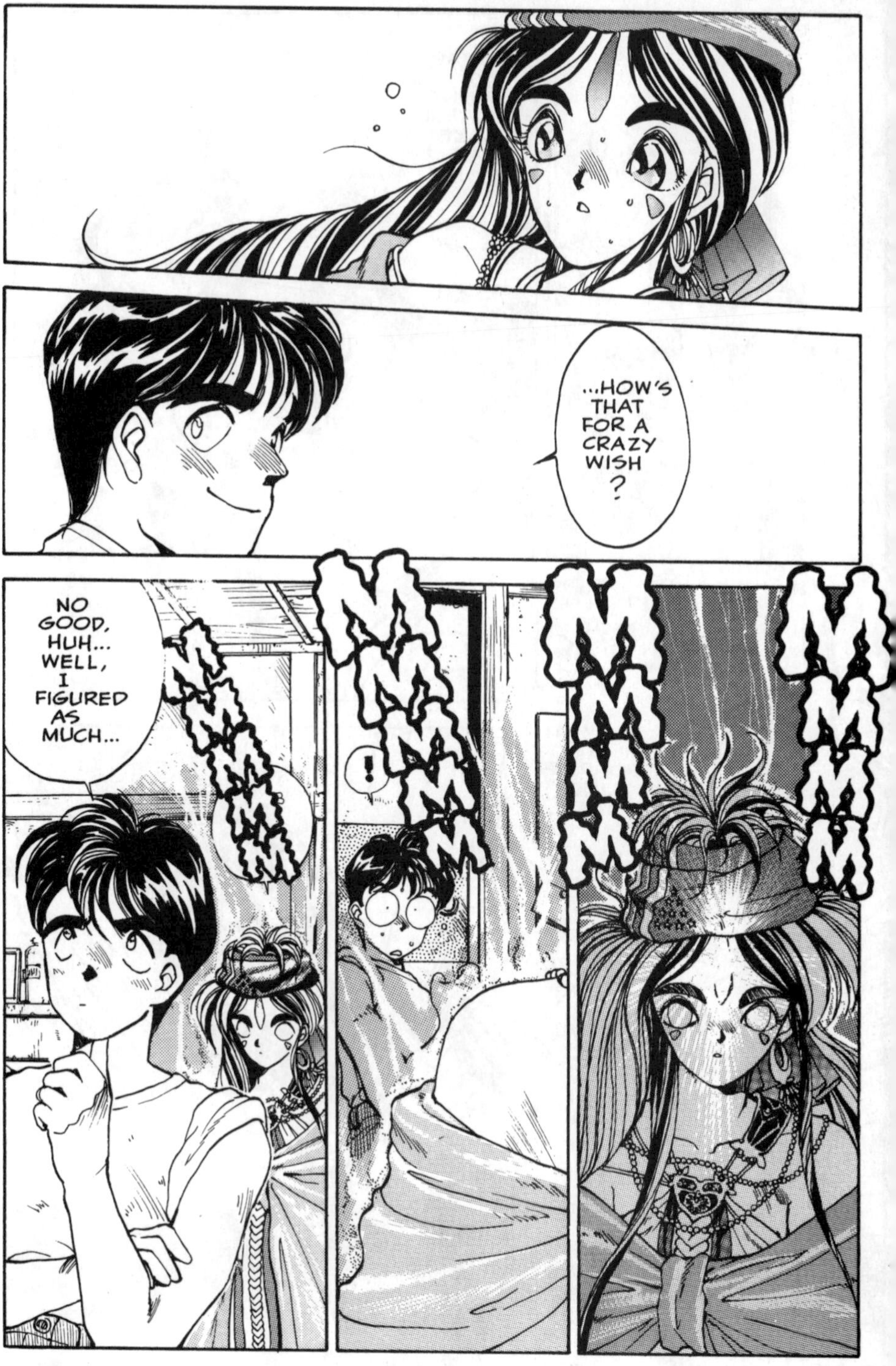
...HOW'S THAT FOR A CRAZY WISH ?
NO GOOD, HUH... WELL, I FIGURED AS MUCH...
MMMMMM
!
MMMMMM
MMMMM
MMMMMM

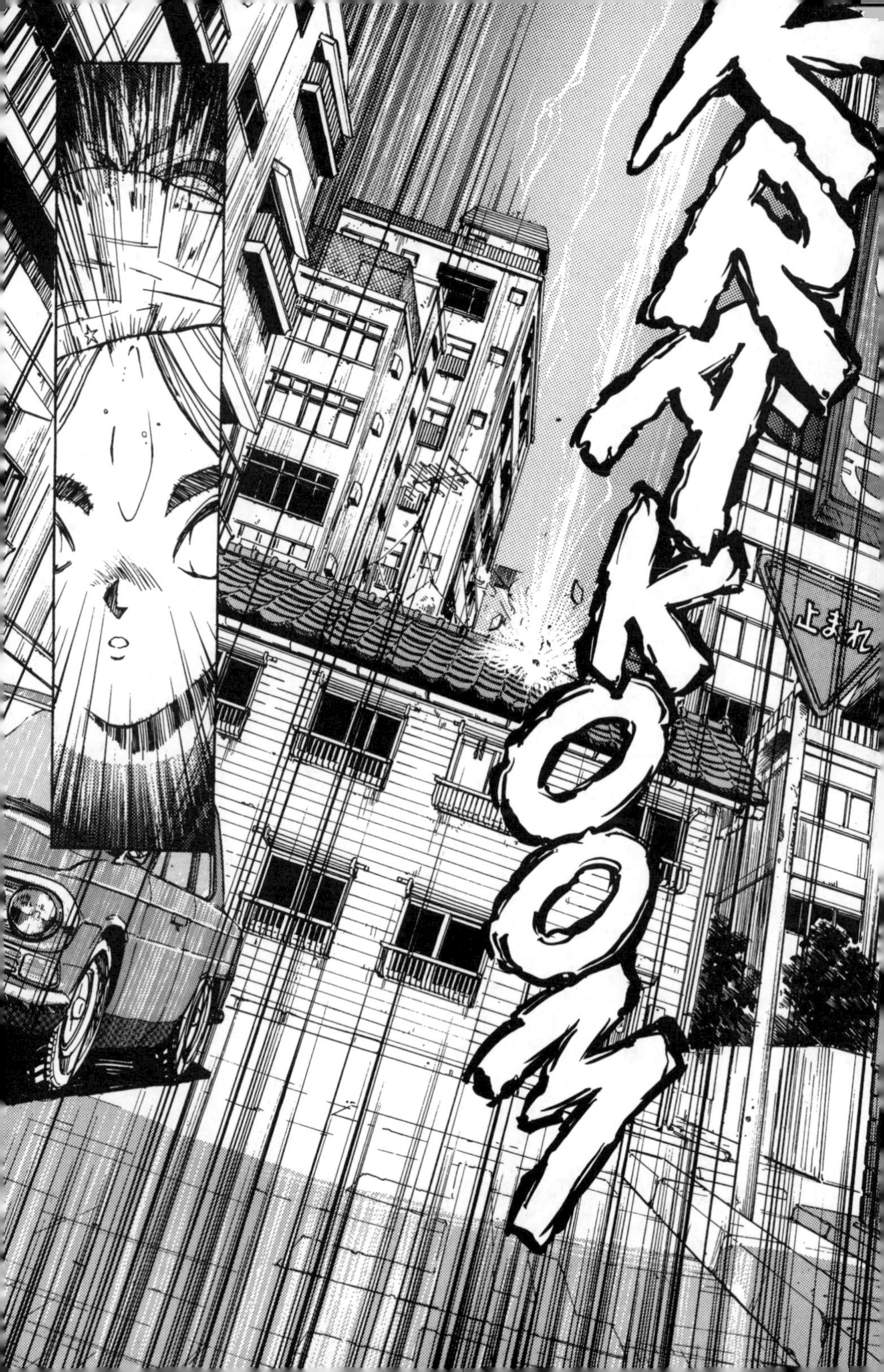
KRAKOOM
止まれ

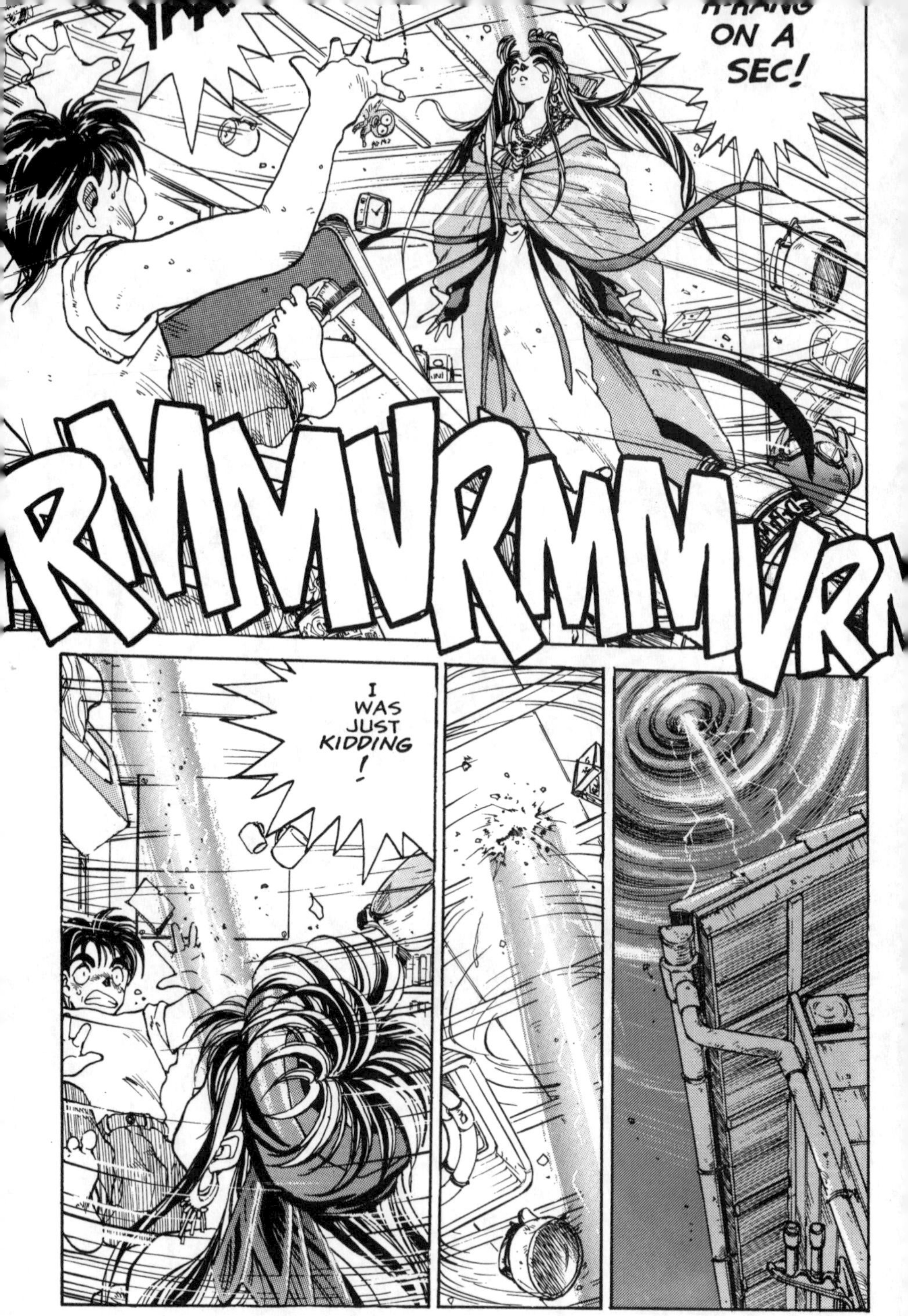
ON A SEC!
RMMVRMMMVR
I WAS JUST KIDDING!

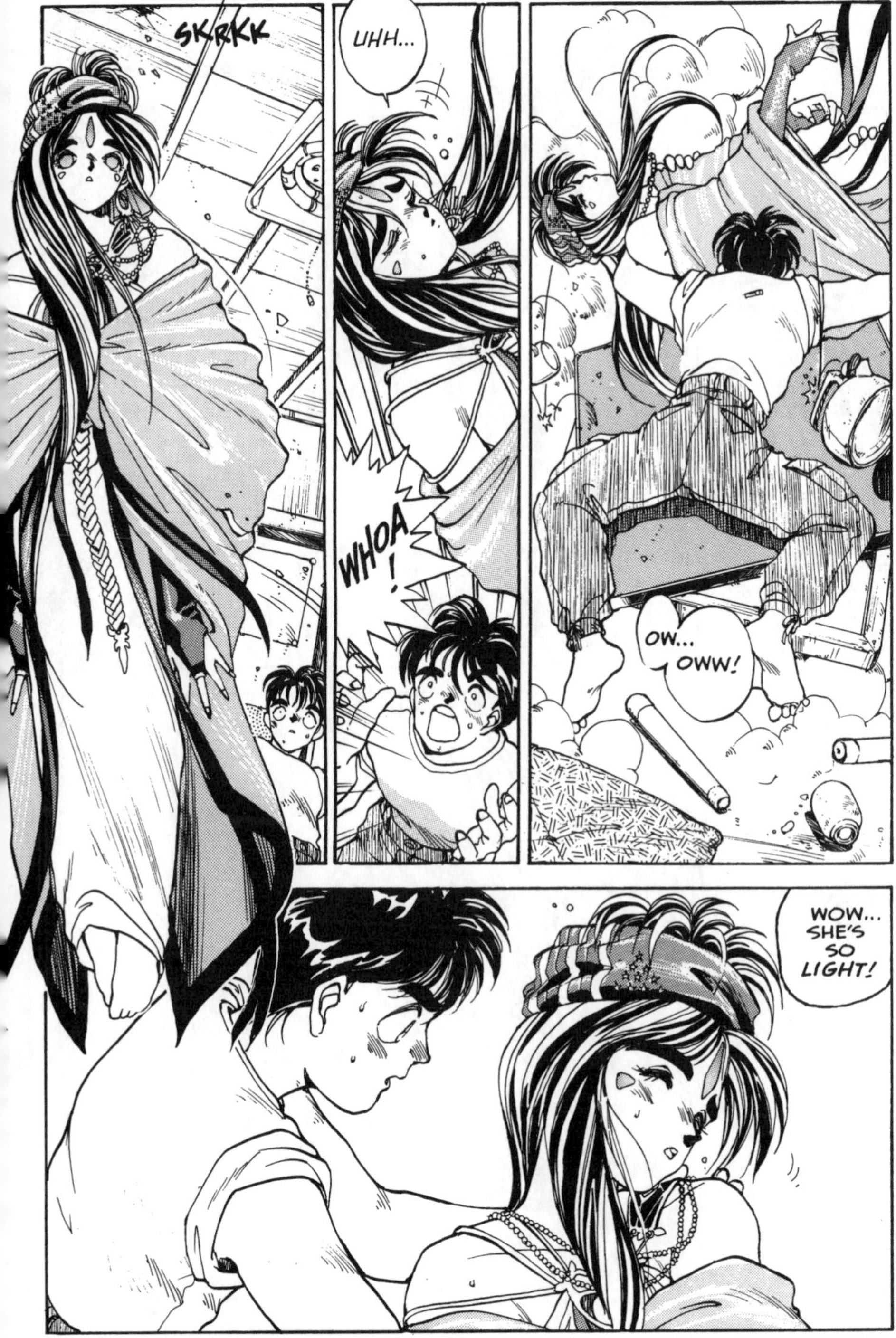
SKRKK
UHH...
WHOA!
OW... OWW!
WOW... SHE'S SO LIGHT!

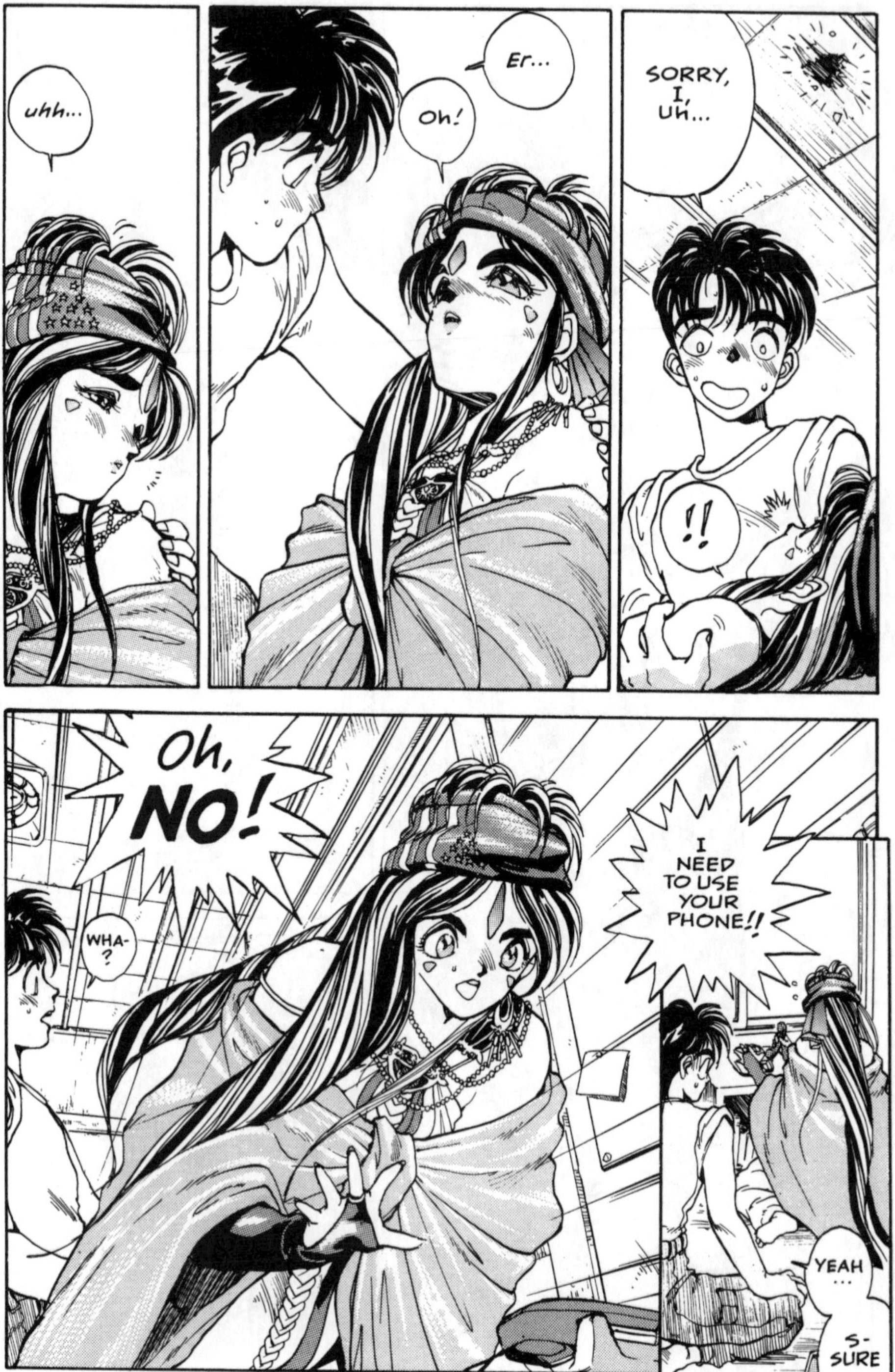
uhh...
Er...
Oh!
SORRY, I, UH...
!!
Oh, NO!
WHA-?
I NEED TO USE YOUR PHONE!!
YEAH...
S-SURE...

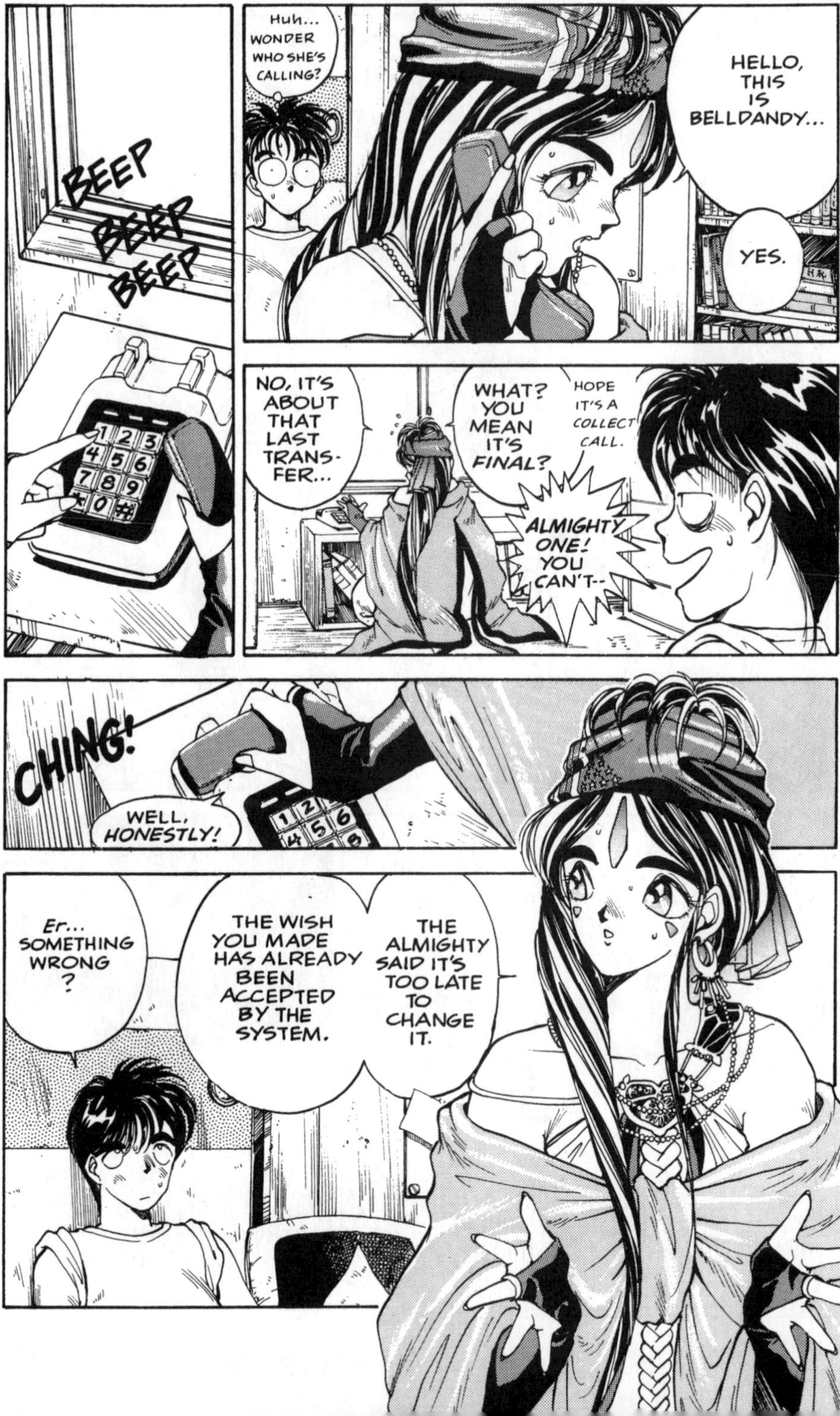
BEEP BEEP BEEP
Huh... WONDER WHO SHE'S CALLING?
HELLO, THIS IS BELLDANDY...
YES.
NO, IT'S ABOUT THAT LAST TRANSFER...
WHAT? YOU MEAN IT'S *FINAL*?
HOPE IT'S A COLLECT CALL.
ALMIGHTY ONE! YOU CAN'T--
CHING!
WELL, *HONESTLY!*
Er... SOMETHING WRONG?
THE WISH YOU MADE HAS ALREADY BEEN ACCEPTED BY THE SYSTEM.
THE ALMIGHTY SAID IT'S TOO LATE TO CHANGE IT.

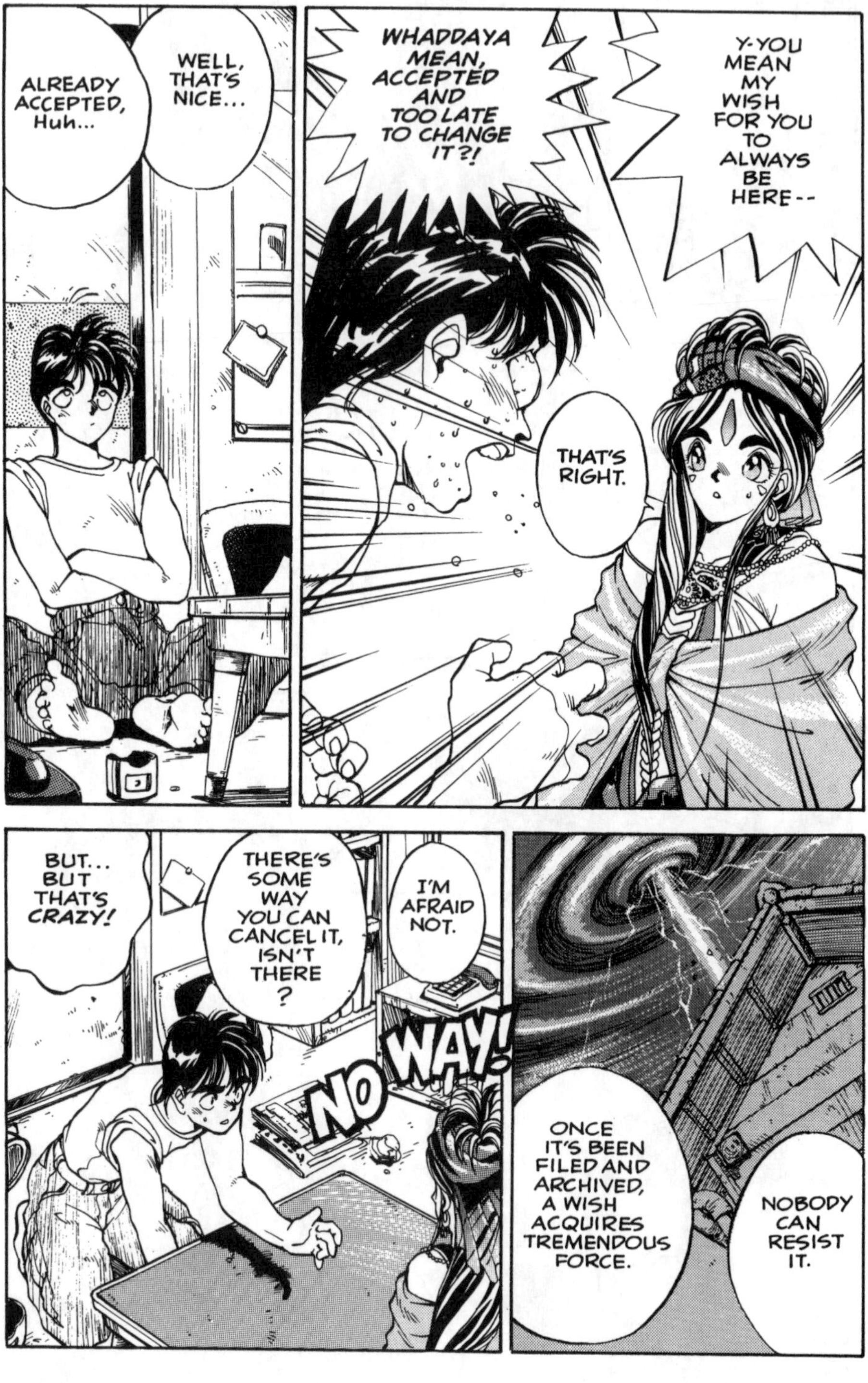
ALREADY ACCEPTED, Huh...
WELL, THAT'S NICE...
WHADDAYA MEAN, ACCEPTED AND TOO LATE TO CHANGE IT?!
Y-YOU MEAN MY WISH FOR YOU TO ALWAYS BE HERE--
THAT'S RIGHT.
BUT... BUT THAT'S CRAZY!
THERE'S SOME WAY YOU CAN CANCEL IT, ISN'T THERE ?
I'M AFRAID NOT.
NO WAY!
ONCE IT'S BEEN FILED AND ARCHIVED, A WISH ACQUIRES TREMENDOUS FORCE.
NOBODY CAN RESIST IT.

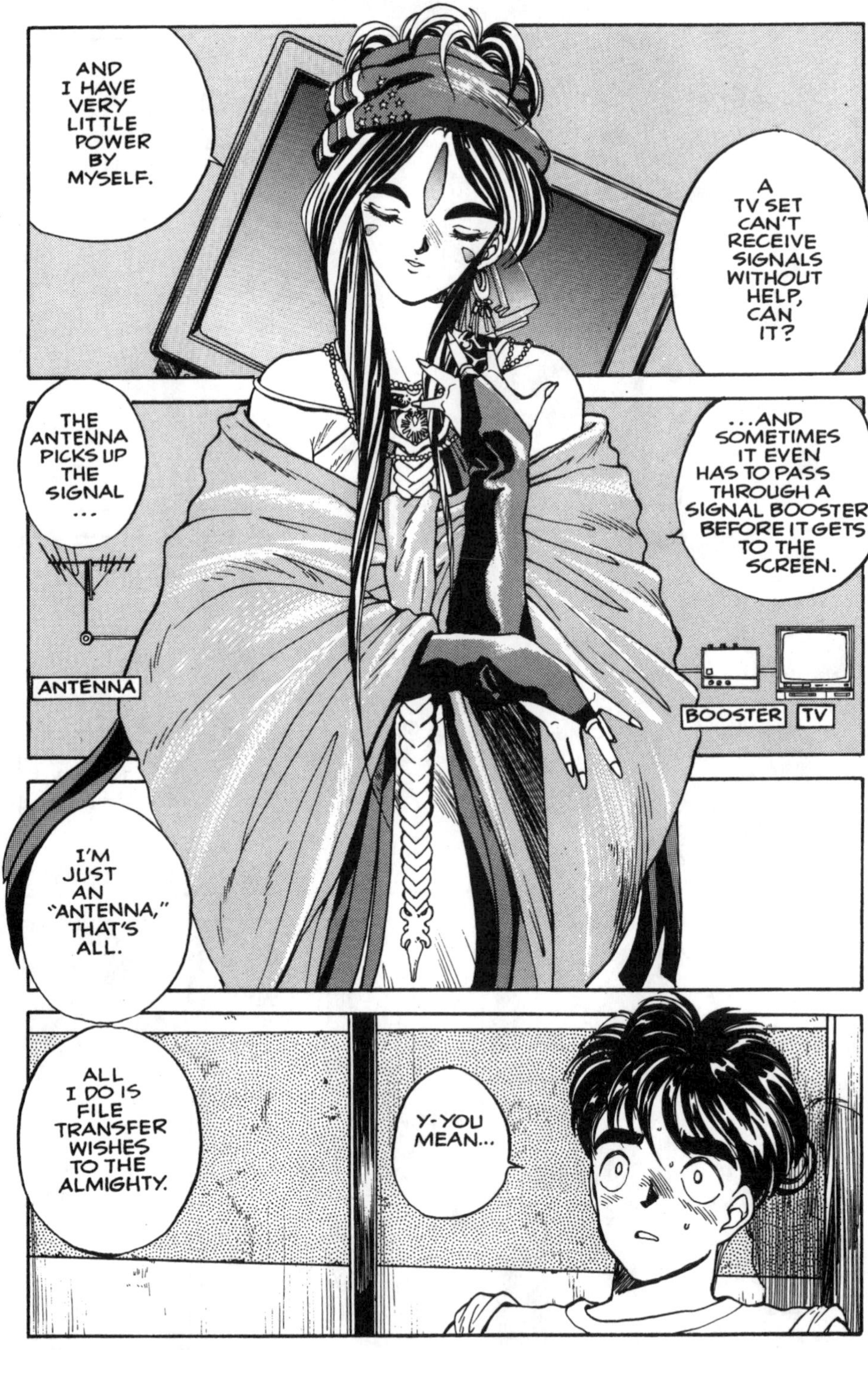
AND I HAVE VERY LITTLE POWER BY MYSELF.
A TV SET CAN'T RECEIVE SIGNALS WITHOUT HELP, CAN IT?
THE ANTENNA PICKS UP THE SIGNAL ...
...AND SOMETIMES IT EVEN HAS TO PASS THROUGH A SIGNAL BOOSTER BEFORE IT GETS TO THE SCREEN.
ANTENNA
BOOSTER
TV
I'M JUST AN "ANTENNA," THAT'S ALL.
ALL I DO IS FILE TRANSFER WISHES TO THE ALMIGHTY.
Y-YOU MEAN...

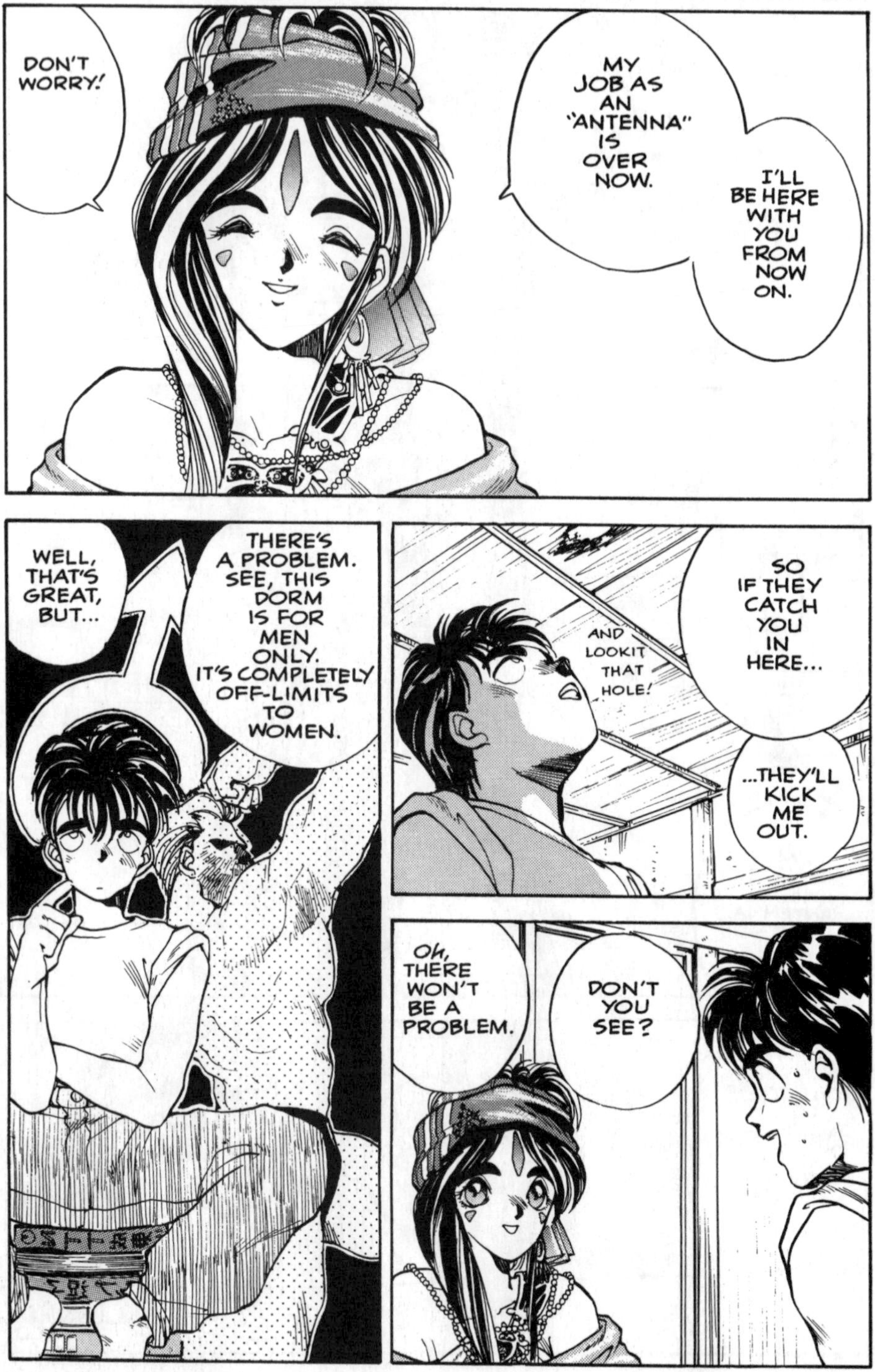
DON'T WORRY!
MY JOB AS AN "ANTENNA" IS OVER NOW.
I'LL BE HERE WITH YOU FROM NOW ON.
WELL, THAT'S GREAT, BUT...
THERE'S A PROBLEM. SEE, THIS DORM IS FOR MEN ONLY. IT'S COMPLETELY OFF-LIMITS TO WOMEN.
AND LOOKIT THAT HOLE!
SO IF THEY CATCH YOU IN HERE...
...THEY'LL KICK ME OUT.
Oh, THERE WON'T BE A PROBLEM.
DON'T YOU SEE?

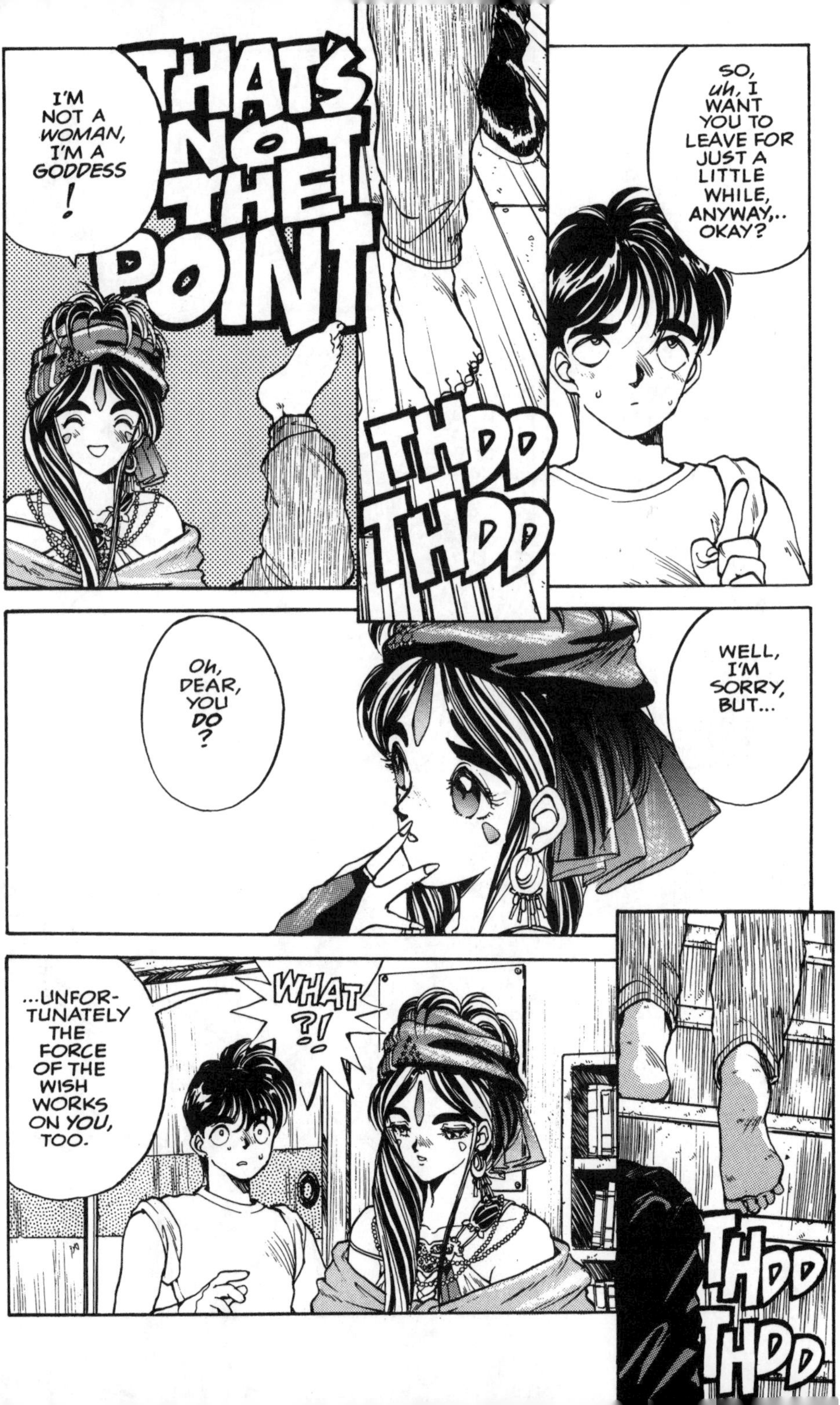
I'M NOT A WOMAN, I'M A GODDESS!
THAT'S NOT THE POINT
THDD THDD
SO, uh, I WANT YOU TO LEAVE FOR JUST A LITTLE WHILE, ANYWAY... OKAY?
Oh, DEAR, YOU DO?
WELL, I'M SORRY, BUT...
...UNFORTUNATELY THE FORCE OF THE WISH WORKS ON YOU, TOO.
WHAT ?!
THDD THDD

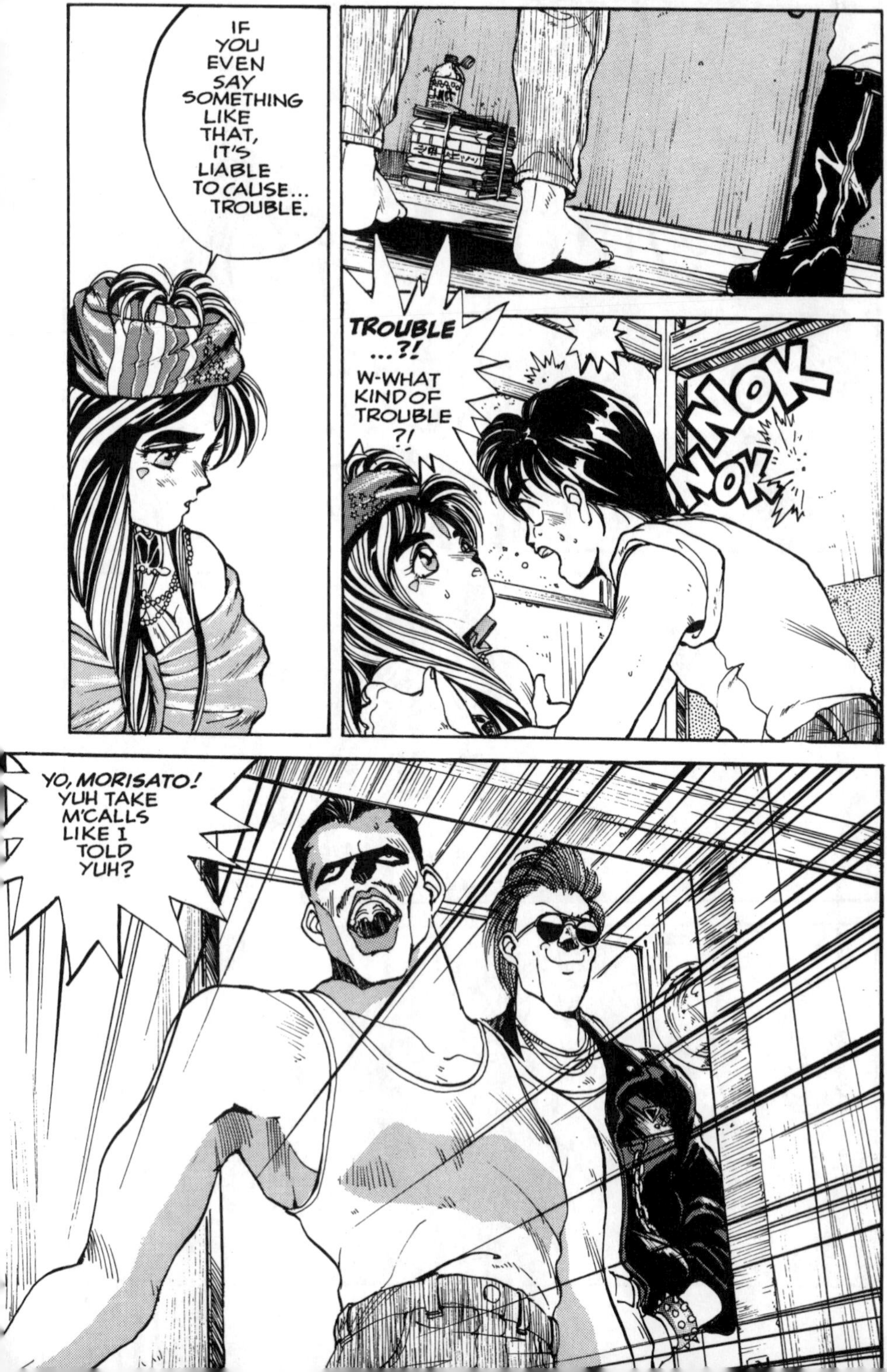
IF YOU EVEN SAY SOMETHING LIKE THAT, IT'S LIABLE TO CAUSE... TROUBLE.
TROUBLE ...?!
W-WHAT KIND OF TROUBLE ?!
NOK NOK
YO, MORISATO! YUH TAKE M'CALLS LIKE I TOLD YUH?

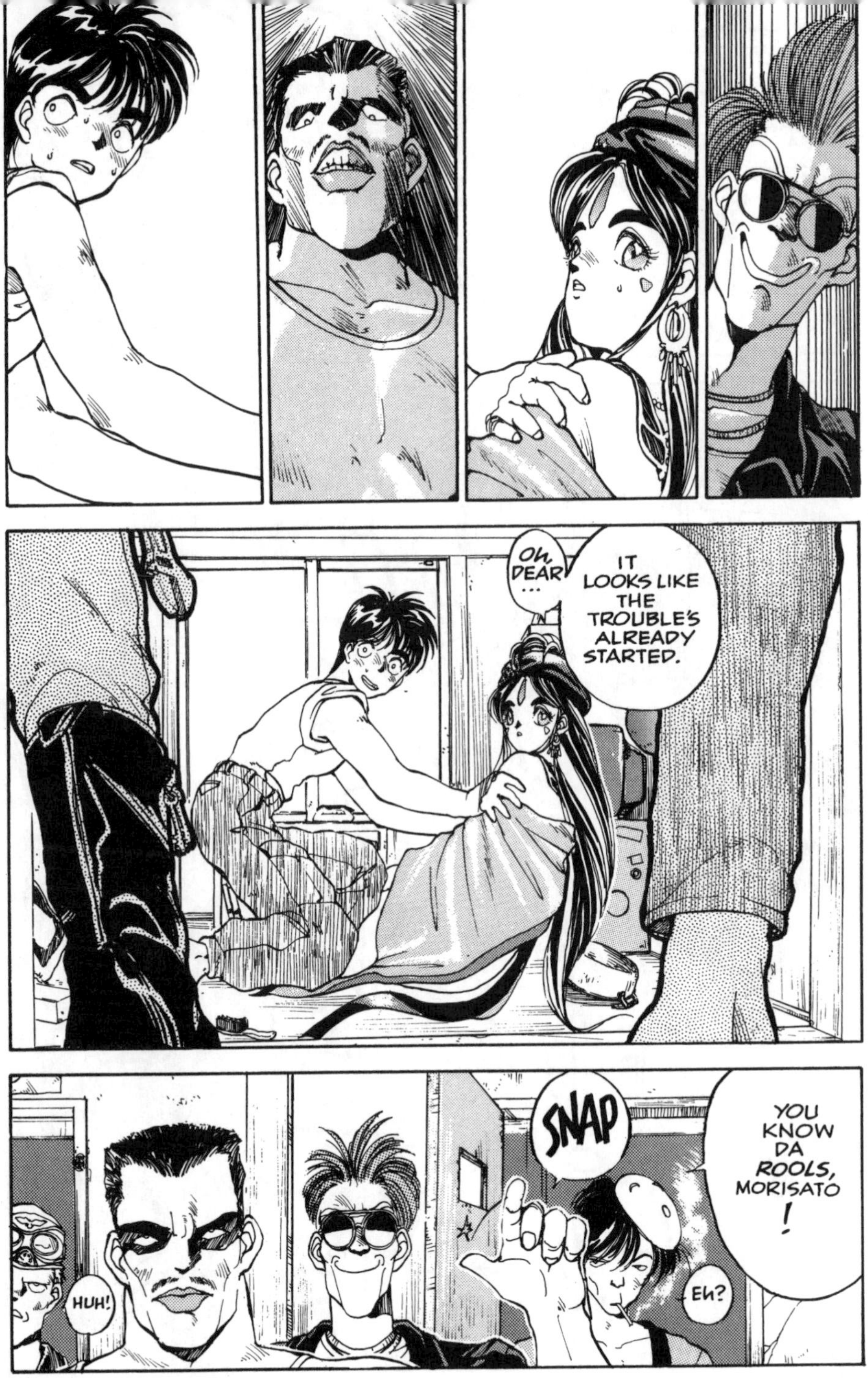
Oh, DEAR ...
IT LOOKS LIKE THE TROUBLE'S ALREADY STARTED.
HUH!
SNAP
YOU KNOW DA ROOLS, MORISATO!
Eh?

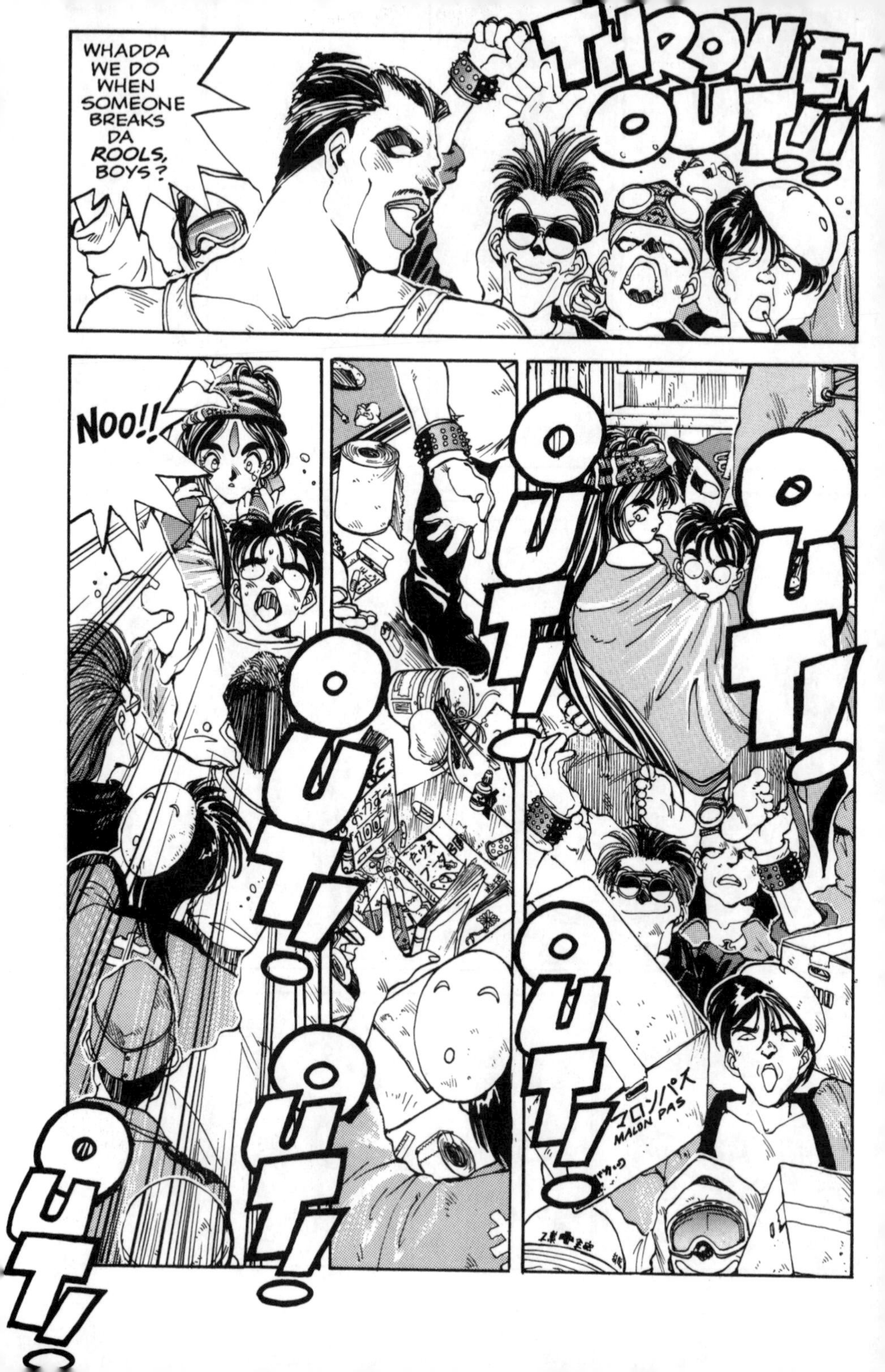
WHADDA WE DO WHEN SOMEONE BREAKS DA ROOLS, BOYS?
THROW 'EM OUT!!
NOO!!
OUT!
OUT!
OUT!
OUT!
OUT!
マロンパス
MALON PAS
OUT!

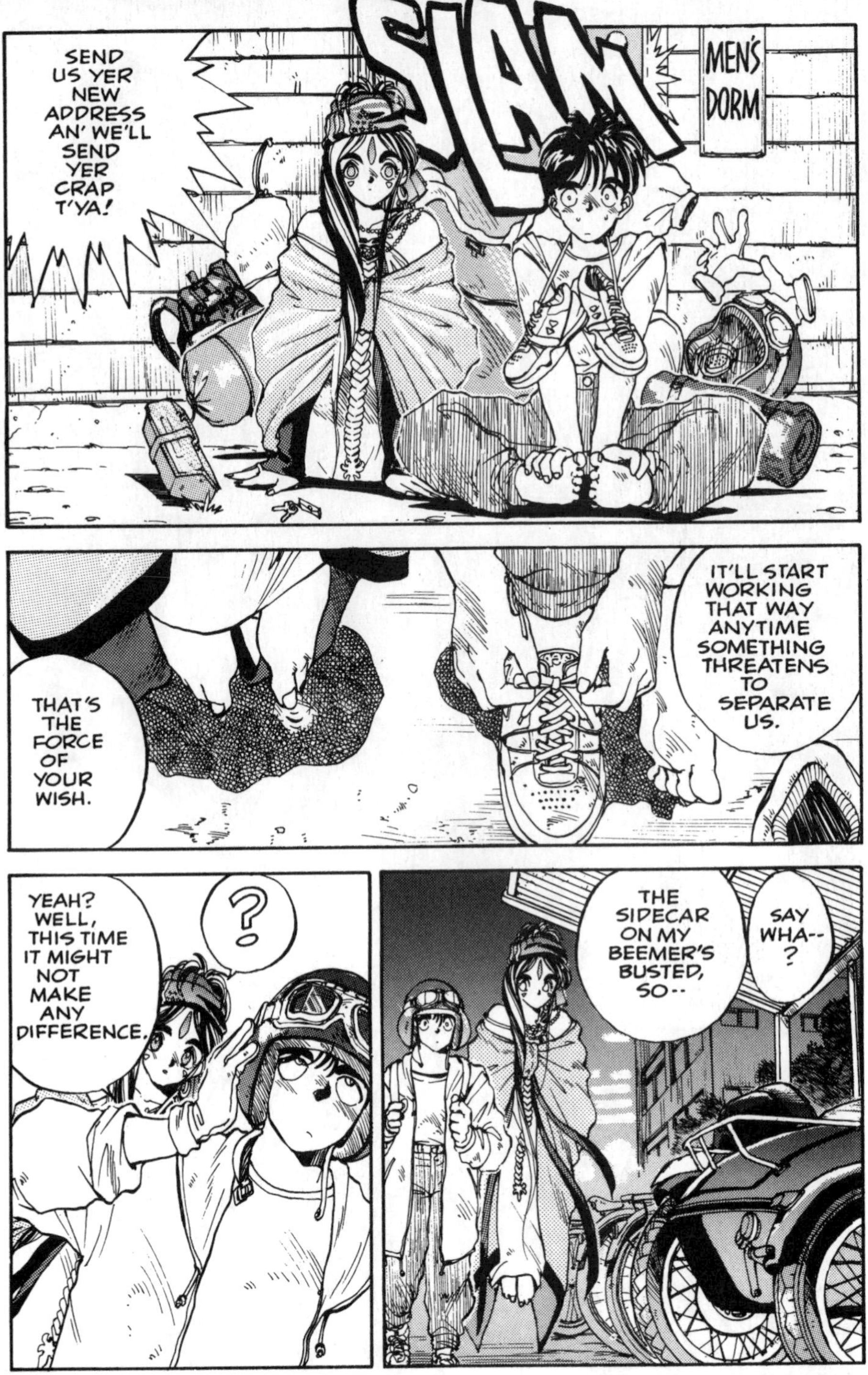
SEND US YER NEW ADDRESS AN' WE'LL SEND YER CRAP T'YA!
SLAM
MEN'S DORM
THAT'S THE FORCE OF YOUR WISH.
IT'LL START WORKING THAT WAY ANYTIME SOMETHING THREATENS TO SEPARATE US.
YEAH? WELL, THIS TIME IT MIGHT NOT MAKE ANY DIFFERENCE.
?
THE SIDECAR ON MY BEEMER'S BUSTED, SO--
SAY WHA--?

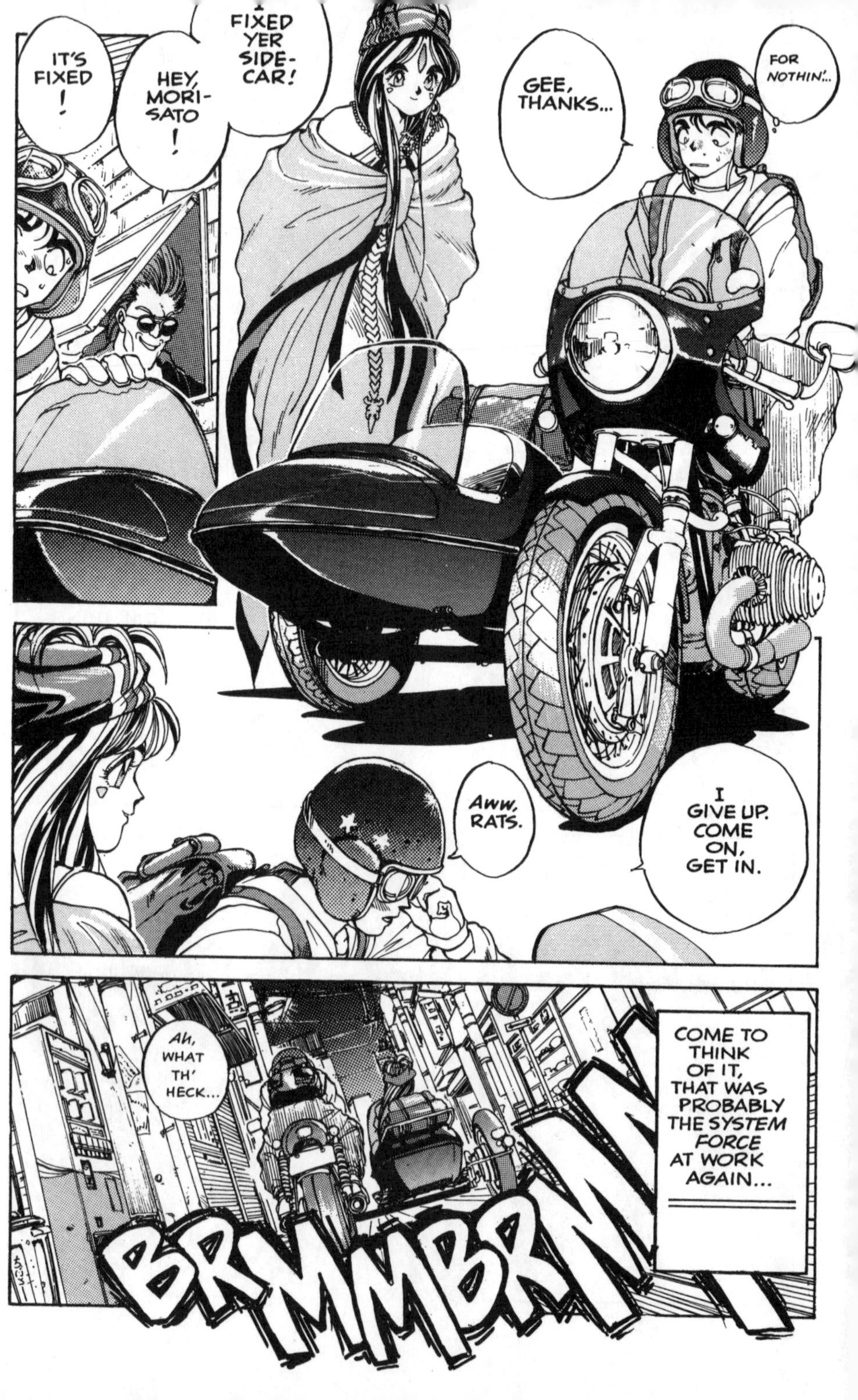
IT'S FIXED!
HEY, MORI-SATO!
FIXED YER SIDE-CAR!
GEE, THANKS...
FOR NOTHIN'...
Aww, RATS.
I GIVE UP. COME ON, GET IN.
Ah, WHAT TH' HECK...
BRMMBRM
COME TO THINK OF IT, THAT WAS PROBABLY THE SYSTEM FORCE AT WORK AGAIN...

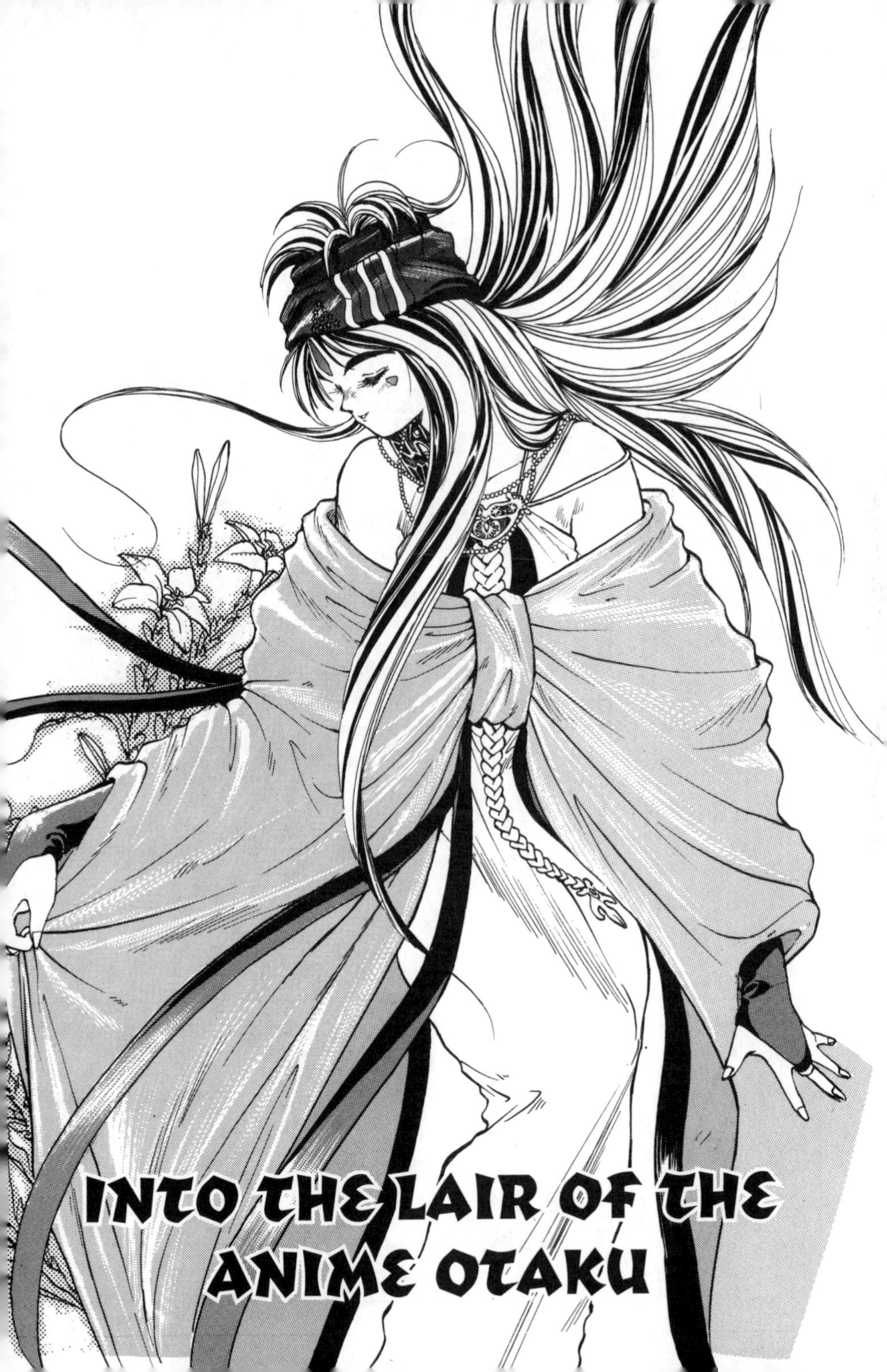

INTO THE LAIR OF THE ANIME OTAKU

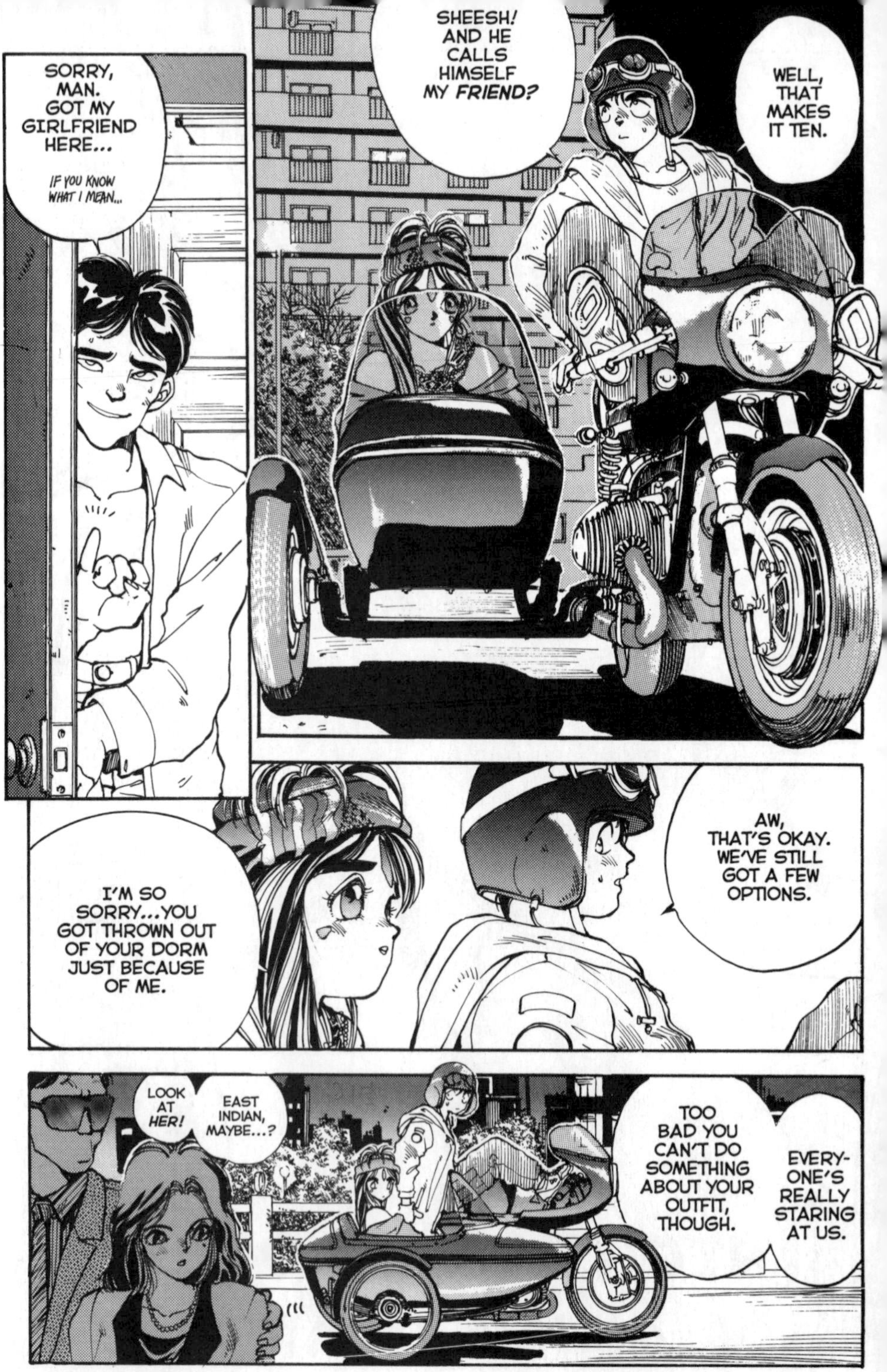
SORRY, MAN. GOT MY GIRLFRIEND HERE...
IF YOU KNOW WHAT I MEAN...
SHEESH! AND HE CALLS HIMSELF MY *FRIEND*?
WELL, THAT MAKES IT TEN.
I'M SO SORRY...YOU GOT THROWN OUT OF YOUR DORM JUST BECAUSE OF ME.
AW, THAT'S OKAY. WE'VE STILL GOT A FEW OPTIONS.
LOOK AT *HER*!
EAST INDIAN, MAYBE...?
TOO BAD YOU CAN'T DO SOMETHING ABOUT YOUR OUTFIT, THOUGH.
EVERY-ONE'S REALLY STARING AT US.

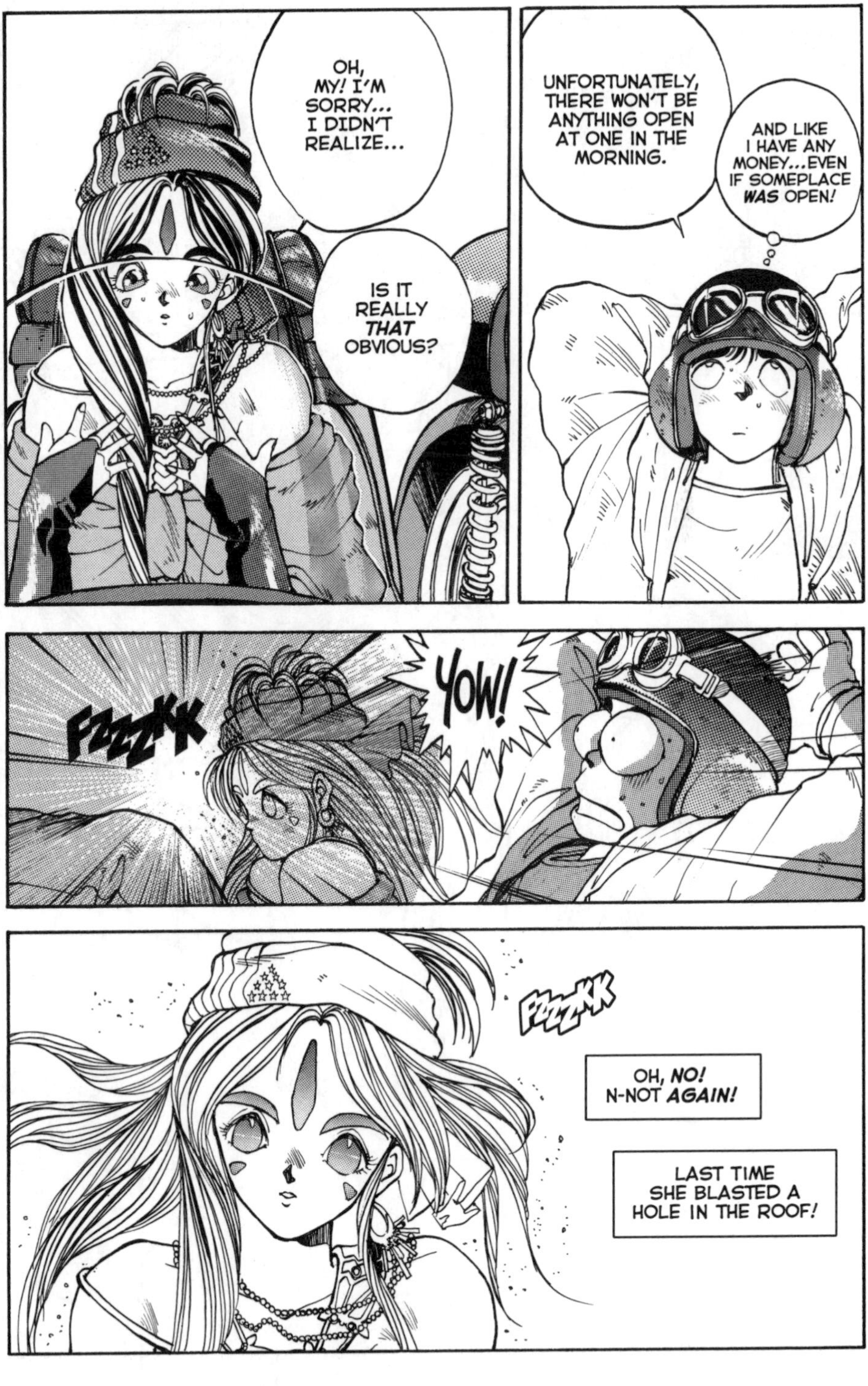
OH, MY! I'M SORRY... I DIDN'T REALIZE...
IS IT REALLY THAT OBVIOUS?
UNFORTUNATELY, THERE WON'T BE ANYTHING OPEN AT ONE IN THE MORNING.
AND LIKE I HAVE ANY MONEY...EVEN IF SOMEPLACE WAS OPEN!
FZZZKK
YOW!
FZZZKK
OH, NO! N-NOT AGAIN!
LAST TIME SHE BLASTED A HOLE IN THE ROOF!

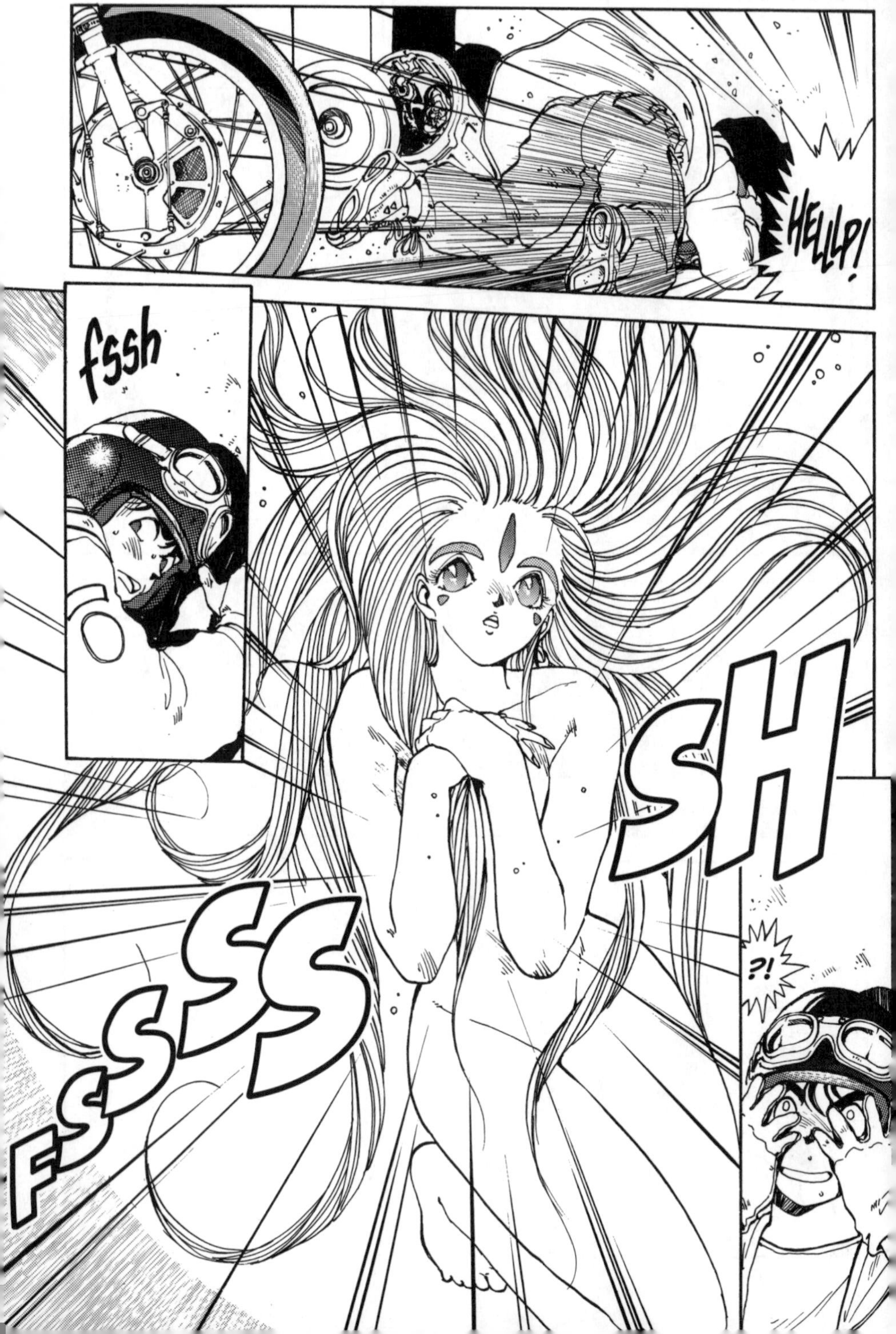
HELLLP!
fssh
FSSSSSH
?!

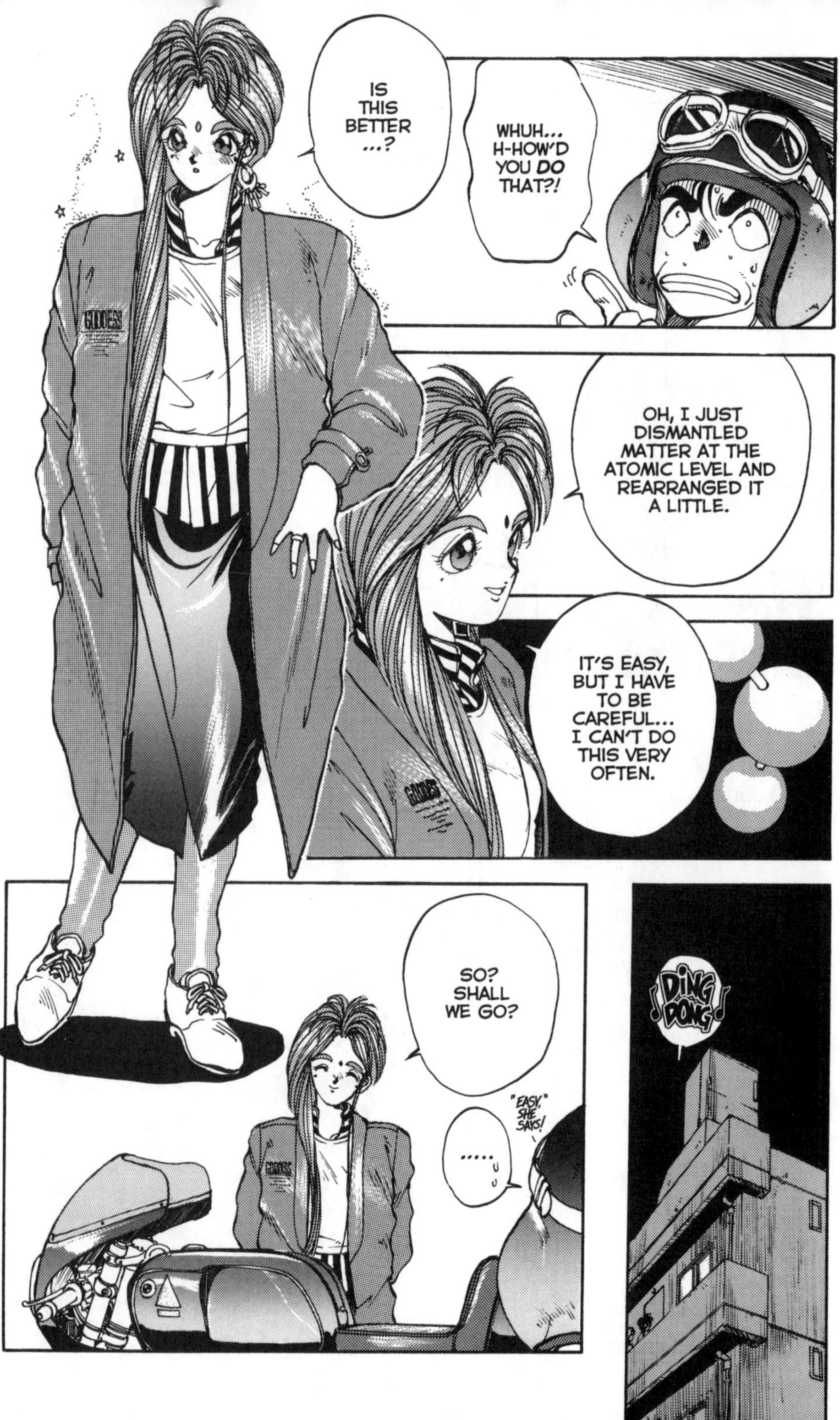
IS THIS BETTER ...?
WHUH... H-HOW'D YOU *DO* THAT?!
OH, I JUST DISMANTLED MATTER AT THE ATOMIC LEVEL AND REARRANGED IT A LITTLE.
IT'S EASY, BUT I HAVE TO BE CAREFUL... I CAN'T DO THIS VERY OFTEN.
SO? SHALL WE GO?
.....
"EASY," SHE SAYS!
DING DONG

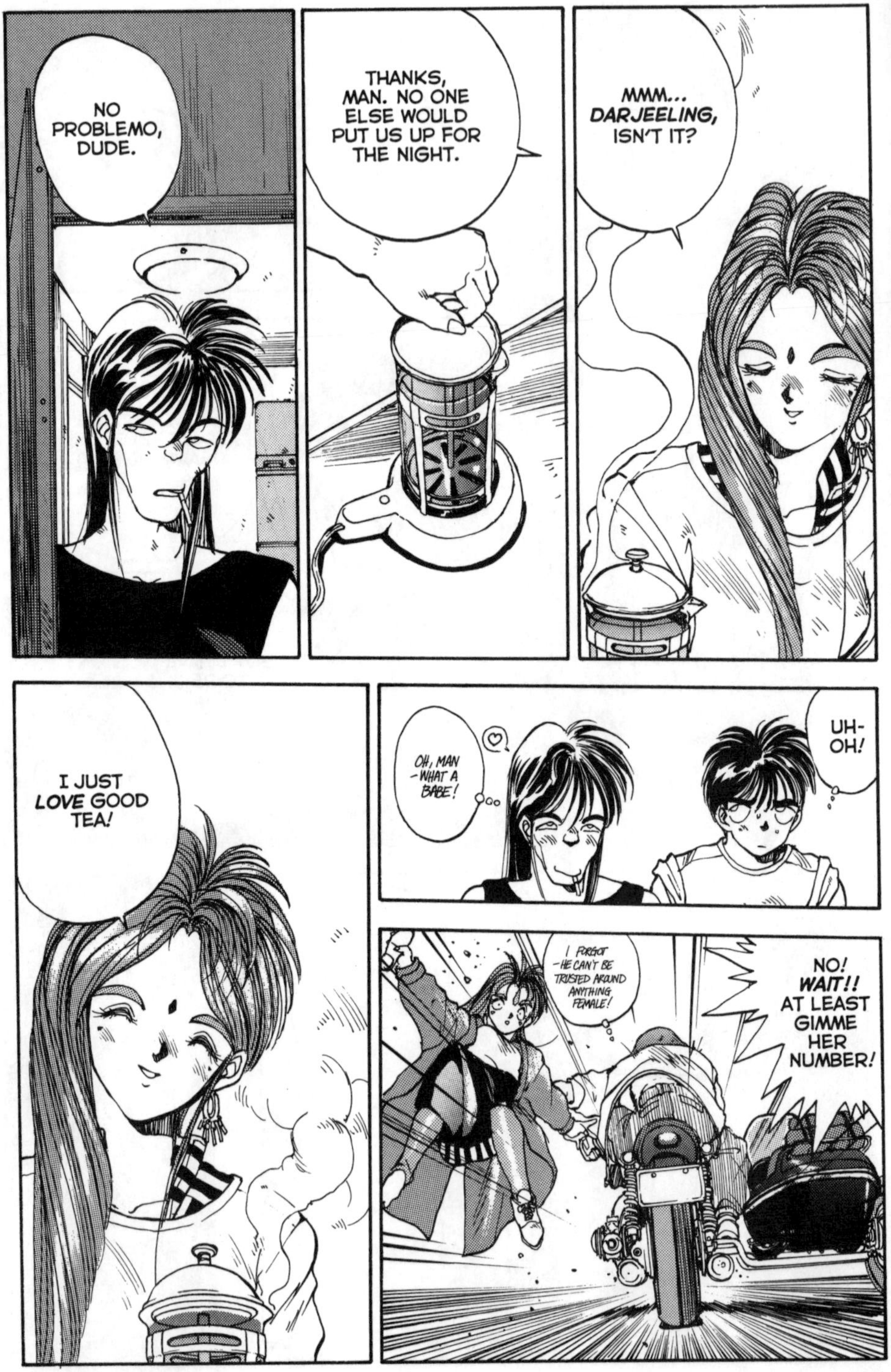
NO PROBLEMO, DUDE.
THANKS, MAN. NO ONE ELSE WOULD PUT US UP FOR THE NIGHT.
MMM... DARJEELING, ISN'T IT?
I JUST LOVE GOOD TEA!
OH, MAN -WHAT A BABE!
UH-OH!
I FORGOT -HE CAN'T BE TRUSTED AROUND ANYTHING FEMALE!
NO! WAIT!! AT LEAST GIMME HER NUMBER!

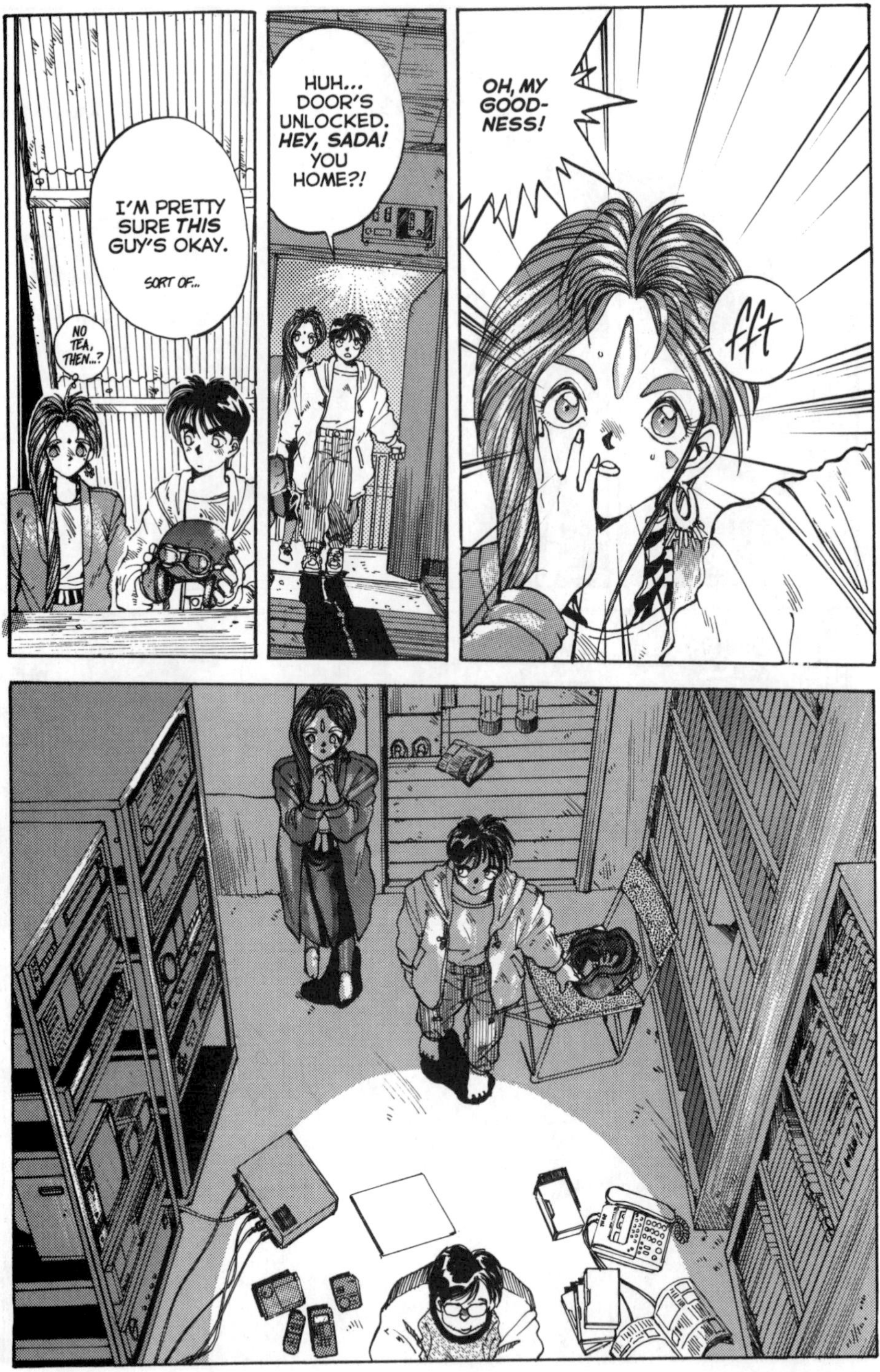
I'M PRETTY SURE THIS GUY'S OKAY.
SORT OF...
NO TEA, THEN...?
HUH... DOOR'S UNLOCKED. HEY, SADA! YOU HOME?!
OH, MY GOODNESS!
fft

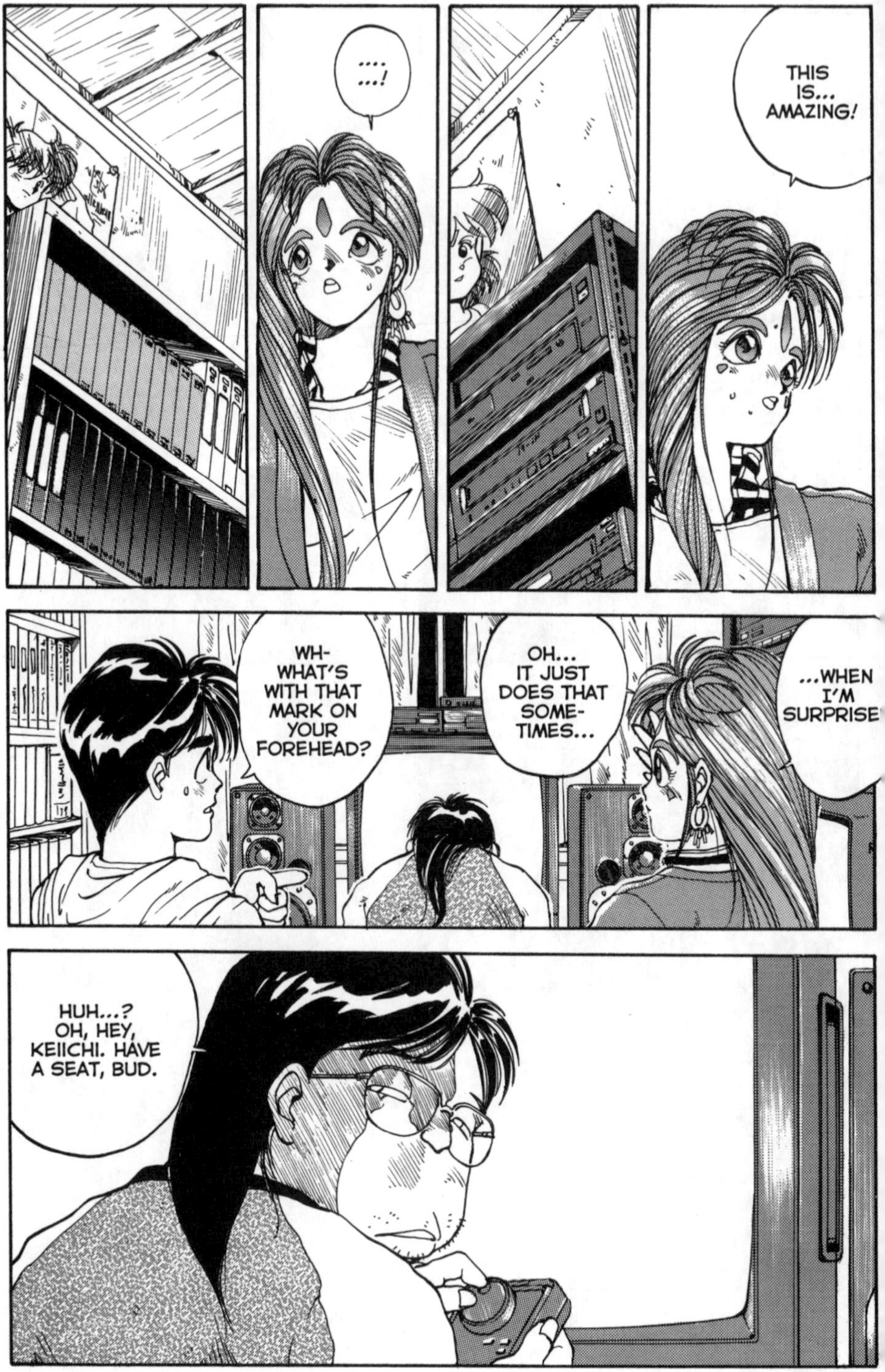

......!
THIS IS... AMAZING!
WH-WHAT'S WITH THAT MARK ON YOUR FOREHEAD?
OH... IT JUST DOES THAT SOME-TIMES...
...WHEN I'M SURPRISE
HUH...? OH, HEY, KEIICHI. HAVE A SEAT, BUD.

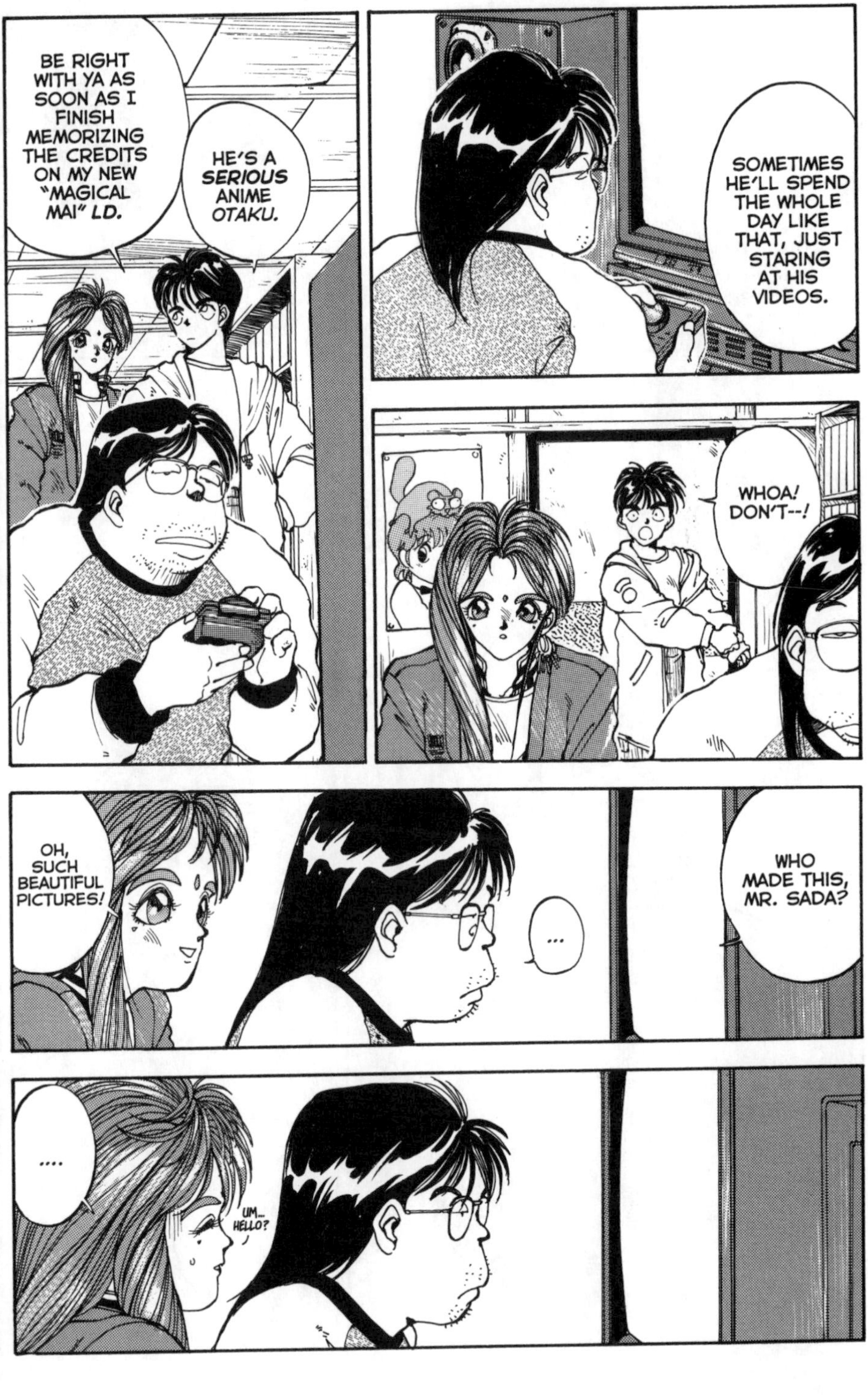
BE RIGHT WITH YA AS SOON AS I FINISH MEMORIZING THE CREDITS ON MY NEW "MAGICAL MAI" LD.
HE'S A SERIOUS ANIME OTAKU.
SOMETIMES HE'LL SPEND THE WHOLE DAY LIKE THAT, JUST STARING AT HIS VIDEOS.
WHOA! DON'T--!
OH, SUCH BEAUTIFUL PICTURES!
...
WHO MADE THIS, MR. SADA?
....
UM... HELLO?

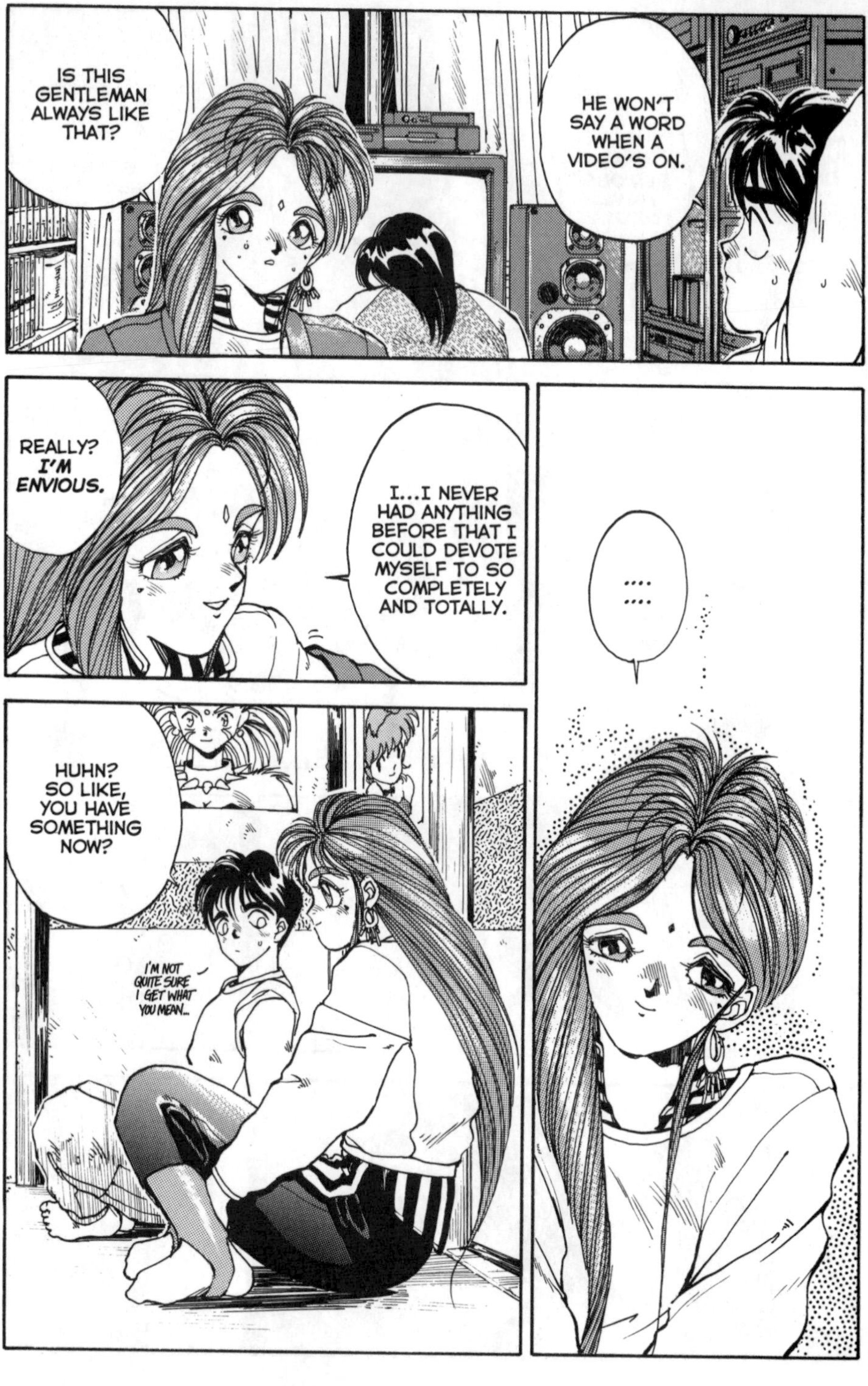
IS THIS GENTLEMAN ALWAYS LIKE THAT?
HE WON'T SAY A WORD WHEN A VIDEO'S ON.
REALLY? *I'M ENVIOUS.*
I...I NEVER HAD ANYTHING BEFORE THAT I COULD DEVOTE MYSELF TO SO COMPLETELY AND TOTALLY.
HUHN? SO LIKE, YOU HAVE SOMETHING NOW?
I'M NOT QUITE SURE I GET WHAT YOU MEAN...
....
....

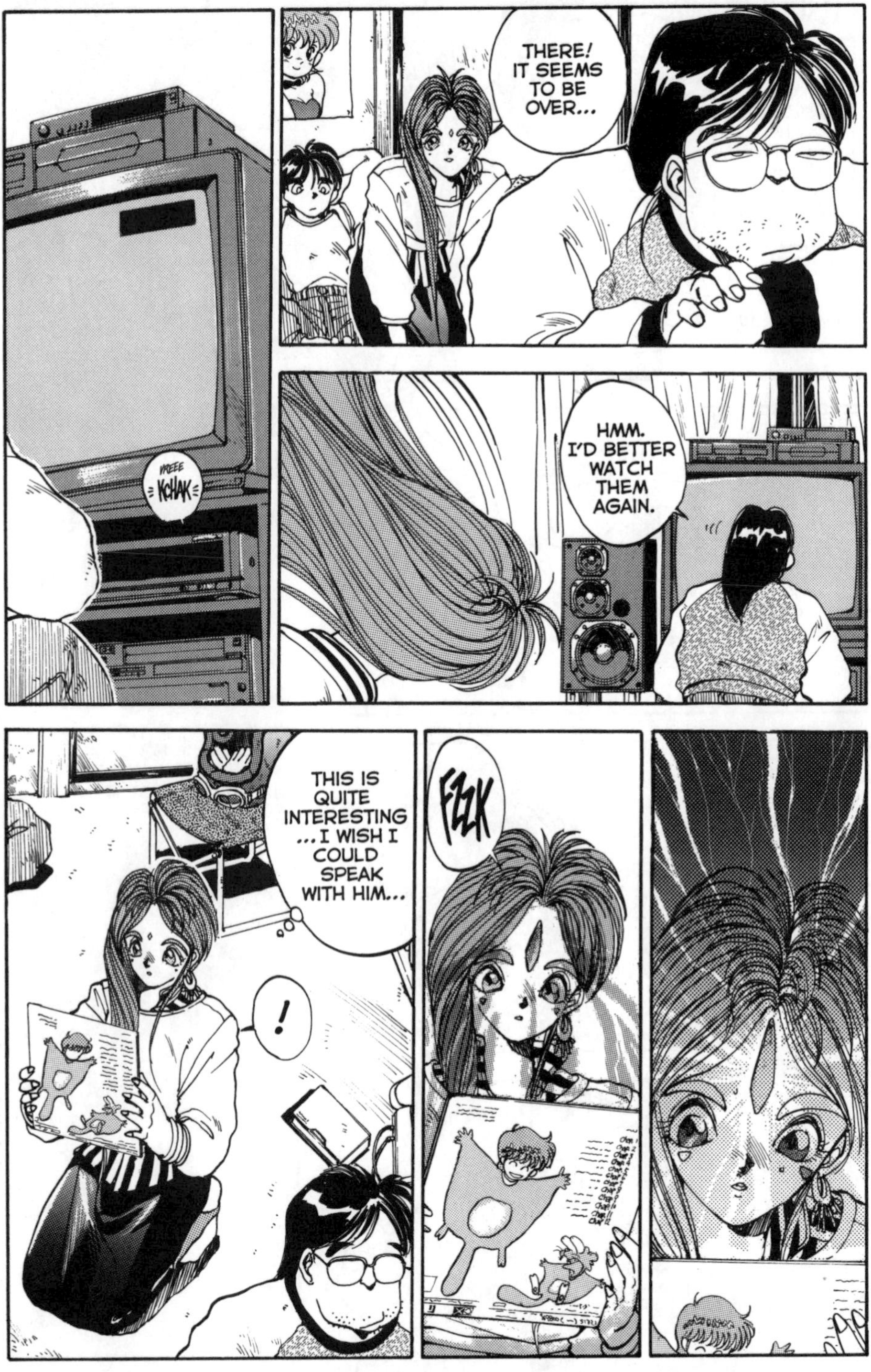
VREEE
KCHAK
THERE! IT SEEMS TO BE OVER...
HMM. I'D BETTER WATCH THEM AGAIN.
THIS IS QUITE INTERESTING ...I WISH I COULD SPEAK WITH HIM...
!
FZZK

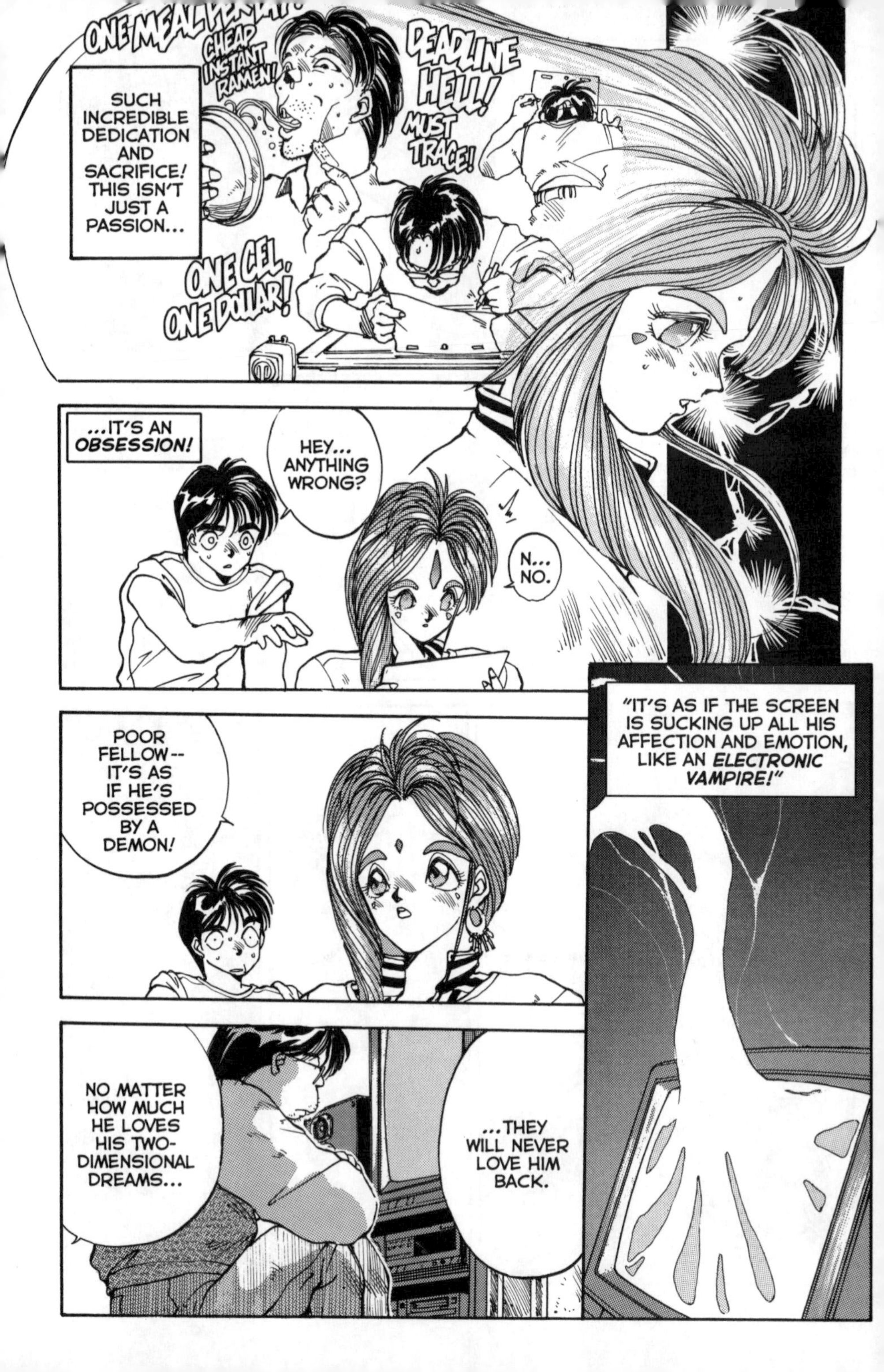
ONE MEAL PER DAY!
CHEAP INSTANT RAMEN!
SUCH INCREDIBLE DEDICATION AND SACRIFICE! THIS ISN'T JUST A PASSION...
DEADLINE HELL!
MUST TRACE!
ONE CEL, ONE DOLLAR!
...IT'S AN *OBSESSION!*
HEY... ANYTHING WRONG?
N... NO.
POOR FELLOW-- IT'S AS IF HE'S POSSESSED BY A DEMON!
NO MATTER HOW MUCH HE LOVES HIS TWO-DIMENSIONAL DREAMS...
...THEY WILL NEVER LOVE HIM BACK.
"IT'S AS IF THE SCREEN IS SUCKING UP ALL HIS AFFECTION AND EMOTION, LIKE AN *ELECTRONIC VAMPIRE!*"

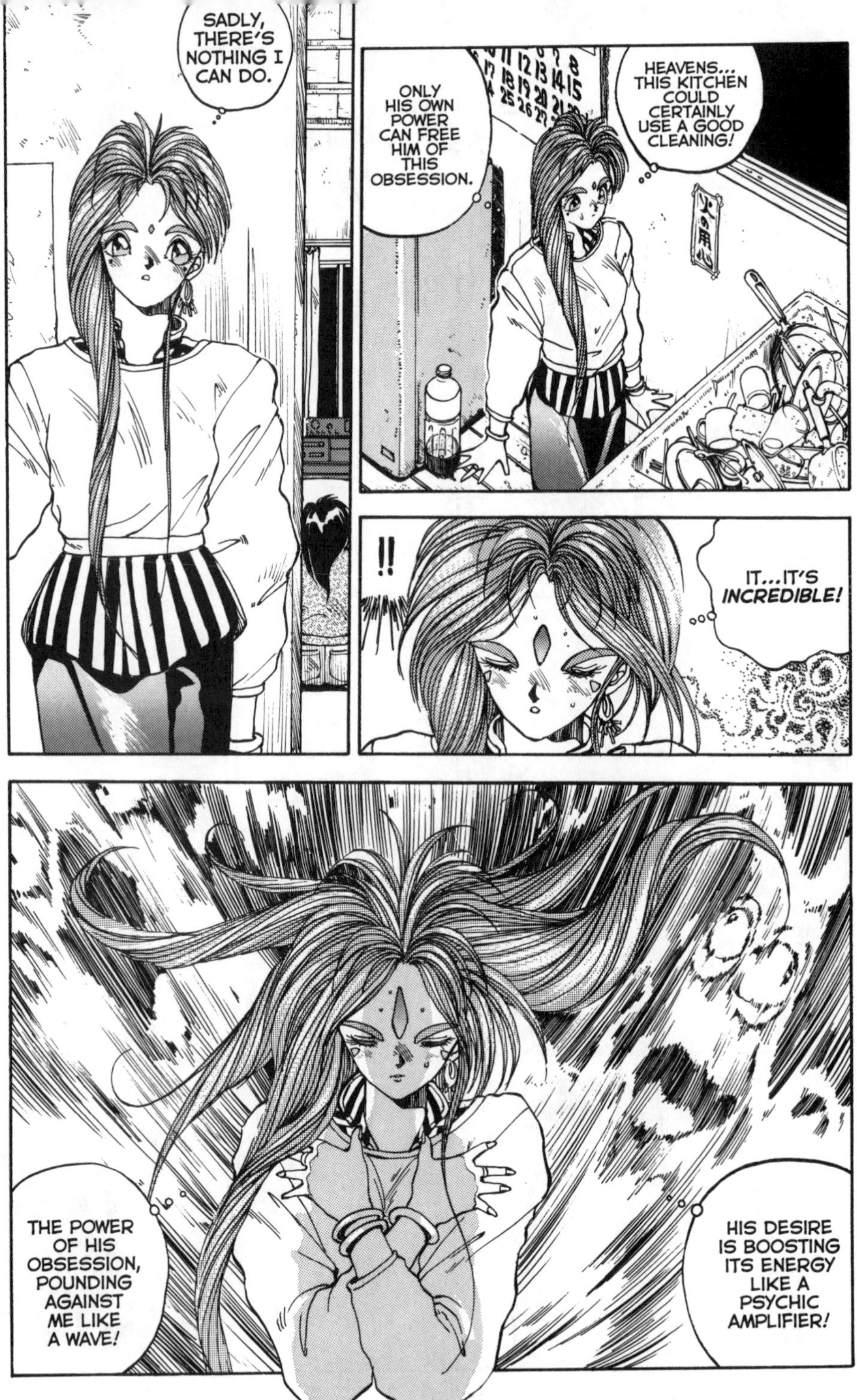
SADLY, THERE'S NOTHING I CAN DO.
ONLY HIS OWN POWER CAN FREE HIM OF THIS OBSESSION.
HEAVENS... THIS KITCHEN COULD CERTAINLY USE A GOOD CLEANING!
!!
IT...IT'S INCREDIBLE!
THE POWER OF HIS OBSESSION, POUNDING AGAINST ME LIKE A WAVE!
HIS DESIRE IS BOOSTING ITS ENERGY LIKE A PSYCHIC AMPLIFIER!

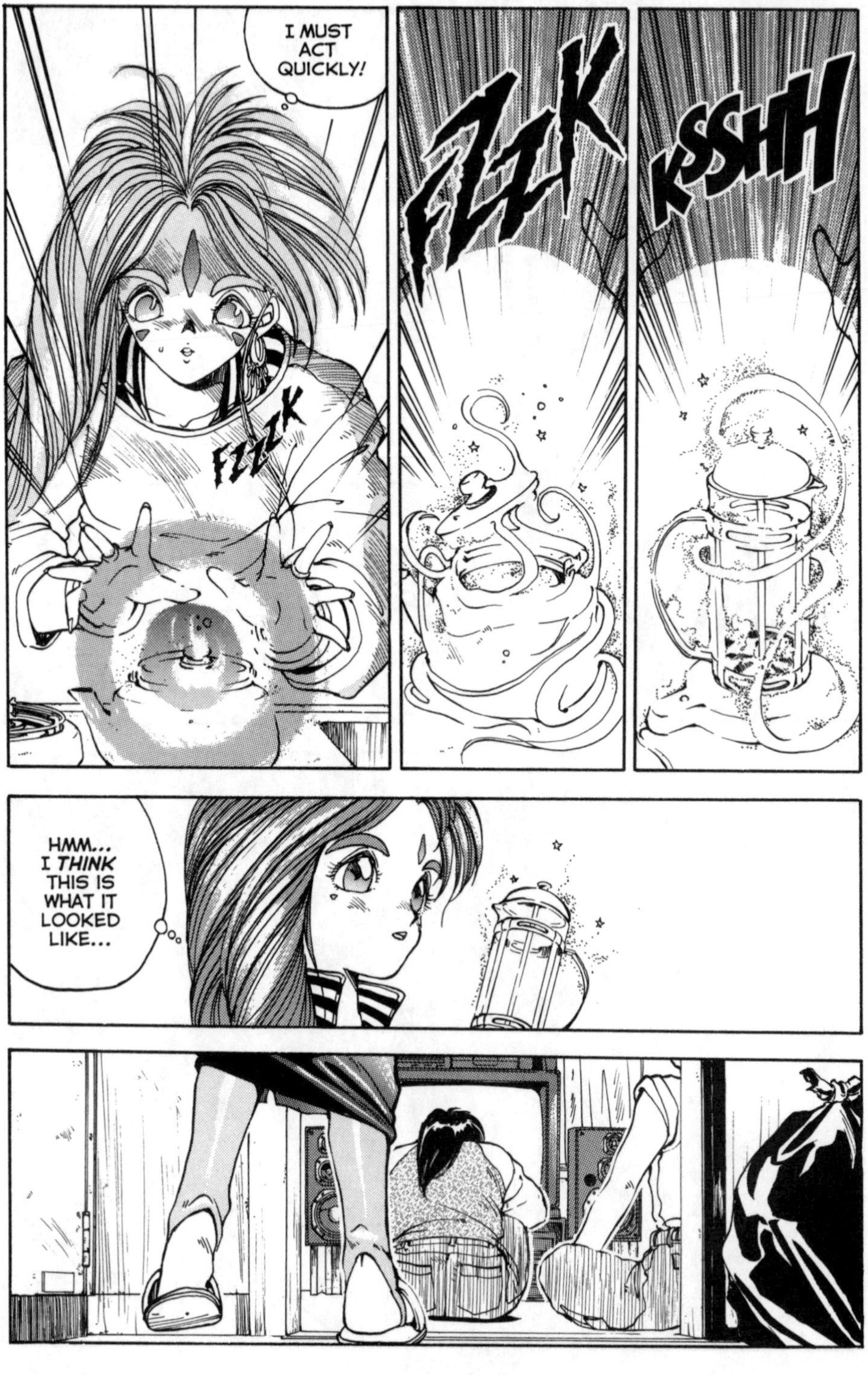
I MUST ACT QUICKLY!
FZZZK
FZZK
KSSHH
HMM... I *THINK* THIS IS WHAT IT LOOKED LIKE...

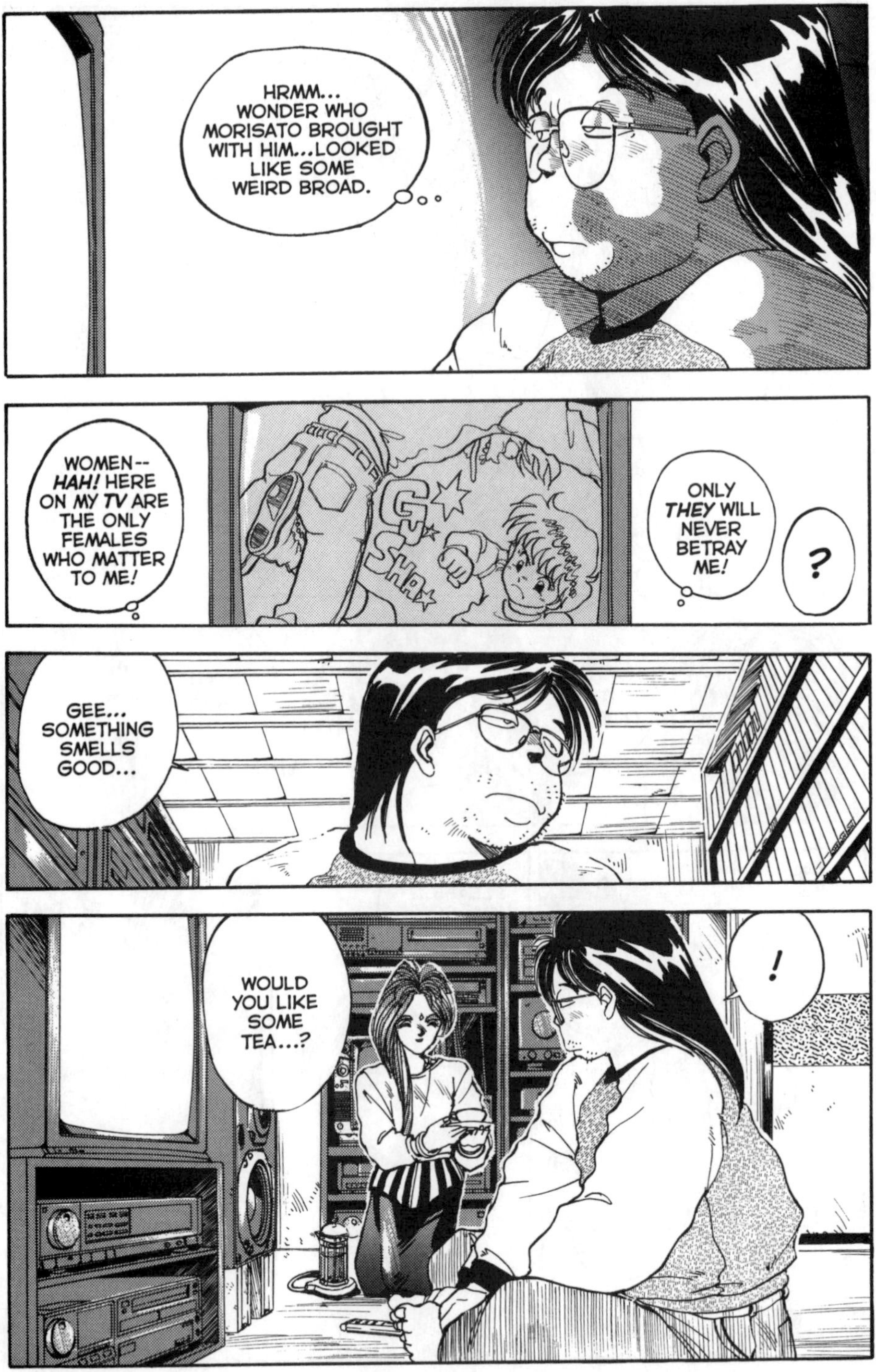
HRMM... WONDER WHO MORISATO BROUGHT WITH HIM...LOOKED LIKE SOME WEIRD BROAD.
WOMEN-- *HAH!* HERE ON MY *TV* ARE THE ONLY FEMALES WHO MATTER TO ME!
G☆ GUSHA☆
ONLY *THEY* WILL NEVER BETRAY ME!
?
GEE... SOMETHING SMELLS GOOD...
WOULD YOU LIKE SOME TEA...?
!

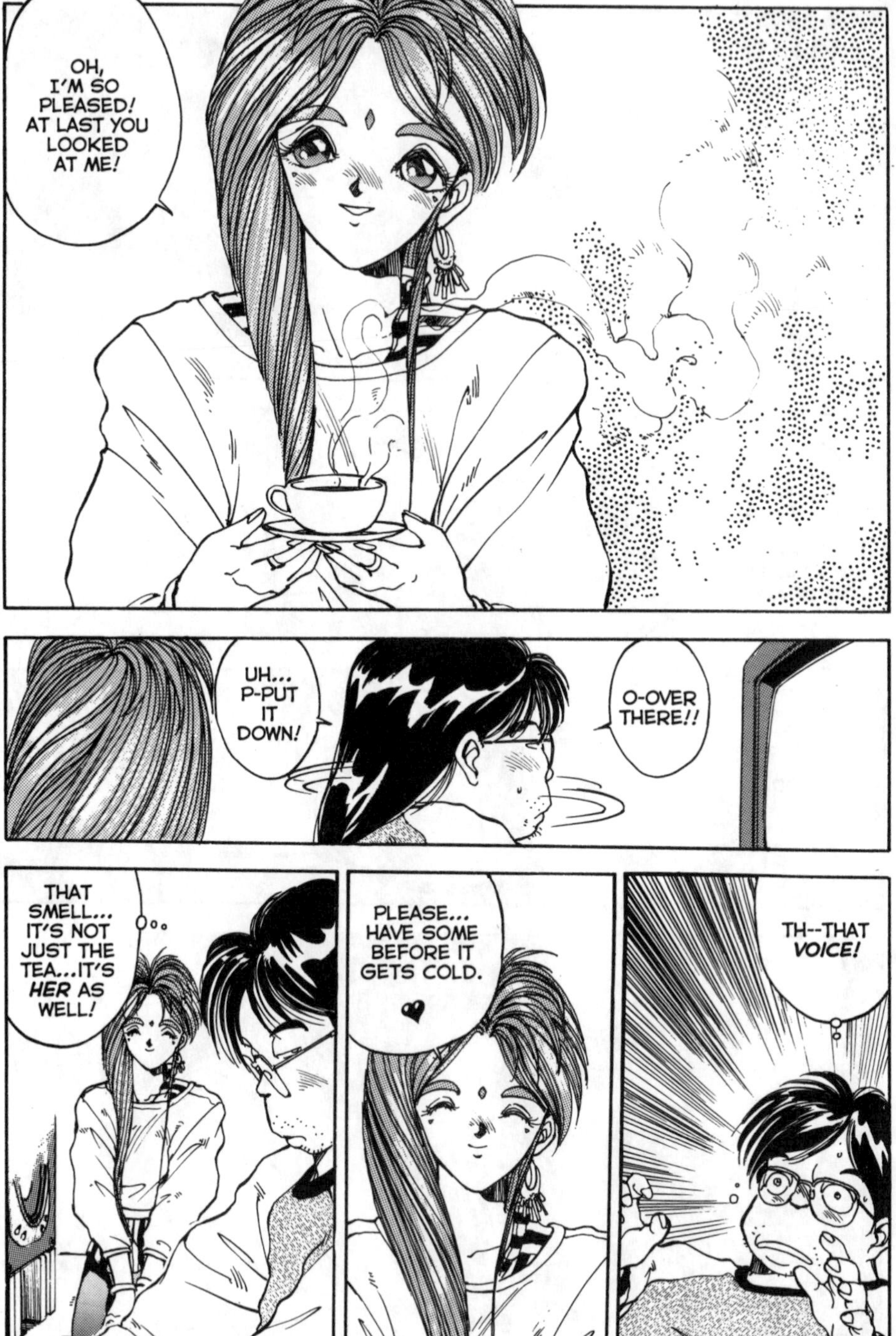
OH, I'M SO PLEASED! AT LAST YOU LOOKED AT ME!
UH... P-PUT IT DOWN!
O-OVER THERE!!
THAT SMELL... IT'S NOT JUST THE TEA...IT'S *HER* AS WELL!
PLEASE... HAVE SOME BEFORE IT GETS COLD.
TH--THAT *VOICE!*

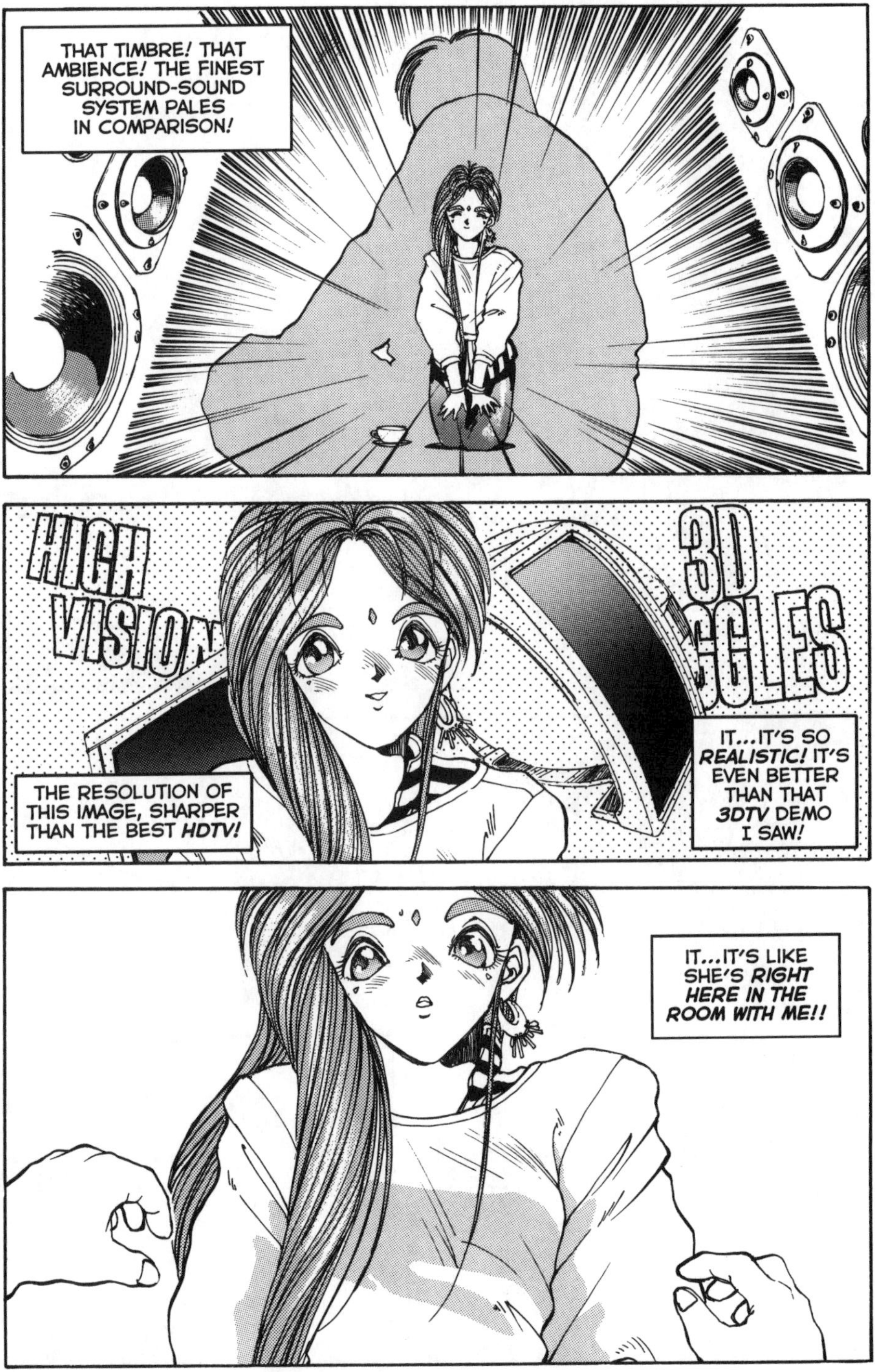
THAT TIMBRE! THAT AMBIENCE! THE FINEST SURROUND-SOUND SYSTEM PALES IN COMPARISON!
HIGH VISION
3D
GGLES
THE RESOLUTION OF THIS IMAGE, SHARPER THAN THE BEST *HDTV!*
IT...IT'S SO *REALISTIC!* IT'S EVEN BETTER THAN THAT *3DTV* DEMO I SAW!
IT...IT'S LIKE SHE'S *RIGHT HERE IN THE ROOM WITH ME!!*

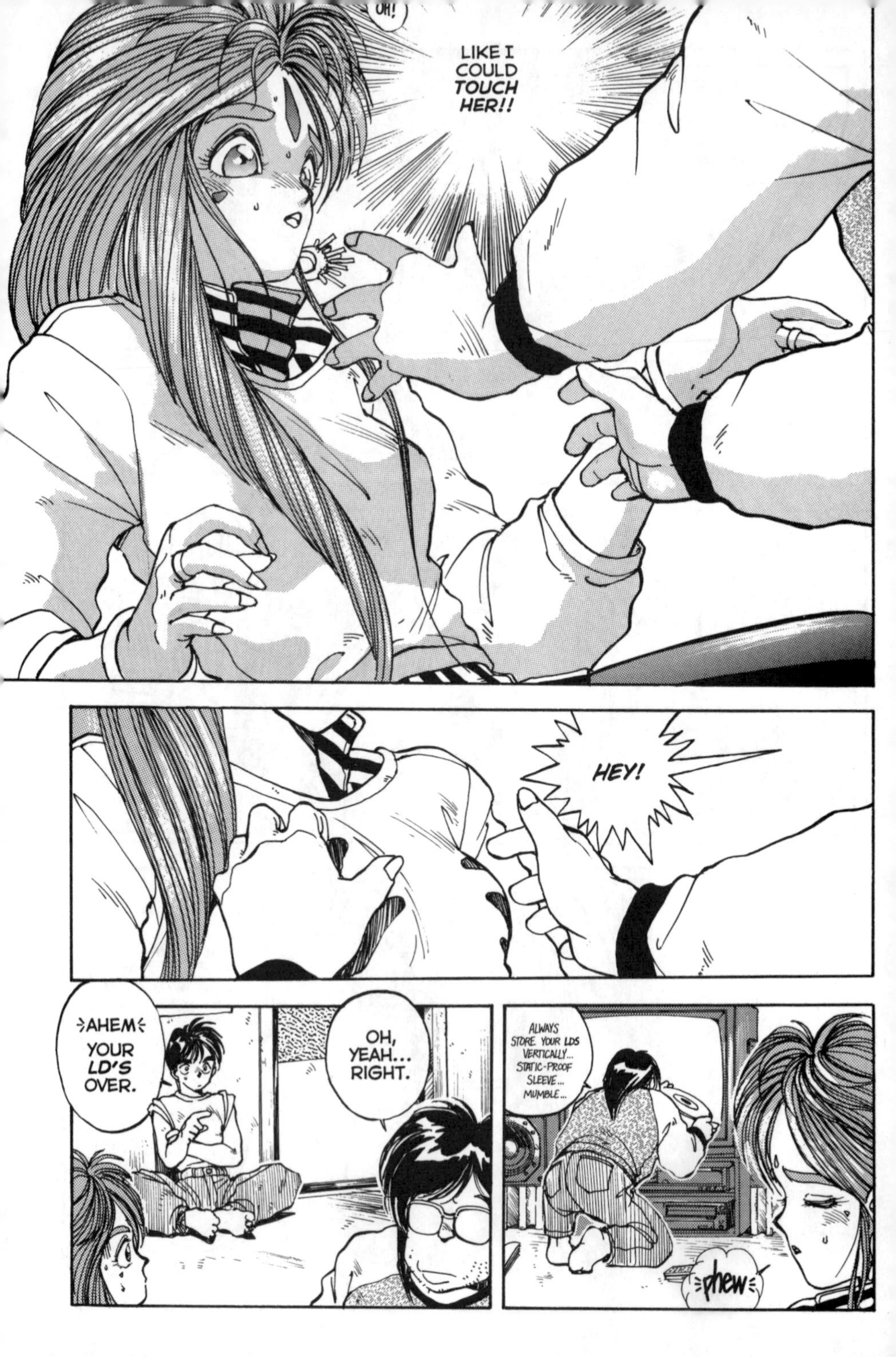

OH!
LIKE I COULD TOUCH HER!!
HEY!
AHEM YOUR LD'S OVER.
OH, YEAH... RIGHT.
ALWAYS STORE YOUR LDS VERTICALLY... STATIC-PROOF SLEEVE... MUMBLE...
phew

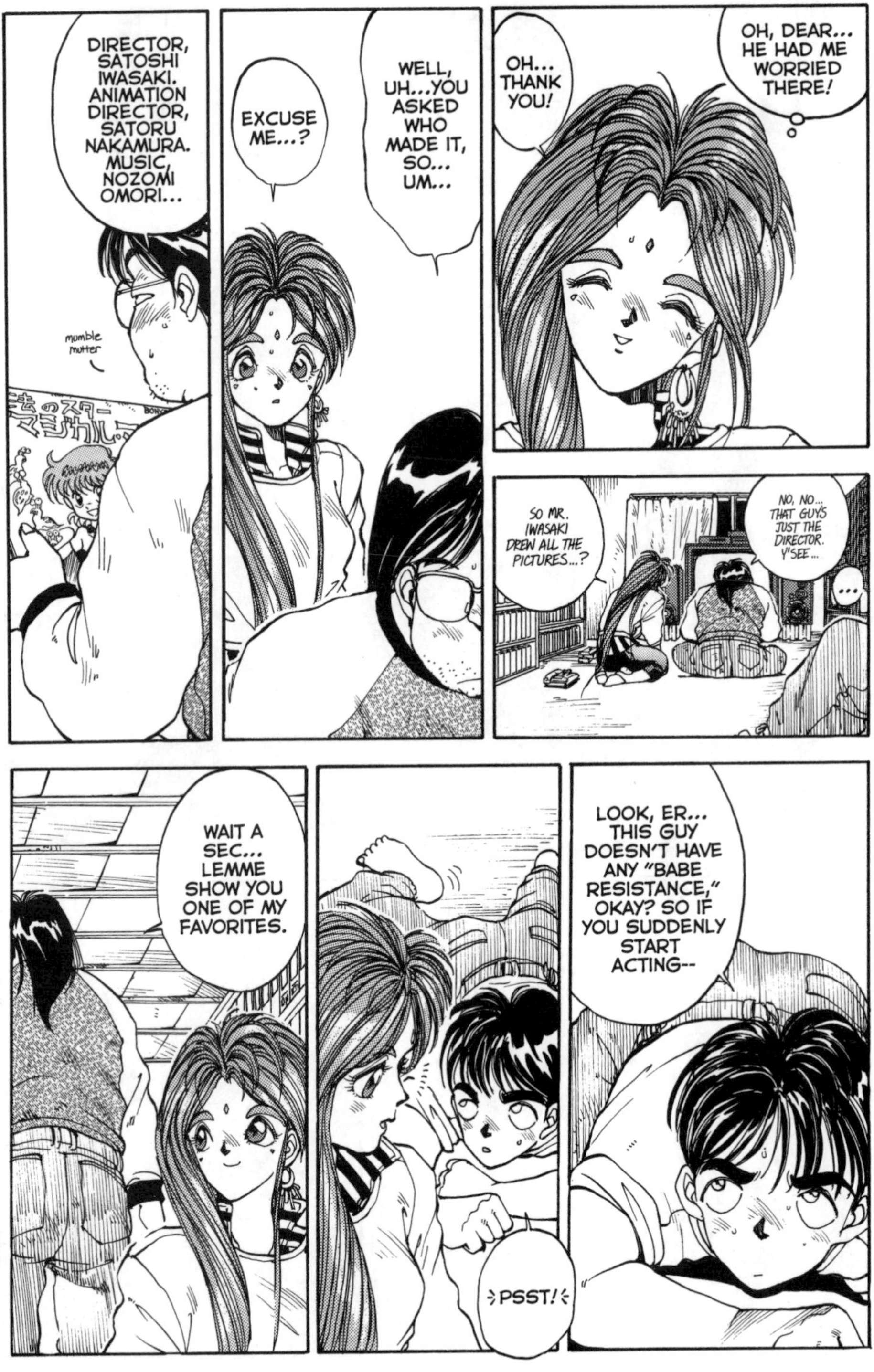
DIRECTOR, SATOSHI IWASAKI. ANIMATION DIRECTOR, SATORU NAKAMURA. MUSIC, NOZOMI OMORI...
mumble mutter
EXCUSE ME...?
WELL, UH...YOU ASKED WHO MADE IT, SO... UM...
OH... THANK YOU!
OH, DEAR... HE HAD ME WORRIED THERE!
SO MR. IWASAKI DREW ALL THE PICTURES...?
NO, NO... THAT GUY'S JUST THE DIRECTOR. Y'SEE...
...
WAIT A SEC... LEMME SHOW YOU ONE OF MY FAVORITES.
PSST!
LOOK, ER... THIS GUY DOESN'T HAVE ANY "BABE RESISTANCE," OKAY? SO IF YOU SUDDENLY START ACTING--

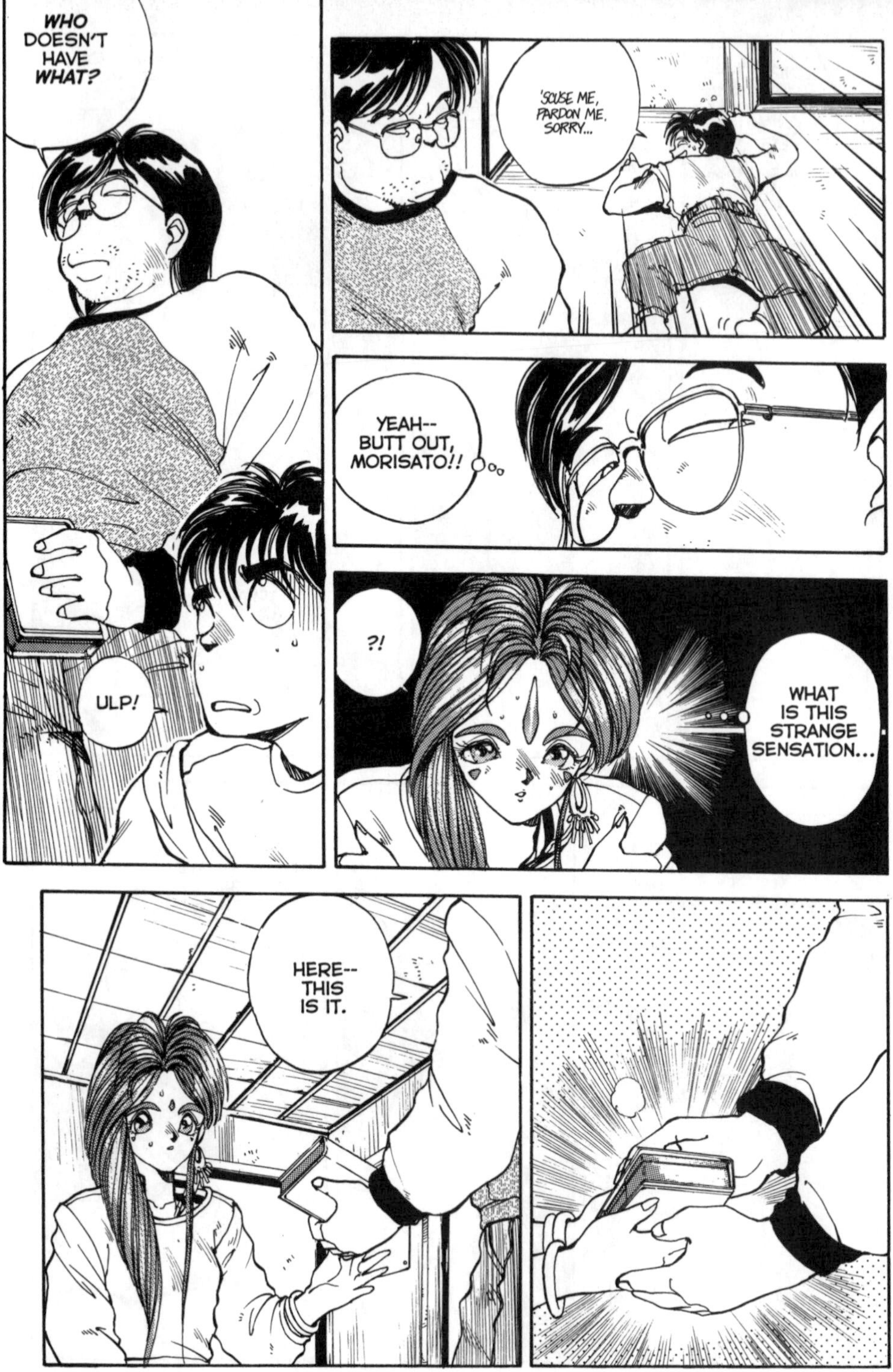
WHO DOESN'T HAVE WHAT?
ULP!
'SCUSE ME, PARDON ME, SORRY...
YEAH-- BUTT OUT, MORISATO!!
?!
WHAT IS THIS STRANGE SENSATION...
HERE-- THIS IS IT.

SUCH SOFT HANDS ...SO NICE AND WARM...

OH! HIS THOUGHTS ARE POURING INTO ME...

HEARING... VISION...SMELL... AND NOW, TOUCH!

THIS IS BETTER THAN MY OLD WORLD IN *EVERY WAY!!* THE ONLY THING I STILL HAVEN'T SAMPLED...

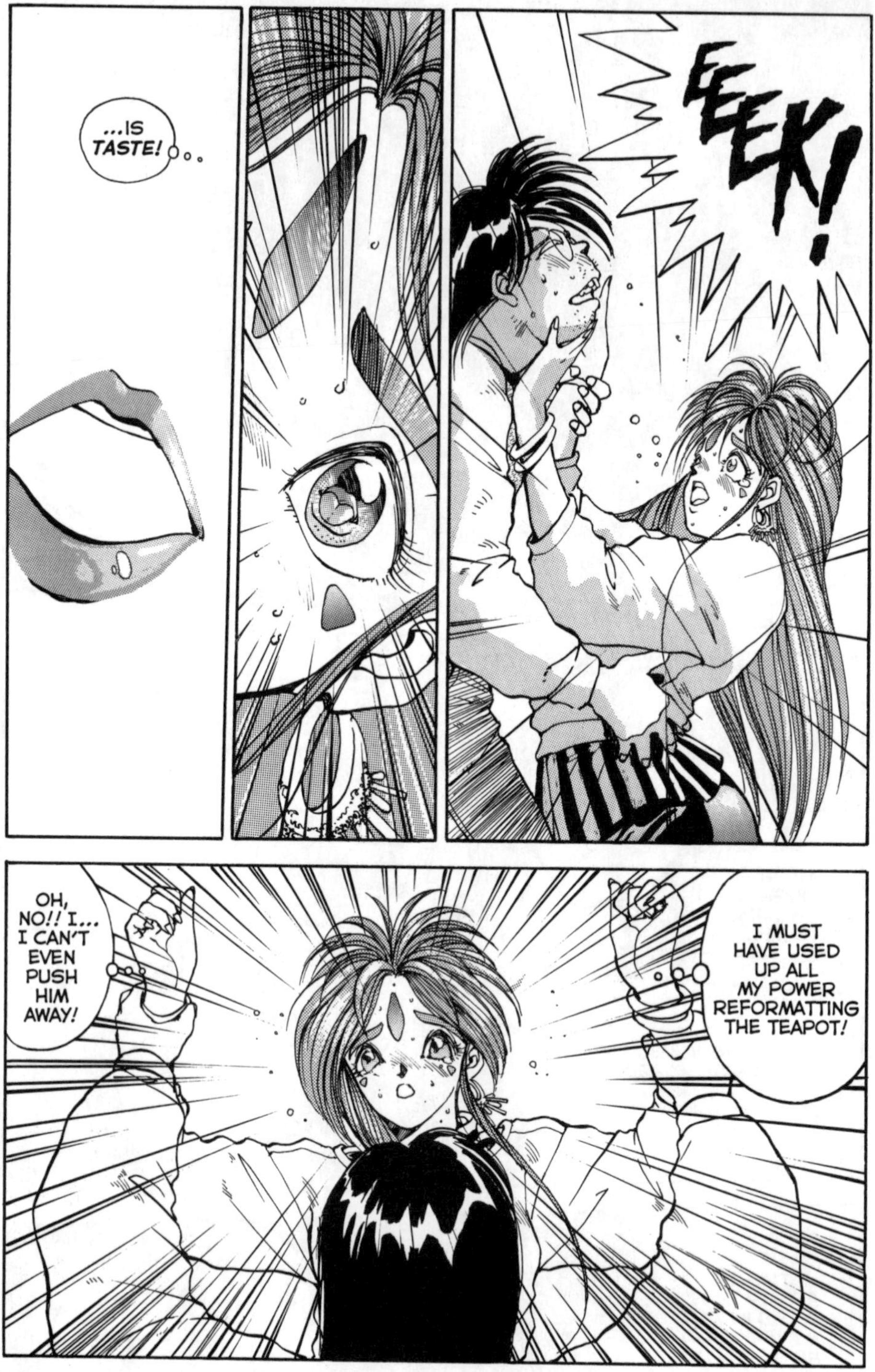
...IS TASTE!
EEEK!
OH, NO!! I... I CAN'T EVEN PUSH HIM AWAY!
I MUST HAVE USED UP ALL MY POWER REFORMATTING THE TEAPOT!

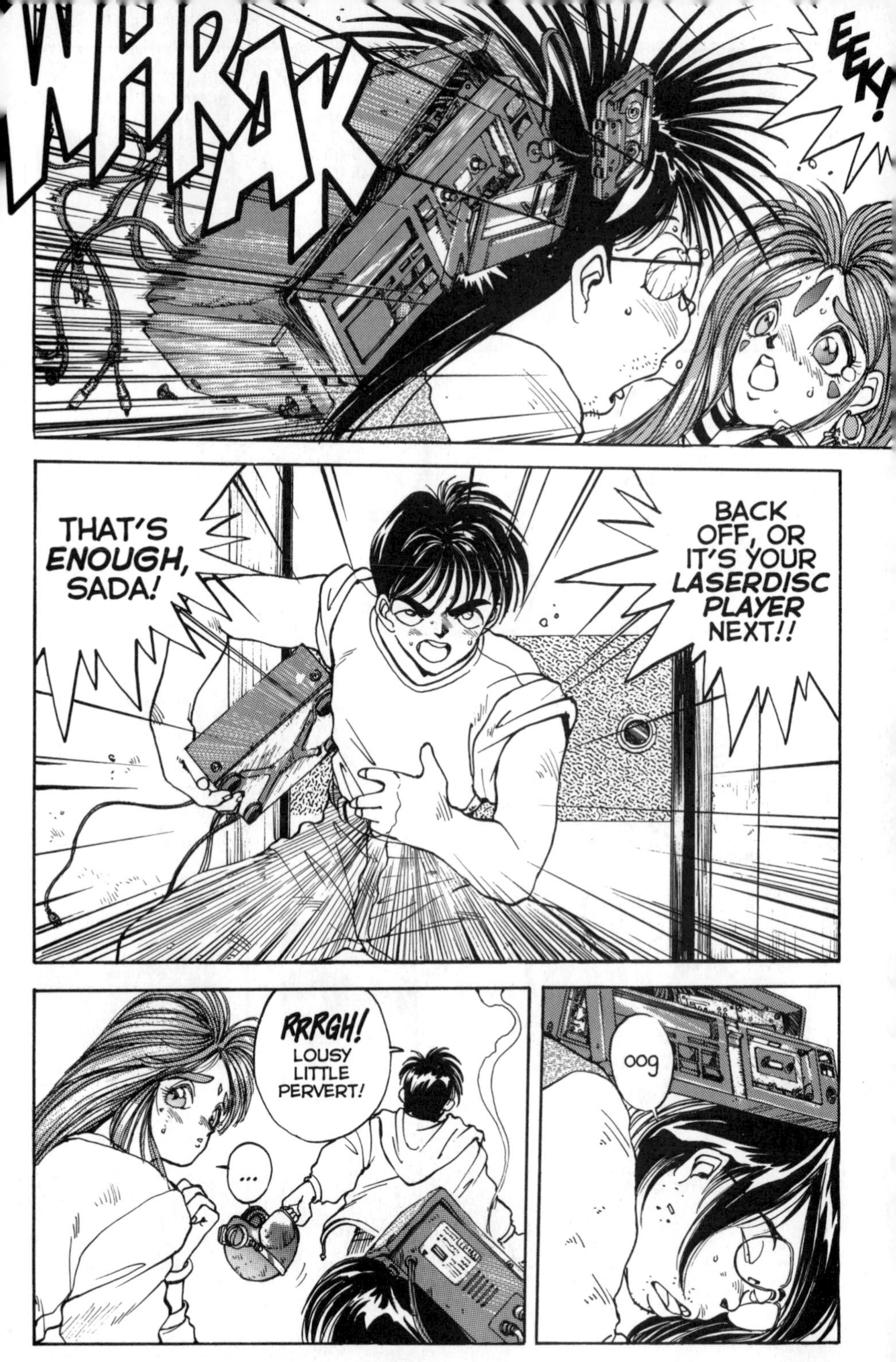
WHRAK
EEEK!
THAT'S ENOUGH, SADA!
BACK OFF, OR IT'S YOUR LASERDISC PLAYER NEXT!!
RRRGH! LOUSY LITTLE PERVERT!
...
oog

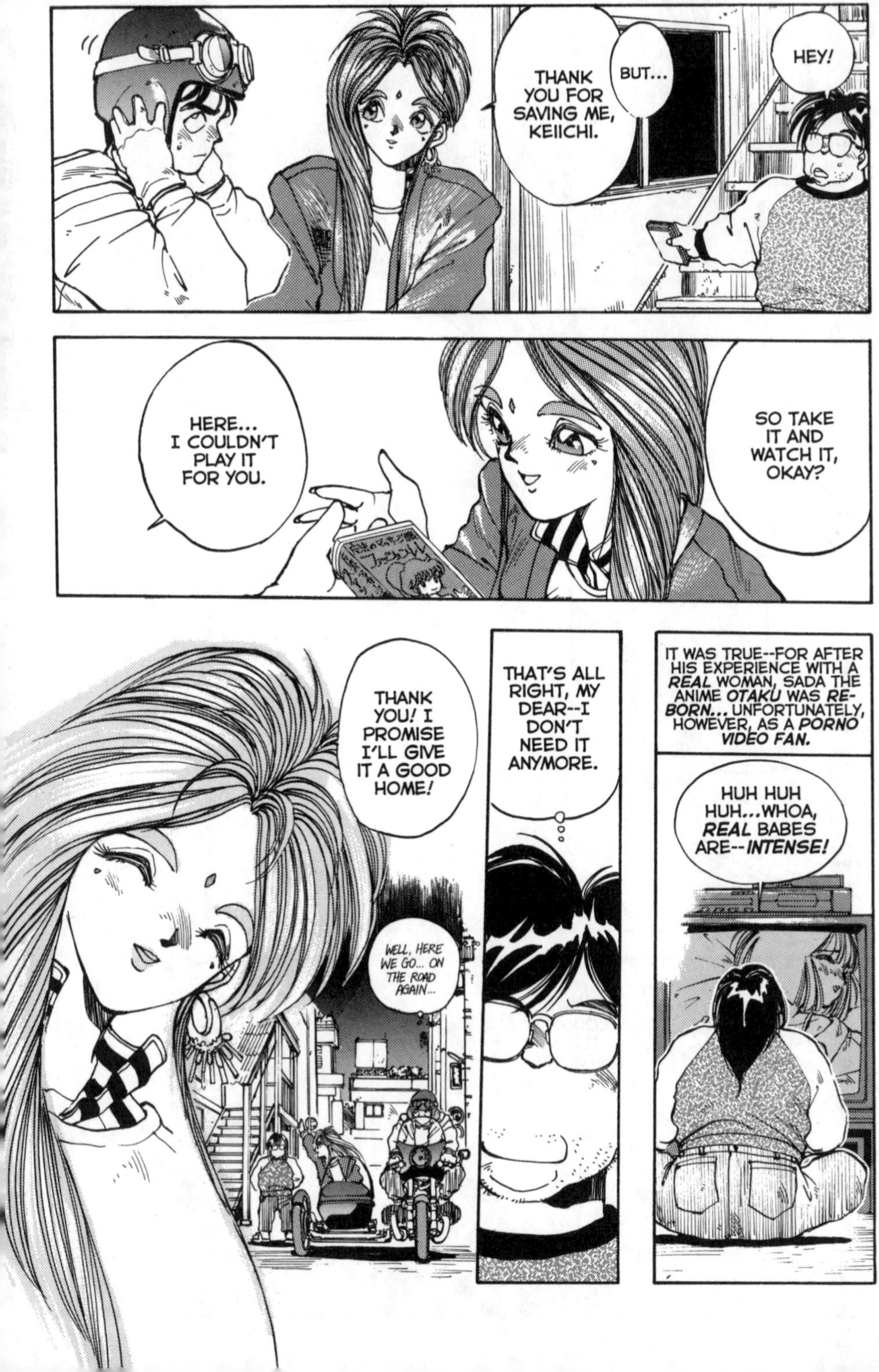
THANK YOU FOR SAVING ME, KEIICHI.
BUT...
HEY!
HERE... I COULDN'T PLAY IT FOR YOU.
SO TAKE IT AND WATCH IT, OKAY?
THANK YOU! I PROMISE I'LL GIVE IT A GOOD HOME!
WELL, HERE WE GO... ON THE ROAD AGAIN...
THAT'S ALL RIGHT, MY DEAR--I DON'T NEED IT ANYMORE.
IT WAS TRUE--FOR AFTER HIS EXPERIENCE WITH A *REAL* WOMAN, SADA THE ANIME *OTAKU* WAS *RE-BORN...* UNFORTUNATELY, HOWEVER, AS A *PORNO VIDEO FAN.*
HUH HUH HUH...WHOA, *REAL* BABES ARE--*INTENSE!*

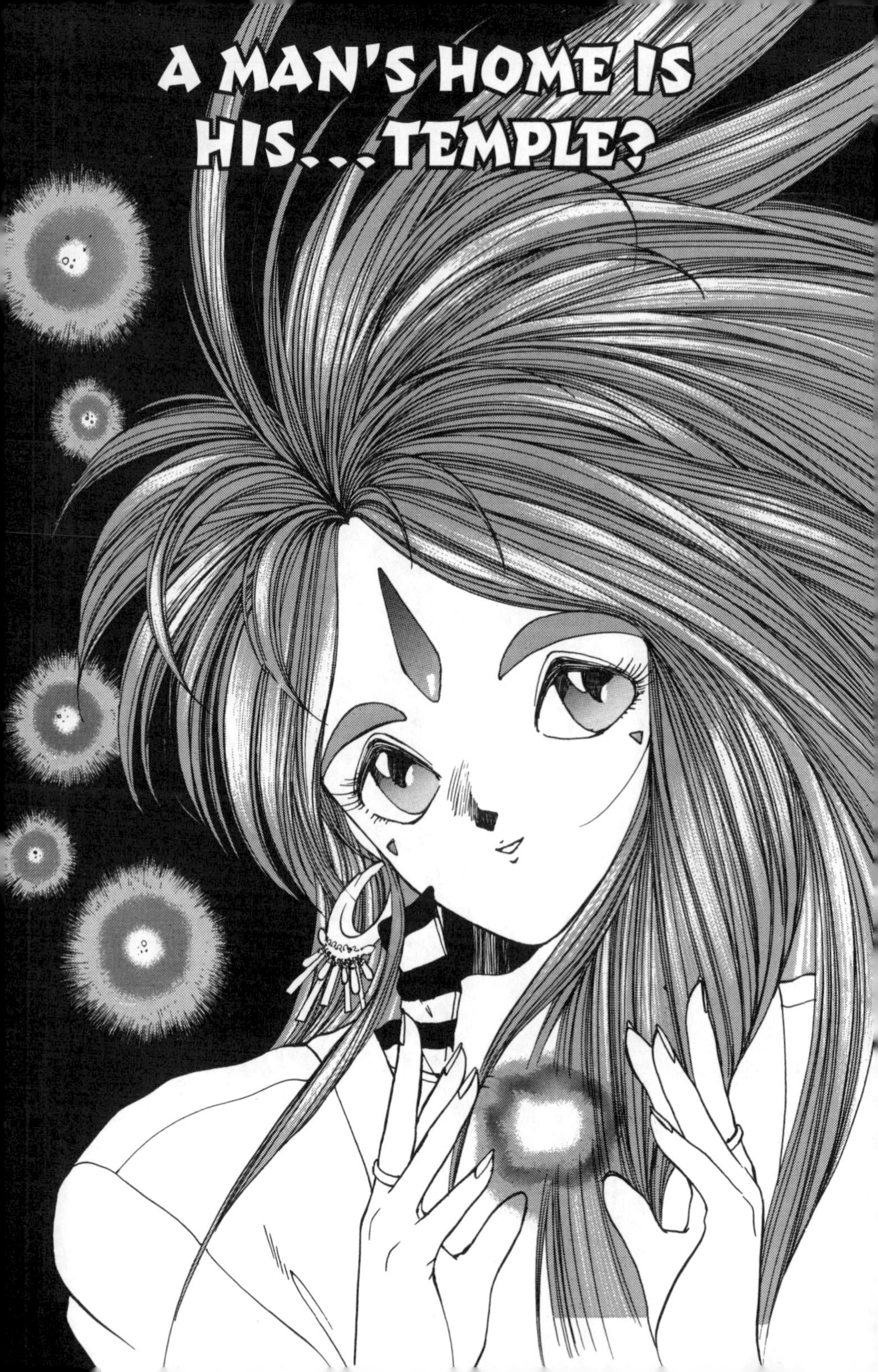
A MAN'S HOME IS
HIS... TEMPLE?

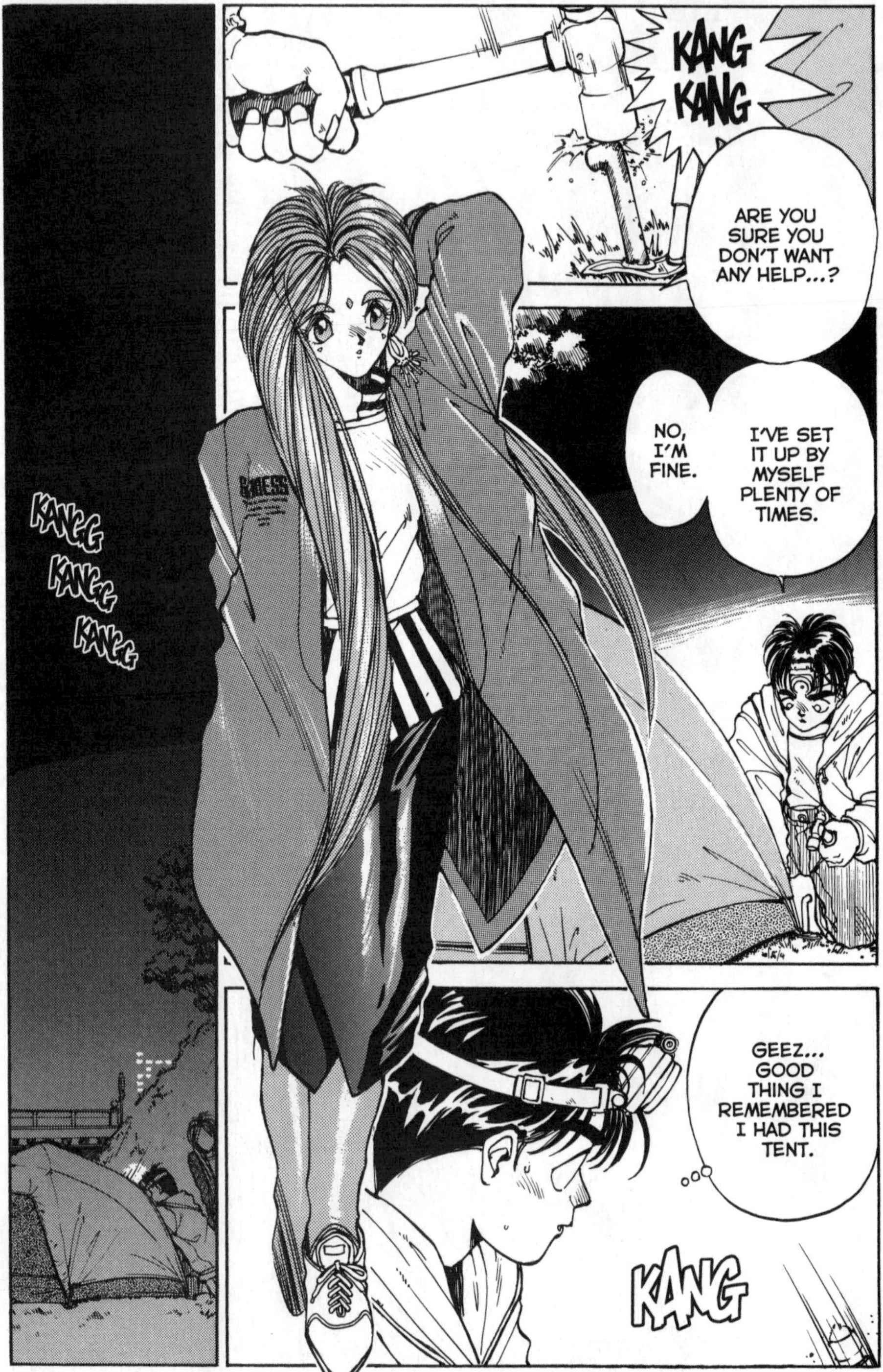
KANGG
KANGG
KANGG
KANG KANG
ARE YOU SURE YOU DON'T WANT ANY HELP...?
NO, I'M FINE.
I'VE SET IT UP BY MYSELF PLENTY OF TIMES.
GEEZ... GOOD THING I REMEMBERED I HAD THIS TENT.
KANG

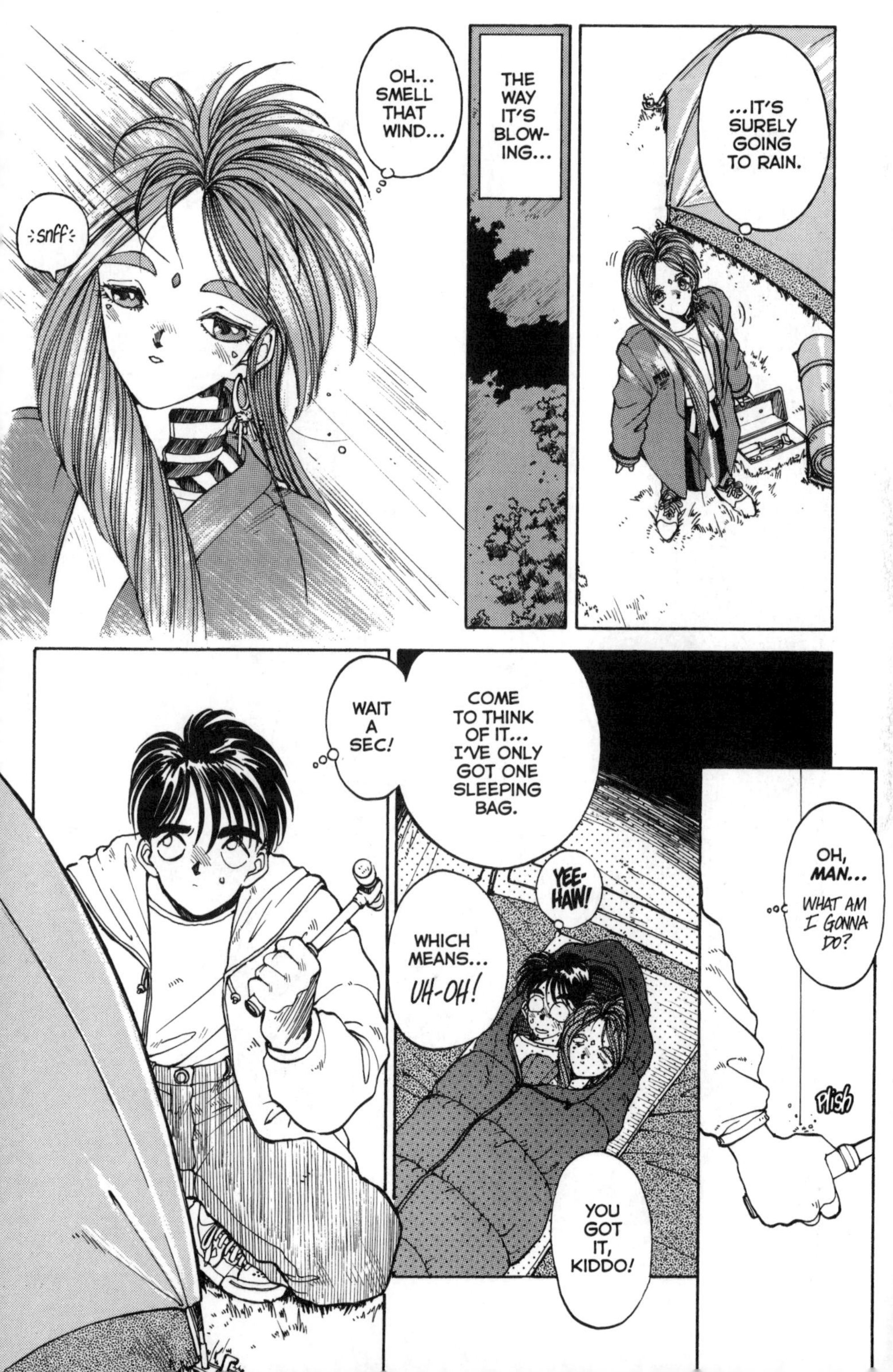
snff
OH... SMELL THAT WIND...
THE WAY IT'S BLOWING...
...IT'S SURELY GOING TO RAIN.
WAIT A SEC!
COME TO THINK OF IT... I'VE ONLY GOT ONE SLEEPING BAG.
WHICH MEANS... UH-OH!
YEE-HAW!
YOU GOT IT, KIDDO!
OH, MAN... WHAT AM I GONNA DO?
Plish

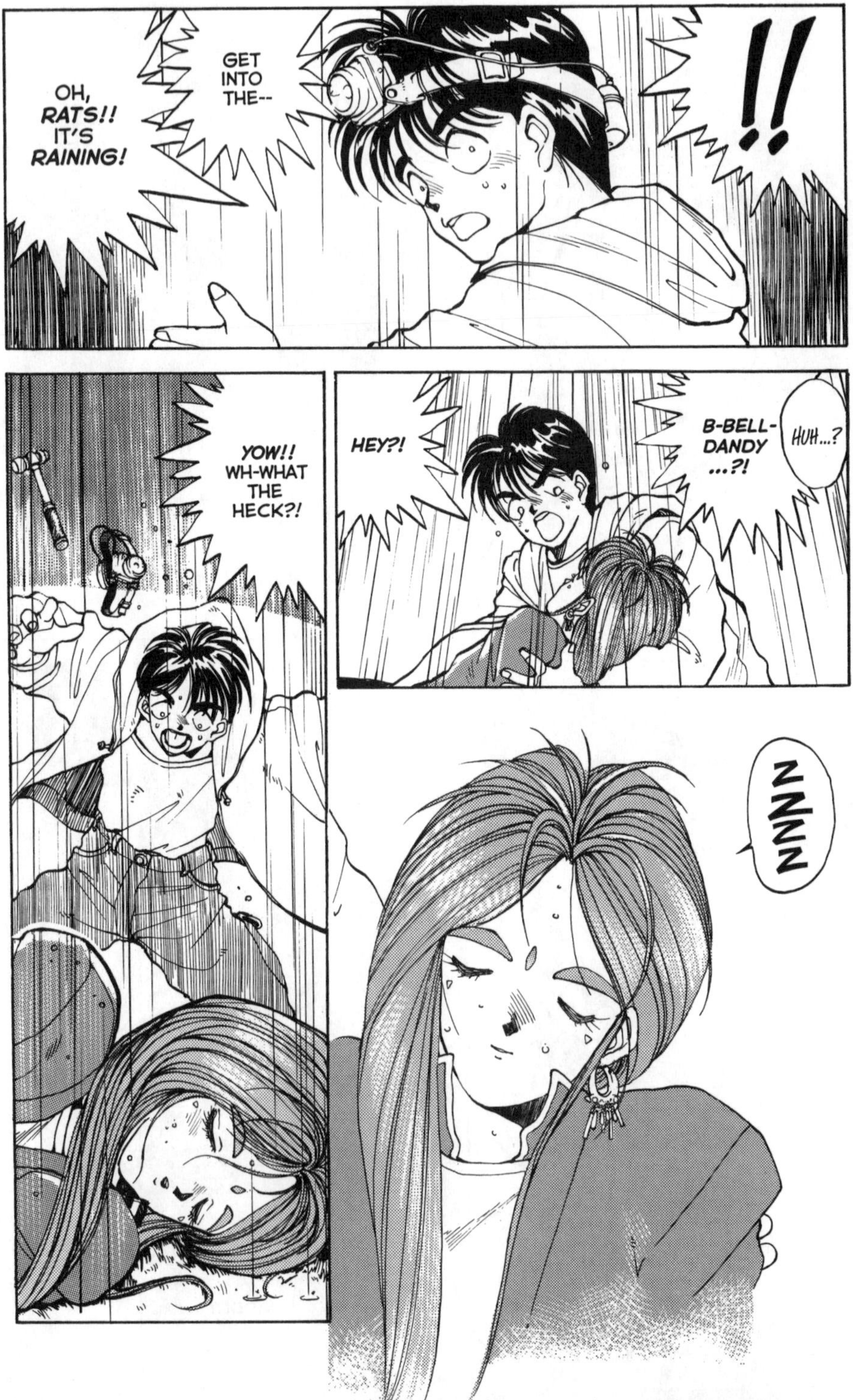
OH, RATS!! IT'S RAINING!
GET INTO THE--
!!
YOW!! WH-WHAT THE HECK?!
HEY?!
B-BELL-DANDY ...?!
HUH...?
NNNN

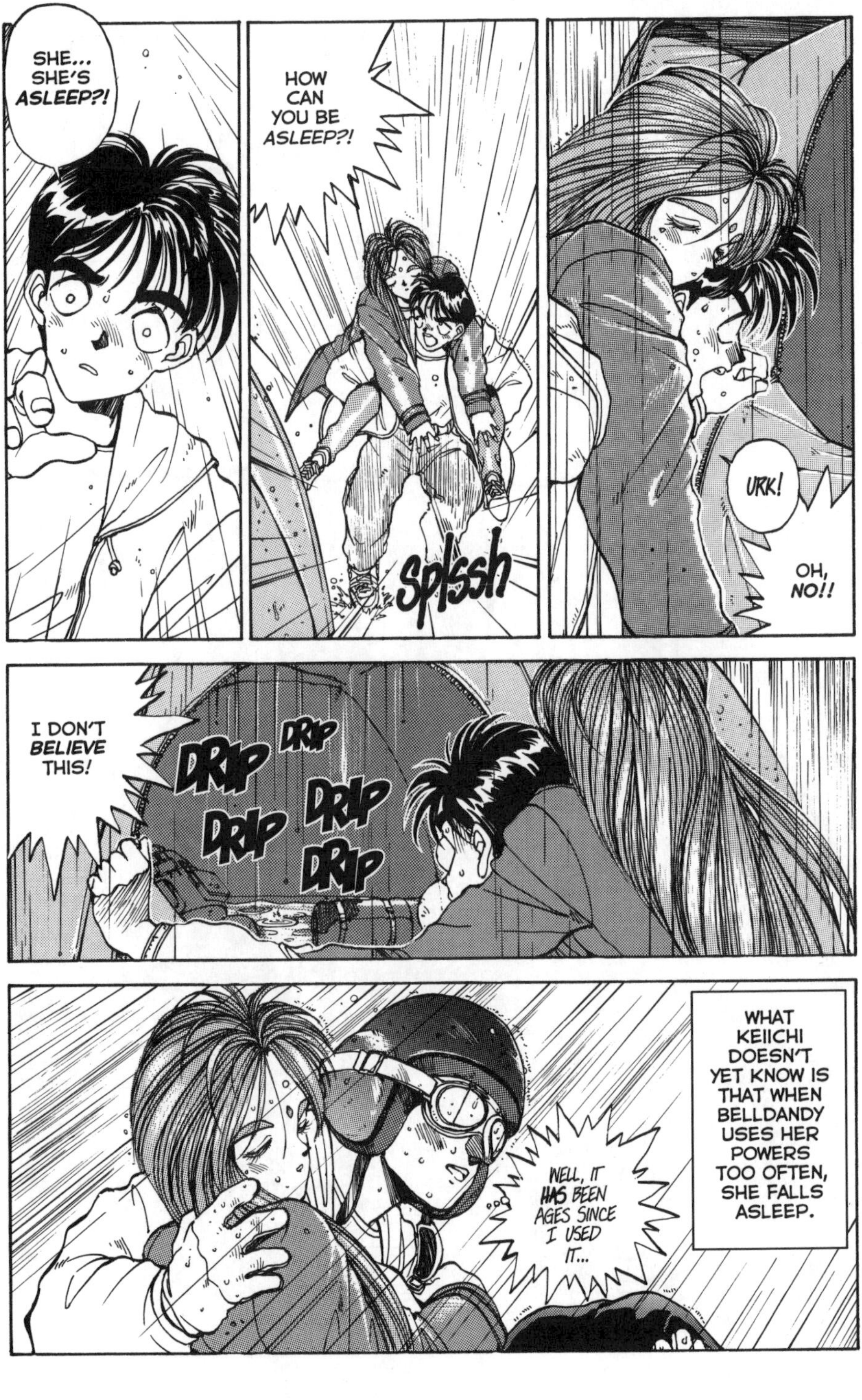
SHE... SHE'S ASLEEP?!
HOW CAN YOU BE ASLEEP?!
SPLSSH
URK!
OH, NO!!
I DON'T BELIEVE THIS!
DRIP DRIP DRIP DRIP DRIP DRIP
WELL, IT HAS BEEN AGES SINCE I USED IT...
WHAT KEIICHI DOESN'T YET KNOW IS THAT WHEN BELLDANDY USES HER POWERS TOO OFTEN, SHE FALLS ASLEEP.

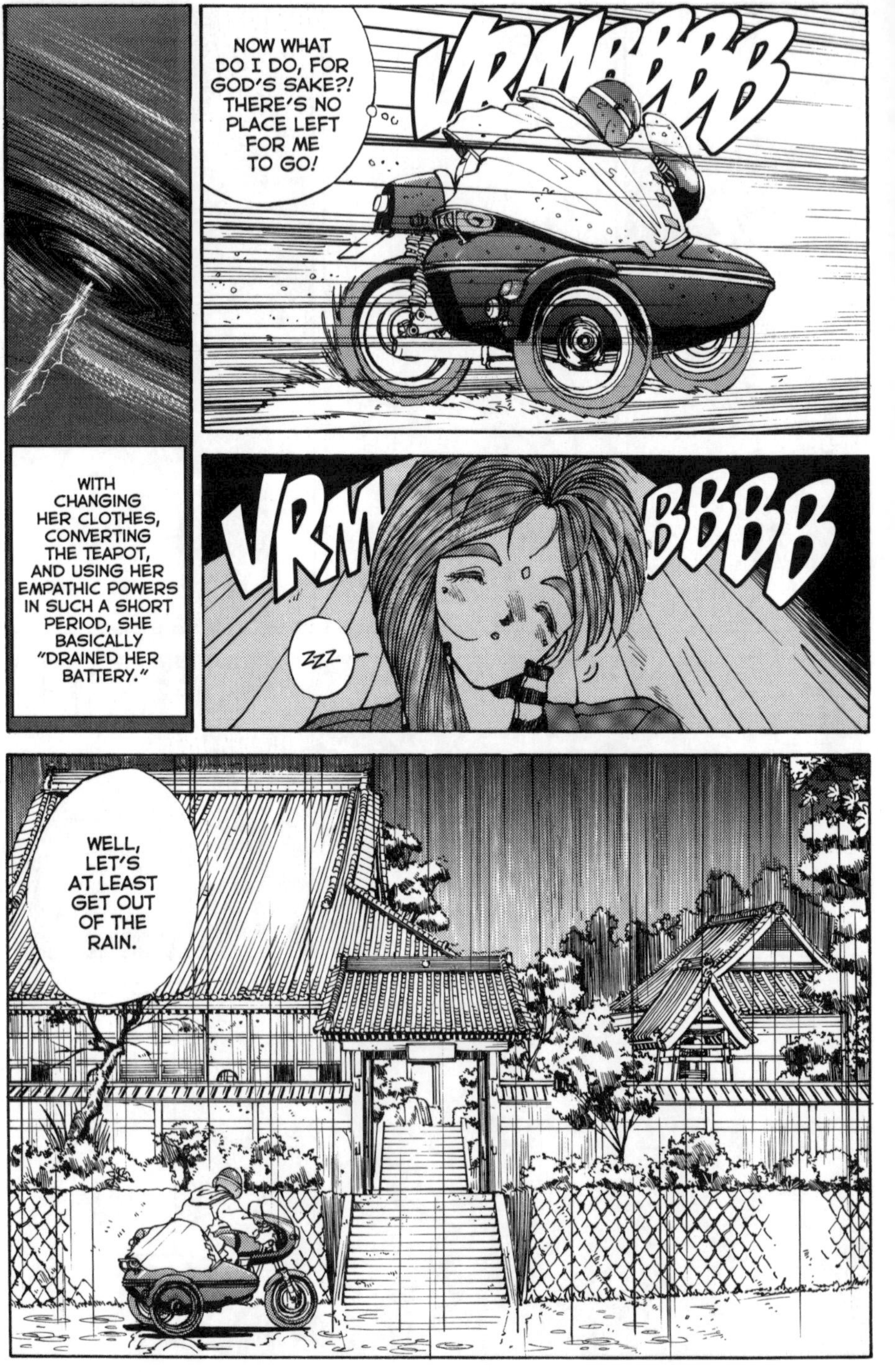
NOW WHAT DO I DO, FOR GOD'S SAKE?! THERE'S NO PLACE LEFT FOR ME TO GO!
VRMBBBB
WITH CHANGING HER CLOTHES, CONVERTING THE TEAPOT, AND USING HER EMPATHIC POWERS IN SUCH A SHORT PERIOD, SHE BASICALLY "DRAINED HER BATTERY."
VRM BBBB
ZZZ
WELL, LET'S AT LEAST GET OUT OF THE RAIN.

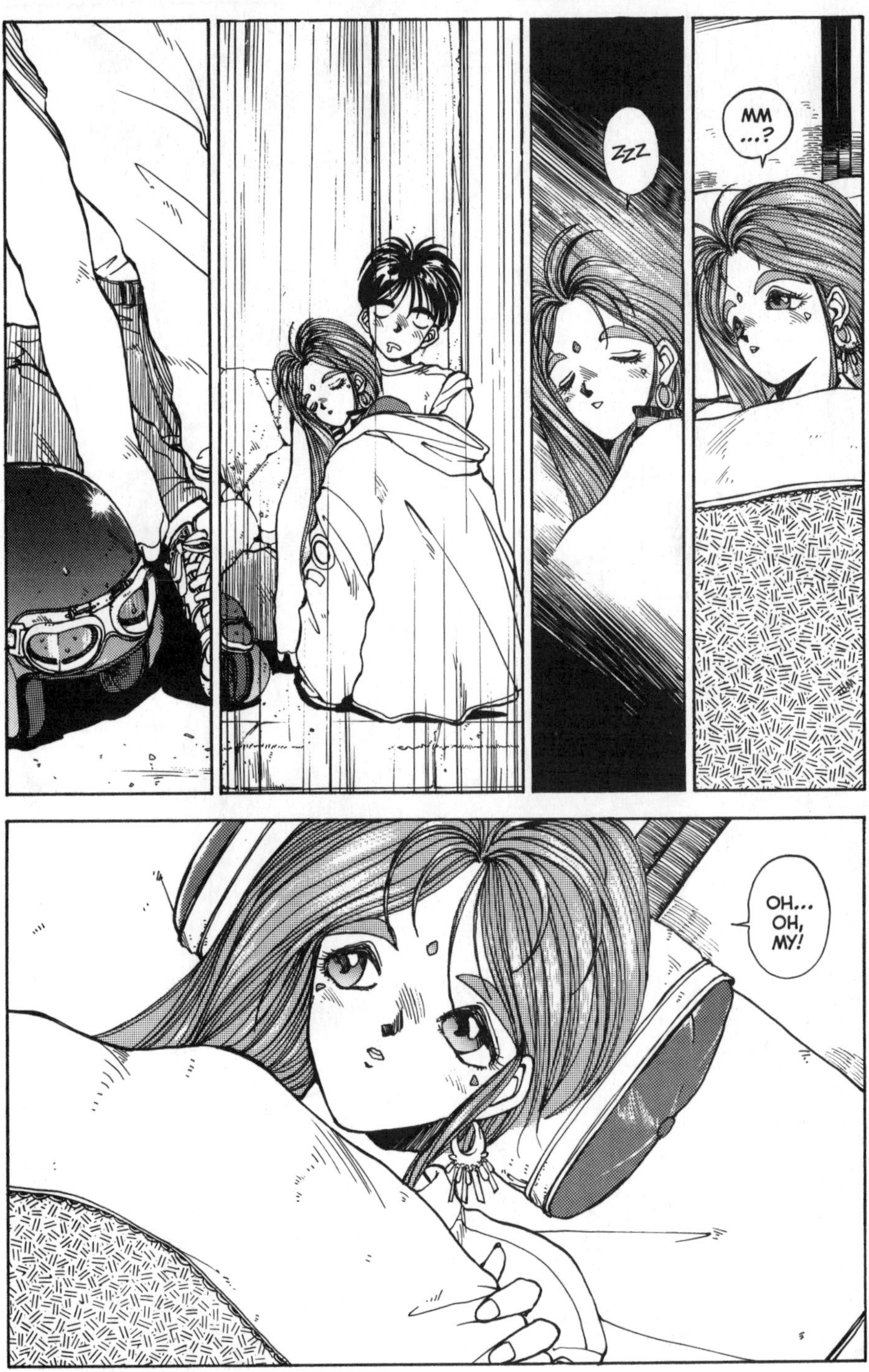
ZZZ
MM ...?
OH... OH, MY!

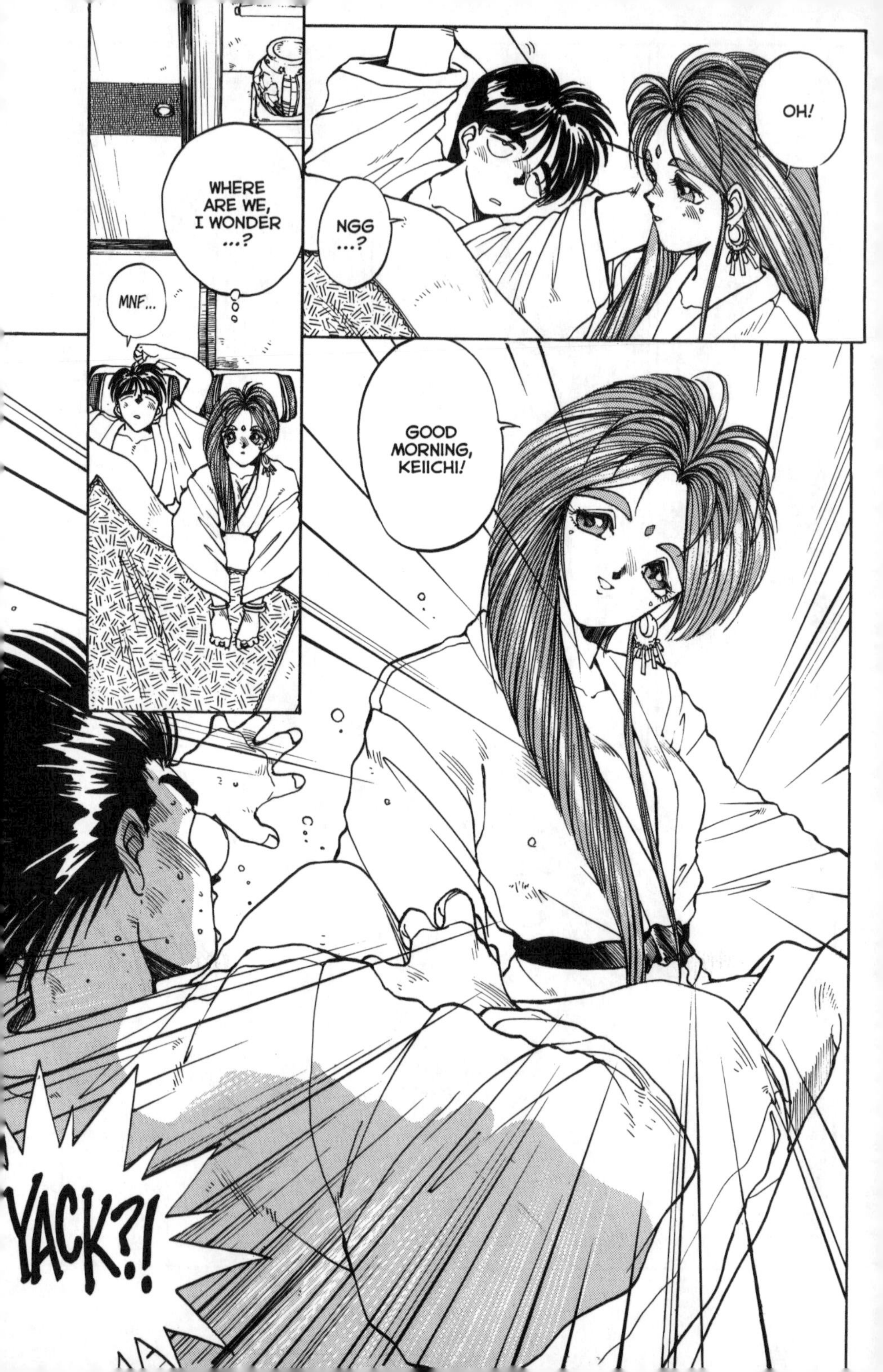
WHERE ARE WE, I WONDER ...?
MNF...
NGG ...?
OH!
GOOD MORNING, KEIICHI!
YACK?!

AIEE!

WE-- WE'RE IN THE *SAME* BED!

FWAK

SMAK KRAK

EXCUSE ME...?

HRM.

MY APOLOGIES, YOUNG LADY. I'M AFRAID I MAY HAVE INADVERTENTLY PUT YOU IN A DIFFICULT POSITION.

WHEN YOU ARRIVED TOGETHER LAST NIGHT, I JUST ASSUMED THE TWO OF YOU WERE... LOVERS.

SORRY ABOUT THAT.

BWAHAHAHA!

THE MORE FOOL ME! HAH--JUMPING TO CONCLUSIONS AGAIN!

ANYWAY, YOUR CLOTHES ARE DRYING.

SIR! SIR!! WAIT!!

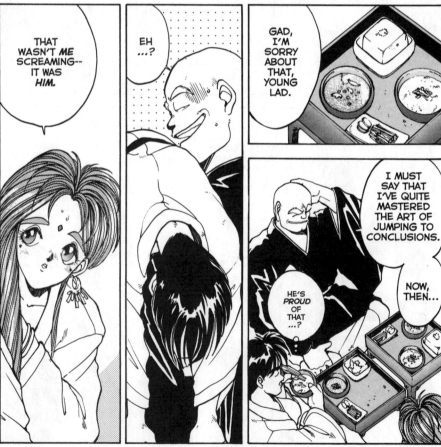

THAT WASN'T *ME* SCREAMING-- IT WAS *HIM*.

EH ...?

GAD, I'M SORRY ABOUT THAT, YOUNG LAD.

I MUST SAY THAT I'VE QUITE MASTERED THE ART OF JUMPING TO CONCLUSIONS.

HE'S *PROUD* OF THAT ...?

NOW, THEN...

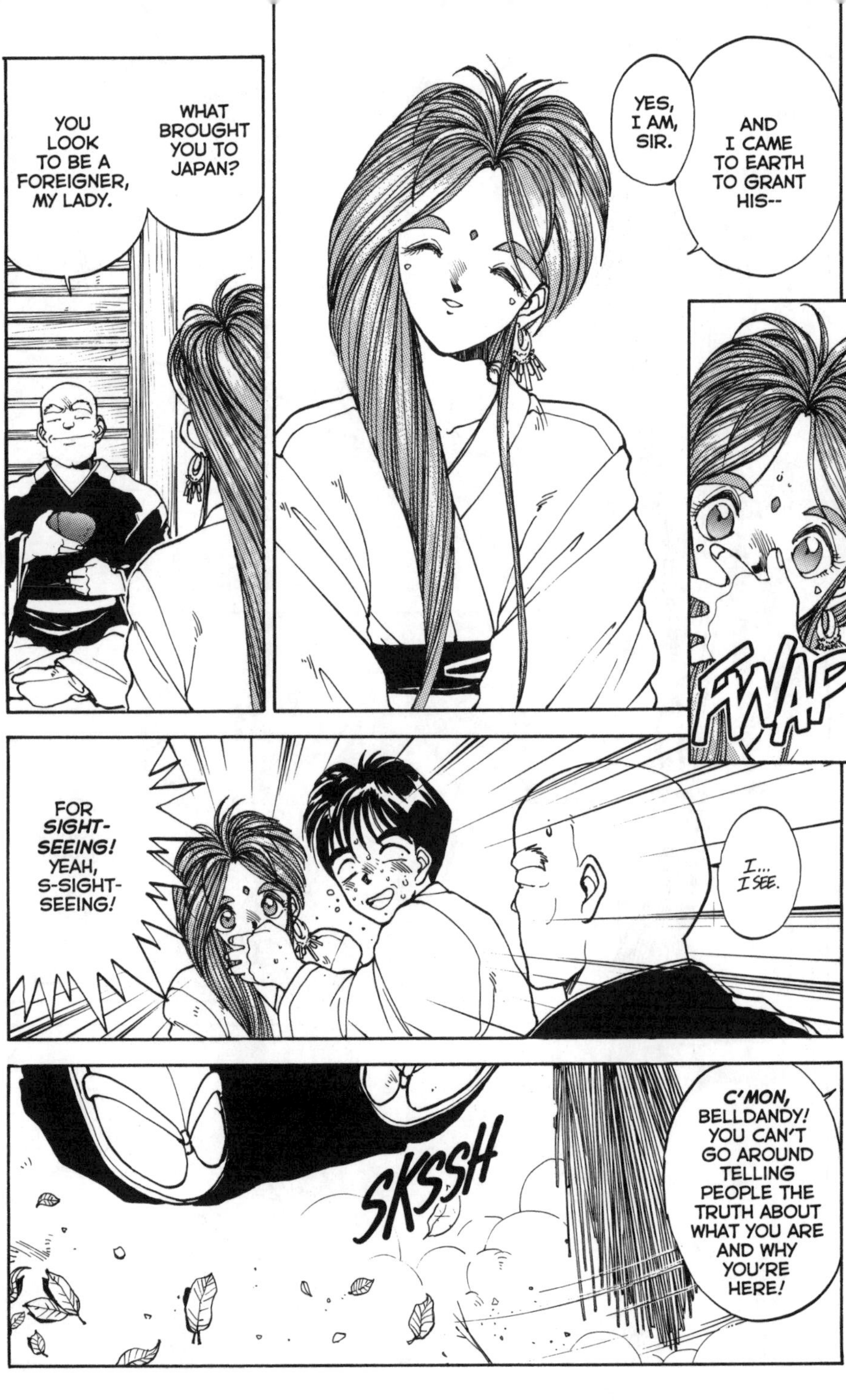
YOU LOOK TO BE A FOREIGNER, MY LADY.
WHAT BROUGHT YOU TO JAPAN?
YES, I AM, SIR.
AND I CAME TO EARTH TO GRANT HIS--
FWAP
FOR *SIGHT-SEEING!* YEAH, S-SIGHT-SEEING!
I... I SEE.
SKSSH
C'MON, BELLDANDY*!* YOU CAN'T GO AROUND TELLING PEOPLE THE TRUTH ABOUT WHAT YOU ARE AND WHY YOU'RE HERE*!*

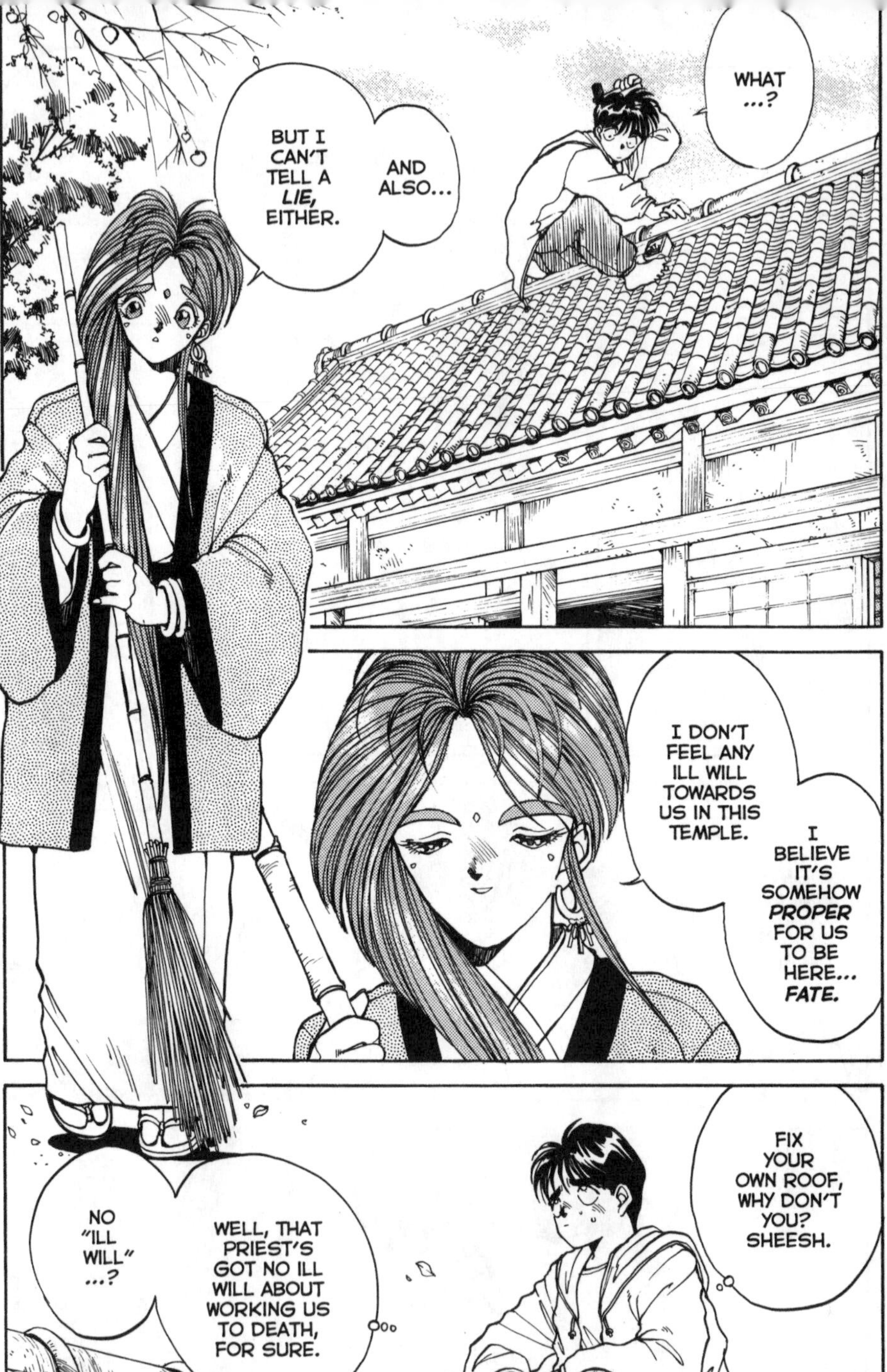
BUT I CAN'T TELL A *LIE,* EITHER.
AND ALSO...
WHAT ...?
I DON'T FEEL ANY ILL WILL TOWARDS US IN THIS TEMPLE.
I BELIEVE IT'S SOMEHOW *PROPER* FOR US TO BE HERE... *FATE.*
NO "ILL WILL" ...?
WELL, THAT PRIEST'S GOT NO ILL WILL ABOUT WORKING US TO DEATH, FOR SURE.
FIX YOUR OWN ROOF, WHY DON'T YOU? SHEESH.

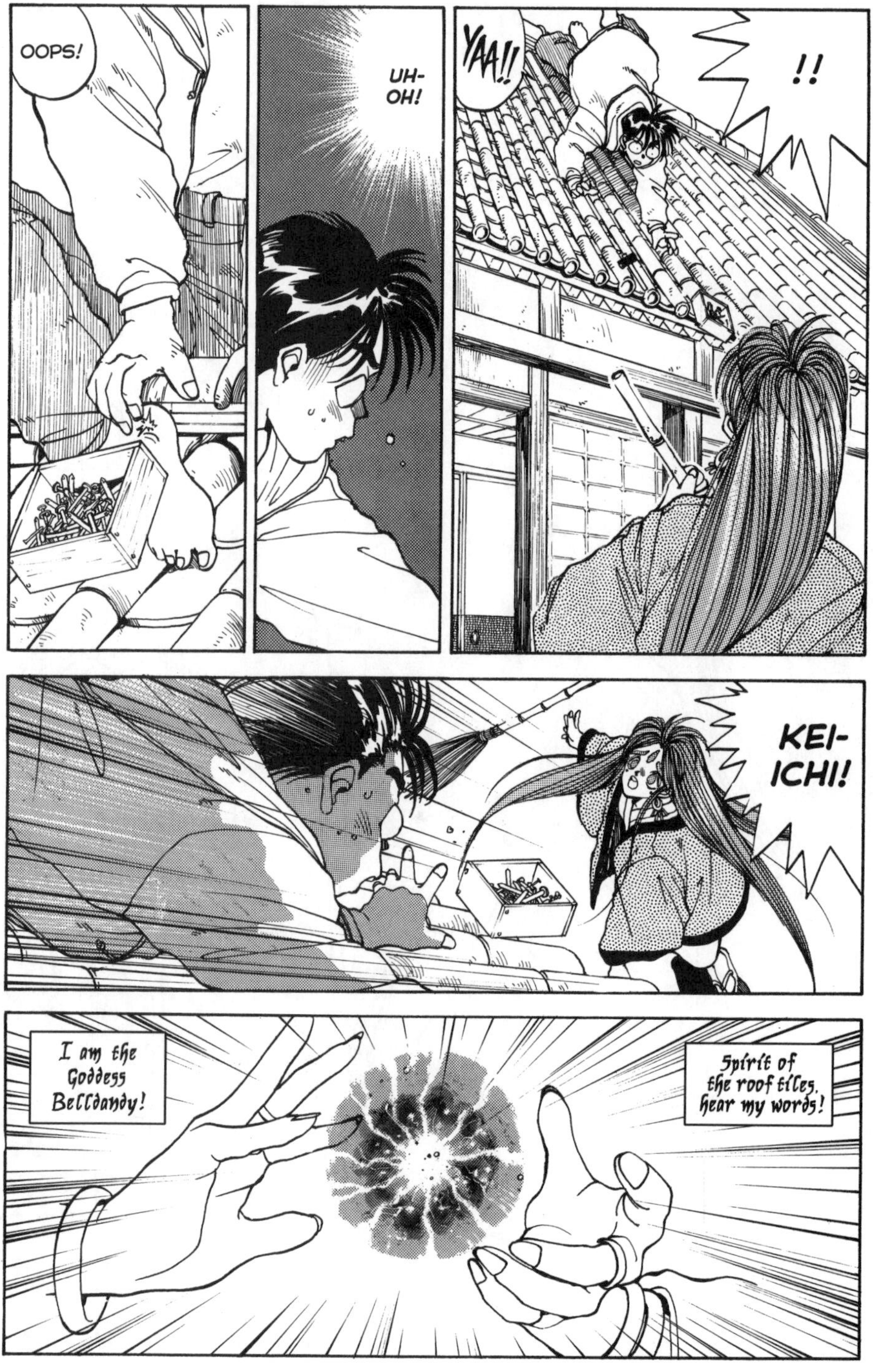
OOPS!
UH-OH!
YAA!!
!!
KEI-ICHI!
I am the Goddess Belldandy!
Spirit of the roof tiles, hear my words!

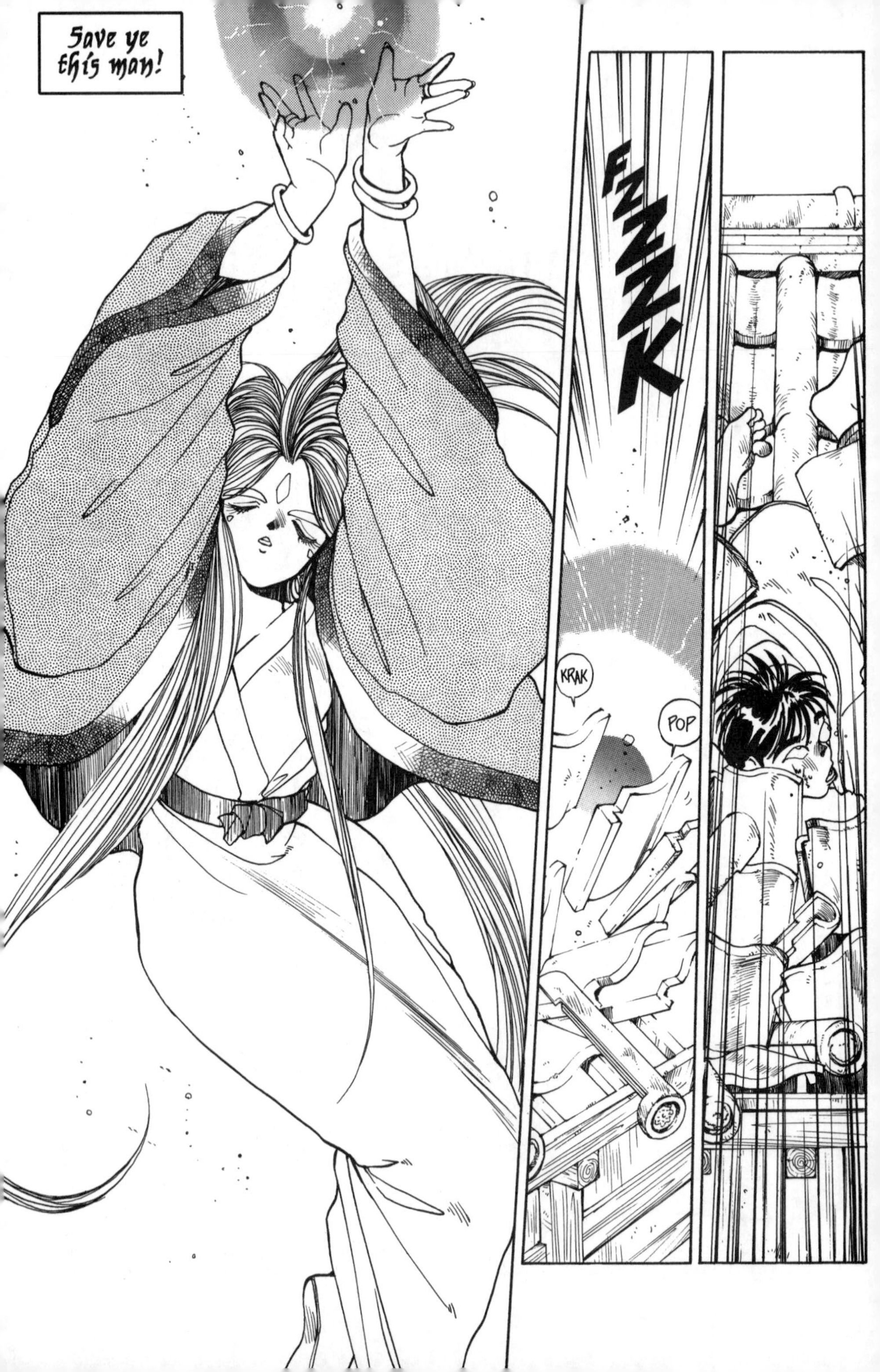
Save ye this man!
FZZZK
KRAK
POP

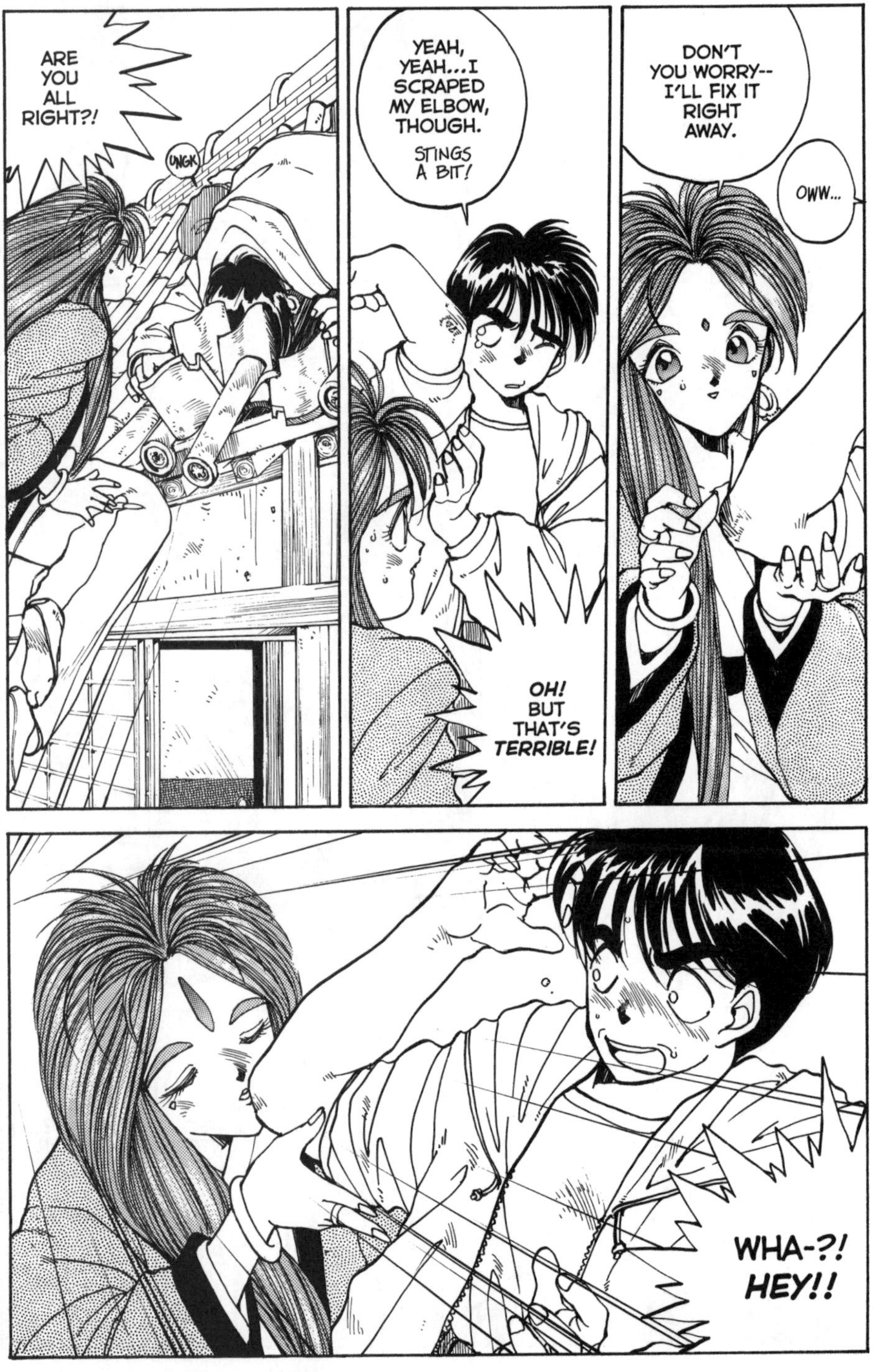
ARE YOU ALL RIGHT?!
UNGK
YEAH, YEAH...I SCRAPED MY ELBOW, THOUGH.
STINGS A BIT!
OH! BUT THAT'S *TERRIBLE!*
DON'T YOU WORRY-- I'LL FIX IT RIGHT AWAY.
OWW...
WHA-?! HEY!!

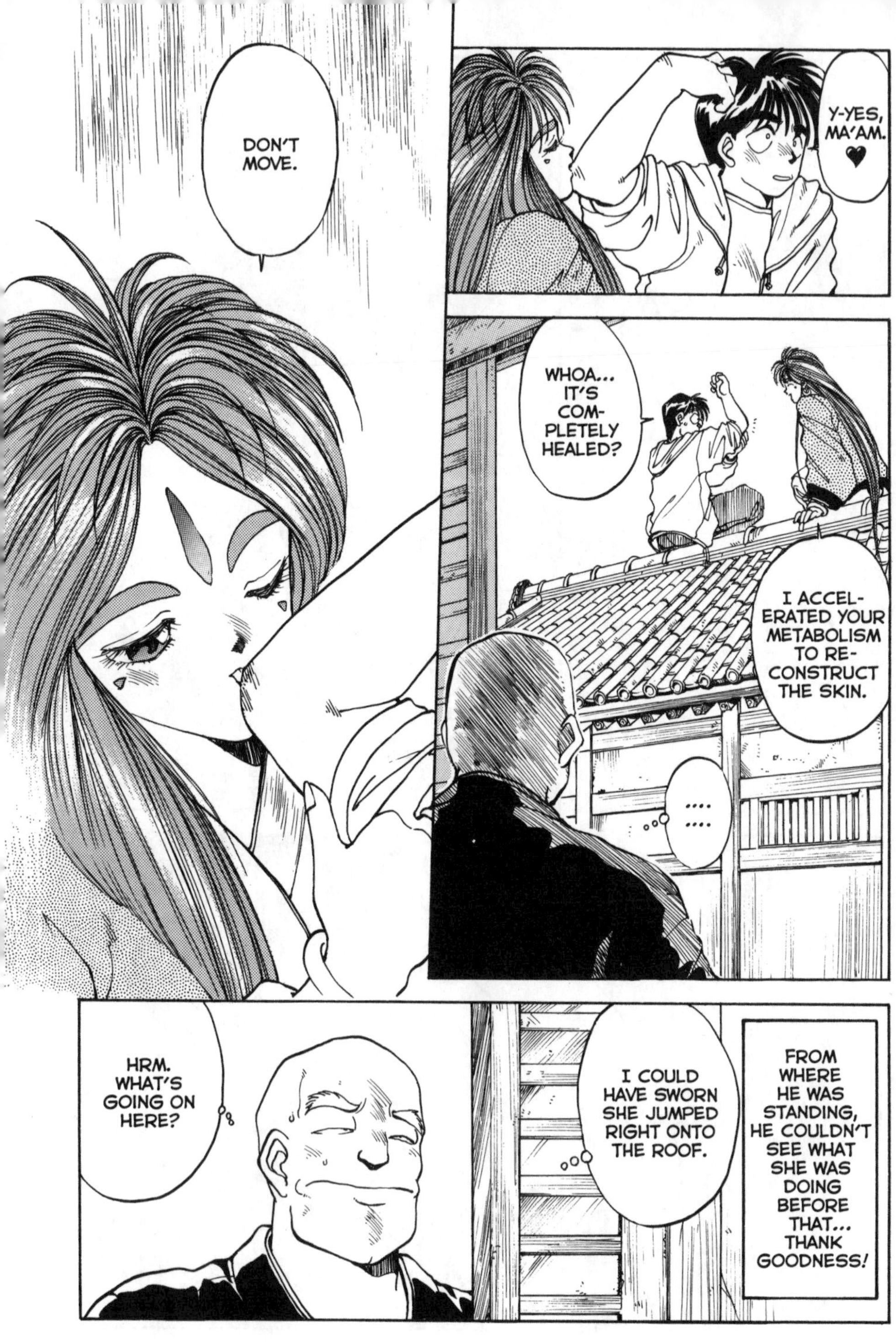
DON'T MOVE.
Y-YES, MA'AM. ♥
WHOA... IT'S COM-PLETELY HEALED?
I ACCEL-ERATED YOUR METABOLISM TO RE-CONSTRUCT THE SKIN.
....
....
HRM. WHAT'S GOING ON HERE?
I COULD HAVE SWORN SHE JUMPED RIGHT ONTO THE ROOF.
FROM WHERE HE WAS STANDING, HE COULDN'T SEE WHAT SHE WAS DOING BEFORE THAT... THANK GOODNESS!

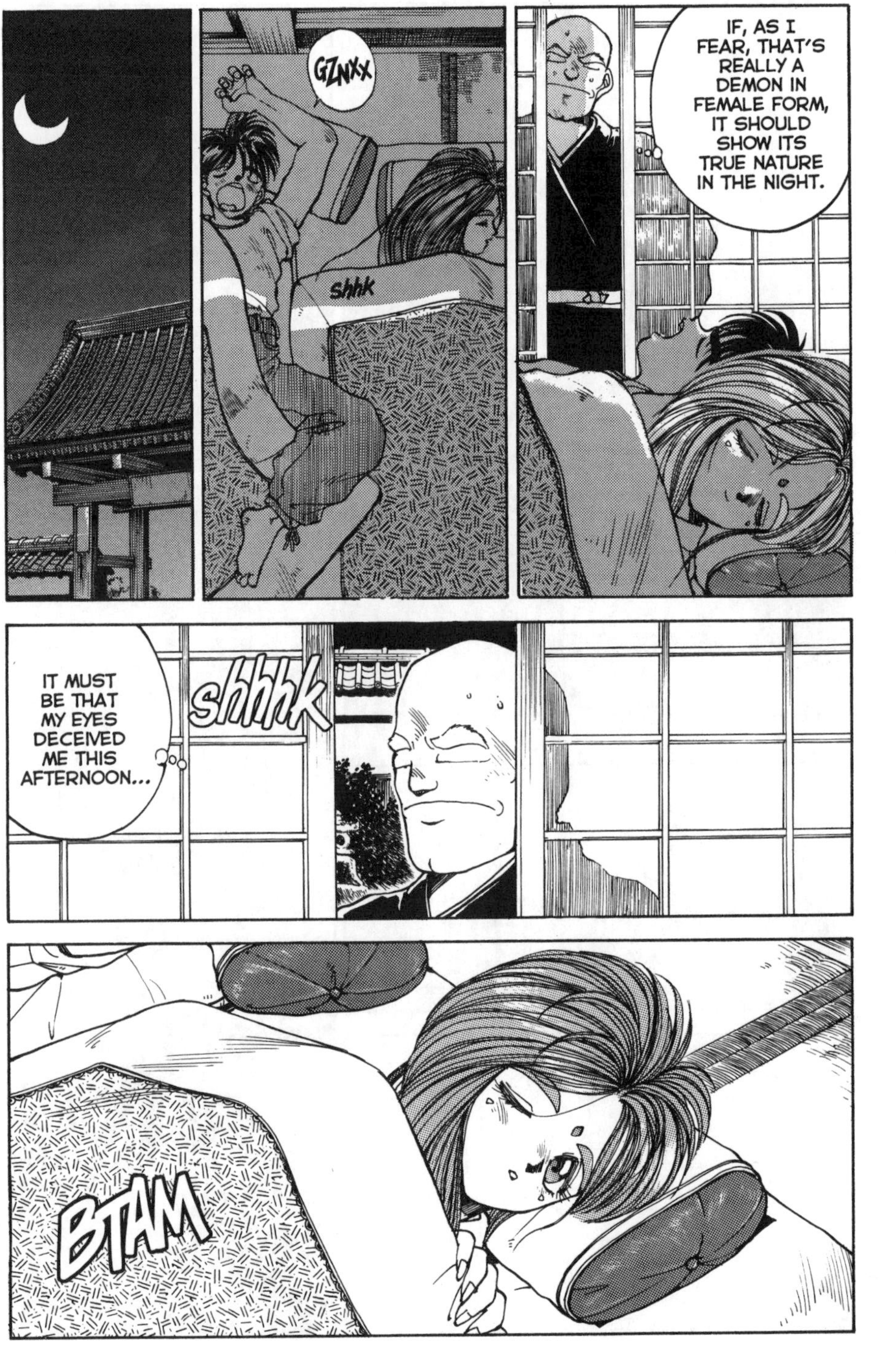
GZNXX
shhk
IF, AS I FEAR, THAT'S REALLY A DEMON IN FEMALE FORM, IT SHOULD SHOW ITS TRUE NATURE IN THE NIGHT.
IT MUST BE THAT MY EYES DECEIVED ME THIS AFTERNOON...
shhhk
BTAM

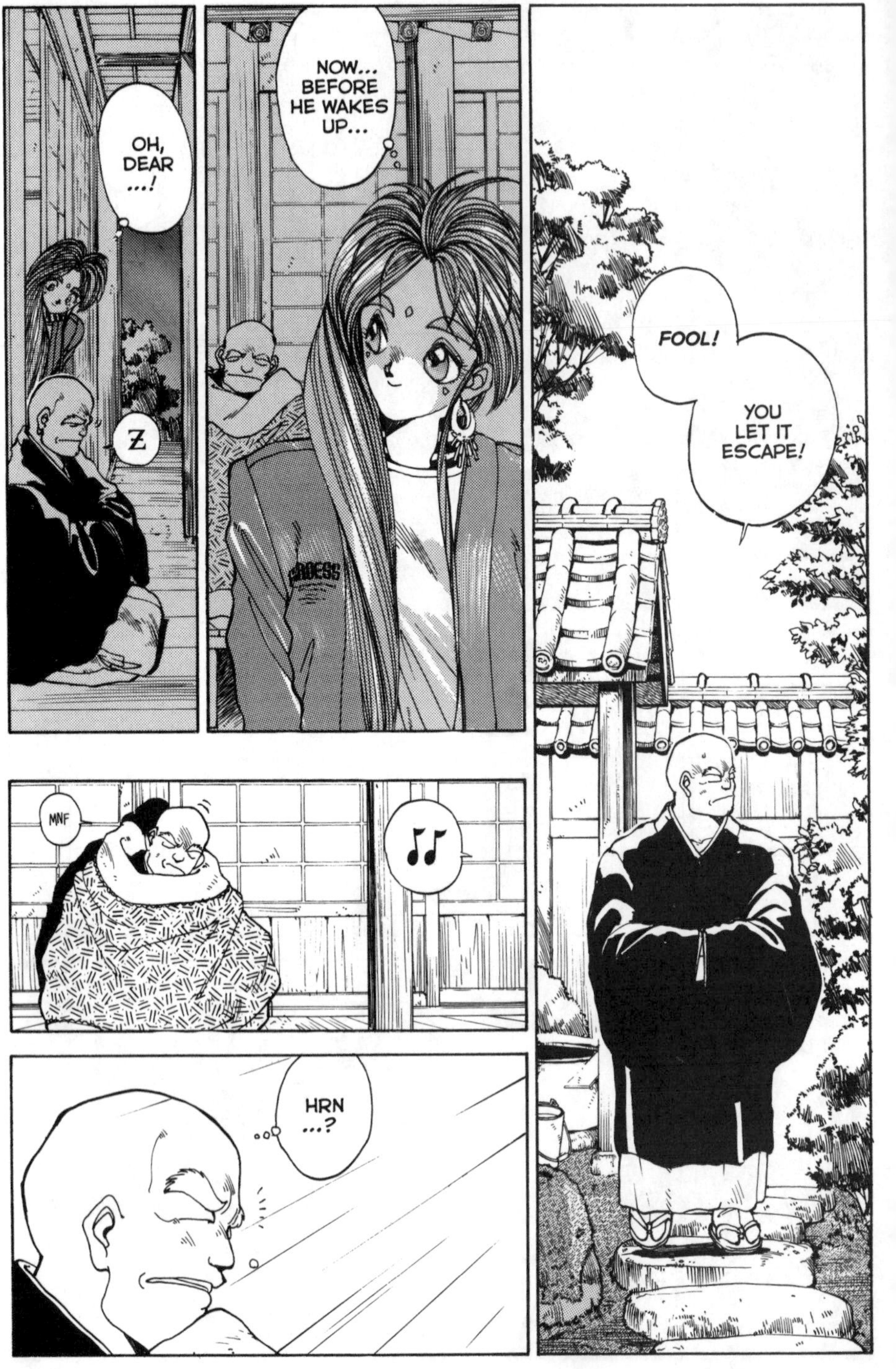
OH, DEAR ...!
Z
NOW... BEFORE HE WAKES UP...
MNF
♫
HRN ...?
FOOL!
YOU LET IT ESCAPE!

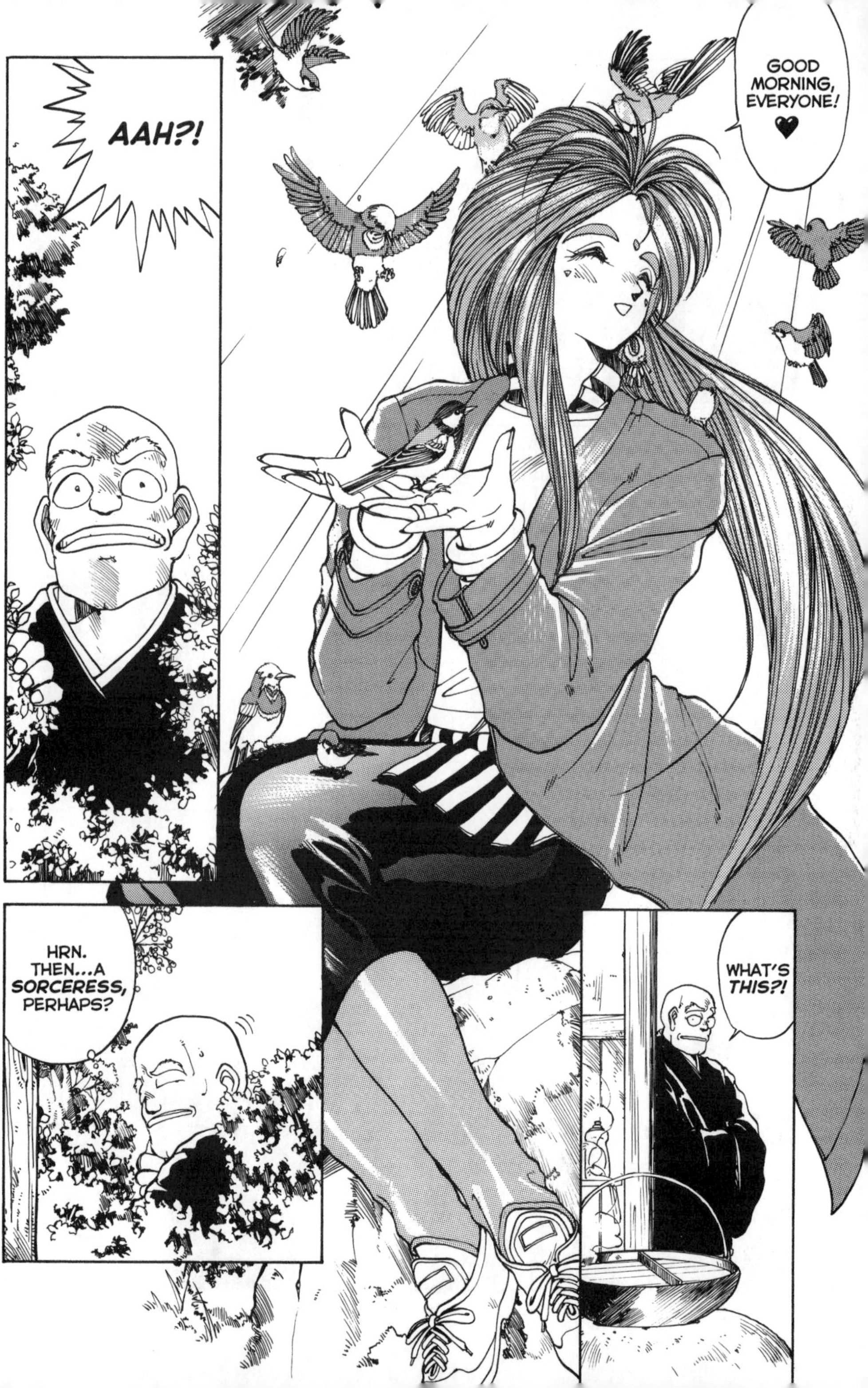
AAH?!
HRN. THEN...A SORCERESS, PERHAPS?
GOOD MORNING, EVERYONE! ♥
WHAT'S THIS?!

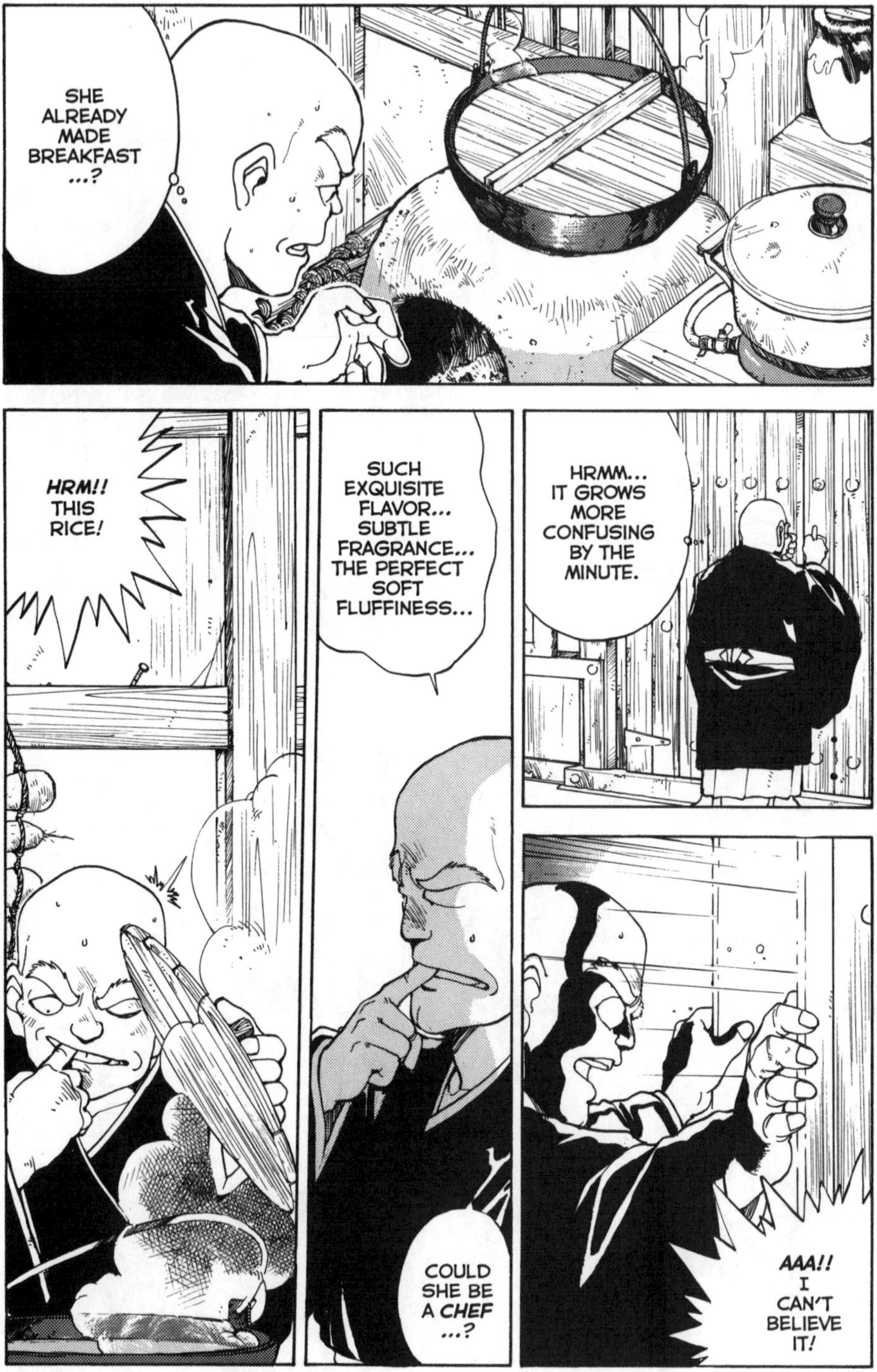
SHE ALREADY MADE BREAKFAST ...?
HRM!! THIS RICE!
SUCH EXQUISITE FLAVOR... SUBTLE FRAGRANCE... THE PERFECT SOFT FLUFFINESS...
COULD SHE BE A *CHEF* ...?
HRMM... IT GROWS MORE CONFUSING BY THE MINUTE.
AAA!! I CAN'T BELIEVE IT!

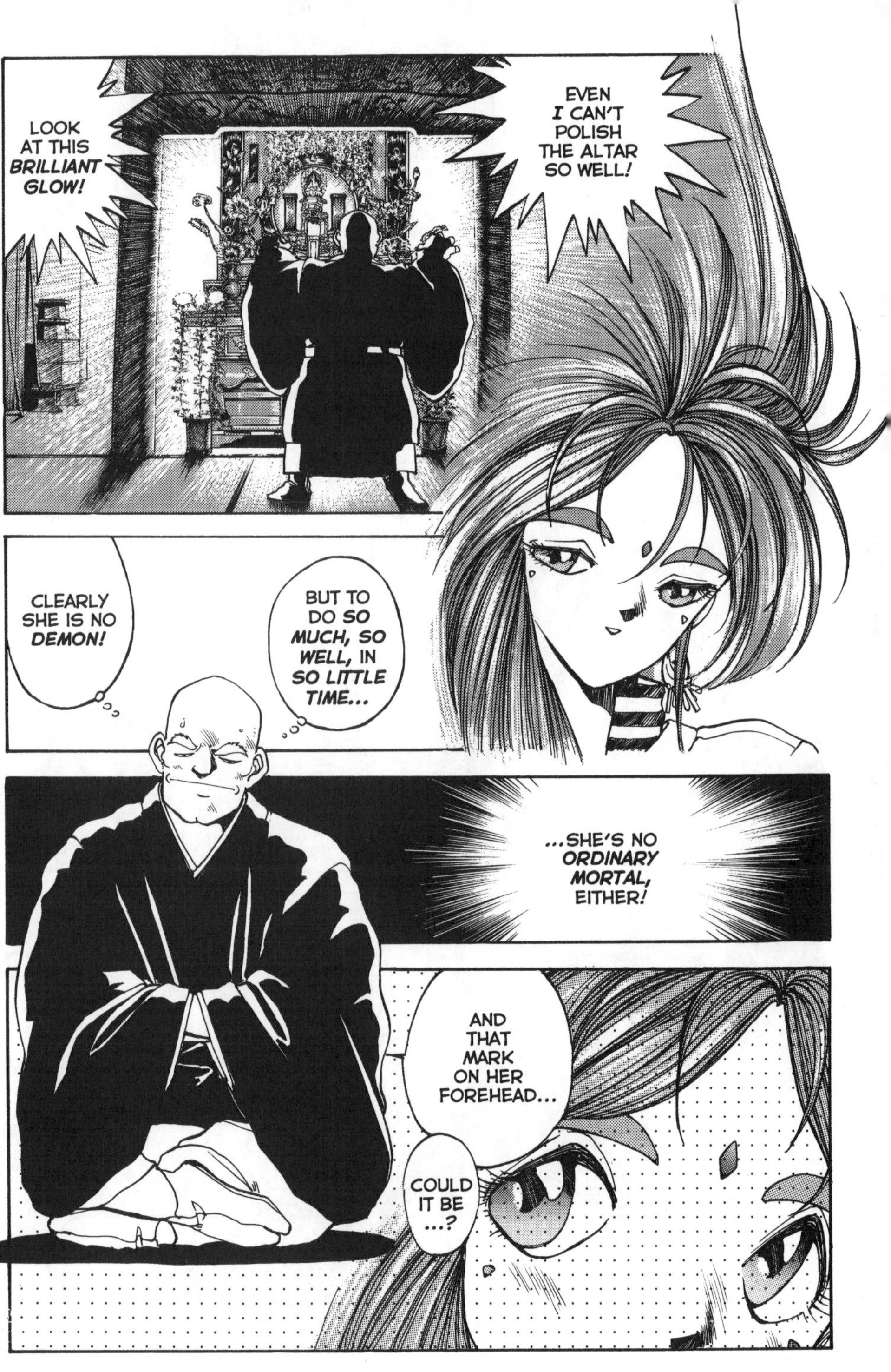
LOOK AT THIS BRILLIANT GLOW!
EVEN I CAN'T POLISH THE ALTAR SO WELL!
CLEARLY SHE IS NO DEMON!
BUT TO DO SO MUCH, SO WELL, IN SO LITTLE TIME...
...SHE'S NO ORDINARY MORTAL, EITHER!
AND THAT MARK ON HER FOREHEAD...
COULD IT BE ...?

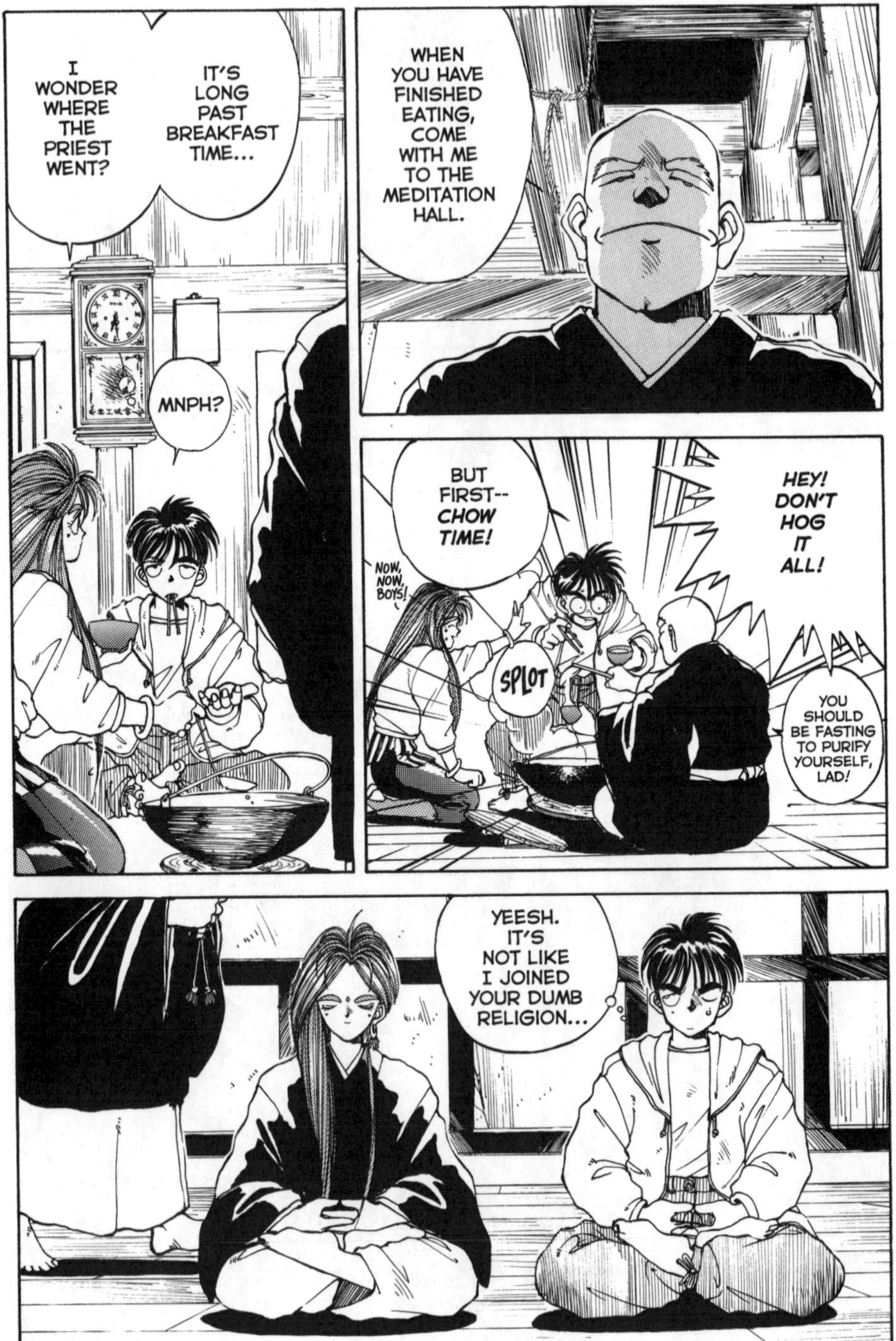
I WONDER WHERE THE PRIEST WENT?
IT'S LONG PAST BREAKFAST TIME...
MNPH?
WHEN YOU HAVE FINISHED EATING, COME WITH ME TO THE MEDITATION HALL.
BUT FIRST-- *CHOW TIME!*
NOW, NOW, BOYS!
HEY! DON'T HOG IT ALL!
SPLOT
YOU SHOULD BE FASTING TO PURIFY YOURSELF, LAD!
YEESH. IT'S NOT LIKE I JOINED YOUR DUMB RELIGION...

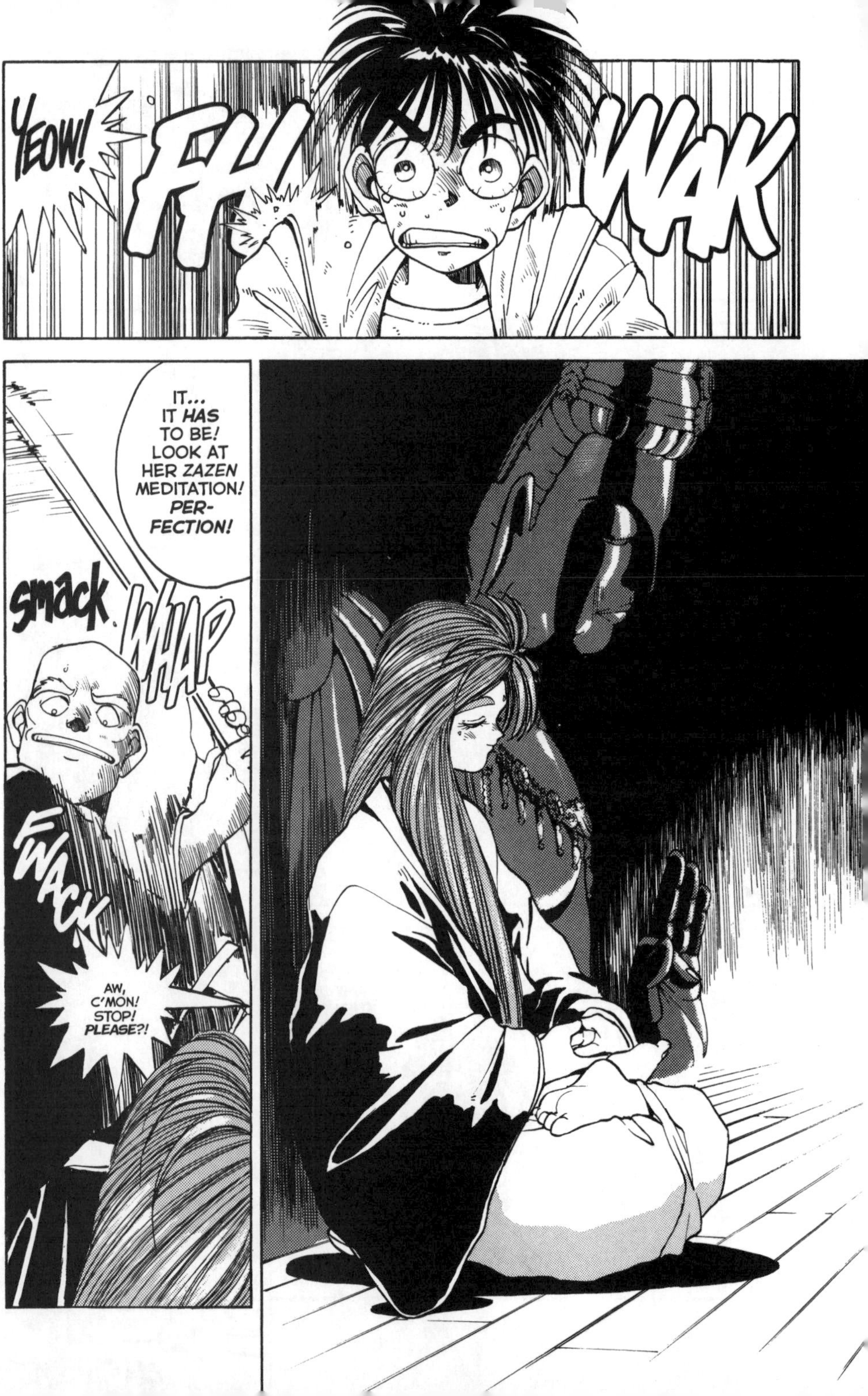
YEOW!
WAK
IT... IT HAS TO BE! LOOK AT HER ZAZEN MEDITATION! PERFECTION!
smack
WHAP
FWACK!
AW, C'MON! STOP! PLEASE?!

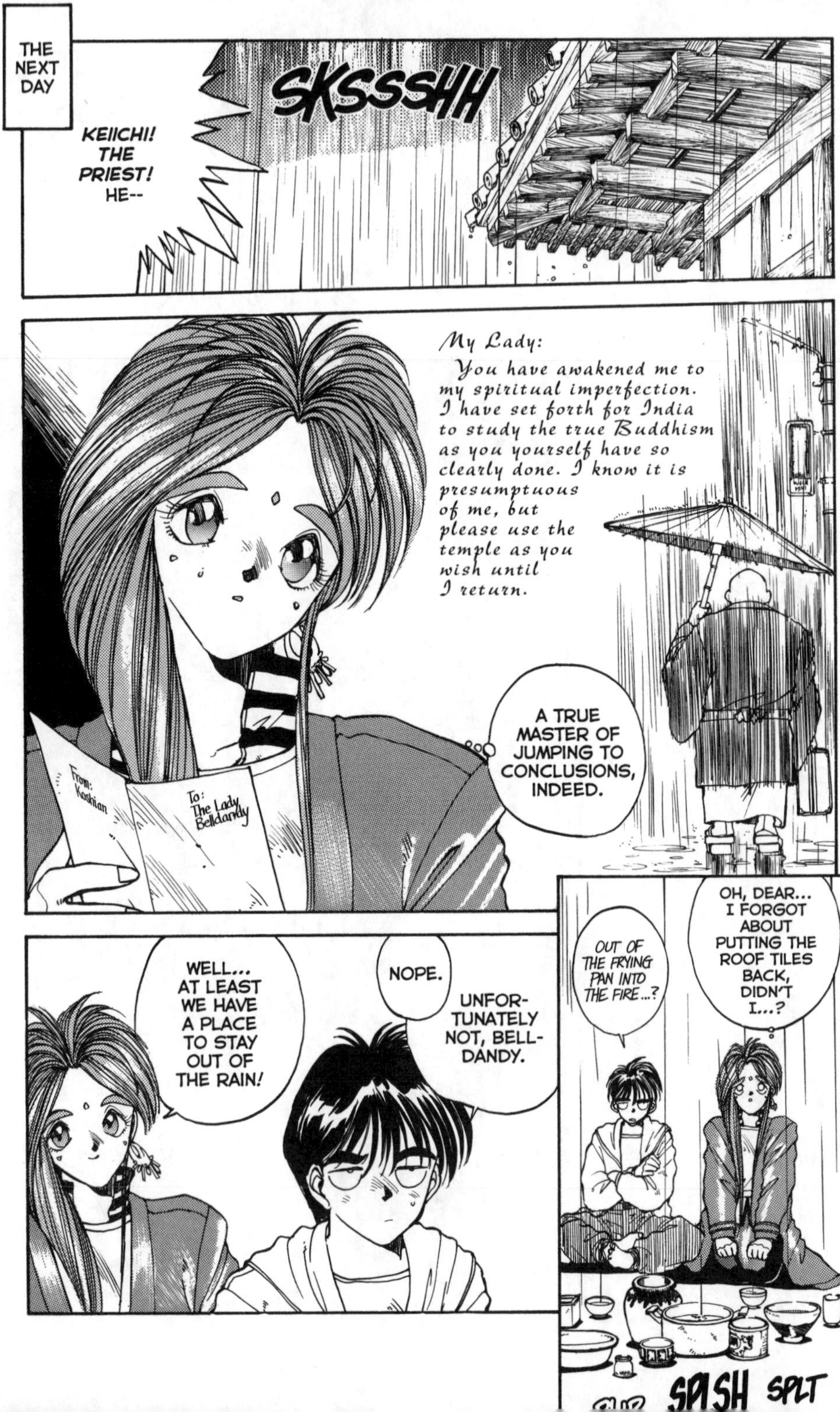
THE NEXT DAY
SKSSSHH
KEIICHI! THE PRIEST! HE--
My Lady:
You have awakened me to my spiritual imperfection. I have set forth for India to study the true Buddhism as you yourself have so clearly done. I know it is presumptuous of me, but please use the temple as you wish until I return.
From: Koshian
To: The Lady Belldandy
A TRUE MASTER OF JUMPING TO CONCLUSIONS, INDEED.
WELL... AT LEAST WE HAVE A PLACE TO STAY OUT OF THE RAIN!
NOPE.
UNFOR-TUNATELY NOT, BELL-DANDY.
OUT OF THE FRYING PAN INTO THE FIRE...?
OH, DEAR... I FORGOT ABOUT PUTTING THE ROOF TILES BACK, DIDN'T I...?
SPISH
SPLT

COLLEGE EXCHANGE.... GODDESS

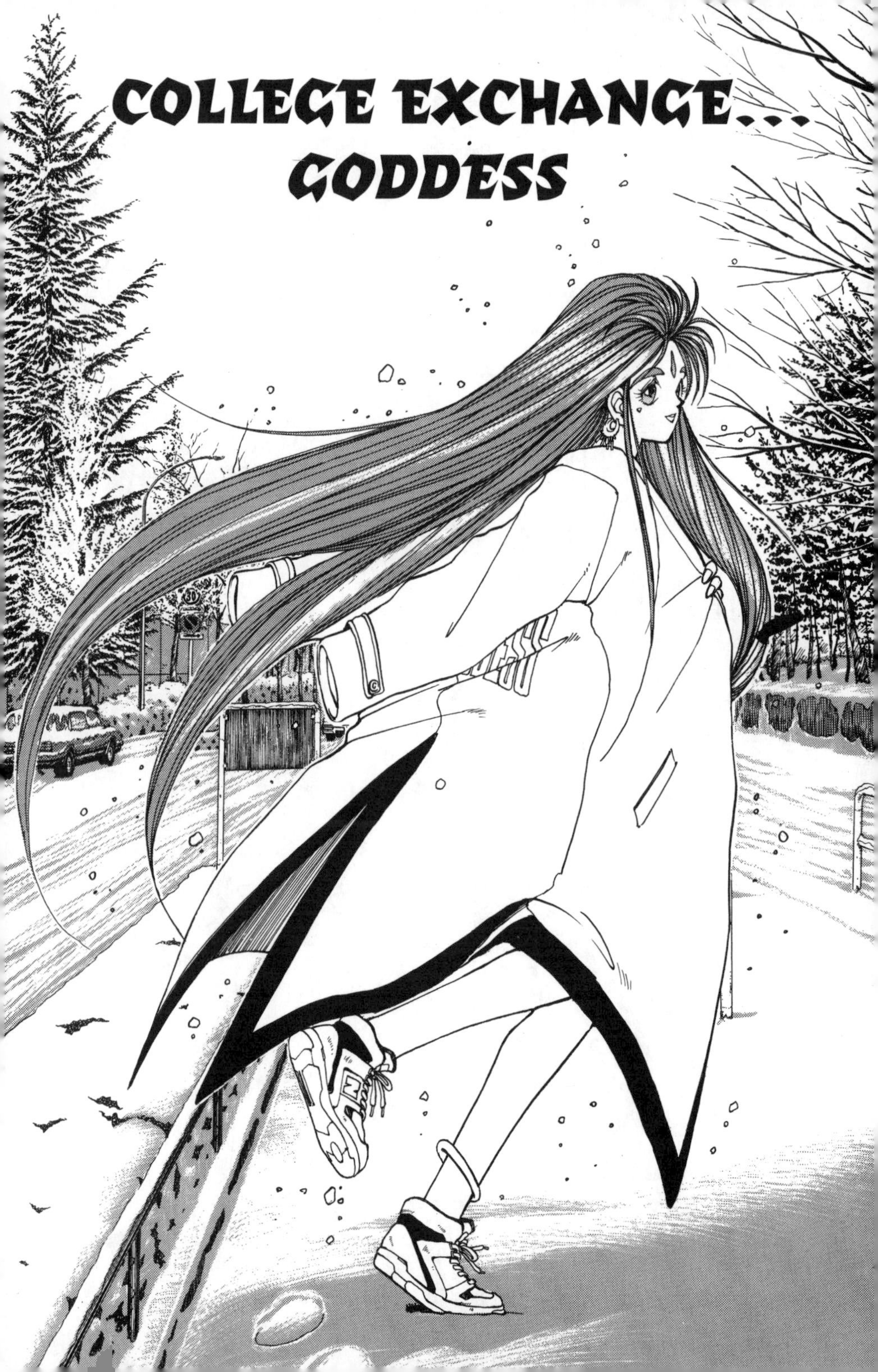

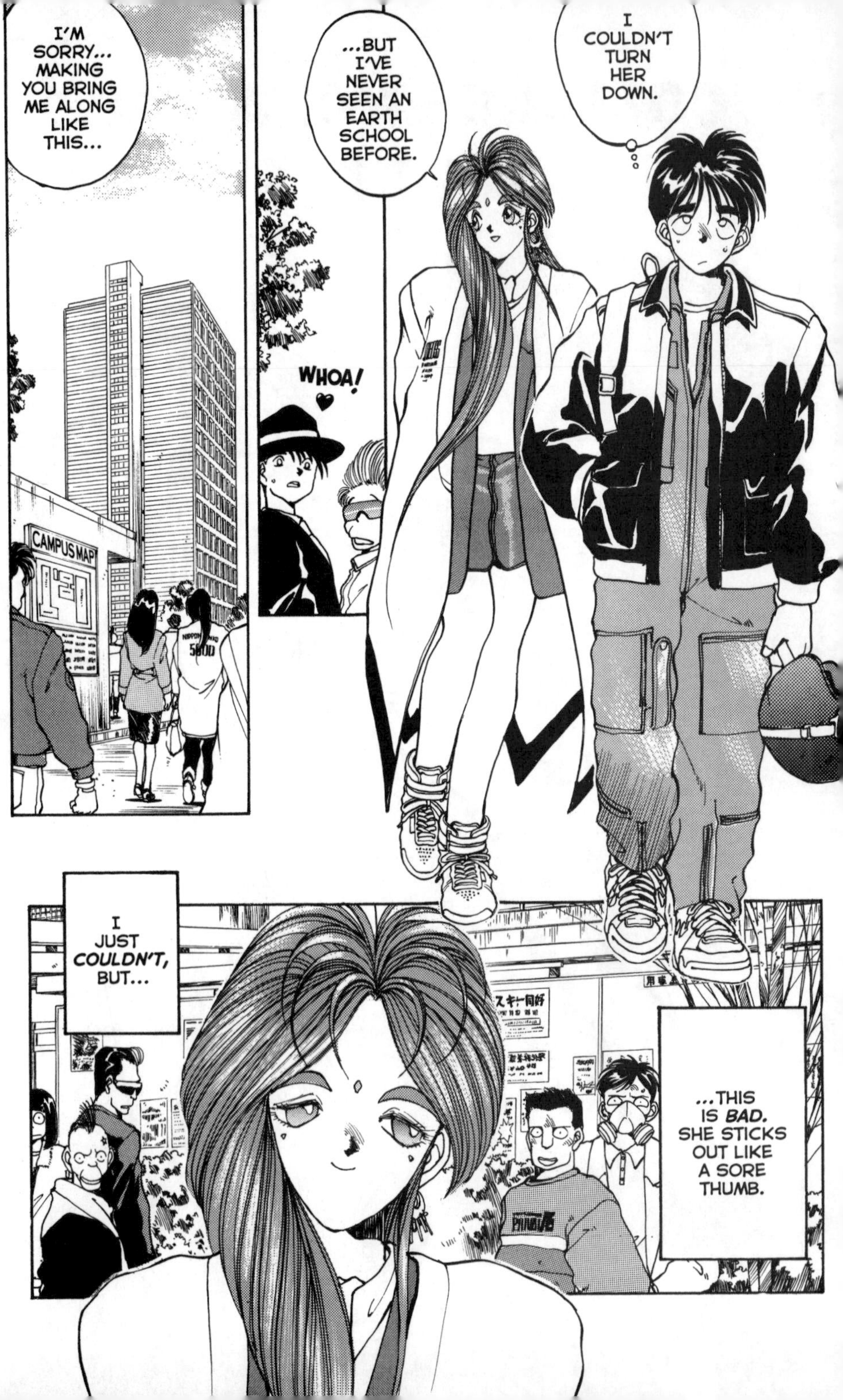
I'M SORRY... MAKING YOU BRING ME ALONG LIKE THIS...
CAMPUS MAP
...BUT I'VE NEVER SEEN AN EARTH SCHOOL BEFORE.
WHOA!
I COULDN'T TURN HER DOWN.
I JUST *COULDN'T*, BUT...
...THIS IS *BAD.* SHE STICKS OUT LIKE A SORE THUMB.

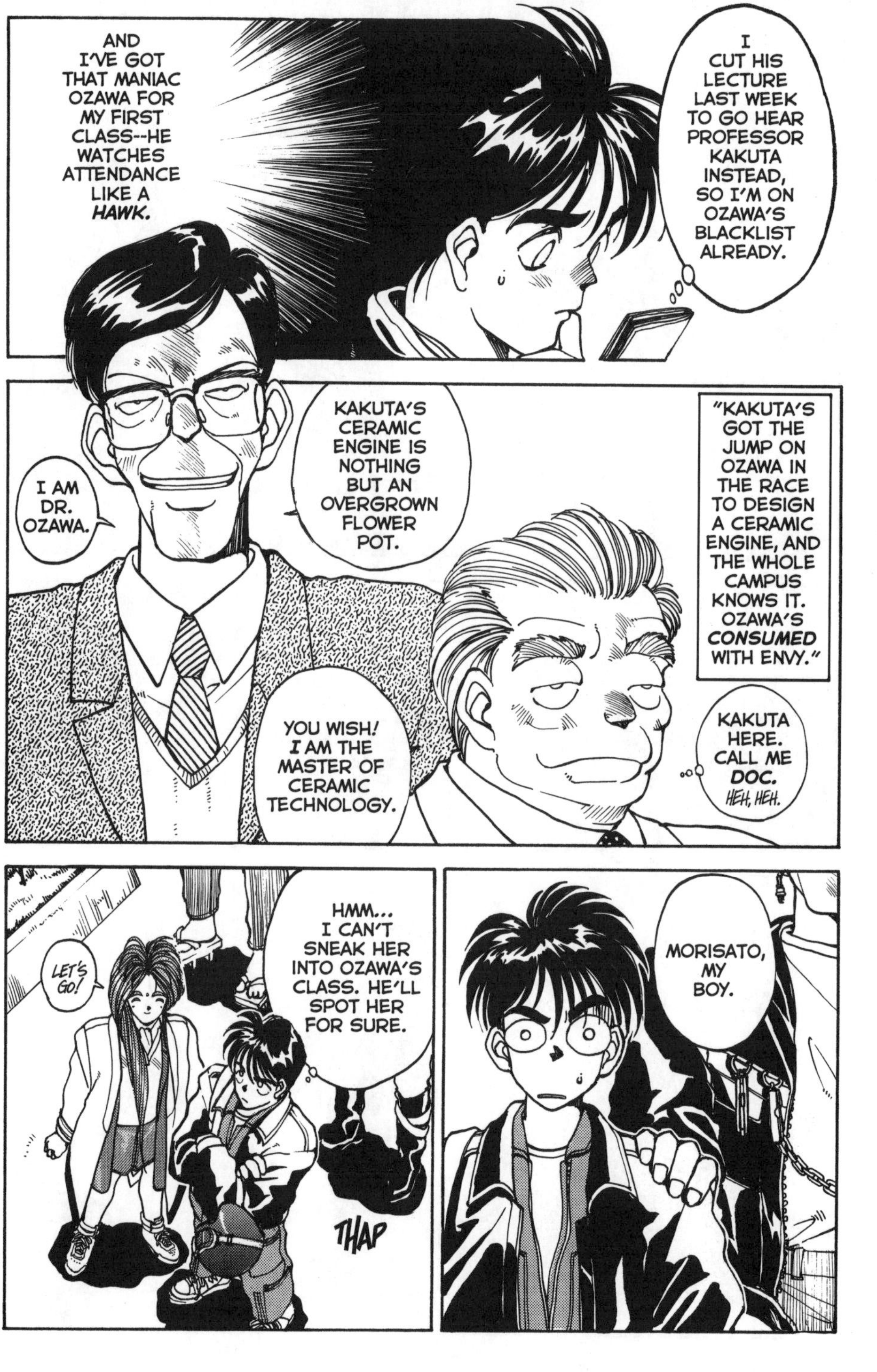
AND I'VE GOT THAT MANIAC OZAWA FOR MY FIRST CLASS--HE WATCHES ATTENDANCE LIKE A *HAWK.*
I CUT HIS LECTURE LAST WEEK TO GO HEAR PROFESSOR KAKUTA INSTEAD, SO I'M ON OZAWA'S BLACKLIST ALREADY.
I AM DR. OZAWA.
KAKUTA'S CERAMIC ENGINE IS NOTHING BUT AN OVERGROWN FLOWER POT.
"KAKUTA'S GOT THE JUMP ON OZAWA IN THE RACE TO DESIGN A CERAMIC ENGINE, AND THE WHOLE CAMPUS KNOWS IT. OZAWA'S *CONSUMED* WITH ENVY."
YOU WISH! *I* AM THE MASTER OF CERAMIC TECHNOLOGY.
KAKUTA HERE. CALL ME *DOC.* HEH, HEH.
LET'S GO!
HMM... I CAN'T SNEAK HER INTO OZAWA'S CLASS. HE'LL SPOT HER FOR SURE.
THAP
MORISATO, MY BOY.

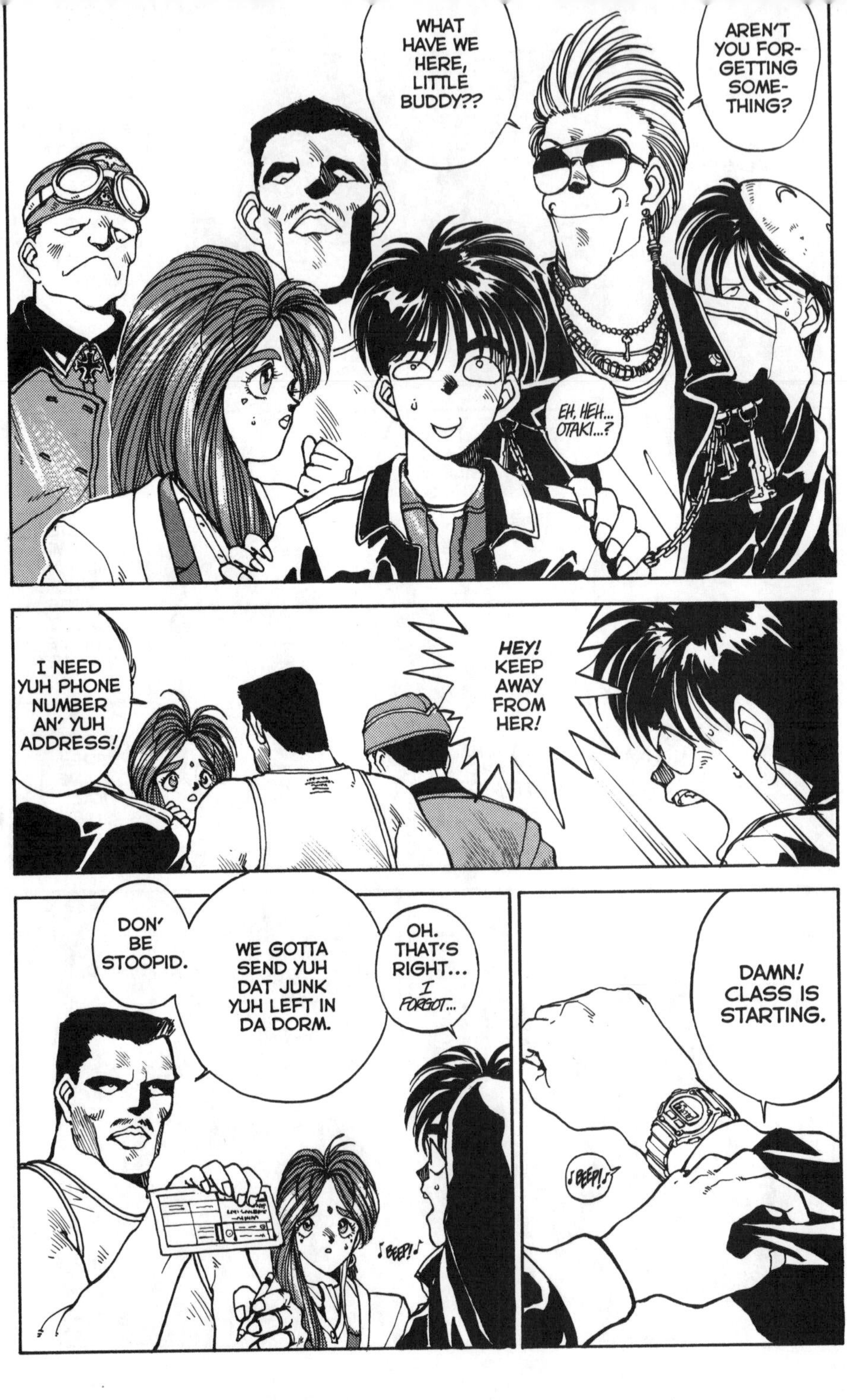
WHAT HAVE WE HERE, LITTLE BUDDY??
AREN'T YOU FOR-GETTING SOME-THING?
EH, HEH... OTAKI...?
I NEED YUH PHONE NUMBER AN' YUH ADDRESS!
HEY! KEEP AWAY FROM HER!
DON' BE STOOPID.
WE GOTTA SEND YUH DAT JUNK YUH LEFT IN DA DORM.
OH. THAT'S RIGHT... I FORGOT...
BEEP!
DAMN! CLASS IS STARTING.
BEEP!

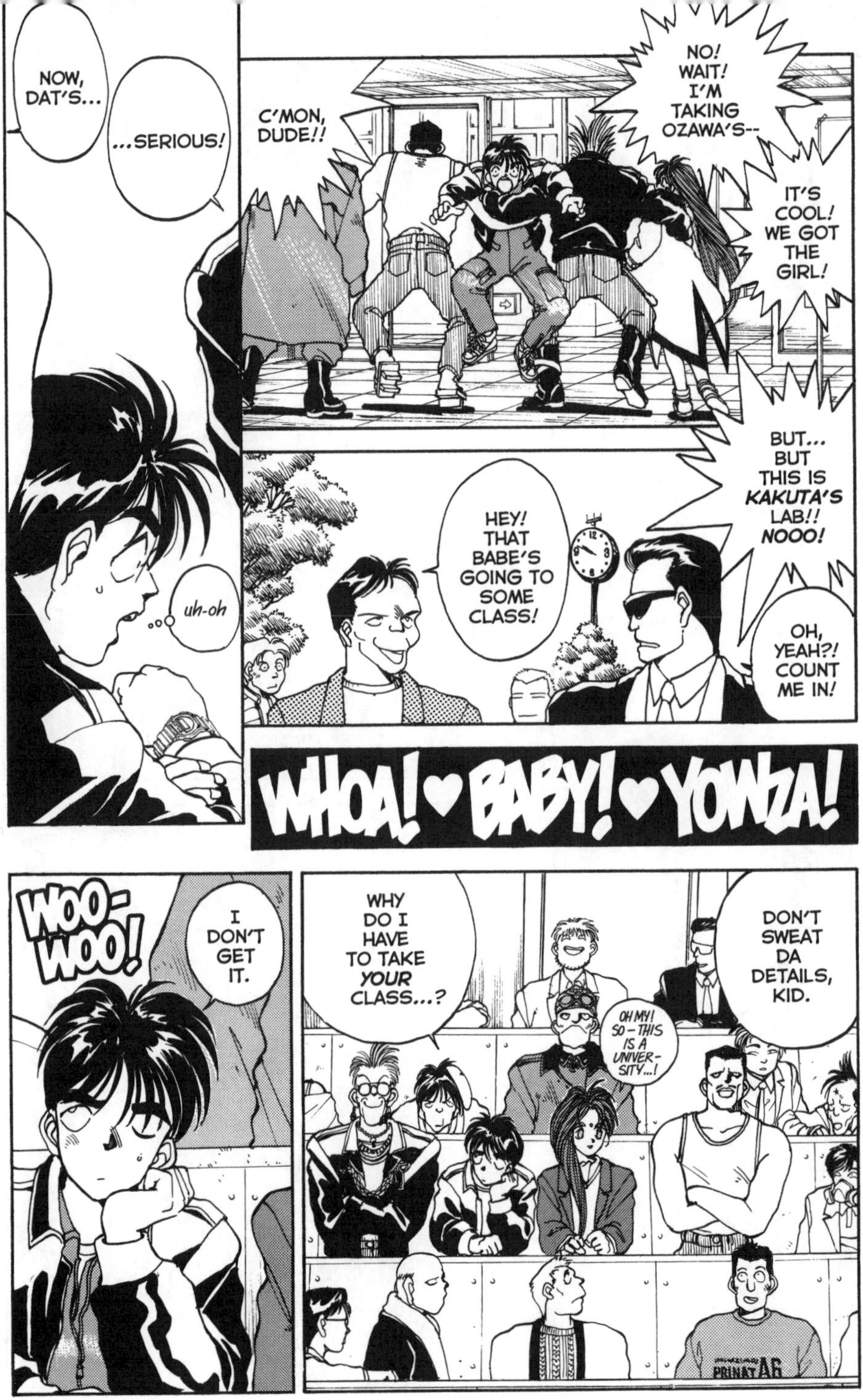
NOW, DAT'S...
...SERIOUS!
uh-oh
C'MON, DUDE!!
NO! WAIT! I'M TAKING OZAWA'S--
IT'S COOL! WE GOT THE GIRL!
HEY! THAT BABE'S GOING TO SOME CLASS!
BUT... BUT THIS IS *KAKUTA'S* LAB!! *NOOO!*
OH, YEAH?! COUNT ME IN!
WHOA! ♥ BABY! ♥ YOWZA!
WOO-WOO!
I DON'T GET IT.
WHY DO I HAVE TO TAKE *YOUR* CLASS...?
OH MY! SO—THIS IS A UNIVER-SITY...!
DON'T SWEAT DA DETAILS, KID.
PRINAT A6

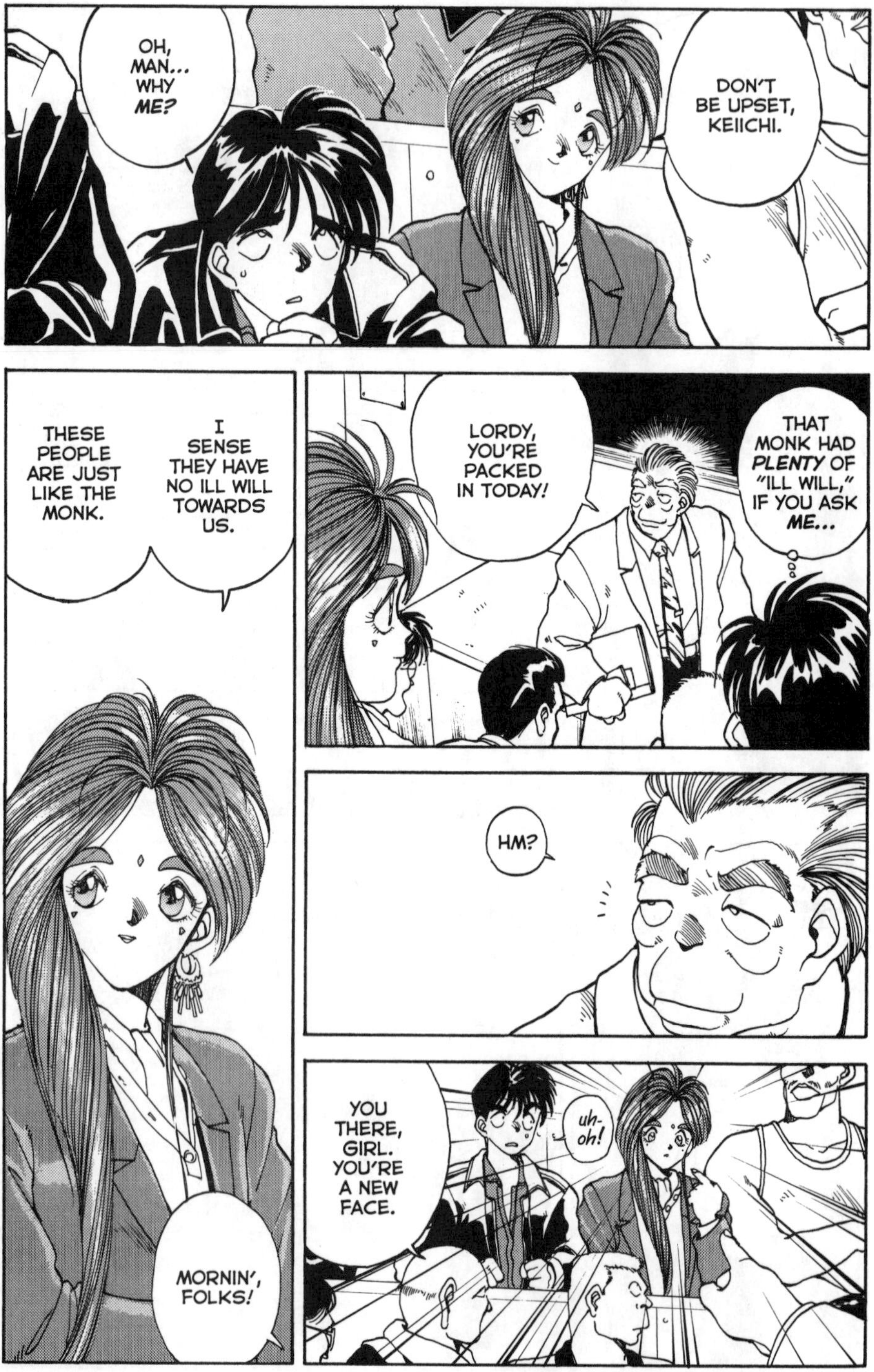
OH, MAN... WHY *ME?*
DON'T BE UPSET, KEIICHI.
THESE PEOPLE ARE JUST LIKE THE MONK.
I SENSE THEY HAVE NO ILL WILL TOWARDS US.
MORNIN', FOLKS!
LORDY, YOU'RE PACKED IN TODAY!
THAT MONK HAD *PLENTY* OF "ILL WILL," IF YOU ASK *ME...*
HM?
YOU THERE, GIRL. YOU'RE A NEW FACE.
uh-oh!

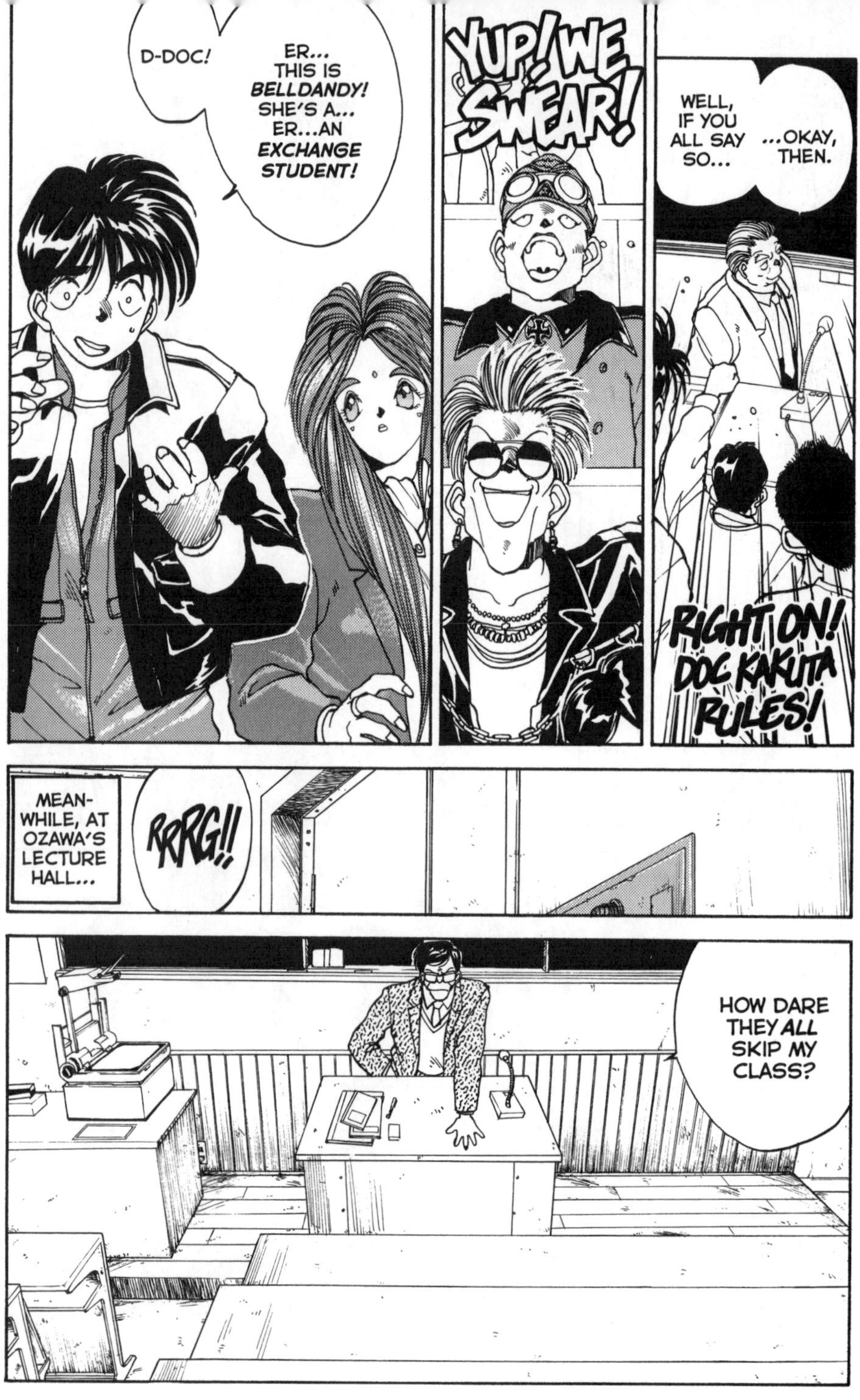
D-DOC!
ER... THIS IS BELLDANDY! SHE'S A... ER...AN EXCHANGE STUDENT!
YUP! WE SWEAR!
WELL, IF YOU ALL SAY SO...
...OKAY, THEN.
RIGHT ON! DOC KAKUTA RULES!
MEAN-WHILE, AT OZAWA'S LECTURE HALL...
RRRG!!
HOW DARE THEY ALL SKIP MY CLASS?

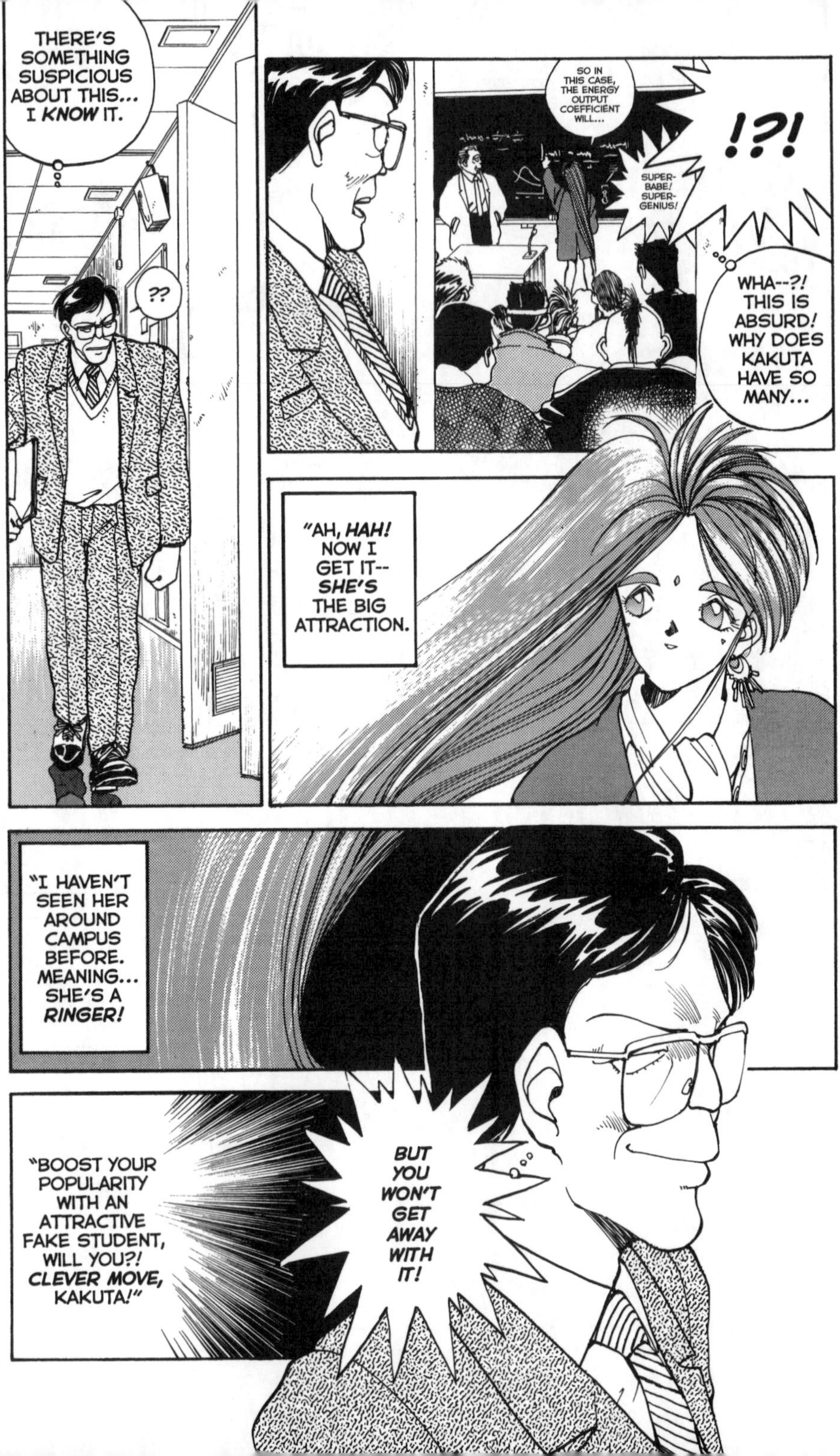
THERE'S SOMETHING SUSPICIOUS ABOUT THIS... I KNOW IT.
??
SO IN THIS CASE, THE ENERGY OUTPUT COEFFICIENT WILL...
SUPER-BABE! SUPER-GENIUS!
!?!
WHA--?! THIS IS ABSURD! WHY DOES KAKUTA HAVE SO MANY...
"AH, HAH! NOW I GET IT-- SHE'S THE BIG ATTRACTION.
"I HAVEN'T SEEN HER AROUND CAMPUS BEFORE. MEANING... SHE'S A RINGER!
"BOOST YOUR POPULARITY WITH AN ATTRACTIVE FAKE STUDENT, WILL YOU?! CLEVER MOVE, KAKUTA!"
BUT YOU WON'T GET AWAY WITH IT!

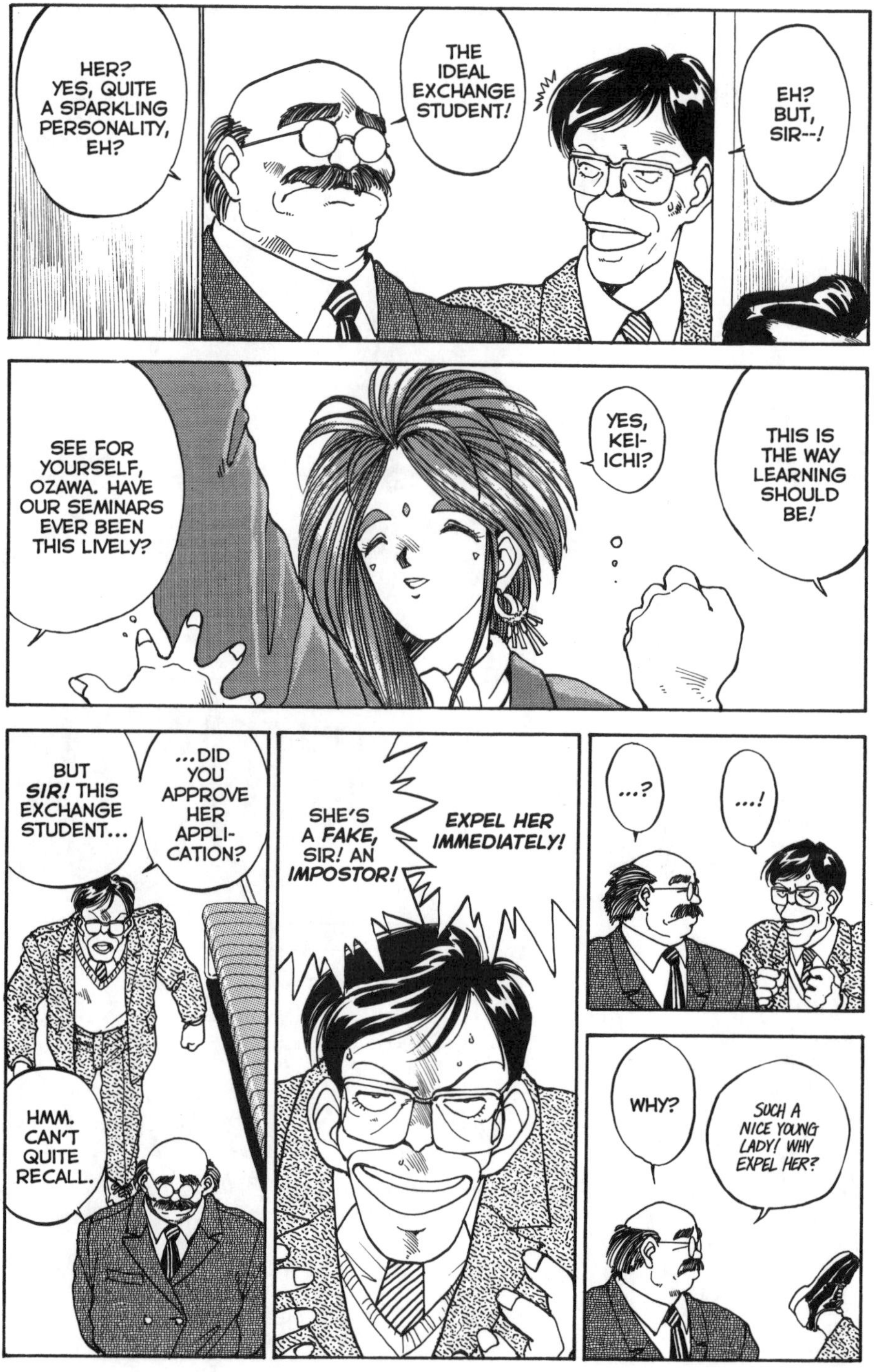
HER? YES, QUITE A SPARKLING PERSONALITY, EH?
THE IDEAL EXCHANGE STUDENT!
EH? BUT, SIR--!
SEE FOR YOURSELF, OZAWA. HAVE OUR SEMINARS EVER BEEN THIS LIVELY?
YES, KEI-ICHI?
THIS IS THE WAY LEARNING SHOULD BE!
BUT SIR! THIS EXCHANGE STUDENT...
...DID YOU APPROVE HER APPLI-CATION?
HMM. CAN'T QUITE RECALL.
SHE'S A FAKE, SIR! AN IMPOSTOR!
EXPEL HER IMMEDIATELY!
...?
...!
WHY?
SUCH A NICE YOUNG LADY! WHY EXPEL HER?

BAH! YOU OLD FOOL! I'LL DO IT *MYSELF!* I'LL FIND ABSOLUTE PROOF...

...AND EXPOSE HER TO THE *WHOLE* UNIVERSITY!

CRUNCH TIME, GUYS! OZAWA'S ON THE MOVE!

WHA--?!

DAT'S *BAD.* OZAWA DON'T *NEVER* GIVE UP...

TAK TAKKA TAK

I BET HE'S GOING TO ACCESS THE MAINFRAME FOR DATA.

WE GOTTA CHANGE THE DATA BEFORE HE LOGS ON.

I'M NO HACKER, BUT...

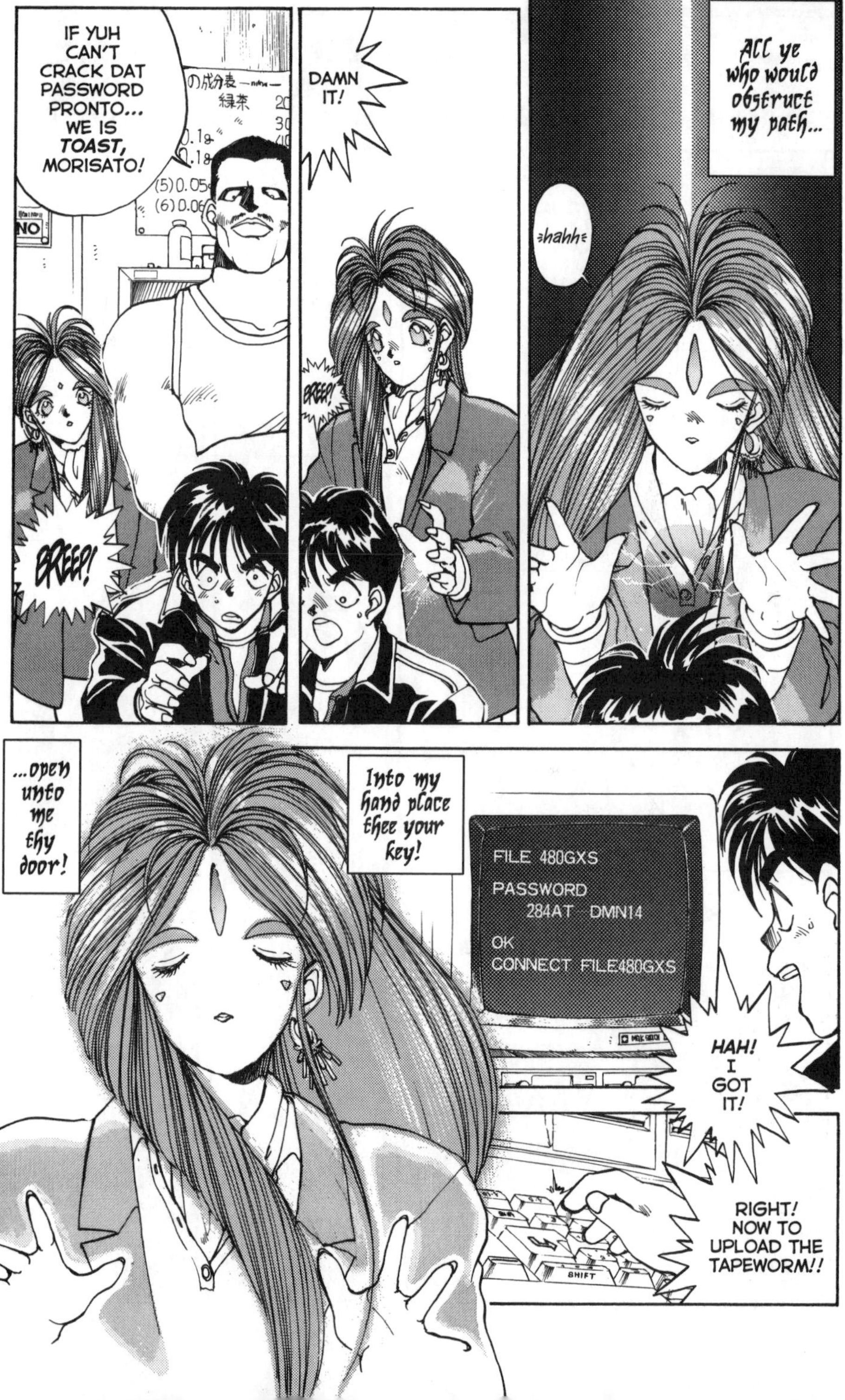
IF YUH CAN'T CRACK DAT PASSWORD PRONTO... WE IS *TOAST*, MORISATO!
BREEP!
DAMN IT!
BREEP!
All ye who would obstruct my path...
hahh
...open unto me thy door!
Into my hand place thee your key!
FILE 480GXS
PASSWORD
284AT DMN14
OK
CONNECT FILE480GXS
HAH! I GOT IT!
RIGHT! NOW TO UPLOAD THE TAPEWORM!!

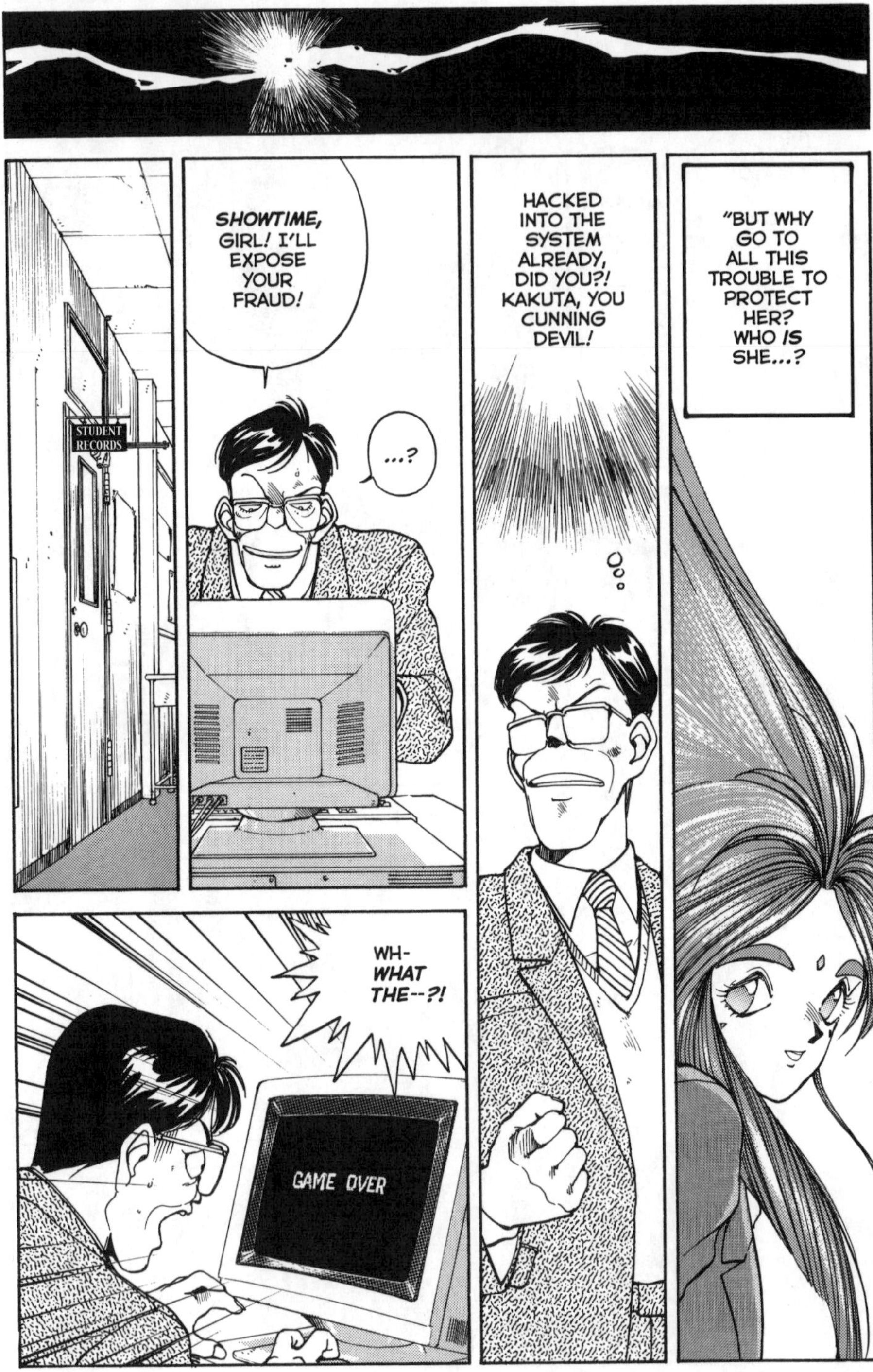
STUDENT RECORDS
SHOWTIME, GIRL! I'LL EXPOSE YOUR FRAUD!
...?
WH- *WHAT THE--?!*
GAME OVER
HACKED INTO THE SYSTEM ALREADY, DID YOU?! KAKUTA, YOU CUNNING DEVIL!
"BUT WHY GO TO ALL THIS TROUBLE TO PROTECT HER? WHO *IS* SHE...?

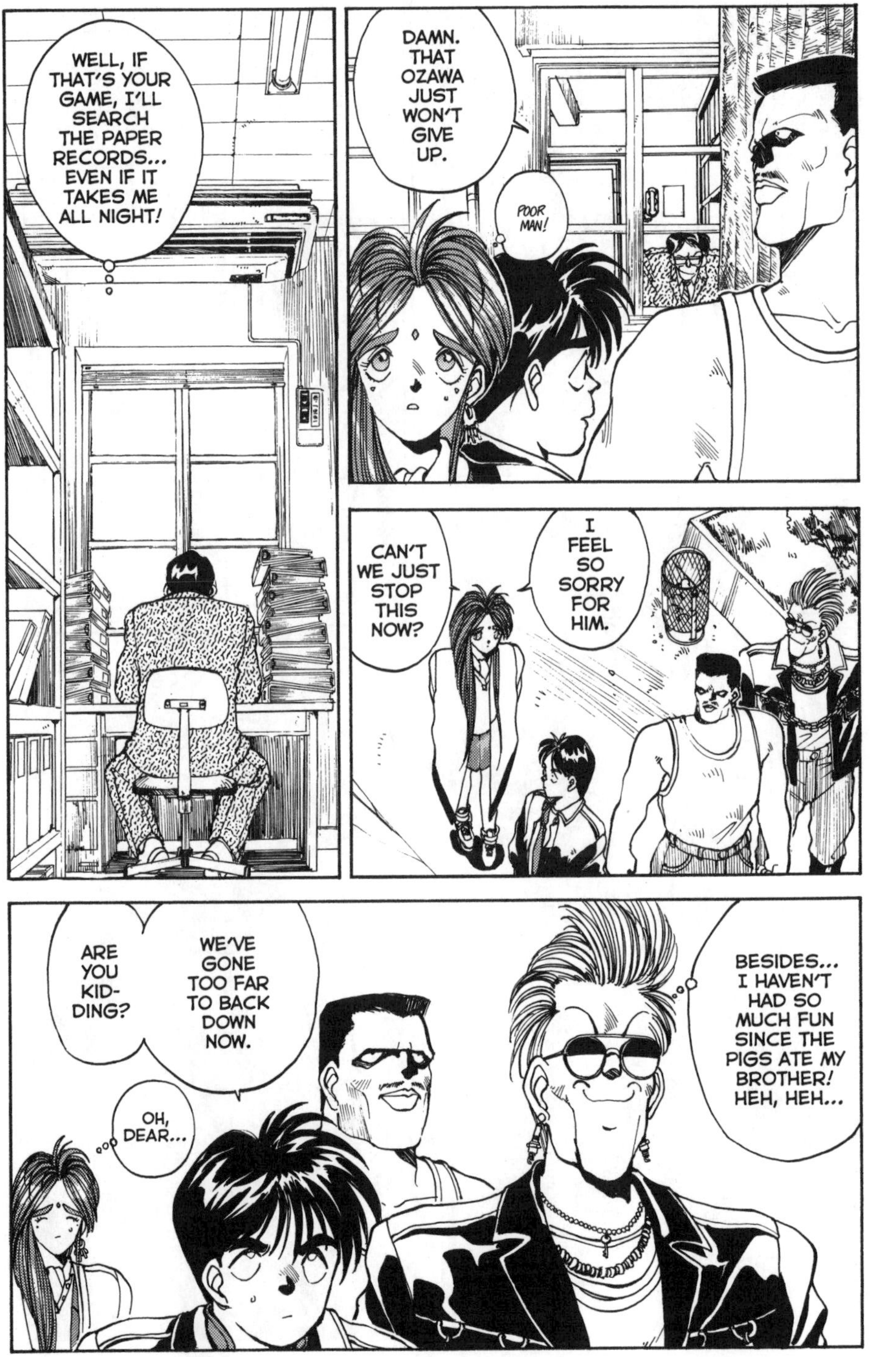
WELL, IF THAT'S YOUR GAME, I'LL SEARCH THE PAPER RECORDS... EVEN IF IT TAKES ME ALL NIGHT!
DAMN. THAT OZAWA JUST WON'T GIVE UP.
POOR MAN!
CAN'T WE JUST STOP THIS NOW?
I FEEL SO SORRY FOR HIM.
ARE YOU KID-DING?
WE'VE GONE TOO FAR TO BACK DOWN NOW.
OH, DEAR...
BESIDES... I HAVEN'T HAD SO MUCH FUN SINCE THE PIGS ATE MY BROTHER! HEH, HEH...

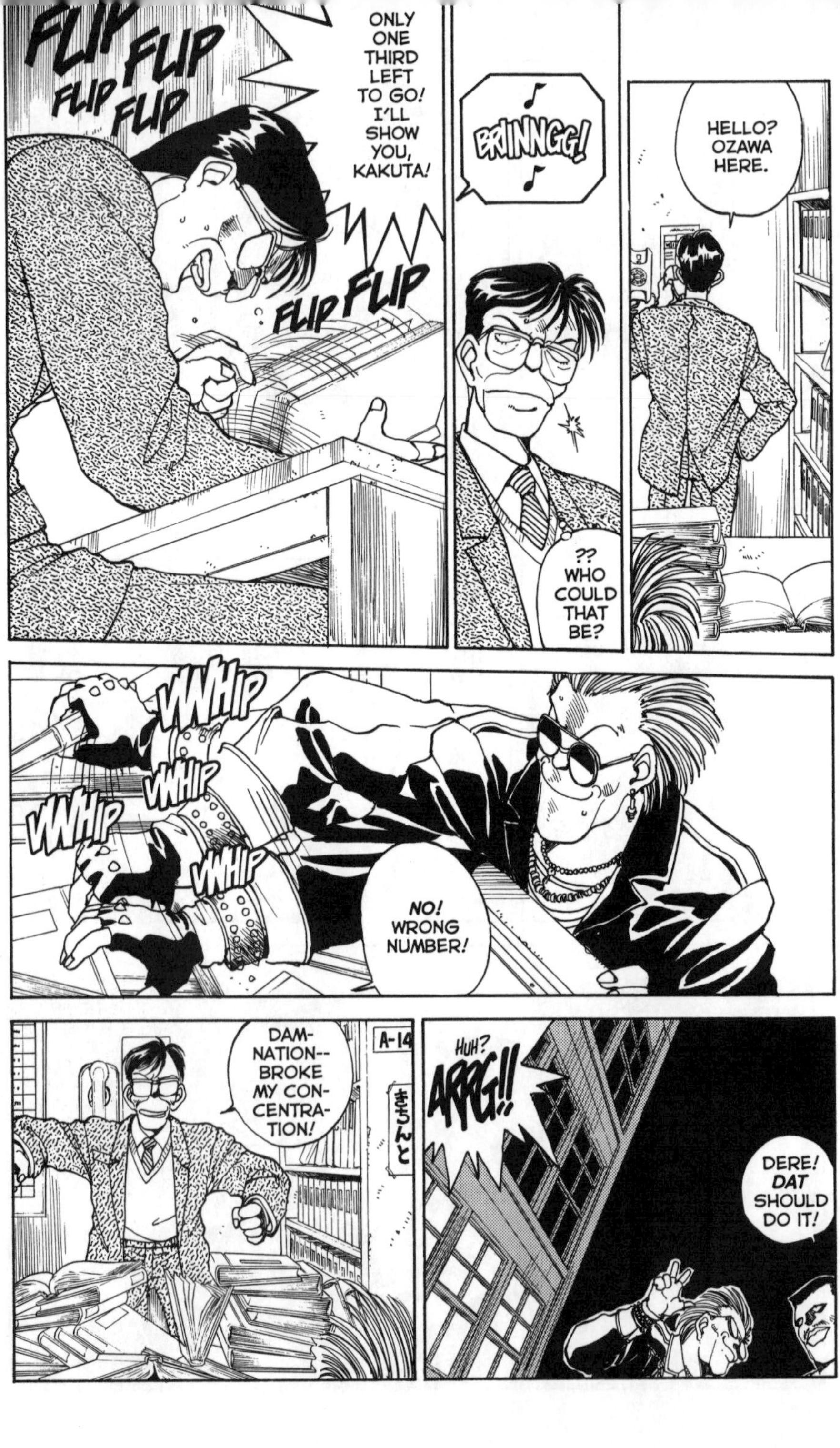
FLIP FLIP FLIP FLIP
ONLY ONE THIRD LEFT TO GO! I'LL SHOW YOU, KAKUTA!
FLIP FLIP
BRIINNGG!
?? WHO COULD THAT BE?
HELLO? OZAWA HERE.
VWHIP
VWHIP
VWHIP
VWHIP
NO! WRONG NUMBER!
DAM-NATION-- BROKE MY CON-CENTRA-TION!
A-14
きちんと
HUH?
ARRG!!
DERE! DAT SHOULD DO IT!

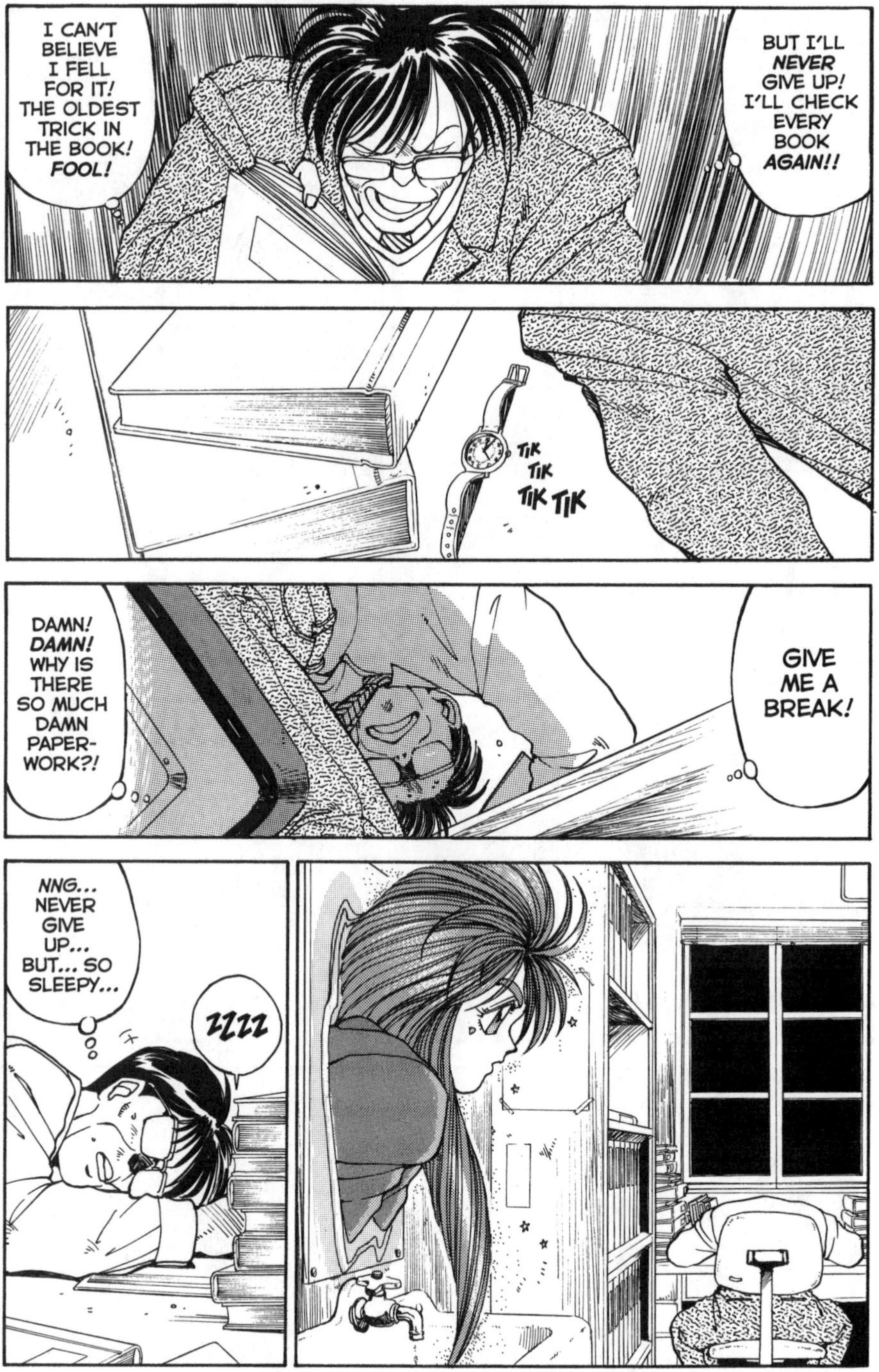
I CAN'T BELIEVE I FELL FOR IT! THE OLDEST TRICK IN THE BOOK! *FOOL!*
BUT I'LL *NEVER* GIVE UP! I'LL CHECK EVERY BOOK *AGAIN!!*
TIK TIK TIK TIK
DAMN! *DAMN!* WHY IS THERE SO MUCH DAMN PAPER-WORK?!
GIVE ME A BREAK!
NNG... NEVER GIVE UP... BUT... SO SLEEPY...
ZZZZ

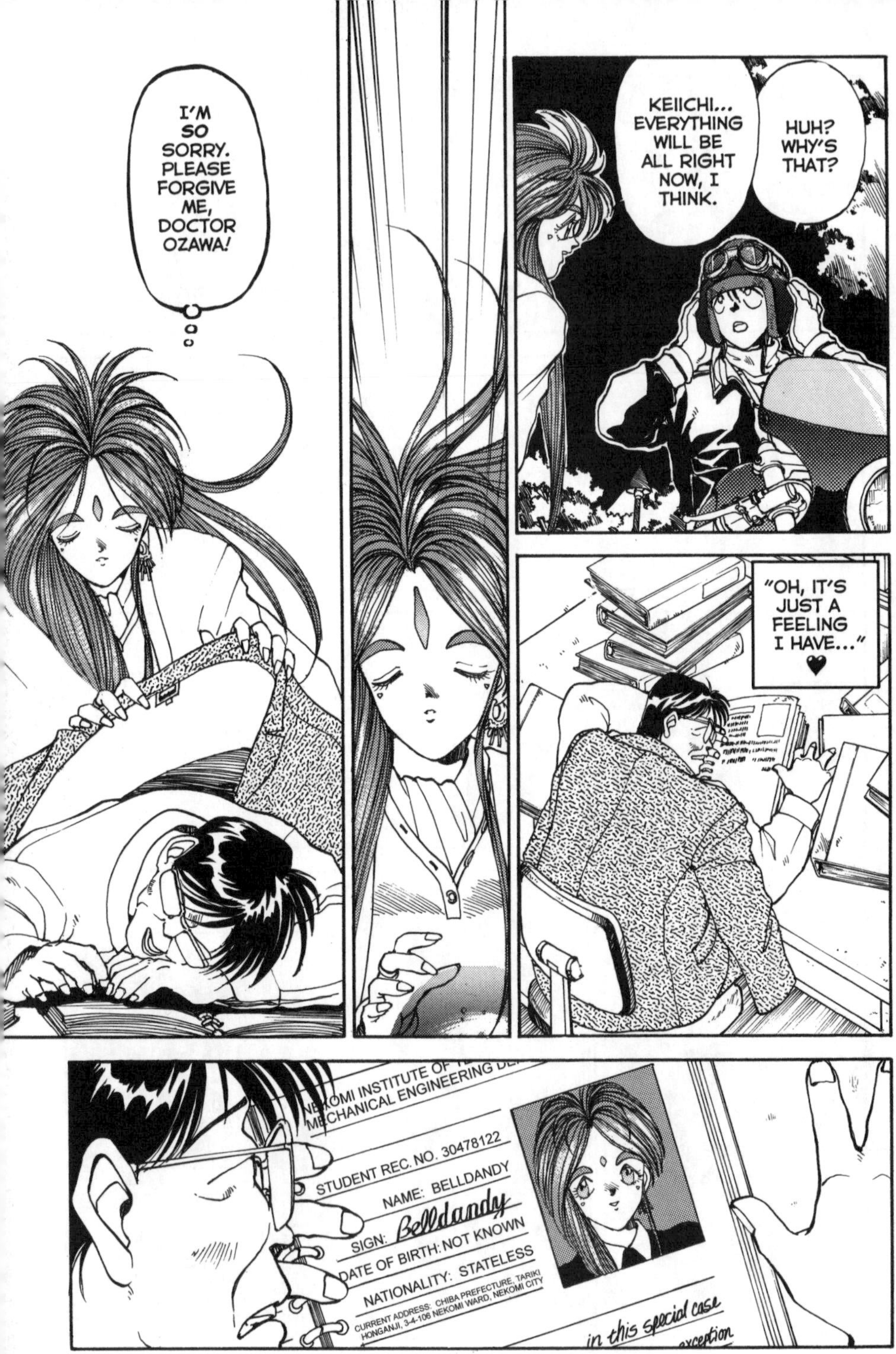
I'M SO SORRY. PLEASE FORGIVE ME, DOCTOR OZAWA!
KEIICHI... EVERYTHING WILL BE ALL RIGHT NOW, I THINK.
HUH? WHY'S THAT?
"OH, IT'S JUST A FEELING I HAVE..." ♥
NEKOMI INSTITUTE OF T
MECHANICAL ENGINEERING DE
STUDENT REC. NO. 30478122
NAME: BELLDANDY
SIGN: Belldandy
DATE OF BIRTH: NOT KNOWN
NATIONALITY: STATELESS
CURRENT ADDRESS: CHIBA PREFECTURE, TARIKI HONGANJI, 3-4-106 NEKOMI WARD, NEKOMI CITY
in this special case
exception

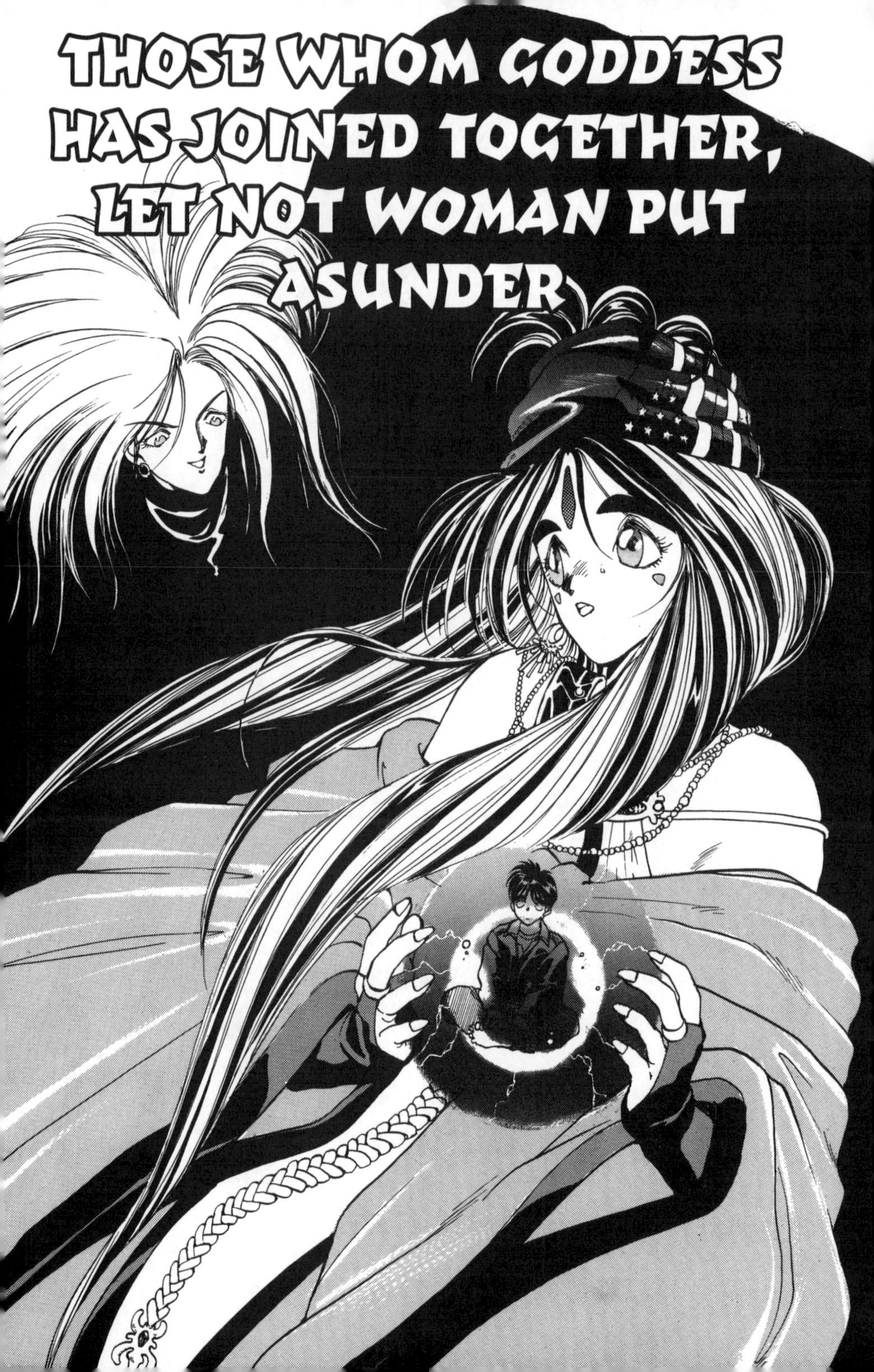
THOSE WHOM GODDESS HAS JOINED TOGETHER, LET NOT WOMAN PUT ASUNDER

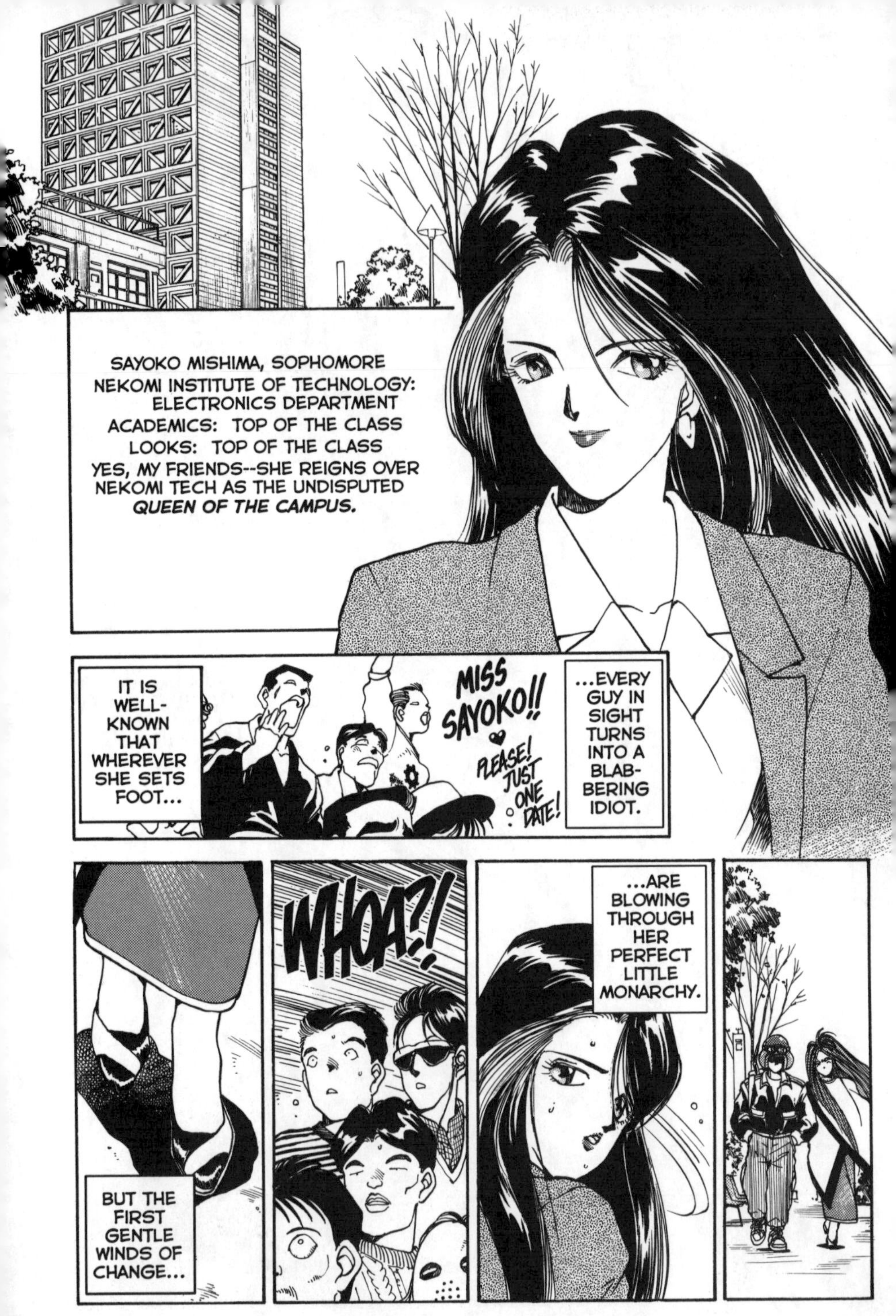
SAYOKO MISHIMA, SOPHOMORE
NEKOMI INSTITUTE OF TECHNOLOGY: ELECTRONICS DEPARTMENT
ACADEMICS: TOP OF THE CLASS
LOOKS: TOP OF THE CLASS
YES, MY FRIENDS--SHE REIGNS OVER NEKOMI TECH AS THE UNDISPUTED *QUEEN OF THE CAMPUS.*
IT IS WELL-KNOWN THAT WHEREVER SHE SETS FOOT...
MISS SAYOKO!!
PLEASE! JUST ONE DATE!
...EVERY GUY IN SIGHT TURNS INTO A BLAB-BERING IDIOT.
BUT THE FIRST GENTLE WINDS OF CHANGE...
WHOA?!
...ARE BLOWING THROUGH HER PERFECT LITTLE MONARCHY.

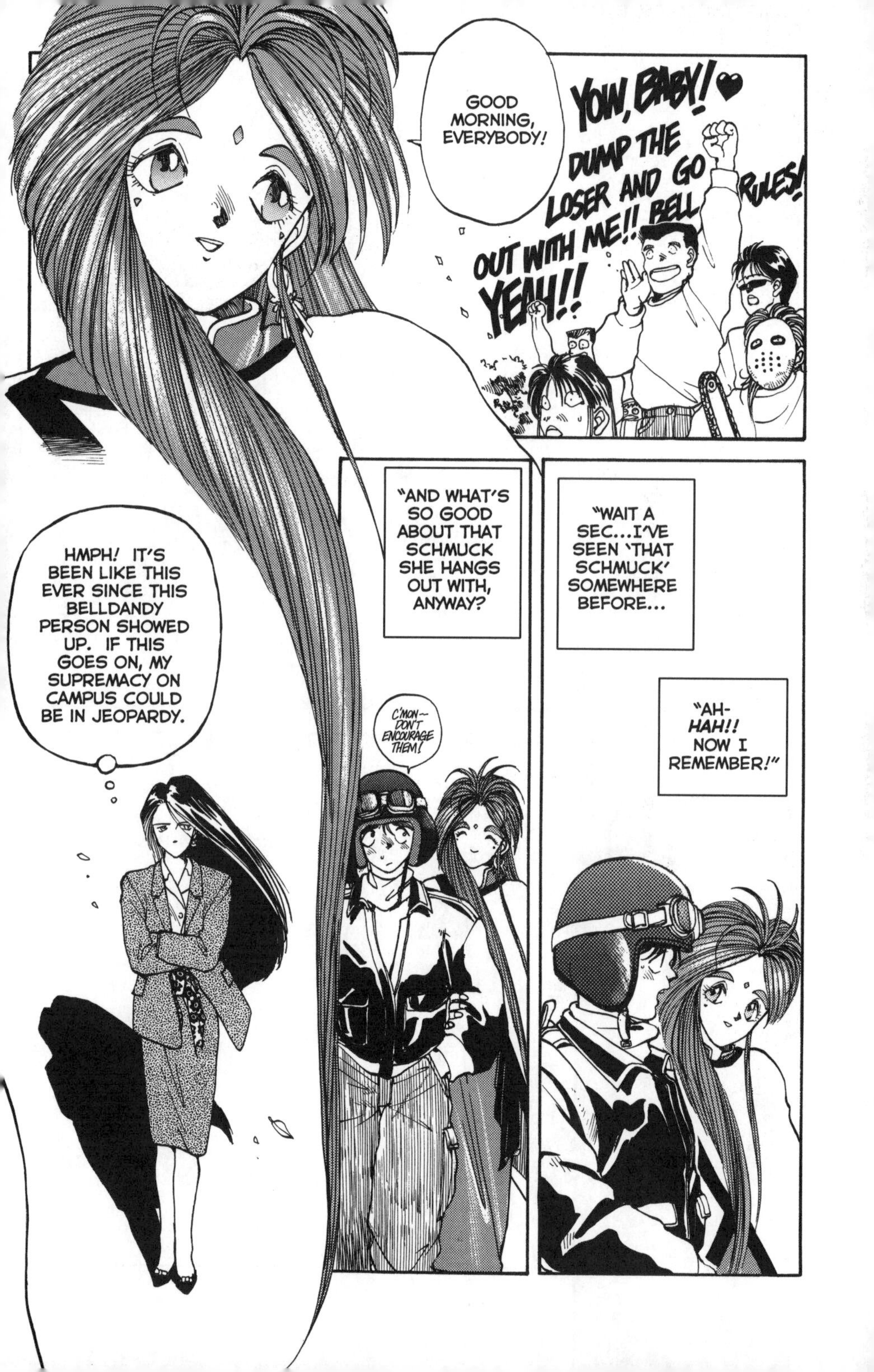
GOOD MORNING, EVERYBODY!
YOW, BABY!♥
DUMP THE LOSER AND GO OUT WITH ME!!
BELL RULES!
YEAH!!
HMPH! IT'S BEEN LIKE THIS EVER SINCE THIS BELLDANDY PERSON SHOWED UP. IF THIS GOES ON, MY SUPREMACY ON CAMPUS COULD BE IN JEOPARDY.
"AND WHAT'S SO GOOD ABOUT THAT SCHMUCK SHE HANGS OUT WITH, ANYWAY?
C'MON-- DON'T ENCOURAGE THEM!
"WAIT A SEC...I'VE SEEN 'THAT SCHMUCK' SOMEWHERE BEFORE...
"AH-HAH!! NOW I REMEMBER!"

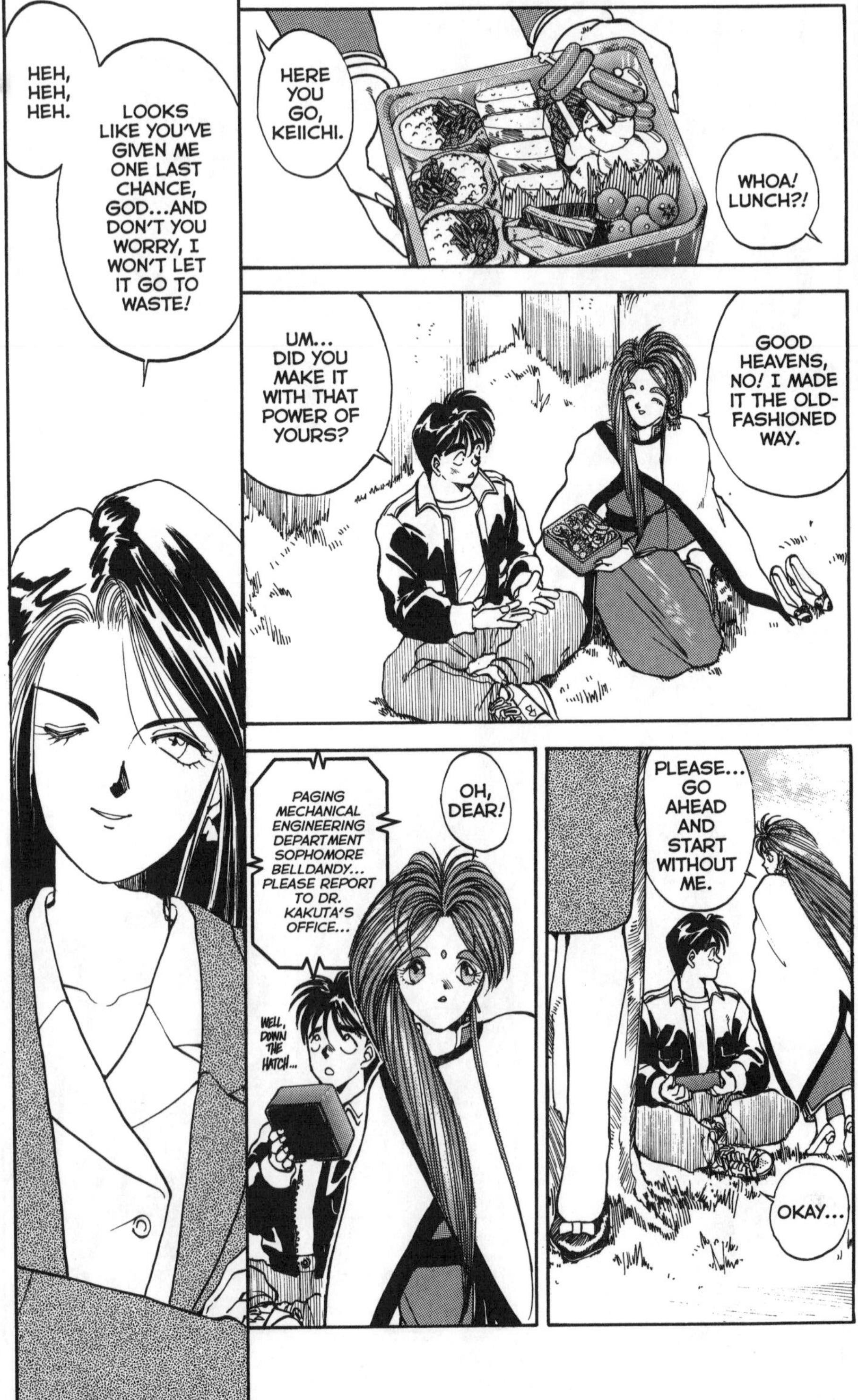
HEH, HEH, HEH.
LOOKS LIKE YOU'VE GIVEN ME ONE LAST CHANCE, GOD...AND DON'T YOU WORRY, I WON'T LET IT GO TO WASTE!
HERE YOU GO, KEIICHI.
WHOA! LUNCH?!
UM... DID YOU MAKE IT WITH THAT POWER OF YOURS?
GOOD HEAVENS, NO! I MADE IT THE OLD-FASHIONED WAY.
PAGING MECHANICAL ENGINEERING DEPARTMENT SOPHOMORE BELLDANDY... PLEASE REPORT TO DR. KAKUTA'S OFFICE...
OH, DEAR!
WELL, DOWN THE HATCH...
PLEASE... GO AHEAD AND START WITHOUT ME.
OKAY...

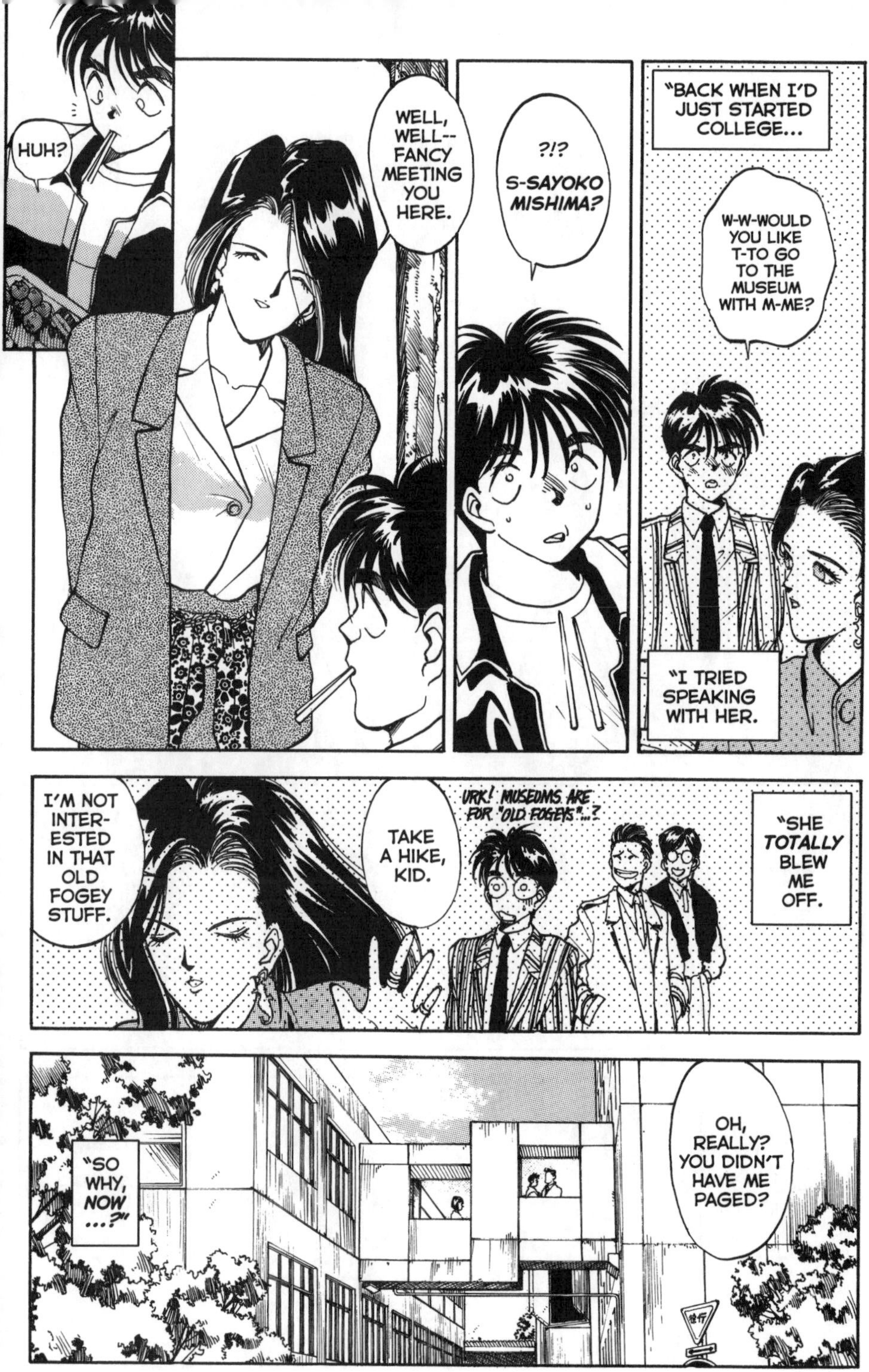
HUH?
WELL, WELL--FANCY MEETING YOU HERE.
?!?
S-SAYOKO MISHIMA?
"BACK WHEN I'D JUST STARTED COLLEGE...
W-W-WOULD YOU LIKE T-TO GO TO THE MUSEUM WITH M-ME?
"I TRIED SPEAKING WITH HER.
I'M NOT INTER-ESTED IN THAT OLD FOGEY STUFF.
TAKE A HIKE, KID.
URK! MUSEUMS ARE FOR "OLD FOGEYS"...?
"SHE *TOTALLY* BLEW ME OFF.
"SO WHY, *NOW*...?"
OH, REALLY? YOU DIDN'T HAVE ME PAGED?

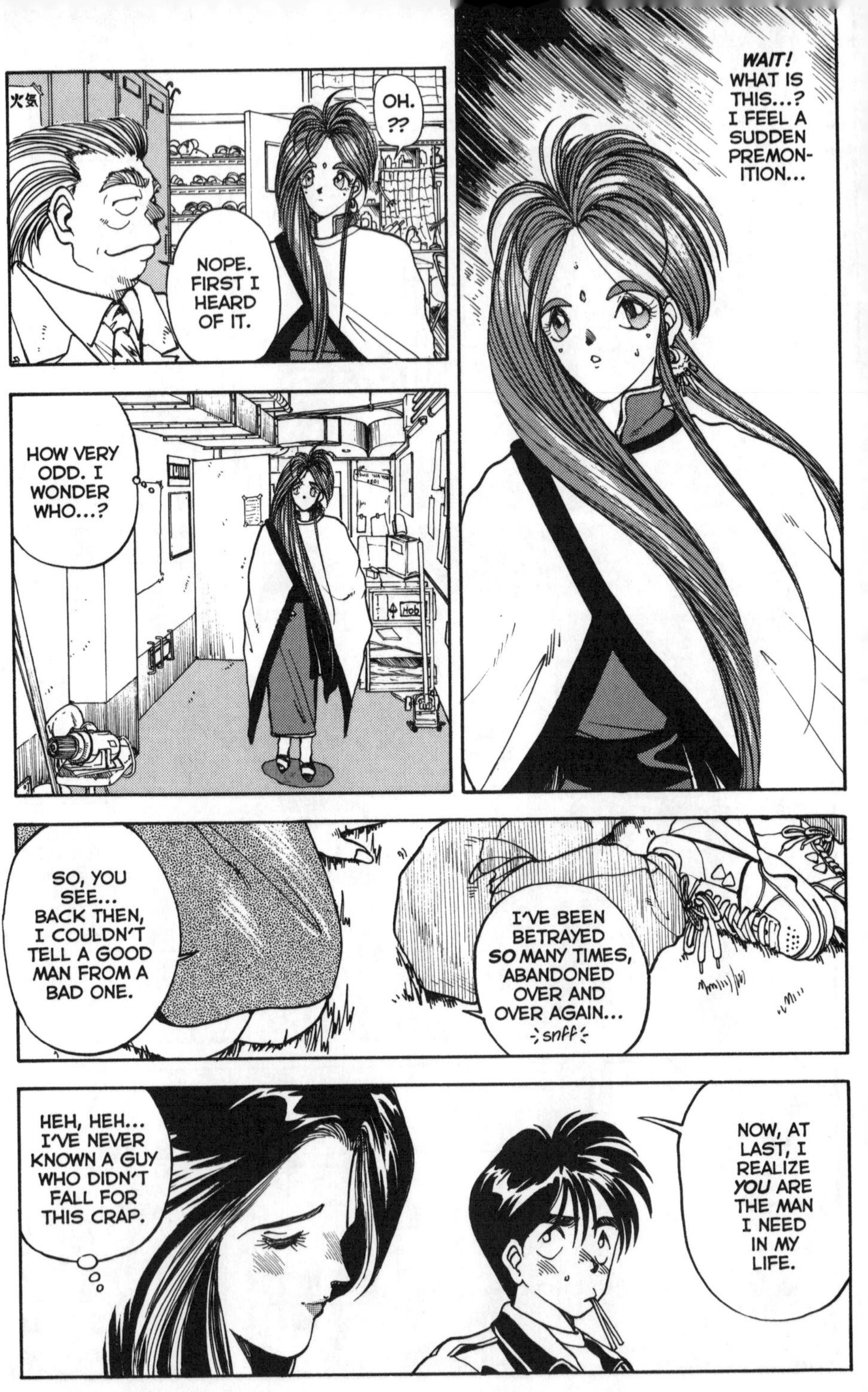
火気
OH. ??
NOPE. FIRST I HEARD OF IT.
HOW VERY ODD. I WONDER WHO...?
WAIT! WHAT IS THIS...? I FEEL A SUDDEN PREMONITION...
SO, YOU SEE... BACK THEN, I COULDN'T TELL A GOOD MAN FROM A BAD ONE.
I'VE BEEN BETRAYED SO MANY TIMES, ABANDONED OVER AND OVER AGAIN...
snff
HEH, HEH... I'VE NEVER KNOWN A GUY WHO DIDN'T FALL FOR THIS CRAP.
NOW, AT LAST, I REALIZE YOU ARE THE MAN I NEED IN MY LIFE.

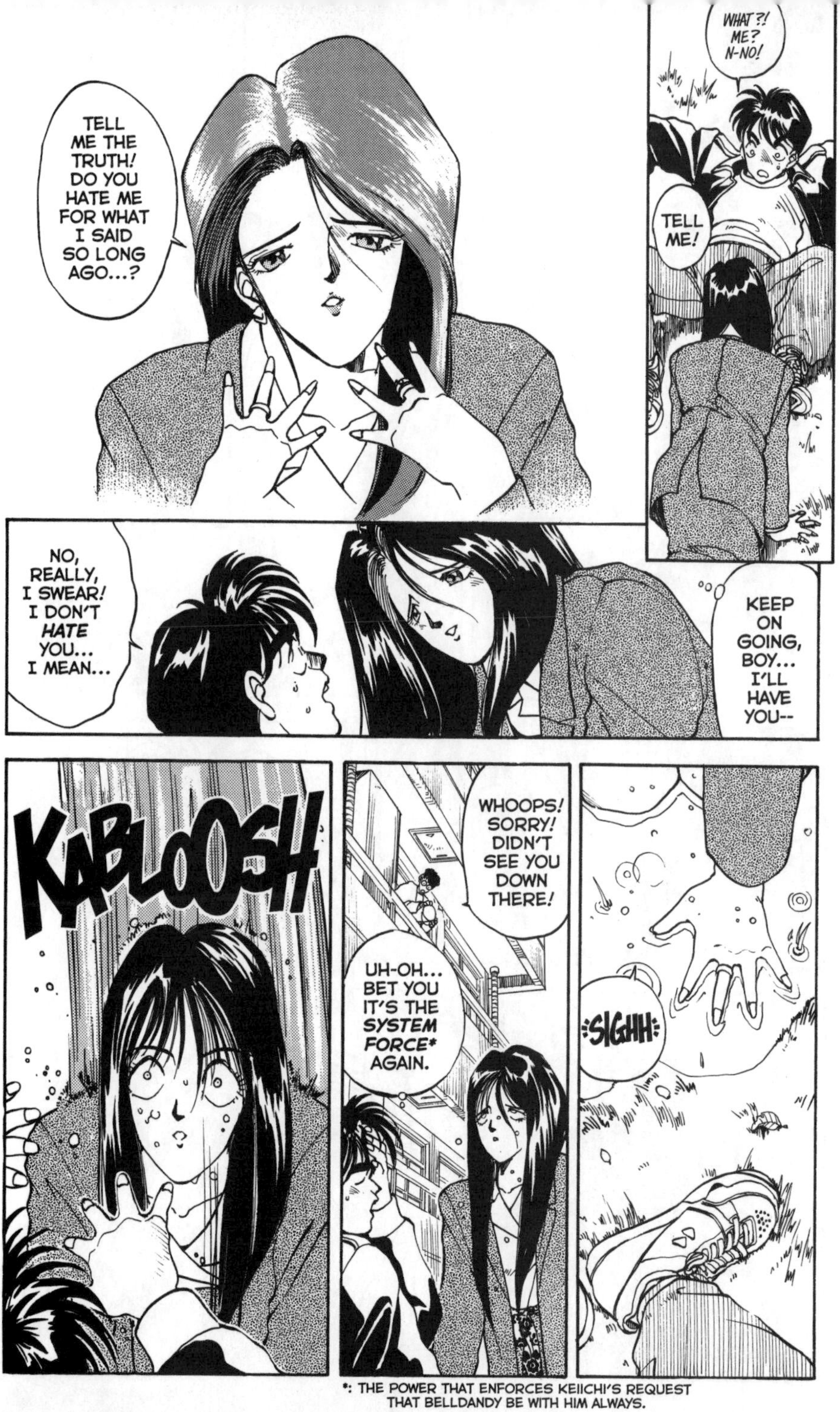
TELL ME THE TRUTH! DO YOU HATE ME FOR WHAT I SAID SO LONG AGO...?
WHAT?! ME? N-NO!
TELL ME!
NO, REALLY, I SWEAR! I DON'T *HATE* YOU... I MEAN...
KEEP ON GOING, BOY... I'LL HAVE YOU--
KABLOOSH
WHOOPS! SORRY! DIDN'T SEE YOU DOWN THERE!
UH-OH... BET YOU IT'S THE *SYSTEM FORCE** AGAIN.
SIGHH

*: THE POWER THAT ENFORCES KEIICHI'S REQUEST THAT BELLDANDY BE WITH HIM ALWAYS.

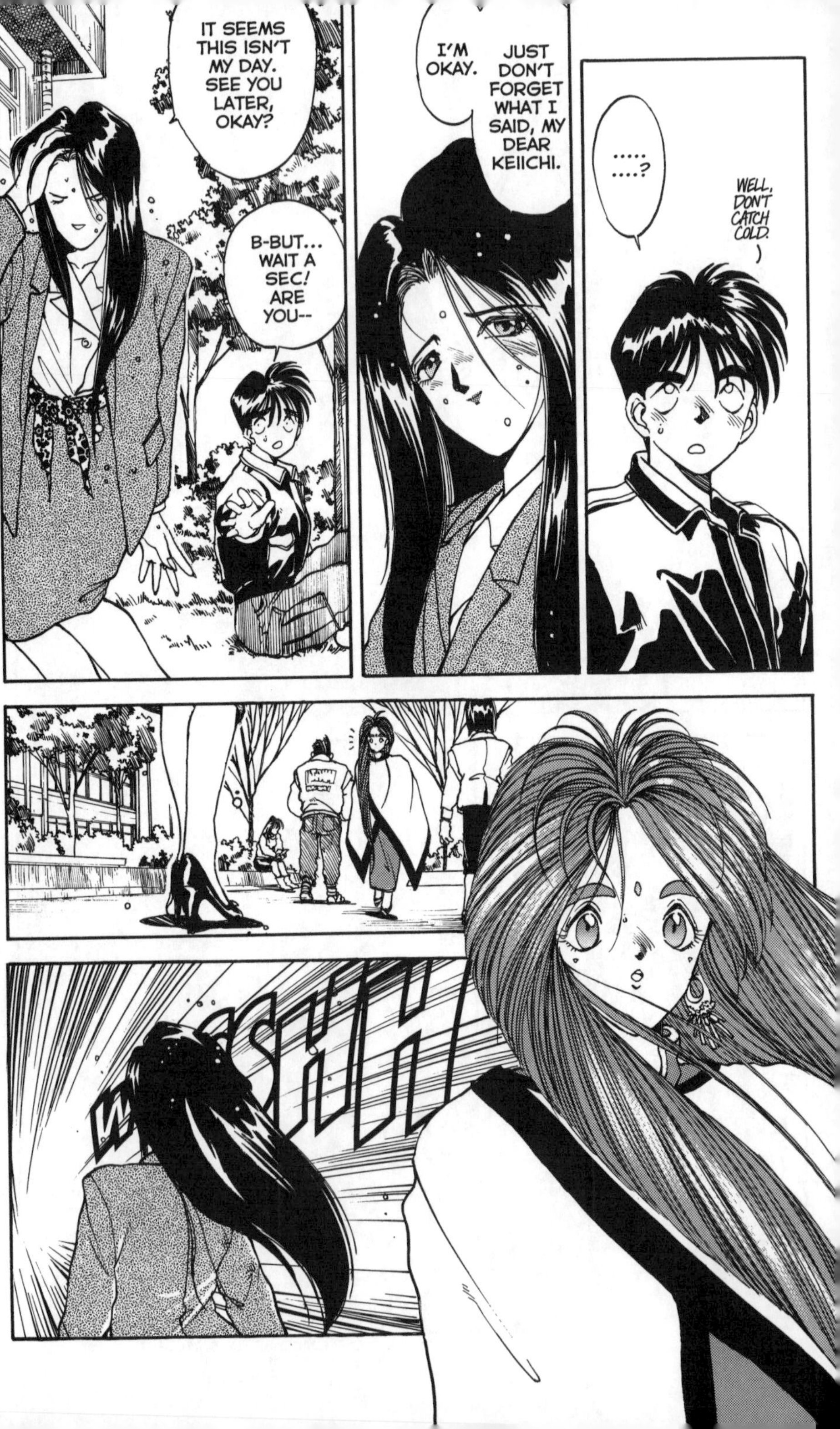
IT SEEMS THIS ISN'T MY DAY. SEE YOU LATER, OKAY?
B-BUT... WAIT A SEC! ARE YOU--
I'M OKAY.
JUST DON'T FORGET WHAT I SAID, MY DEAR KEIICHI.
.....
....?
WELL, DON'T CATCH COLD.
WHOOSHH!

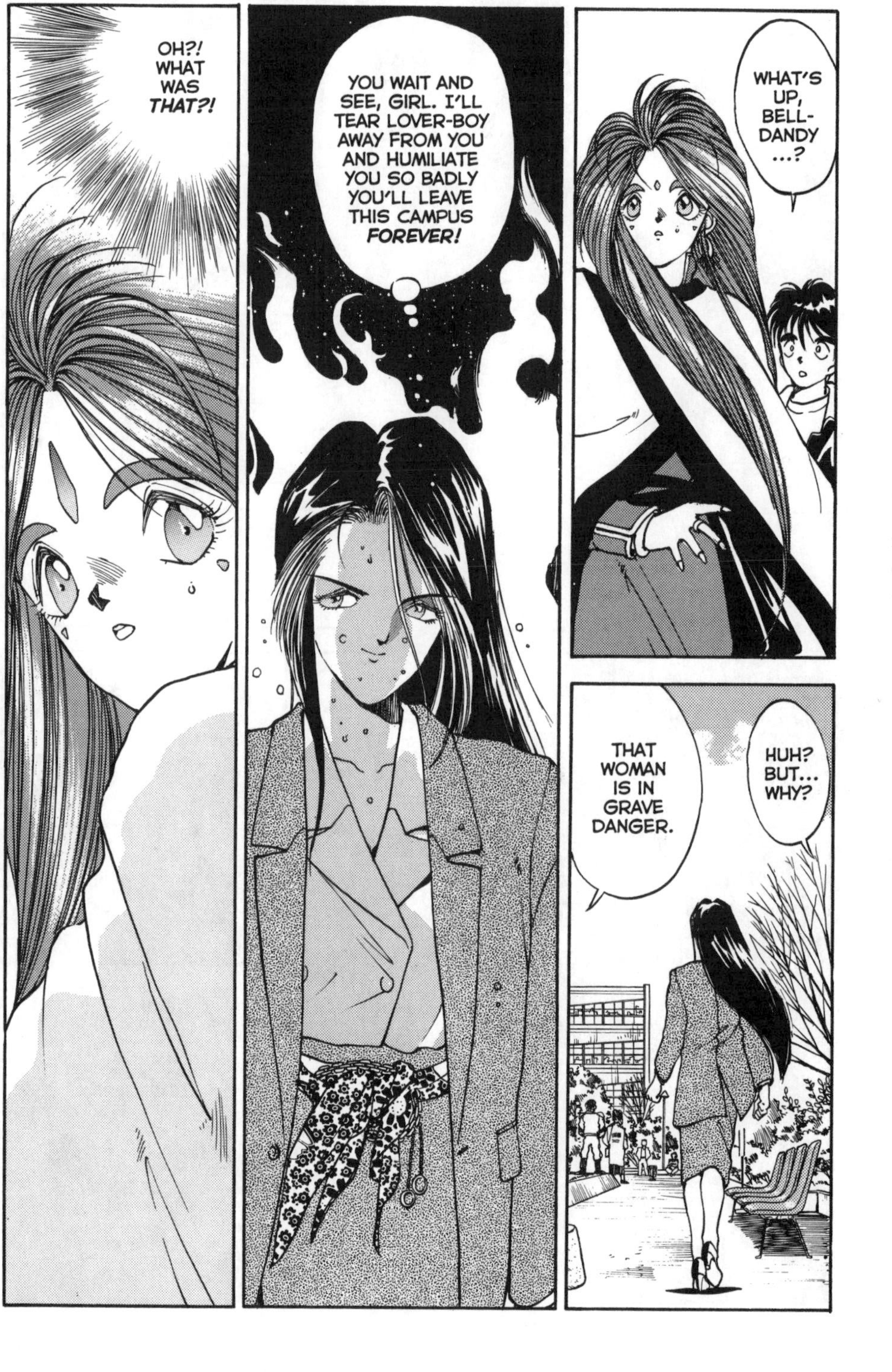
OH?! WHAT WAS *THAT?!*
YOU WAIT AND SEE, GIRL. I'LL TEAR LOVER-BOY AWAY FROM YOU AND HUMILIATE YOU SO BADLY YOU'LL LEAVE THIS CAMPUS *FOREVER!*
WHAT'S UP, BELL-DANDY ...?
THAT WOMAN IS IN GRAVE DANGER.
HUH? BUT... WHY?

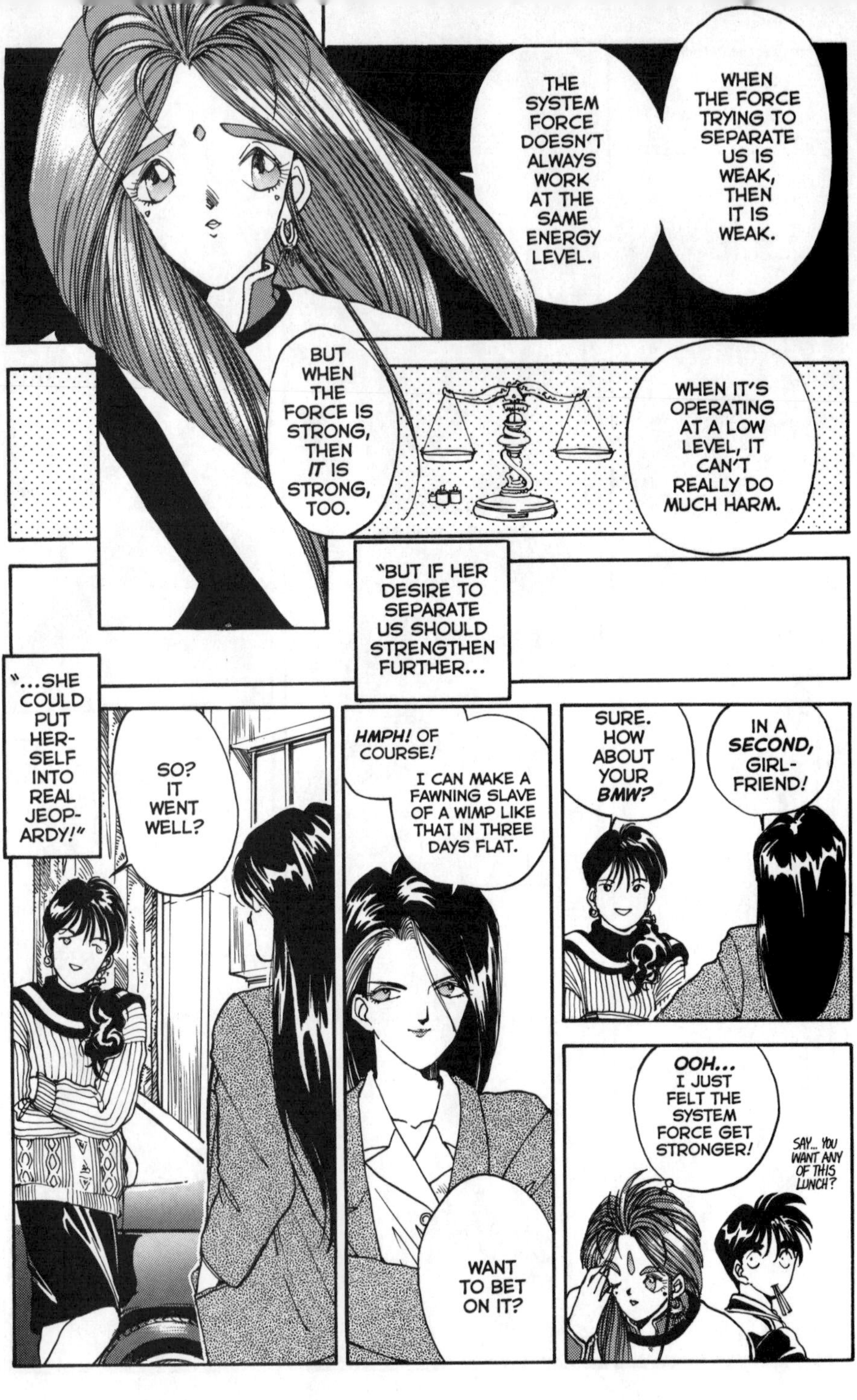
THE SYSTEM FORCE DOESN'T ALWAYS WORK AT THE SAME ENERGY LEVEL.
WHEN THE FORCE TRYING TO SEPARATE US IS WEAK, THEN IT IS WEAK.
BUT WHEN THE FORCE IS STRONG, THEN *IT* IS STRONG, TOO.
WHEN IT'S OPERATING AT A LOW LEVEL, IT CAN'T REALLY DO MUCH HARM.
"BUT IF HER DESIRE TO SEPARATE US SHOULD STRENGTHEN FURTHER...
"...SHE COULD PUT HER-SELF INTO REAL JEOP-ARDY!"
SO? IT WENT WELL?
HMPH! OF COURSE!
I CAN MAKE A FAWNING SLAVE OF A WIMP LIKE THAT IN THREE DAYS FLAT.
WANT TO BET ON IT?
SURE. HOW ABOUT YOUR *BMW?*
IN A *SECOND,* GIRL-FRIEND!
OOH... I JUST FELT THE SYSTEM FORCE GET STRONGER!
SAY... YOU WANT ANY OF THIS LUNCH?

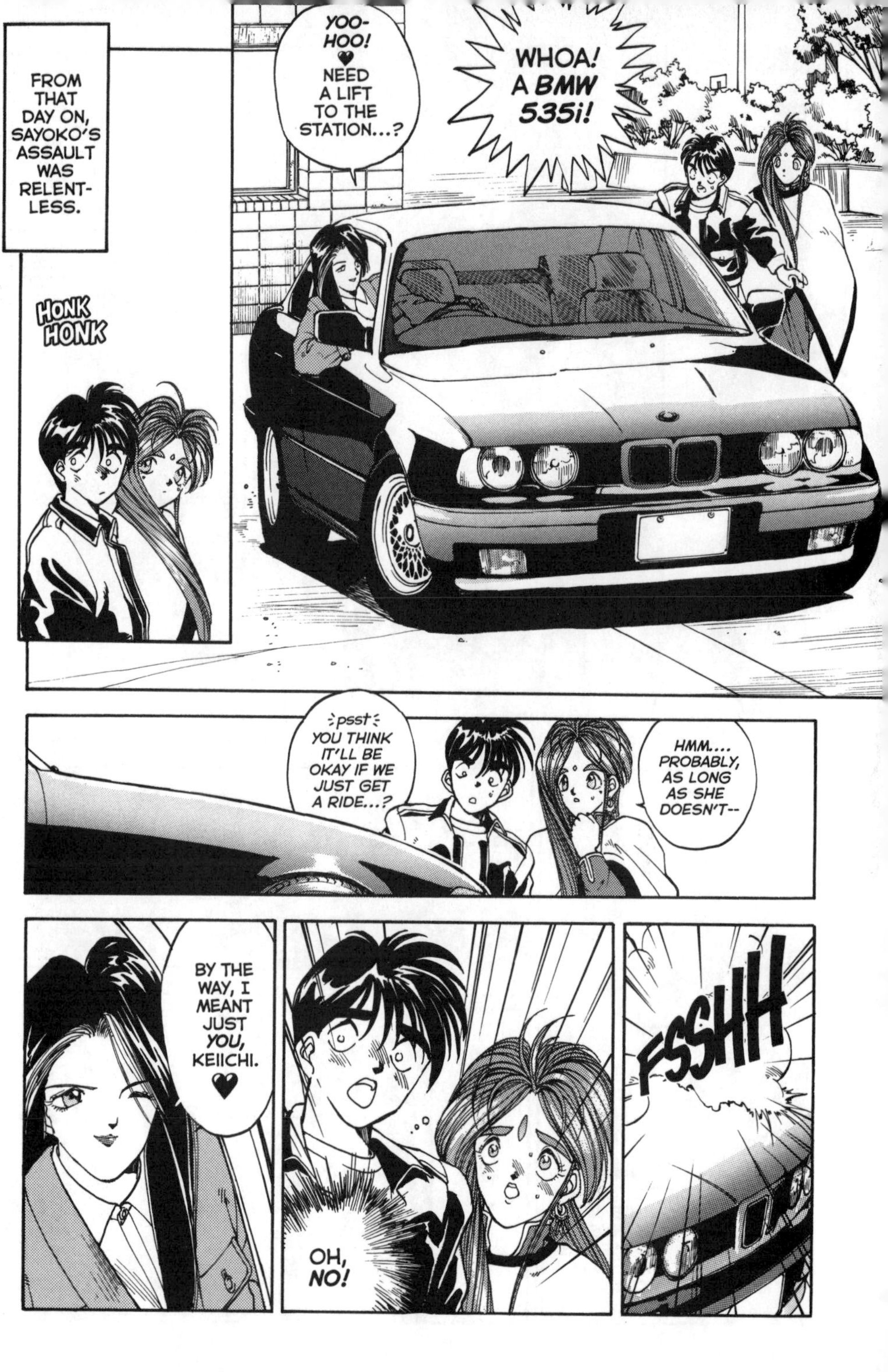
FROM THAT DAY ON, SAYOKO'S ASSAULT WAS RELENT-LESS.
YOO-HOO! ♥ NEED A LIFT TO THE STATION...?
WHOA! A BMW 535i!
HONK HONK
psst YOU THINK IT'LL BE OKAY IF WE JUST GET A RIDE...?
HMM.... PROBABLY, AS LONG AS SHE DOESN'T--
BY THE WAY, I MEANT JUST YOU, KEIICHI. ♥
OH, NO!
FSSHH

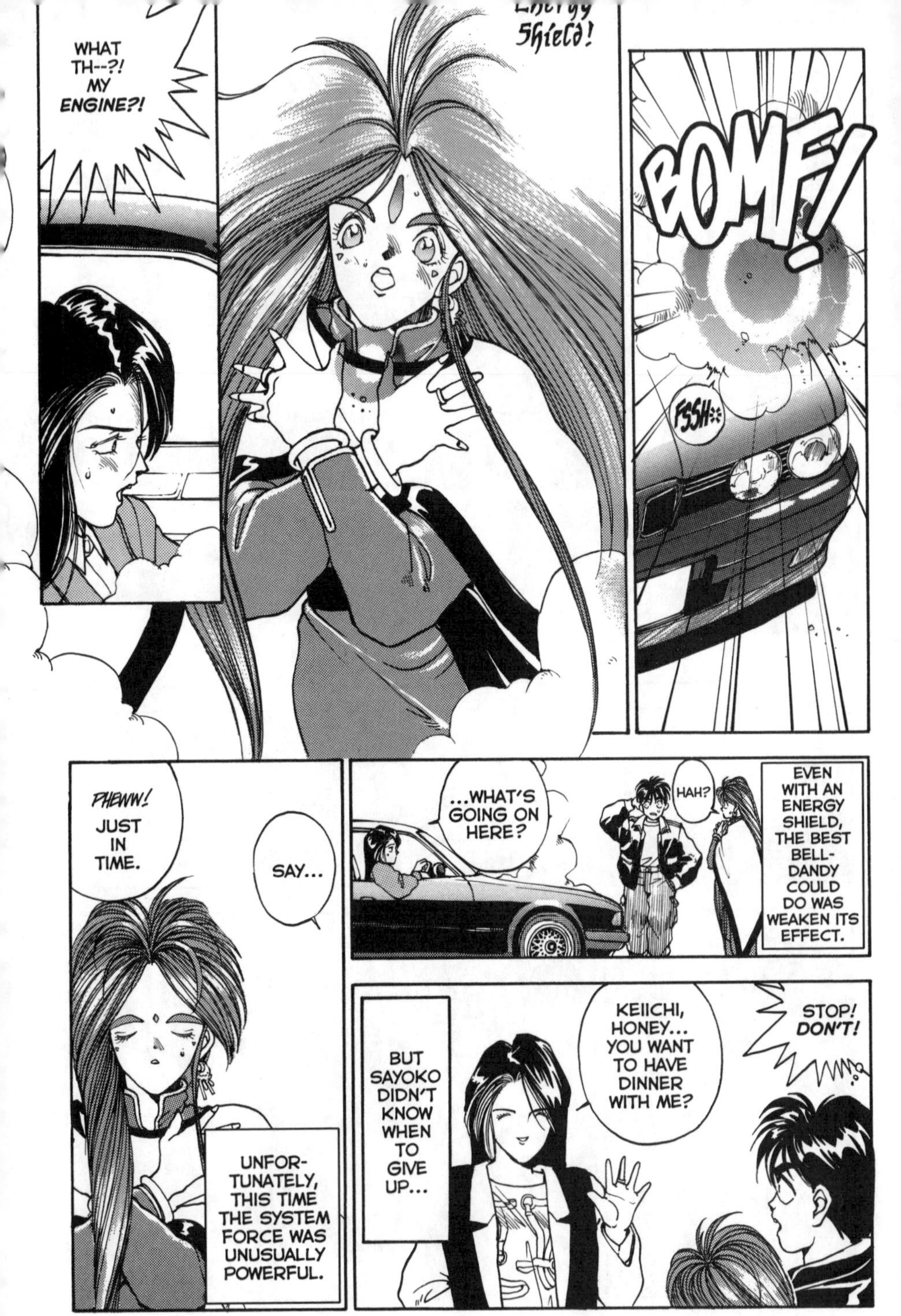

WHAT TH--?! MY ENGINE?!
Energy Shield!
BOMF!
FSSH
PHEWW! JUST IN TIME.
SAY...
UNFOR-TUNATELY, THIS TIME THE SYSTEM FORCE WAS UNUSUALLY POWERFUL.
...WHAT'S GOING ON HERE?
HAH?
EVEN WITH AN ENERGY SHIELD, THE BEST BELL-DANDY COULD DO WAS WEAKEN ITS EFFECT.
BUT SAYOKO DIDN'T KNOW WHEN TO GIVE UP...
KEIICHI, HONEY... YOU WANT TO HAVE DINNER WITH ME?
STOP! DON'T!

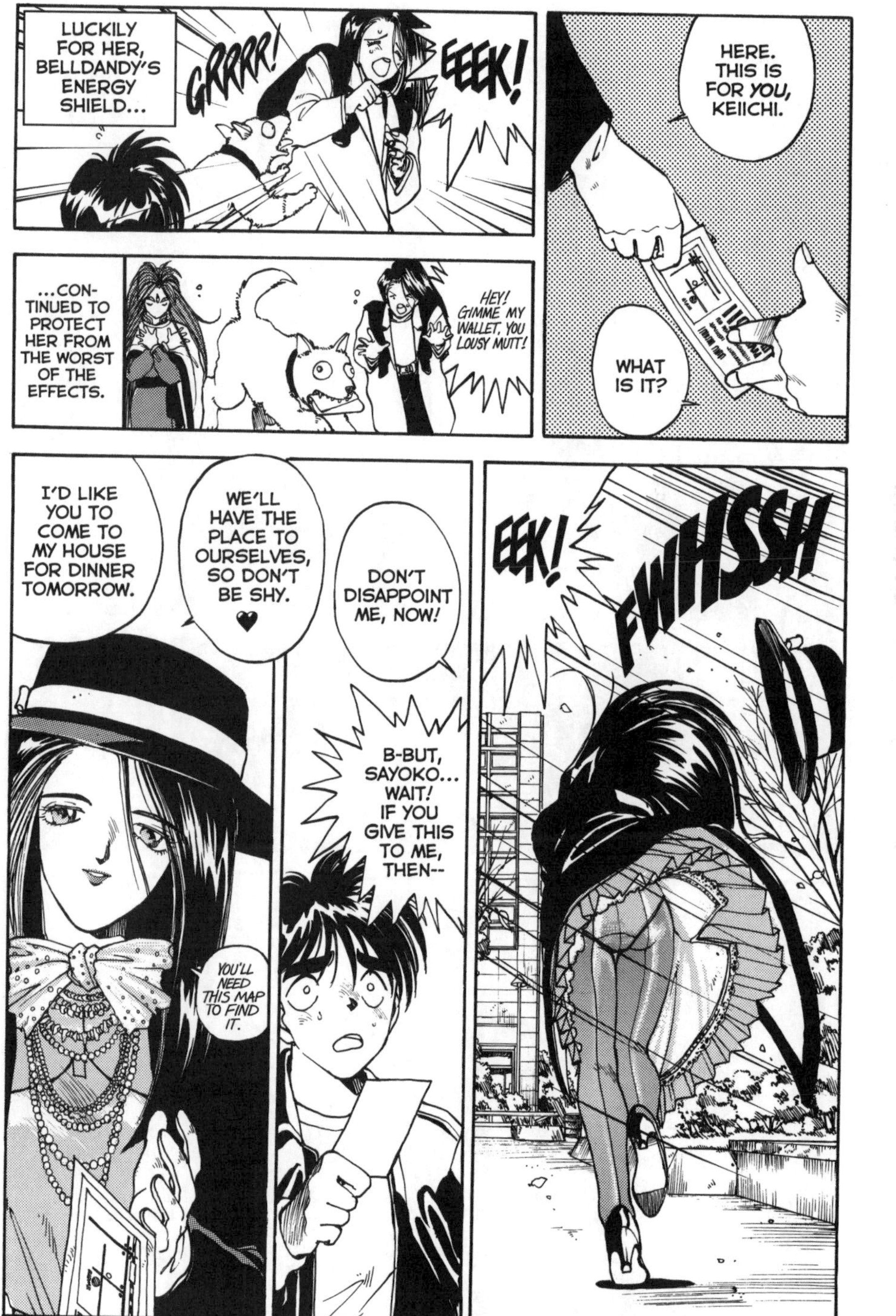
LUCKILY FOR HER, BELLDANDY'S ENERGY SHIELD...
GRRRR!
EEEK!
...CONTINUED TO PROTECT HER FROM THE WORST OF THE EFFECTS.
HEY! GIMME MY WALLET, YOU LOUSY MUTT!
HERE. THIS IS FOR *YOU*, KEIICHI.
WHAT IS IT?
I'D LIKE YOU TO COME TO MY HOUSE FOR DINNER TOMORROW.
WE'LL HAVE THE PLACE TO OURSELVES, SO DON'T BE SHY. ♥
YOU'LL NEED THIS MAP TO FIND IT.
DON'T DISAPPOINT ME, NOW!
B-BUT, SAYOKO... WAIT! IF YOU GIVE THIS TO ME, THEN--
EEK!
FWHSSH

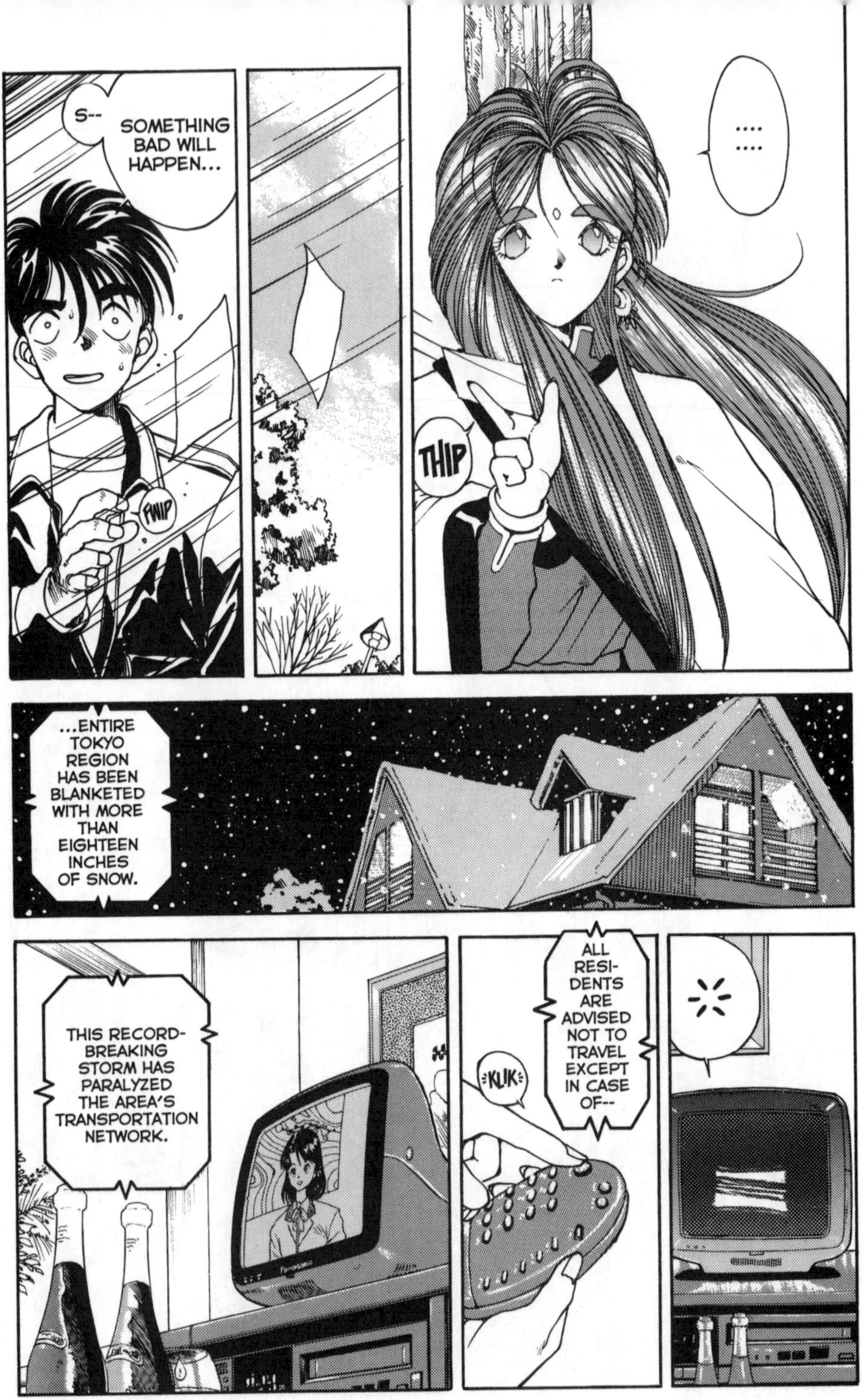
S--
SOMETHING BAD WILL HAPPEN...
FWIP
THIP
....
....
...ENTIRE TOKYO REGION HAS BEEN BLANKETED WITH MORE THAN EIGHTEEN INCHES OF SNOW.
THIS RECORD-BREAKING STORM HAS PARALYZED THE AREA'S TRANSPORTATION NETWORK.
KLIK
ALL RESI-DENTS ARE ADVISED NOT TO TRAVEL EXCEPT IN CASE OF--

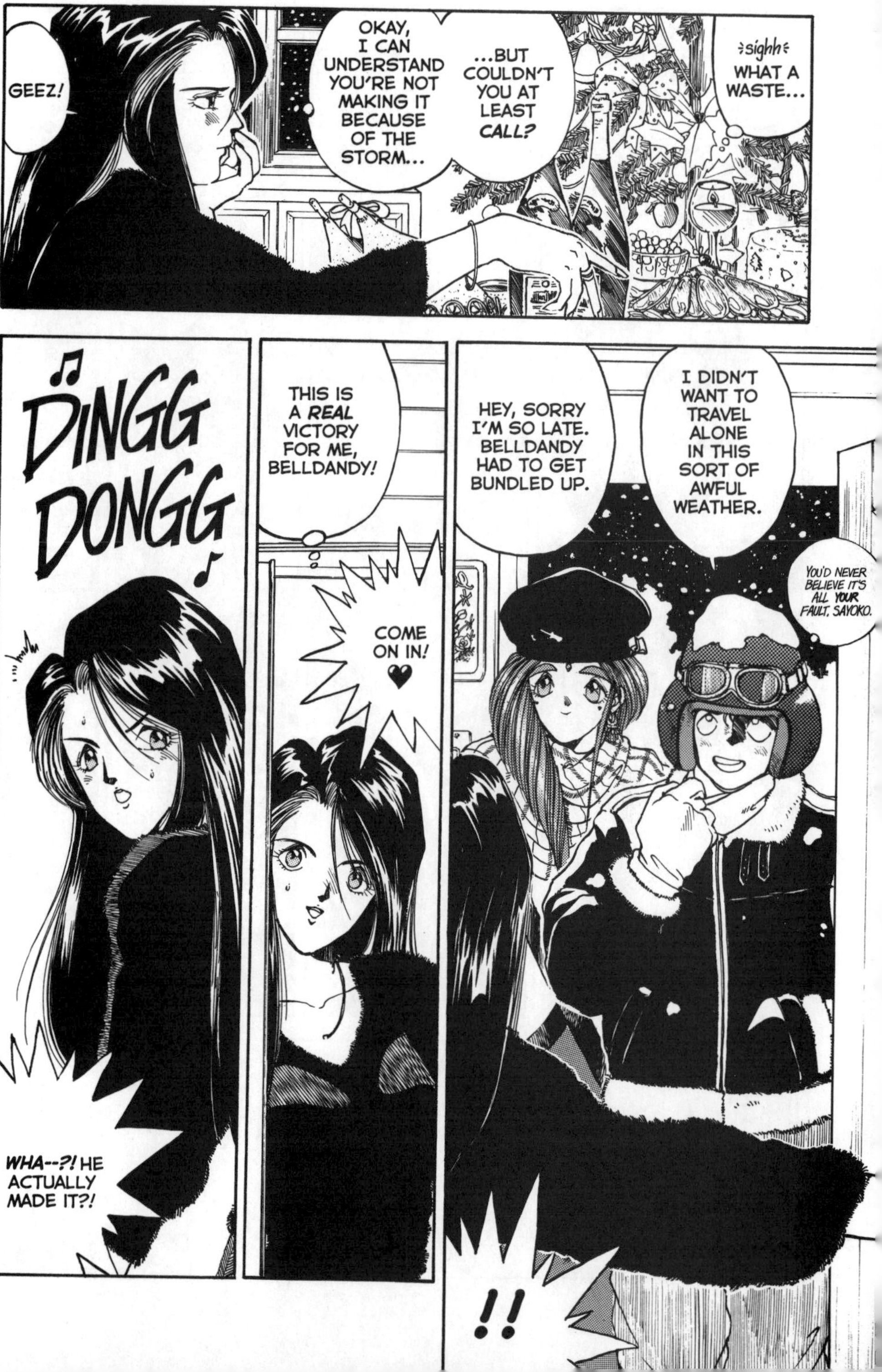
GEEZ!
OKAY, I CAN UNDERSTAND YOU'RE NOT MAKING IT BECAUSE OF THE STORM...
...BUT COULDN'T YOU AT LEAST *CALL?*
⸗sighh⸗ WHAT A WASTE...
DINGG DONGG
WHA--?! HE ACTUALLY MADE IT?!
THIS IS A *REAL* VICTORY FOR ME, BELLDANDY!
COME ON IN!
HEY, SORRY I'M SO LATE. BELLDANDY HAD TO GET BUNDLED UP.
I DIDN'T WANT TO TRAVEL ALONE IN THIS SORT OF AWFUL WEATHER.
YOU'D NEVER BELIEVE IT'S ALL **YOUR** FAULT, SAYOKO.
!!

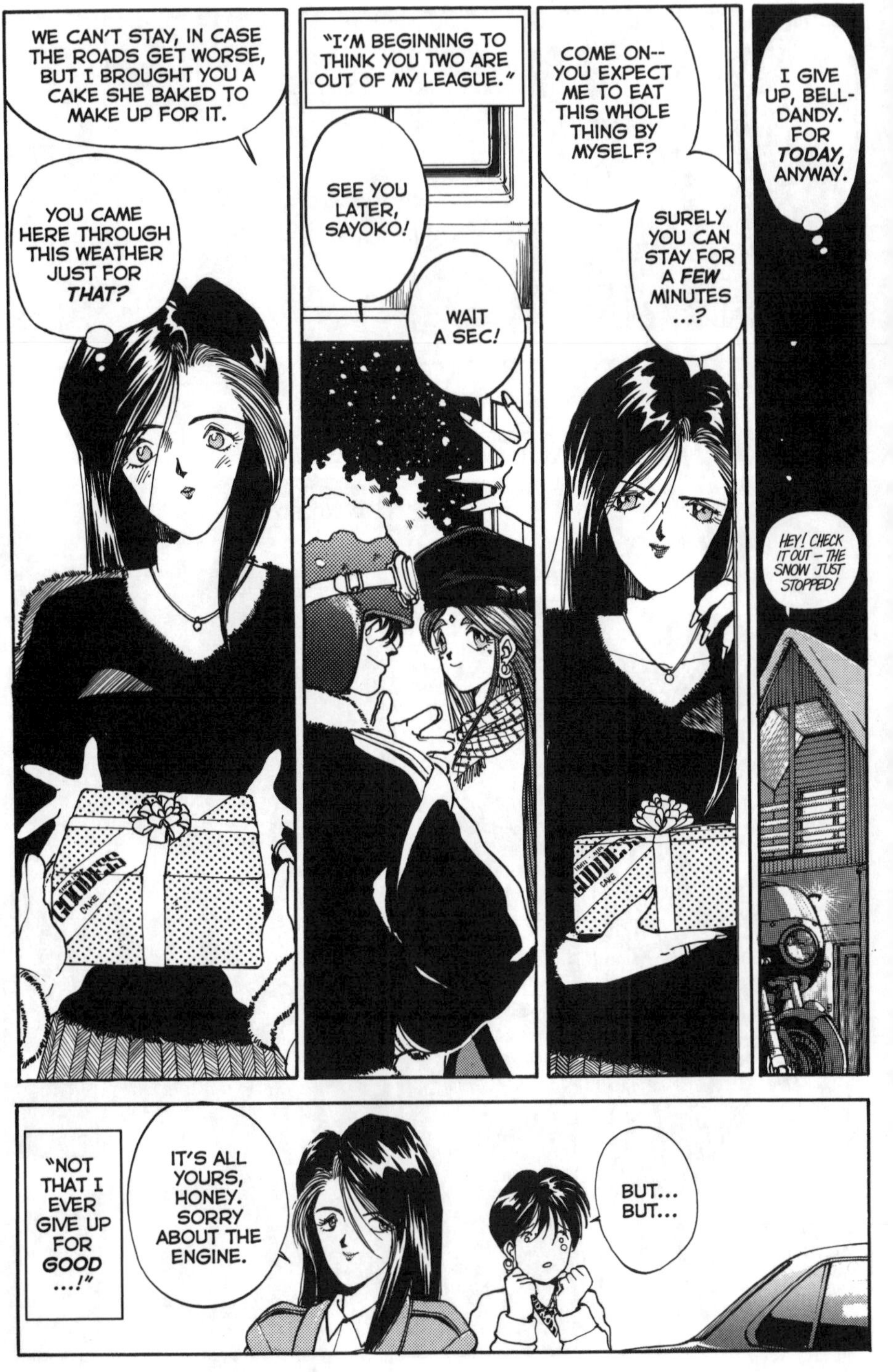
WE CAN'T STAY, IN CASE THE ROADS GET WORSE, BUT I BROUGHT YOU A CAKE SHE BAKED TO MAKE UP FOR IT.
YOU CAME HERE THROUGH THIS WEATHER JUST FOR *THAT?*
"I'M BEGINNING TO THINK YOU TWO ARE OUT OF MY LEAGUE."
SEE YOU LATER, SAYOKO!
WAIT A SEC!
COME ON-- YOU EXPECT ME TO EAT THIS WHOLE THING BY MYSELF?
SURELY YOU CAN STAY FOR A *FEW* MINUTES ...?
I GIVE UP, BELL-DANDY. FOR *TODAY,* ANYWAY.
HEY! CHECK IT OUT – THE SNOW JUST STOPPED!
"NOT THAT I EVER GIVE UP FOR *GOOD* ...!"
IT'S ALL YOURS, HONEY. SORRY ABOUT THE ENGINE.
BUT... BUT...

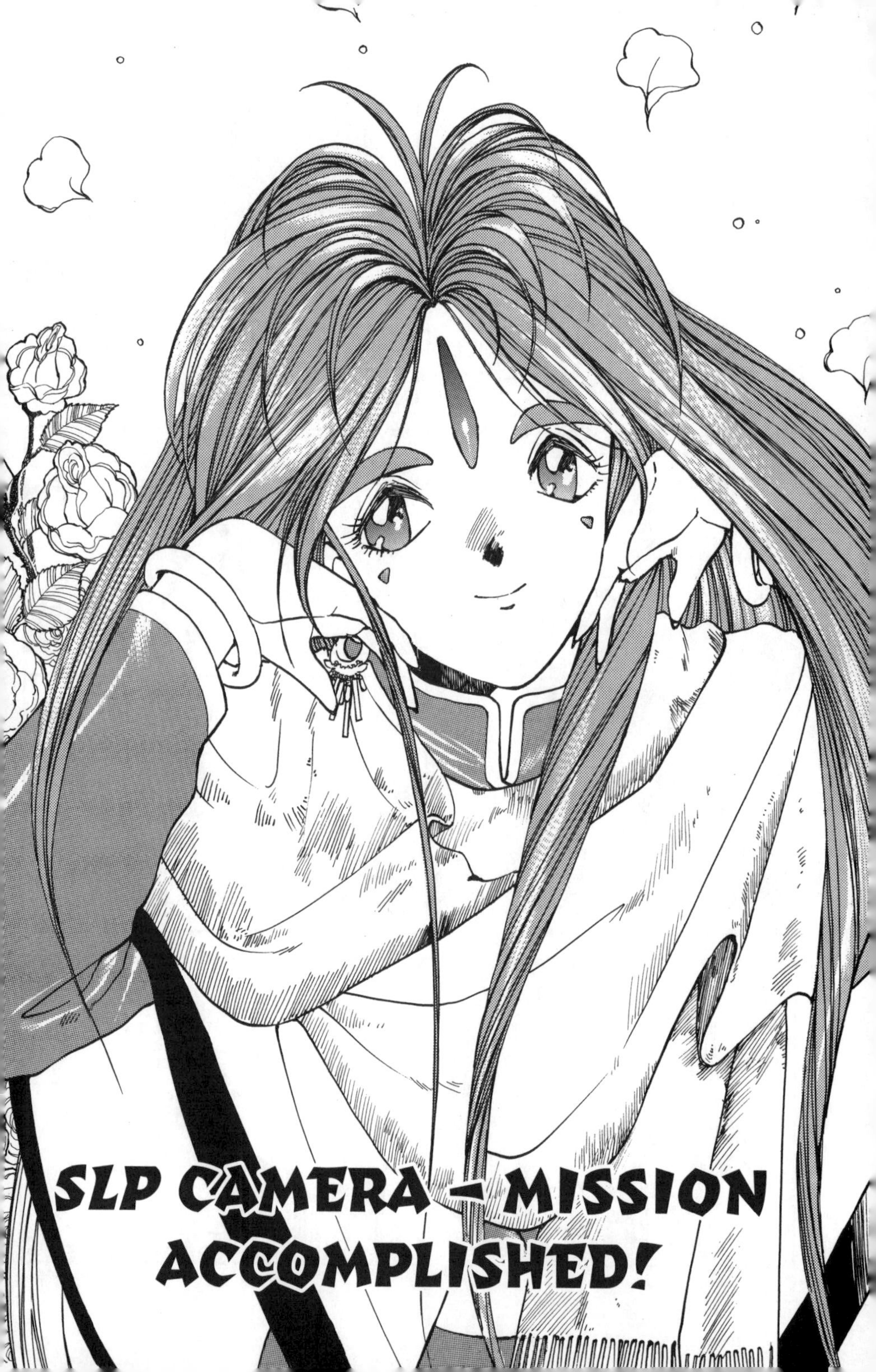
SLP CAMERA – MISSION
ACCOMPLISHED!

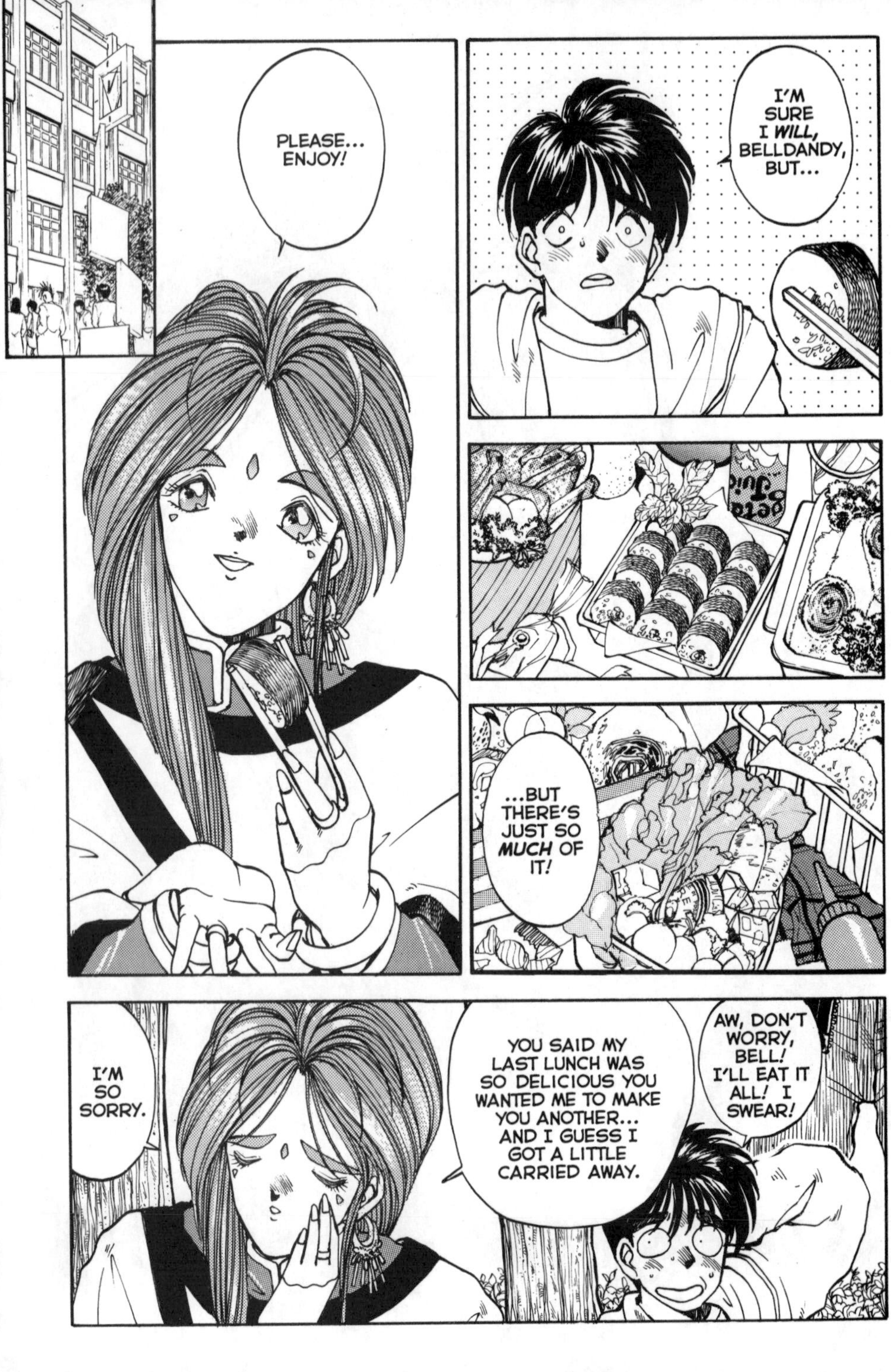
PLEASE... ENJOY!
I'M SURE I *WILL*, BELLDANDY, BUT...
...BUT THERE'S JUST SO *MUCH* OF IT!
I'M SO SORRY.
YOU SAID MY LAST LUNCH WAS SO DELICIOUS YOU WANTED ME TO MAKE YOU ANOTHER... AND I GUESS I GOT A LITTLE CARRIED AWAY.
AW, DON'T WORRY, BELL! I'LL EAT IT ALL! I SWEAR!

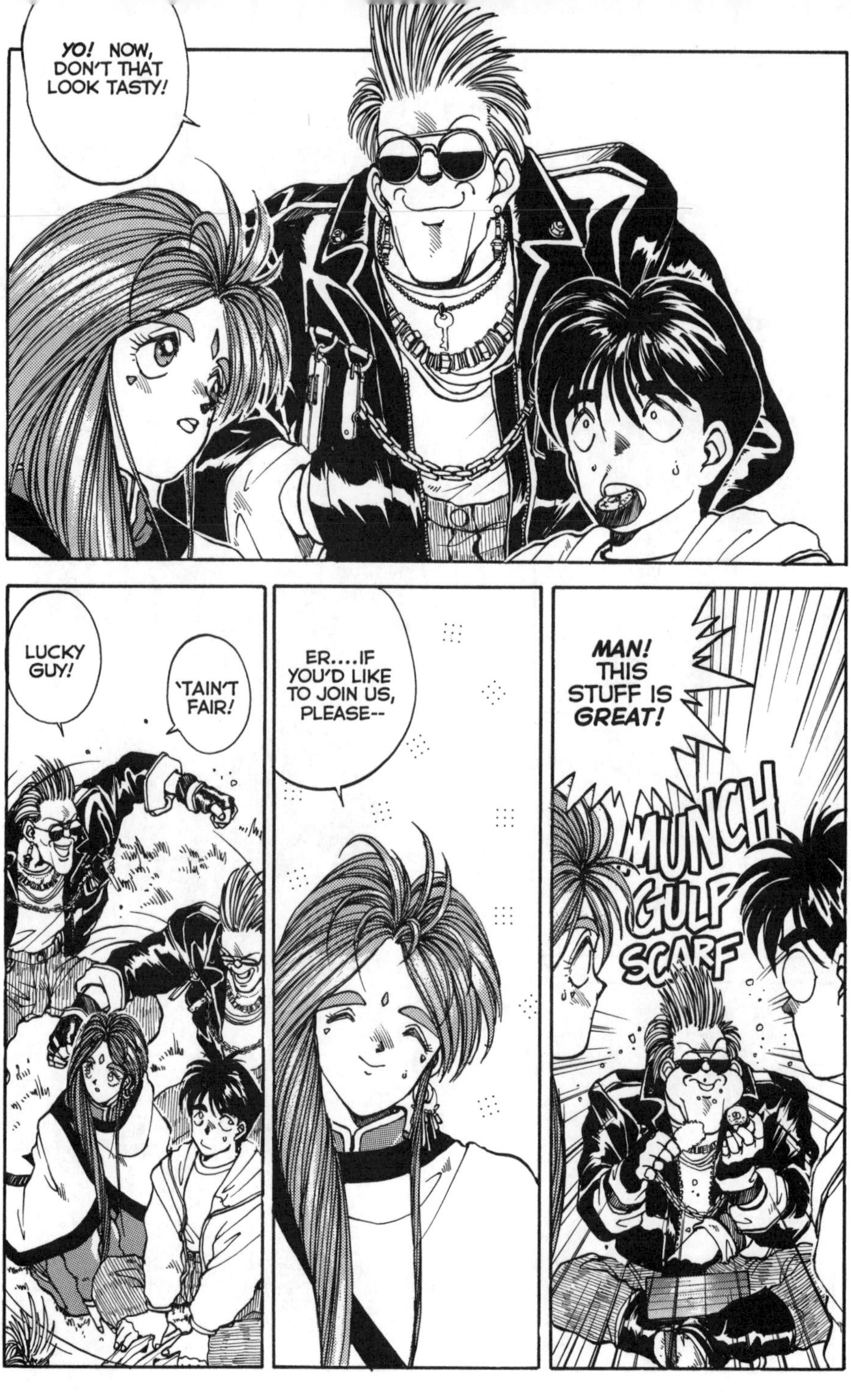
YO! NOW, DON'T THAT LOOK TASTY!
LUCKY GUY!
'TAIN'T FAIR!
ER....IF YOU'D LIKE TO JOIN US, PLEASE--
MAN! THIS STUFF IS GREAT!
MUNCH GULP SCARF

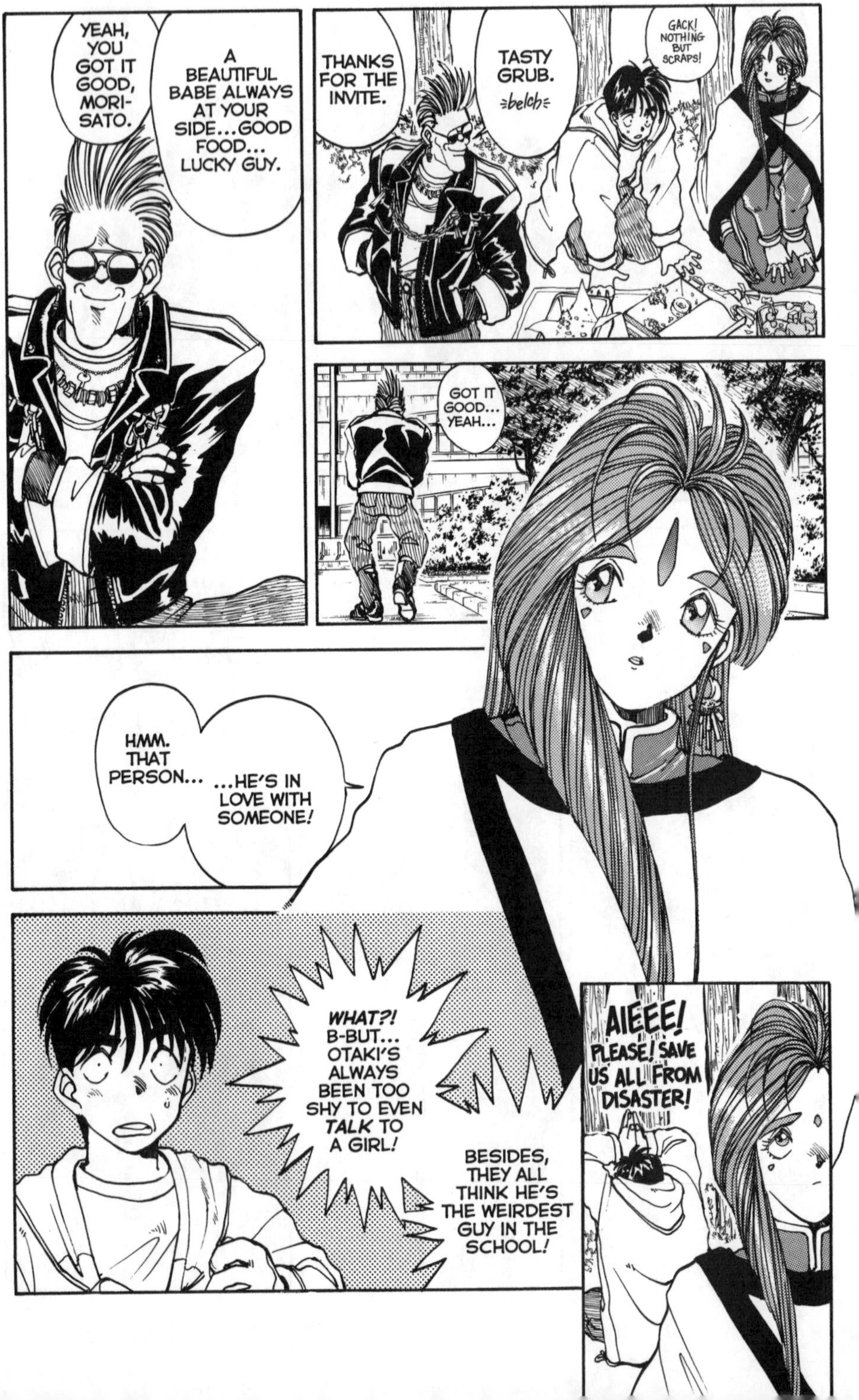
YEAH, YOU GOT IT GOOD, MORI-SATO.
A BEAUTIFUL BABE ALWAYS AT YOUR SIDE...GOOD FOOD... LUCKY GUY.
THANKS FOR THE INVITE.
TASTY GRUB.
belch
GACK! NOTHING BUT SCRAPS!
GOT IT GOOD... YEAH...
HMM. THAT PERSON... ...HE'S IN LOVE WITH SOMEONE!
WHAT?! B-BUT... OTAKI'S ALWAYS BEEN TOO SHY TO EVEN TALK TO A GIRL!
BESIDES, THEY ALL THINK HE'S THE WEIRDEST GUY IN THE SCHOOL!
AIEEE! PLEASE! SAVE US ALL FROM DISASTER!

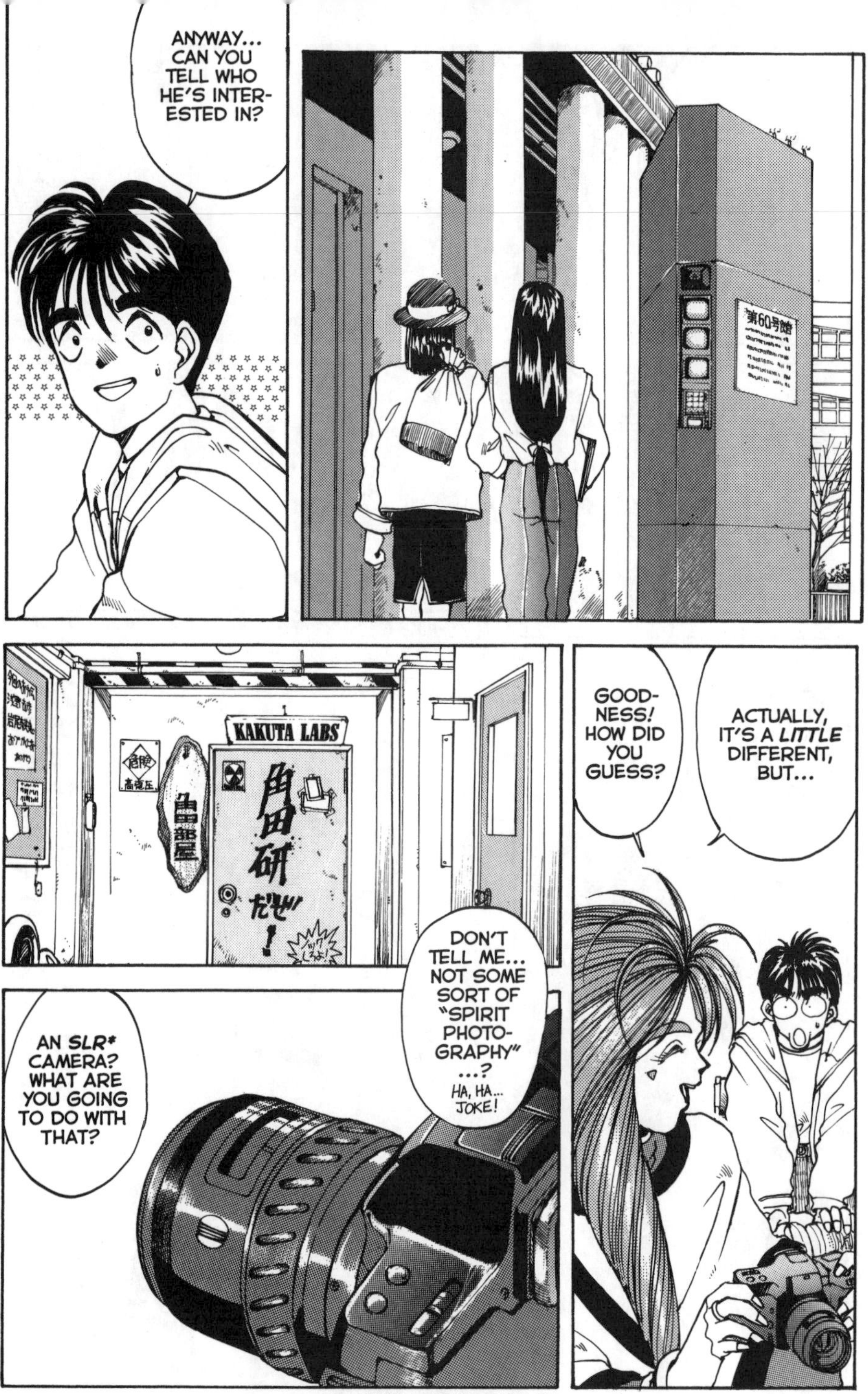
ANYWAY... CAN YOU TELL WHO HE'S INTERESTED IN?
KAKUTA LABS
AN SLR* CAMERA? WHAT ARE YOU GOING TO DO WITH THAT?
DON'T TELL ME... NOT SOME SORT OF "SPIRIT PHOTOGRAPHY" ...?
HA, HA... JOKE!
GOODNESS! HOW DID YOU GUESS?
ACTUALLY, IT'S A *LITTLE* DIFFERENT, BUT...

*: SINGLE LENS REFLEX

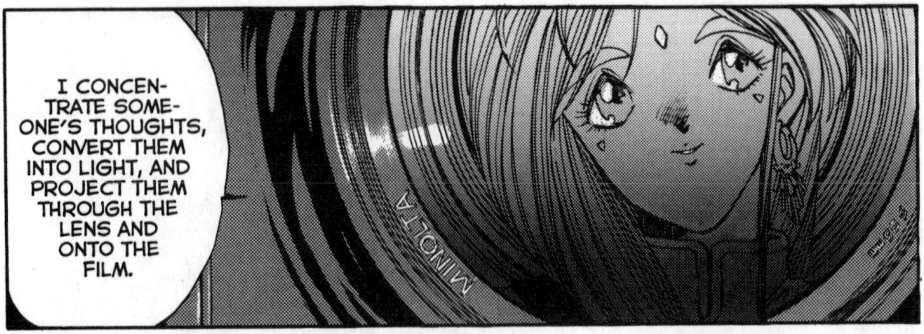
I CONCENTRATE SOMEONE'S THOUGHTS, CONVERT THEM INTO LIGHT, AND PROJECT THEM THROUGH THE LENS AND ONTO THE FILM.

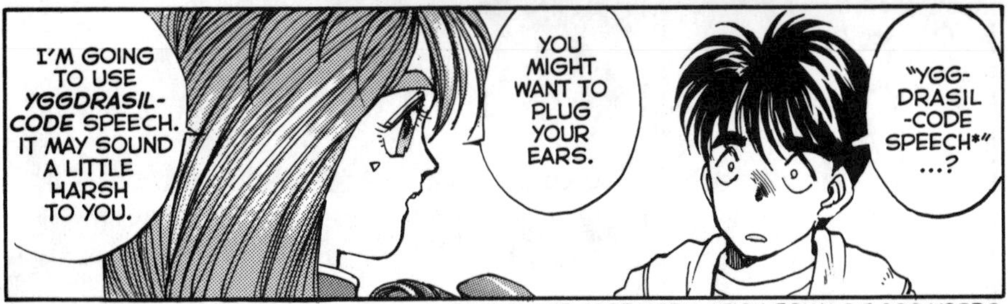
I'M GOING TO USE *YGGDRASIL-CODE* SPEECH. IT MAY SOUND A LITTLE HARSH TO YOU.
YOU MIGHT WANT TO PLUG YOUR EARS.
"YGGDRASIL-CODE SPEECH*"...?

*: EACH PULSE-CODE MODULATION EQUALS 5,000 WORDS.

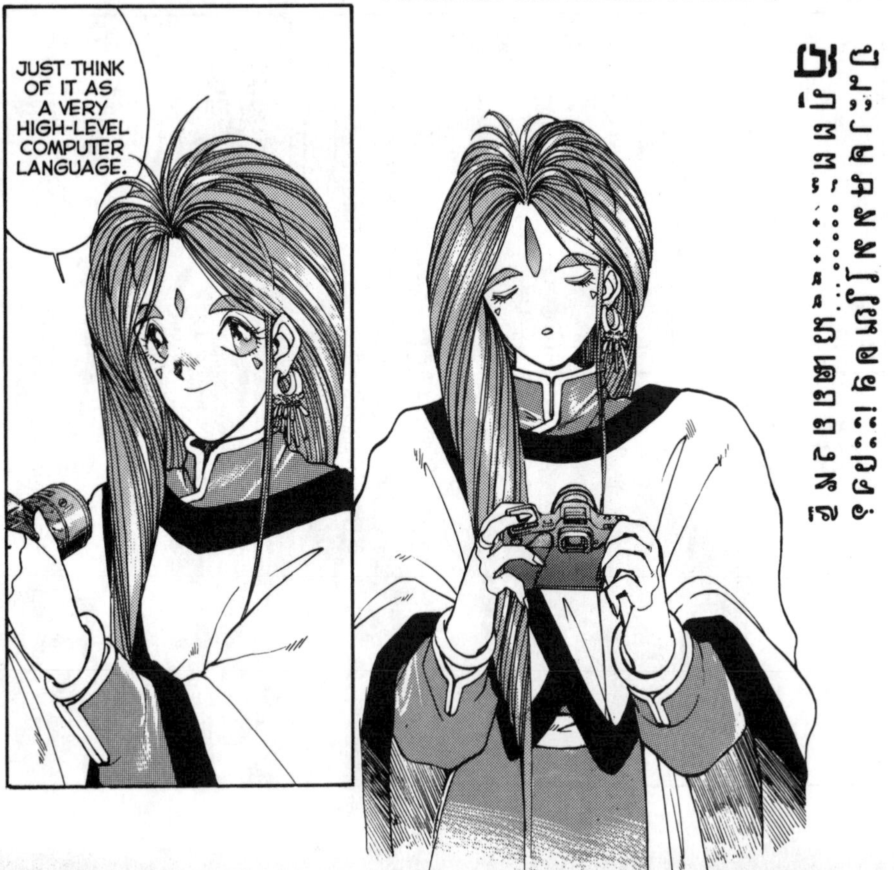
JUST THINK OF IT AS A VERY HIGH-LEVEL COMPUTER LANGUAGE.

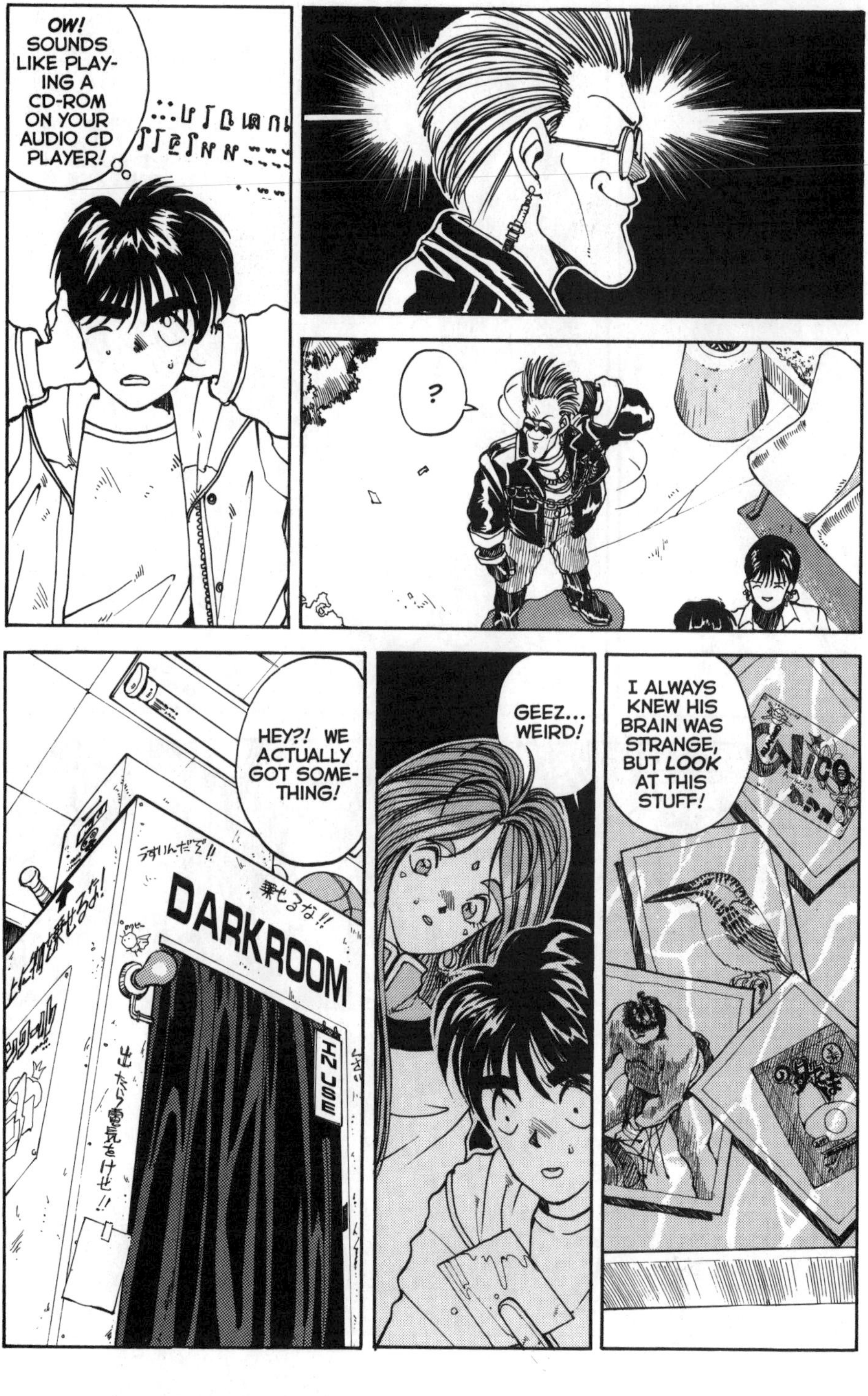
OW! SOUNDS LIKE PLAY-ING A CD-ROM ON YOUR AUDIO CD PLAYER!
?
HEY?! WE ACTUALLY GOT SOME-THING!
DARKROOM
IN USE
GEEZ... WEIRD!
I ALWAYS KNEW HIS BRAIN WAS STRANGE, BUT LOOK AT THIS STUFF!

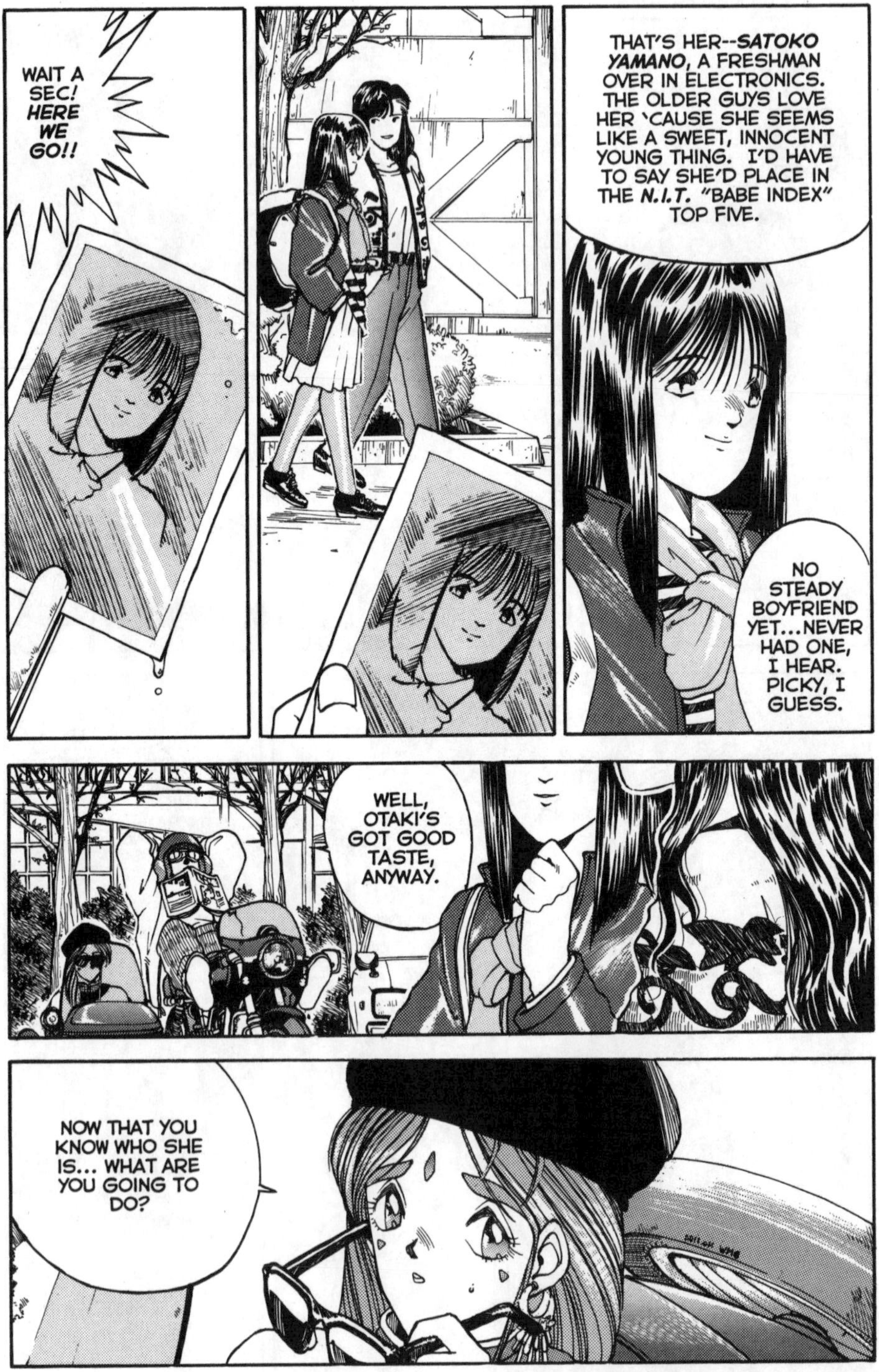
WAIT A SEC! HERE WE GO!!
THAT'S HER--SATOKO YAMANO, A FRESHMAN OVER IN ELECTRONICS. THE OLDER GUYS LOVE HER 'CAUSE SHE SEEMS LIKE A SWEET, INNOCENT YOUNG THING. I'D HAVE TO SAY SHE'D PLACE IN THE N.I.T. "BABE INDEX" TOP FIVE.
NO STEADY BOYFRIEND YET...NEVER HAD ONE, I HEAR. PICKY, I GUESS.
WELL, OTAKI'S GOT GOOD TASTE, ANYWAY.
NOW THAT YOU KNOW WHO SHE IS... WHAT ARE YOU GOING TO DO?

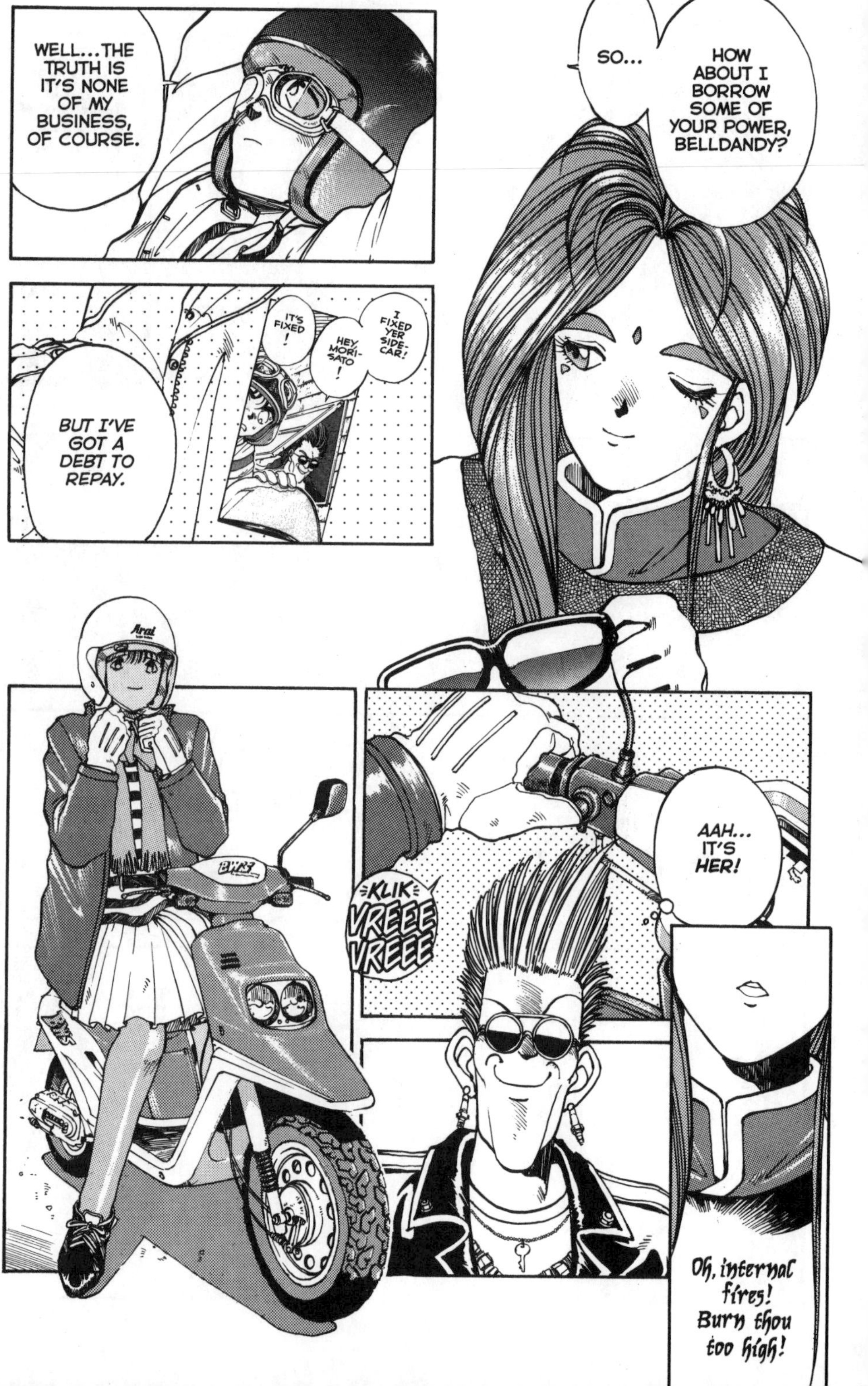
WELL...THE TRUTH IS IT'S NONE OF MY BUSINESS, OF COURSE.
BUT I'VE GOT A DEBT TO REPAY.
IT'S FIXED!
HEY, MORI-SATO!
I FIXED YER SIDE-CAR!
SO...
HOW ABOUT I BORROW SOME OF YOUR POWER, BELLDANDY?
KLIK
VREEE VREEE
AAH... IT'S HER!
Oh, internal fires! Burn thou too high!

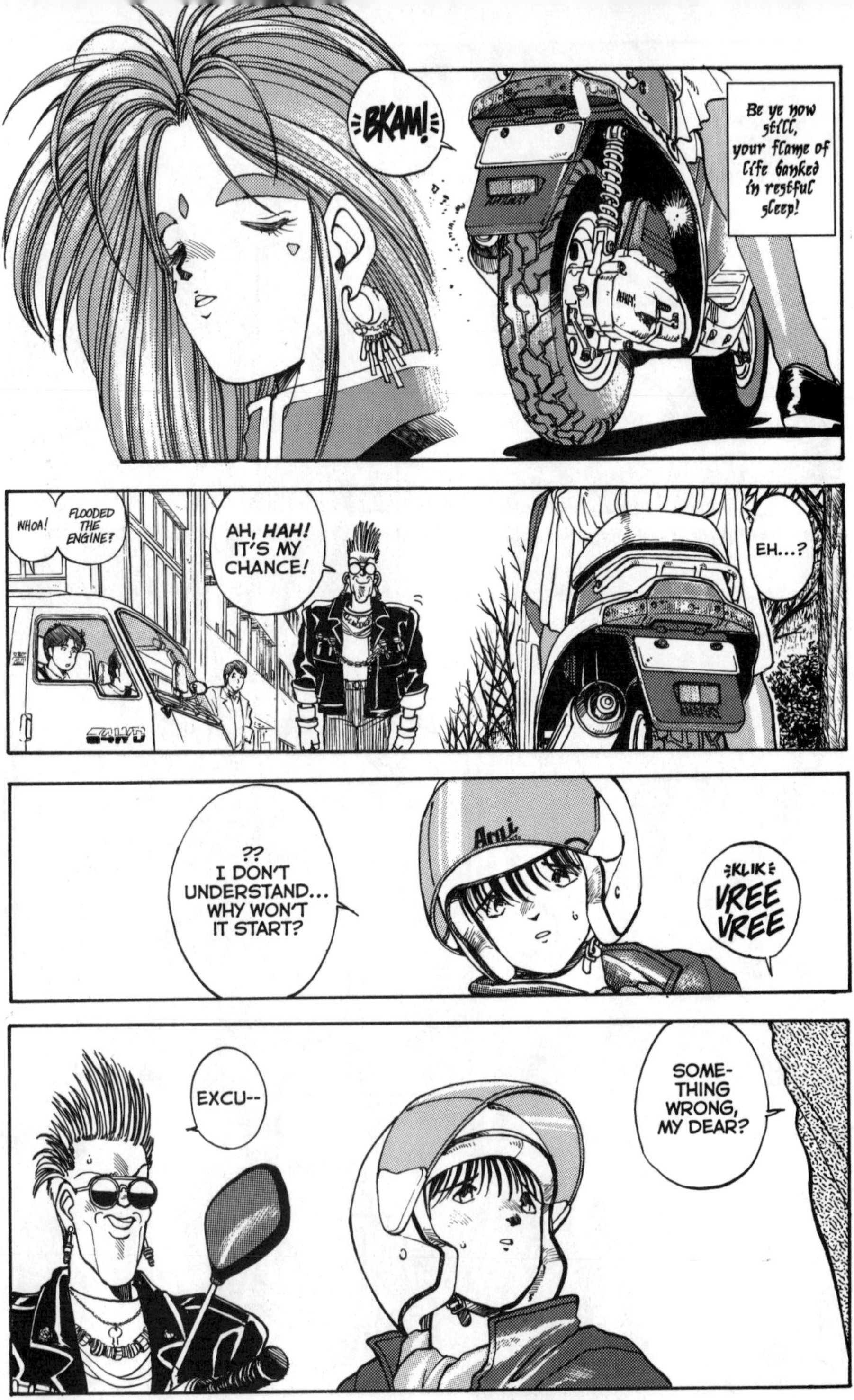
BKAM!
Be ye now still, your flame of life banked in restful sleep!
WHOA!
FLOODED THE ENGINE?
AH, HAH! IT'S MY CHANCE!
EH...?
?? I DON'T UNDERSTAND... WHY WON'T IT START?
KLIK
VREE VREE
EXCU--
SOME-THING WRONG, MY DEAR?

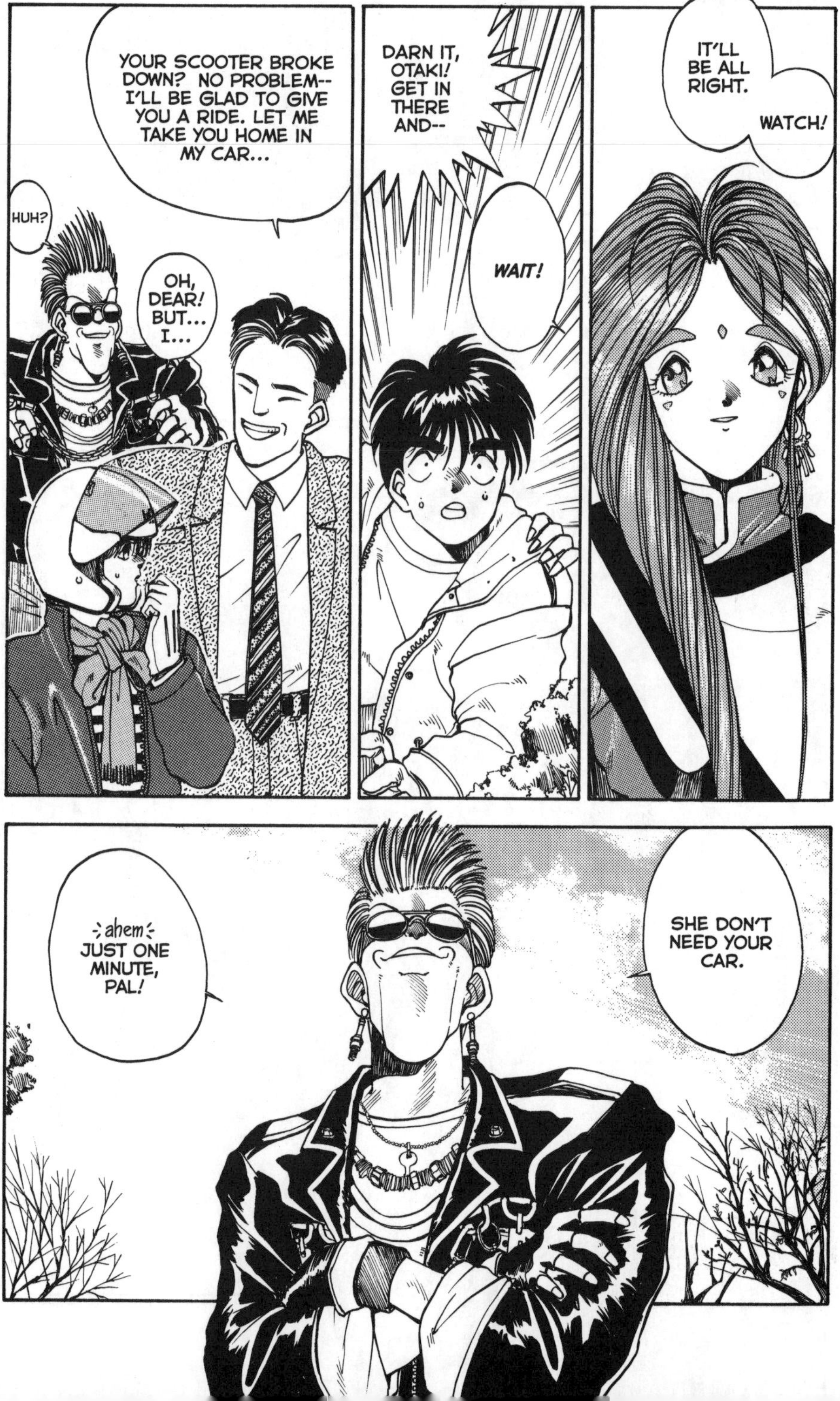
YOUR SCOOTER BROKE DOWN? NO PROBLEM-- I'LL BE GLAD TO GIVE YOU A RIDE. LET ME TAKE YOU HOME IN MY CAR...
HUH?
OH, DEAR! BUT... I...
DARN IT, OTAKI! GET IN THERE AND--
WAIT!
IT'LL BE ALL RIGHT.
WATCH!
ahem JUST ONE MINUTE, PAL!
SHE DON'T NEED YOUR CAR.

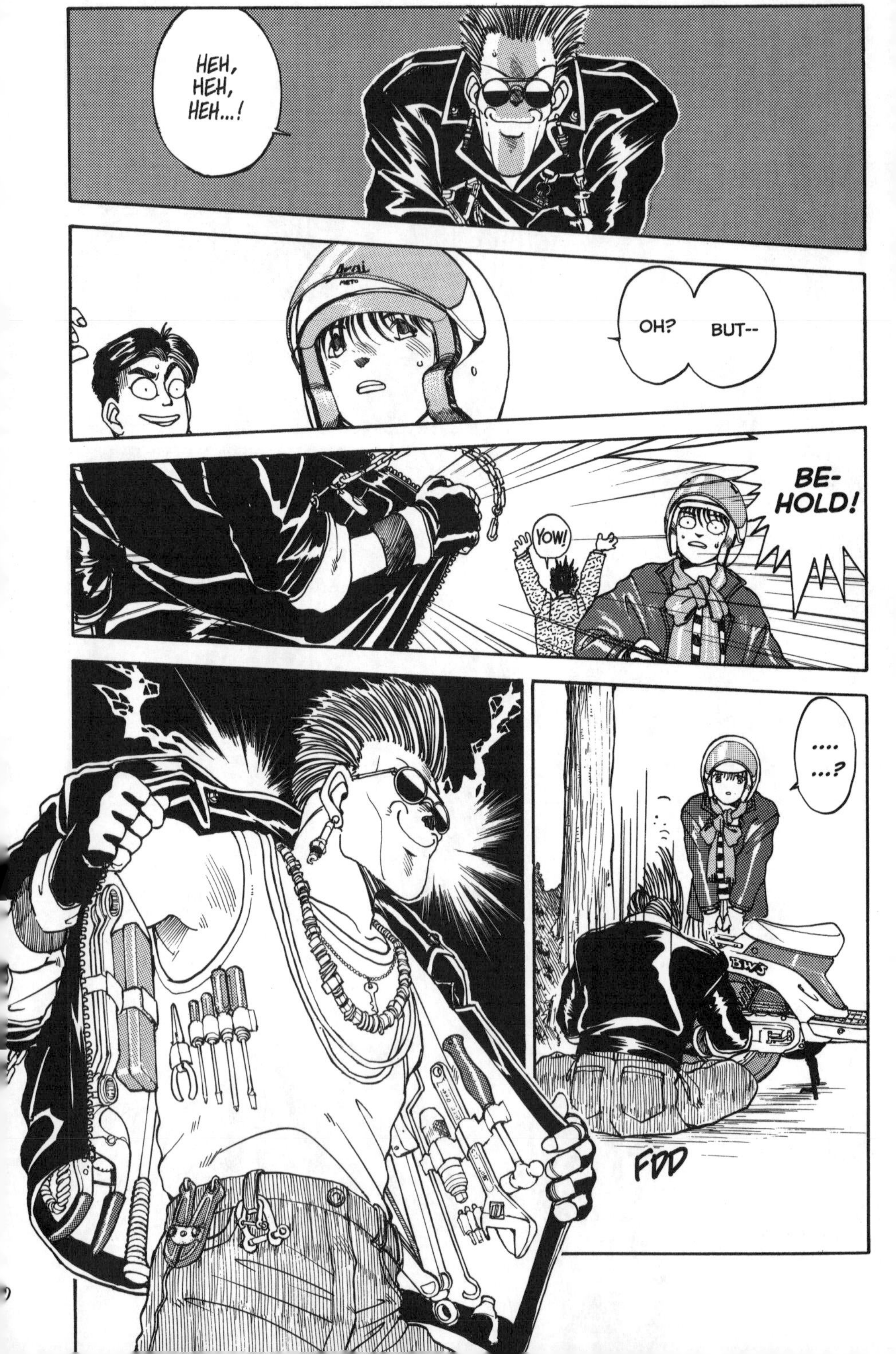
HEH, HEH, HEH...!
OH?
BUT--
YOW!
BE-HOLD!
....?
FDD

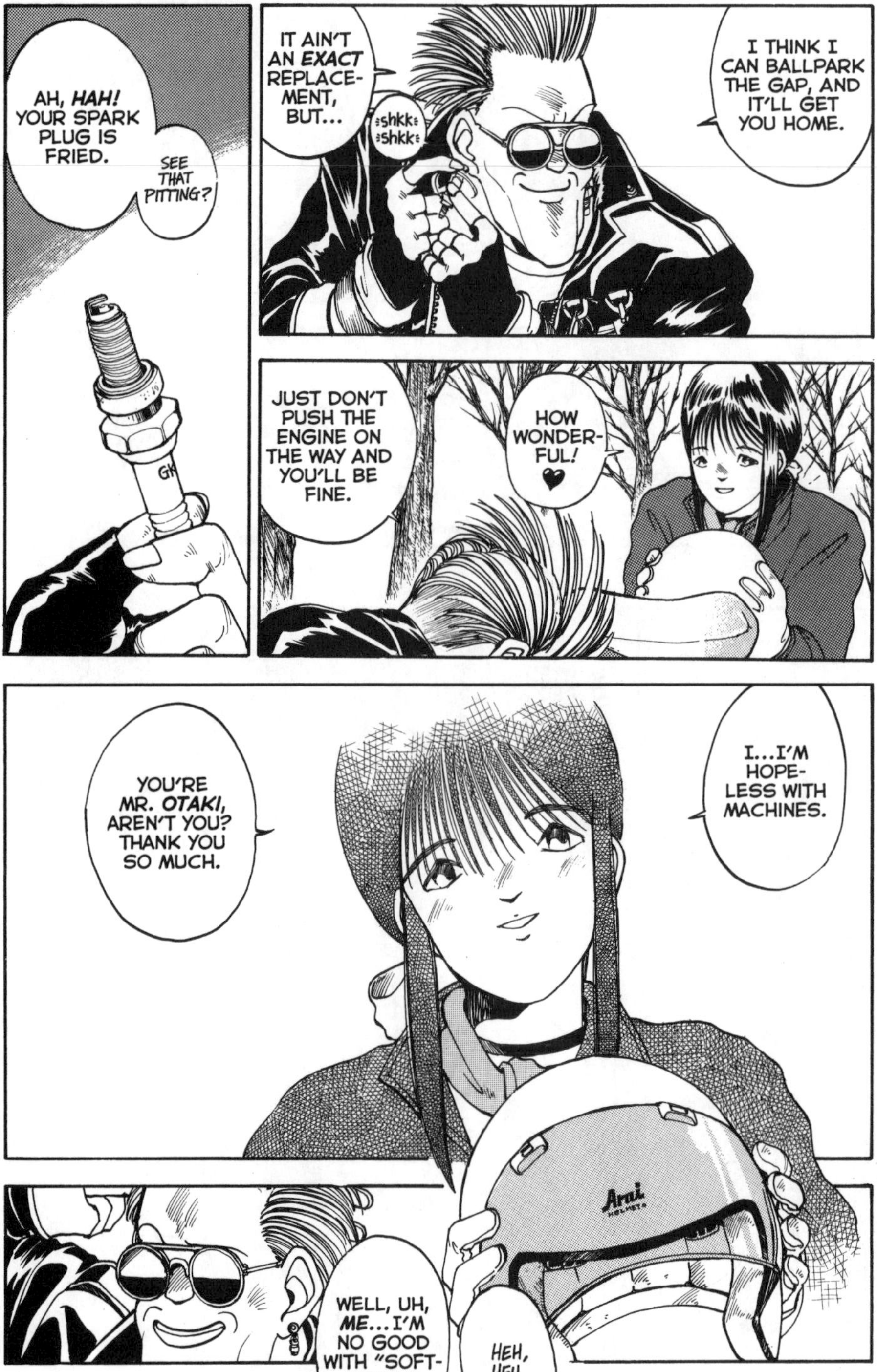
AH, HAH! YOUR SPARK PLUG IS FRIED.
SEE THAT PITTING?
IT AIN'T AN EXACT REPLACEMENT, BUT...
shkk shkk
I THINK I CAN BALLPARK THE GAP, AND IT'LL GET YOU HOME.
JUST DON'T PUSH THE ENGINE ON THE WAY AND YOU'LL BE FINE.
HOW WONDERFUL! ♥
YOU'RE MR. OTAKI, AREN'T YOU? THANK YOU SO MUCH.
I...I'M HOPELESS WITH MACHINES.
Arai
WELL, UH, ME... I'M NO GOOD WITH "SOFTWARE."
HEH, HEH...

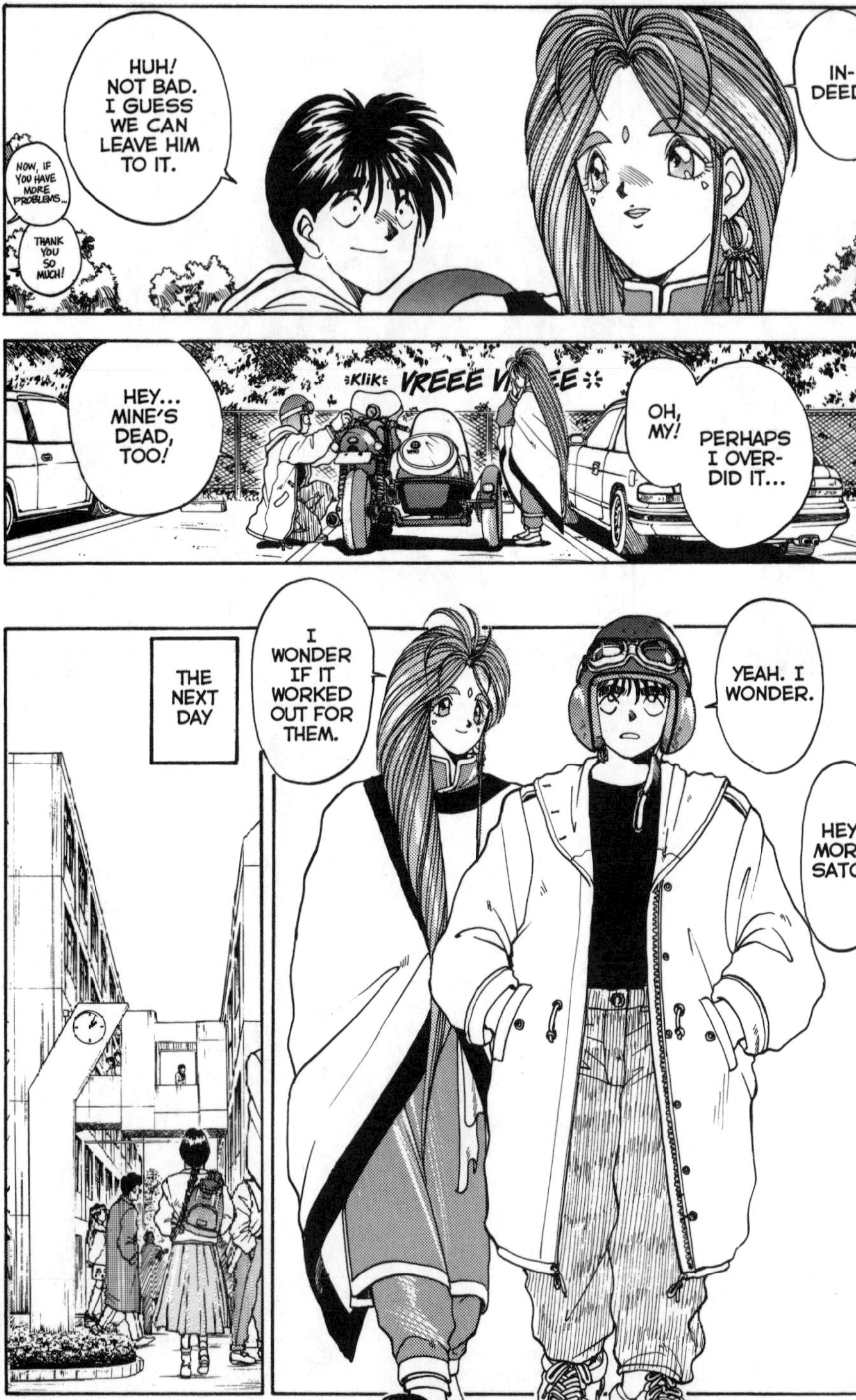
HUH! NOT BAD. I GUESS WE CAN LEAVE HIM TO IT.
NOW, IF YOU HAVE MORE PROBLEMS...
THANK YOU SO MUCH!
IN-DEED.
HEY... MINE'S DEAD, TOO!
KLIK
VREEE
OH, MY!
PERHAPS I OVER-DID IT...
THE NEXT DAY
I WONDER IF IT WORKED OUT FOR THEM.
YEAH. I WONDER.
HEY, MORI-SATO!

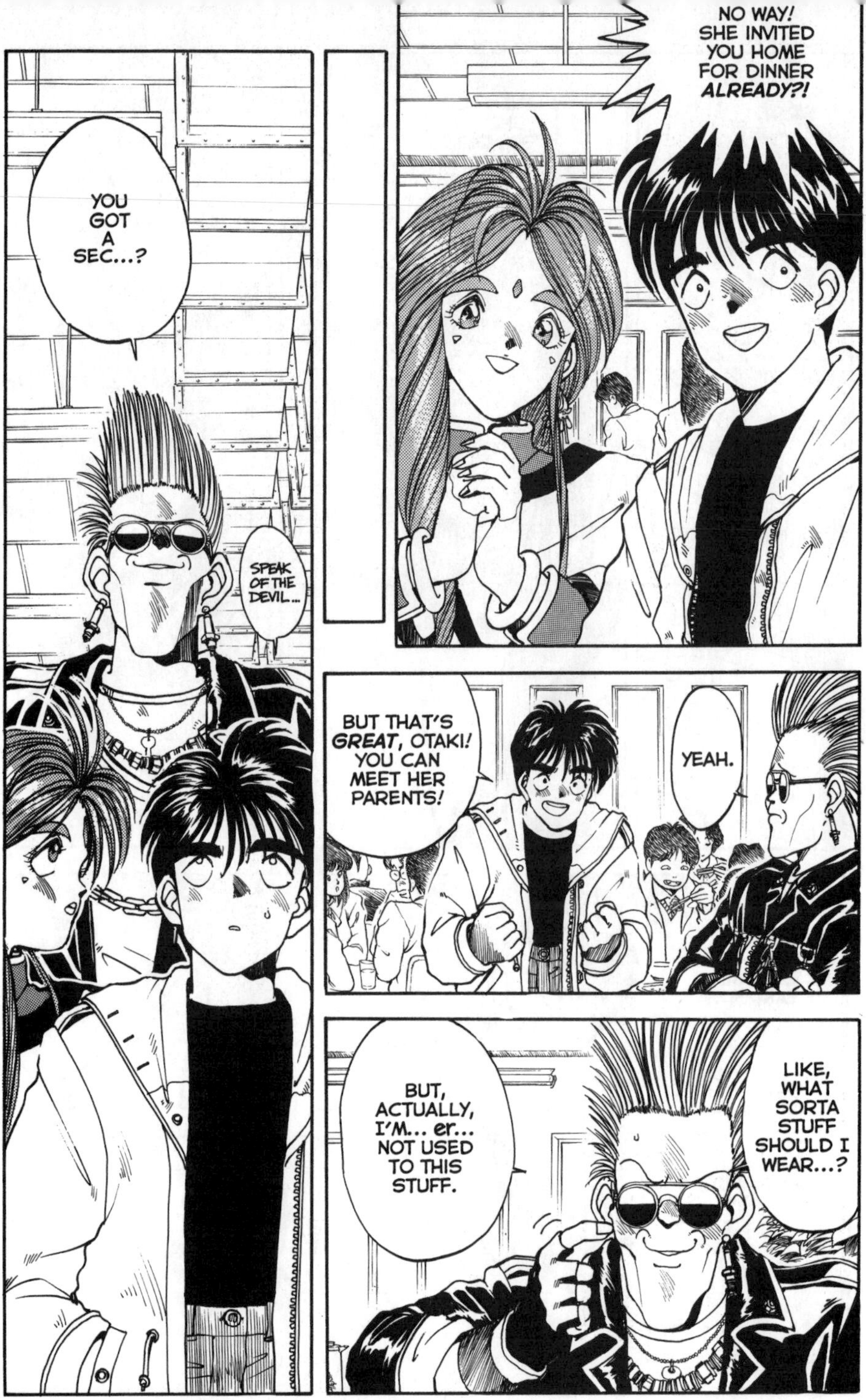
YOU GOT A SEC...?
SPEAK OF THE DEVIL...
NO WAY! SHE INVITED YOU HOME FOR DINNER *ALREADY?!*
BUT THAT'S *GREAT*, OTAKI! YOU CAN MEET HER PARENTS!
YEAH.
BUT, ACTUALLY, I'M... er... NOT USED TO THIS STUFF.
LIKE, WHAT SORTA STUFF SHOULD I WEAR...?

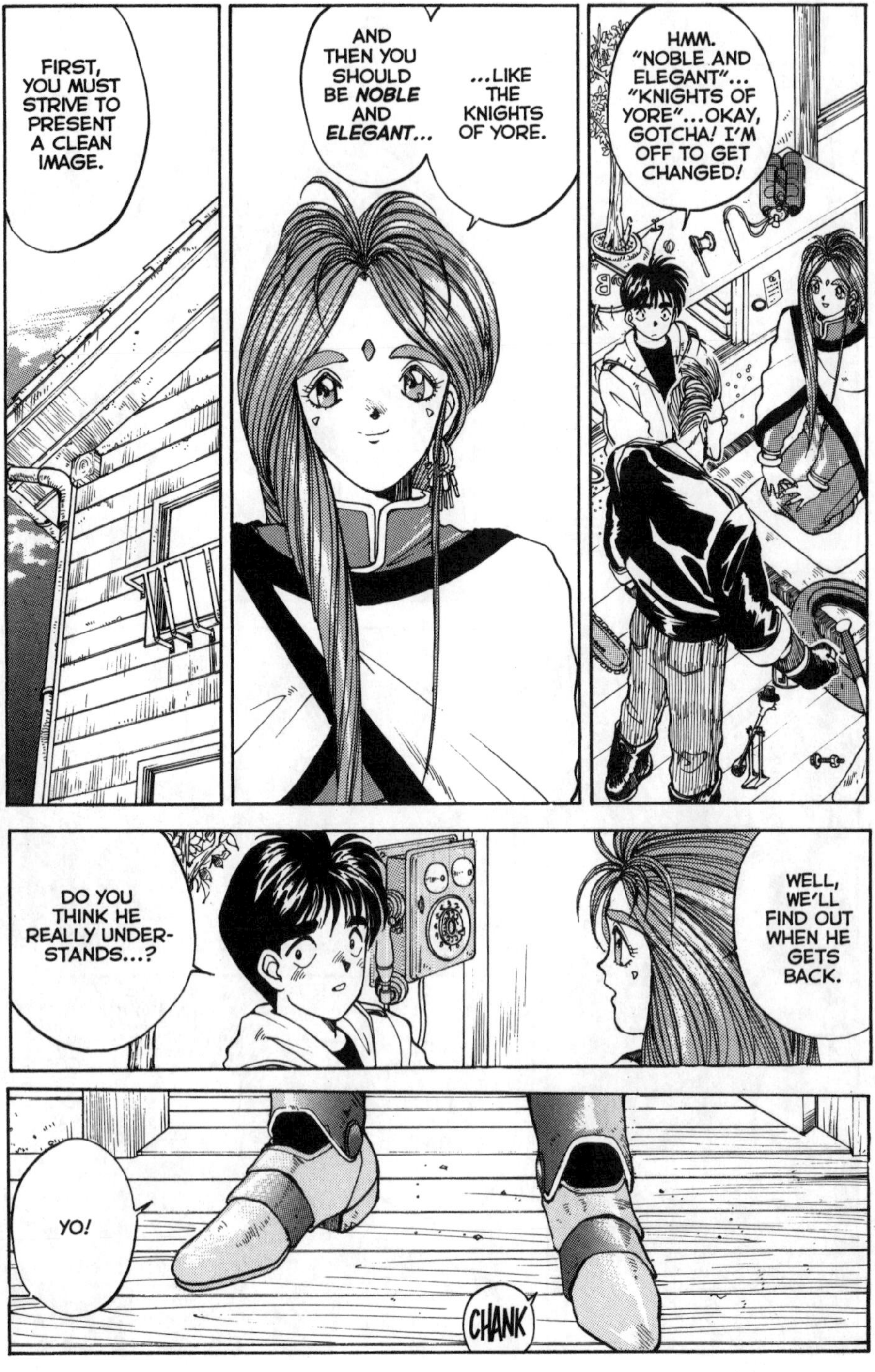
FIRST, YOU MUST STRIVE TO PRESENT A CLEAN IMAGE.
AND THEN YOU SHOULD BE *NOBLE* AND *ELEGANT...*
...LIKE THE KNIGHTS OF YORE.
HMM. "NOBLE AND ELEGANT"... "KNIGHTS OF YORE"...OKAY, GOTCHA! I'M OFF TO GET CHANGED!
DO YOU THINK HE REALLY UNDER-STANDS...?
WELL, WE'LL FIND OUT WHEN HE GETS BACK.
YO!
CHANK

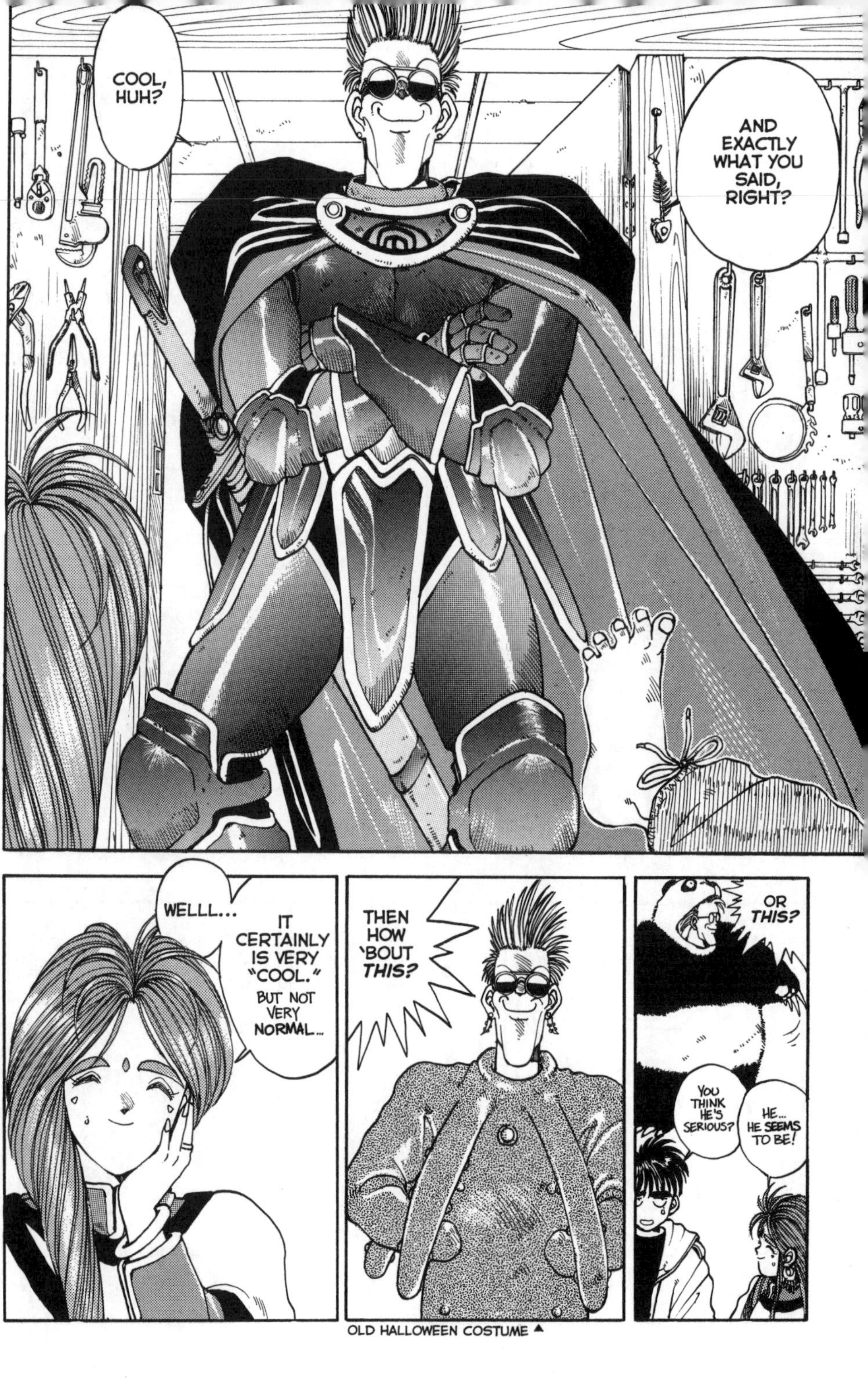
COOL, HUH?
AND EXACTLY WHAT YOU SAID, RIGHT?
WELLL...
IT CERTAINLY IS VERY "COOL."
BUT NOT VERY NORMAL...
THEN HOW 'BOUT *THIS?*
OR *THIS?*
YOU THINK HE'S SERIOUS?
HE... HE SEEMS TO BE!

OLD HALLOWEEN COSTUME ▲

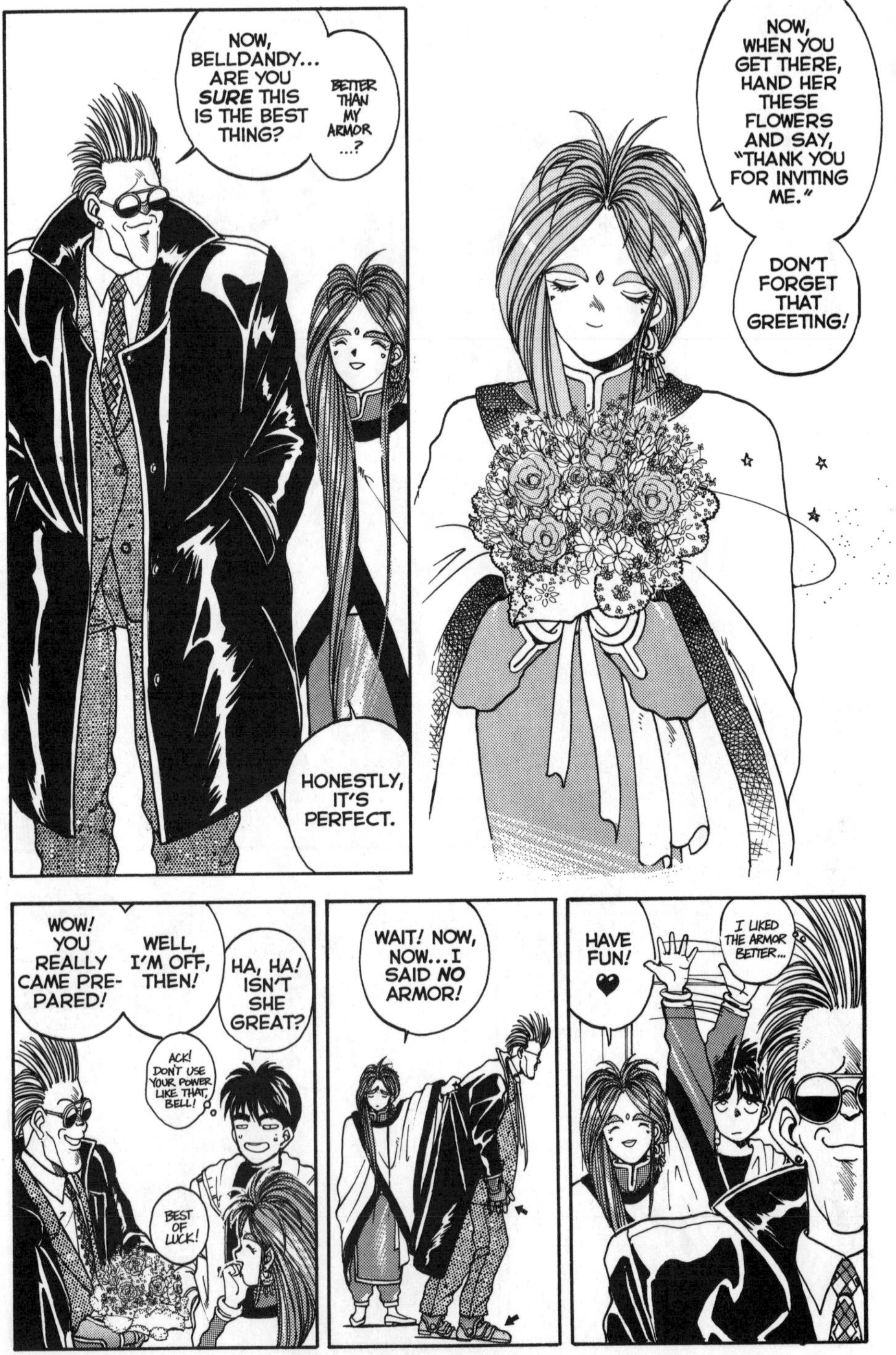
NOW, BELLDANDY... ARE YOU SURE THIS IS THE BEST THING?
BETTER THAN MY ARMOR ...?
HONESTLY, IT'S PERFECT.
NOW, WHEN YOU GET THERE, HAND HER THESE FLOWERS AND SAY, "THANK YOU FOR INVITING ME."
DON'T FORGET THAT GREETING!
WOW! YOU REALLY CAME PRE-PARED!
WELL, I'M OFF, THEN!
HA, HA! ISN'T SHE GREAT?
ACK! DON'T USE YOUR POWER LIKE THAT, BELL!
BEST OF LUCK!
WAIT! NOW, NOW... I SAID NO ARMOR!
HAVE FUN! ♥
I LIKED THE ARMOR BETTER...

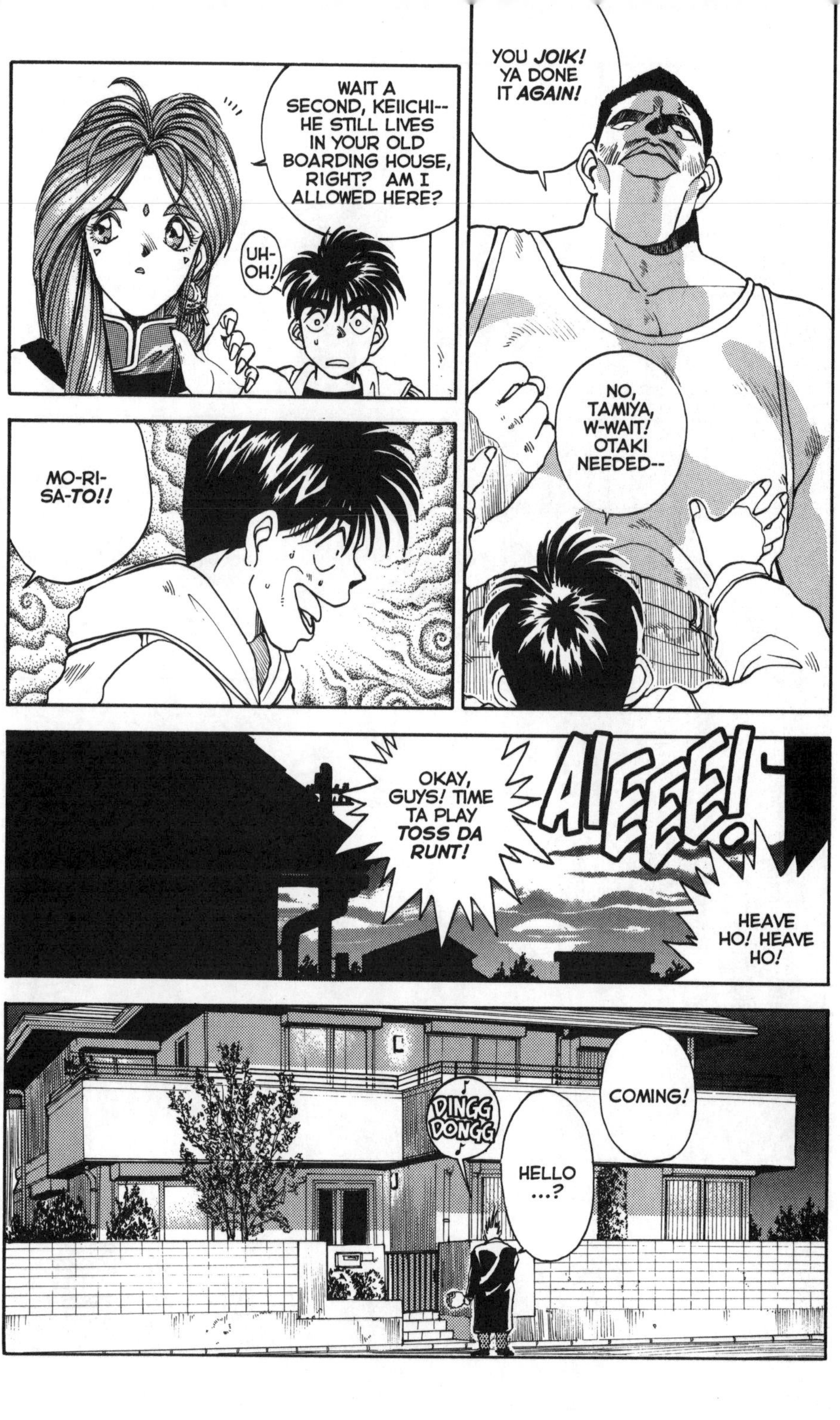
WAIT A SECOND, KEIICHI-- HE STILL LIVES IN YOUR OLD BOARDING HOUSE, RIGHT? AM I ALLOWED HERE?
UH-OH!
MO-RI-SA-TO!!
YOU JOIK! YA DONE IT AGAIN!
NO, TAMIYA, W-WAIT! OTAKI NEEDED--
OKAY, GUYS! TIME TA PLAY TOSS DA RUNT!
AIEEE!
HEAVE HO! HEAVE HO!
DINGG DONGG
COMING!
HELLO ...?

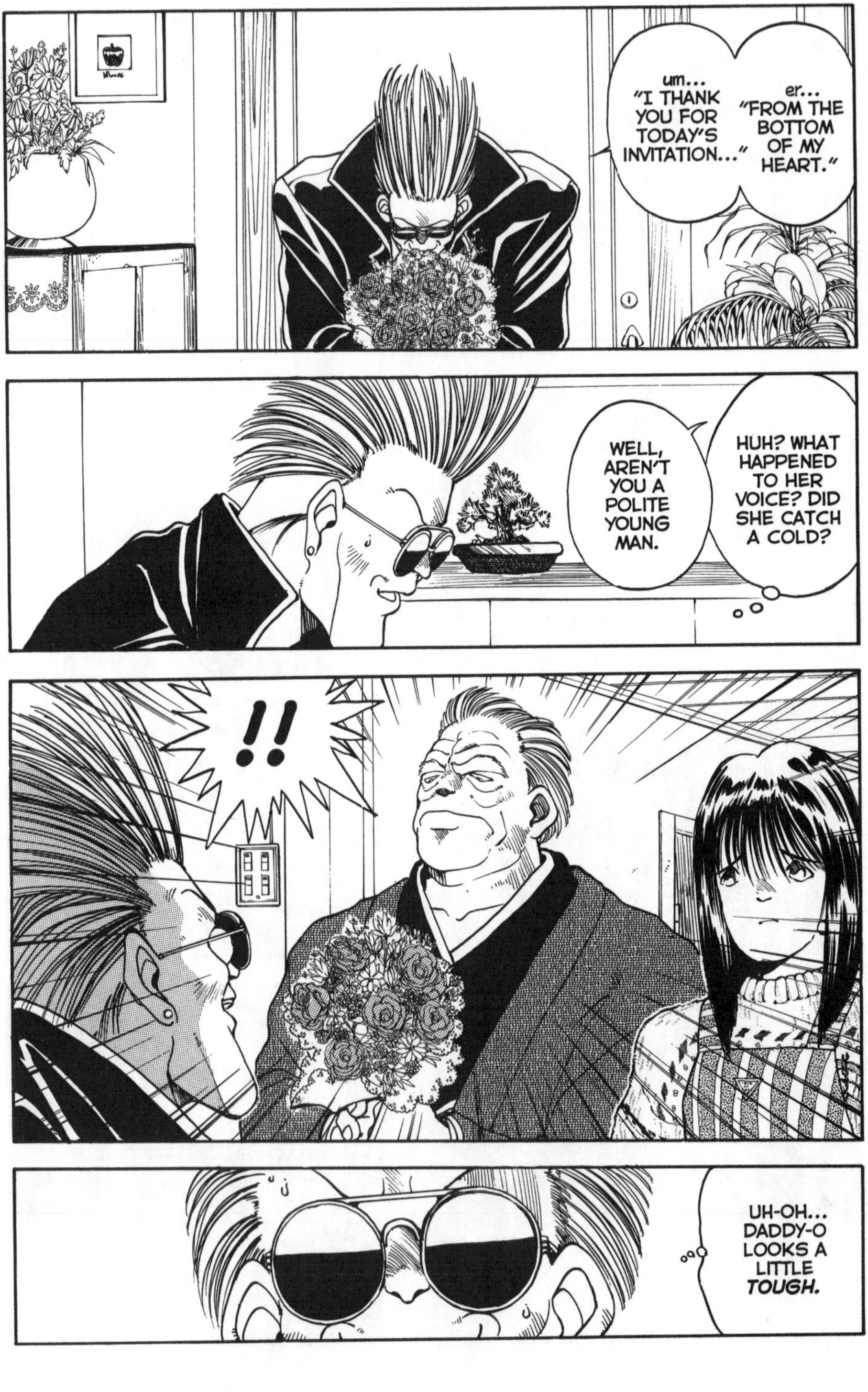
um... "I THANK YOU FOR TODAY'S INVITATION..."
er... "FROM THE BOTTOM OF MY HEART."
WELL, AREN'T YOU A POLITE YOUNG MAN.
HUH? WHAT HAPPENED TO HER VOICE? DID SHE CATCH A COLD?
!!
UH-OH... DADDY-O LOOKS A LITTLE *TOUGH.*

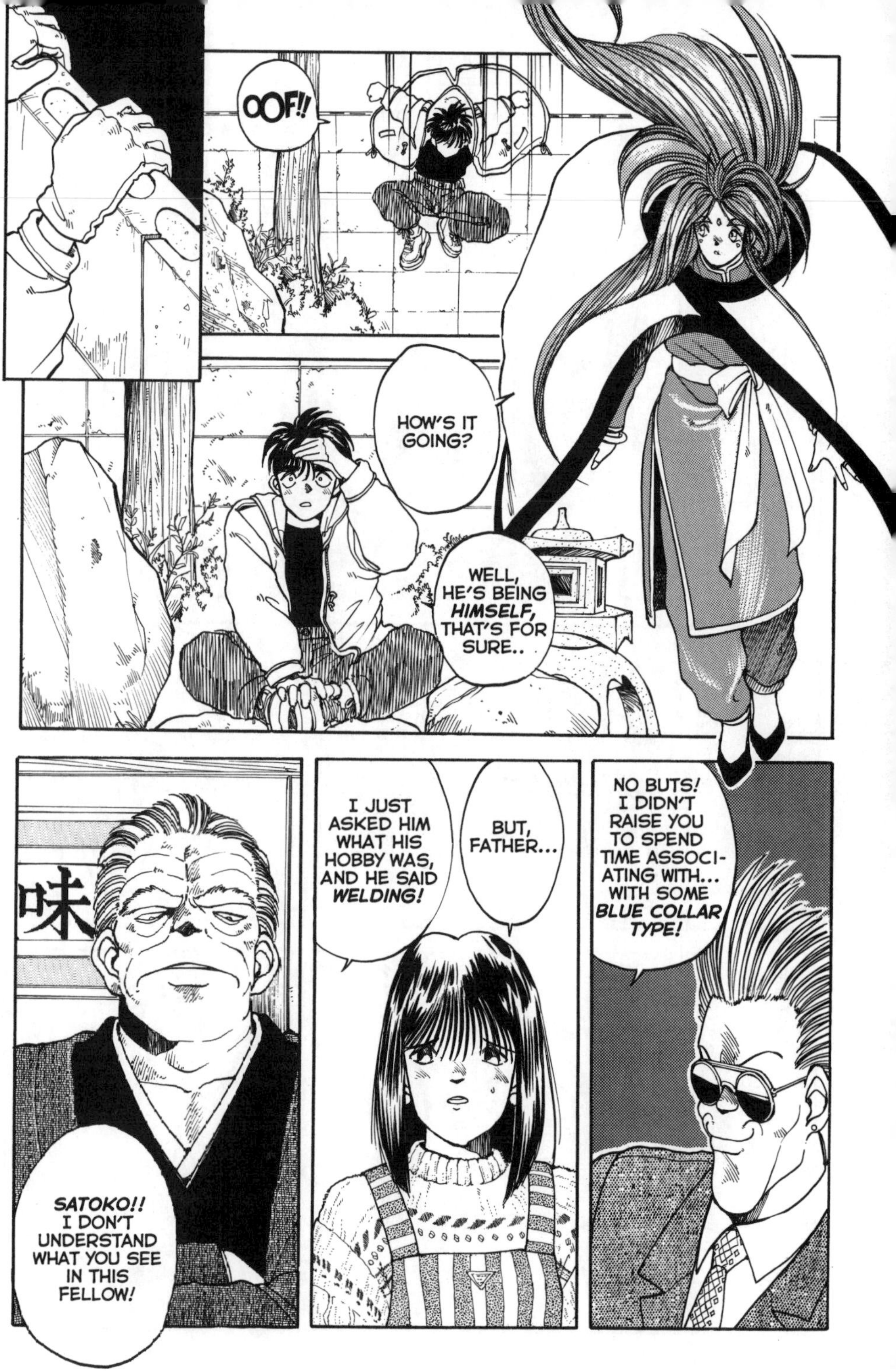
OOF!!
HOW'S IT GOING?
WELL, HE'S BEING *HIMSELF*, THAT'S FOR SURE..
SATOKO!! I DON'T UNDERSTAND WHAT YOU SEE IN THIS FELLOW!
味
I JUST ASKED HIM WHAT HIS HOBBY WAS, AND HE SAID *WELDING!*
BUT, FATHER...
NO BUTS! I DIDN'T RAISE YOU TO SPEND TIME ASSOCI-ATING WITH... WITH SOME *BLUE COLLAR TYPE!*

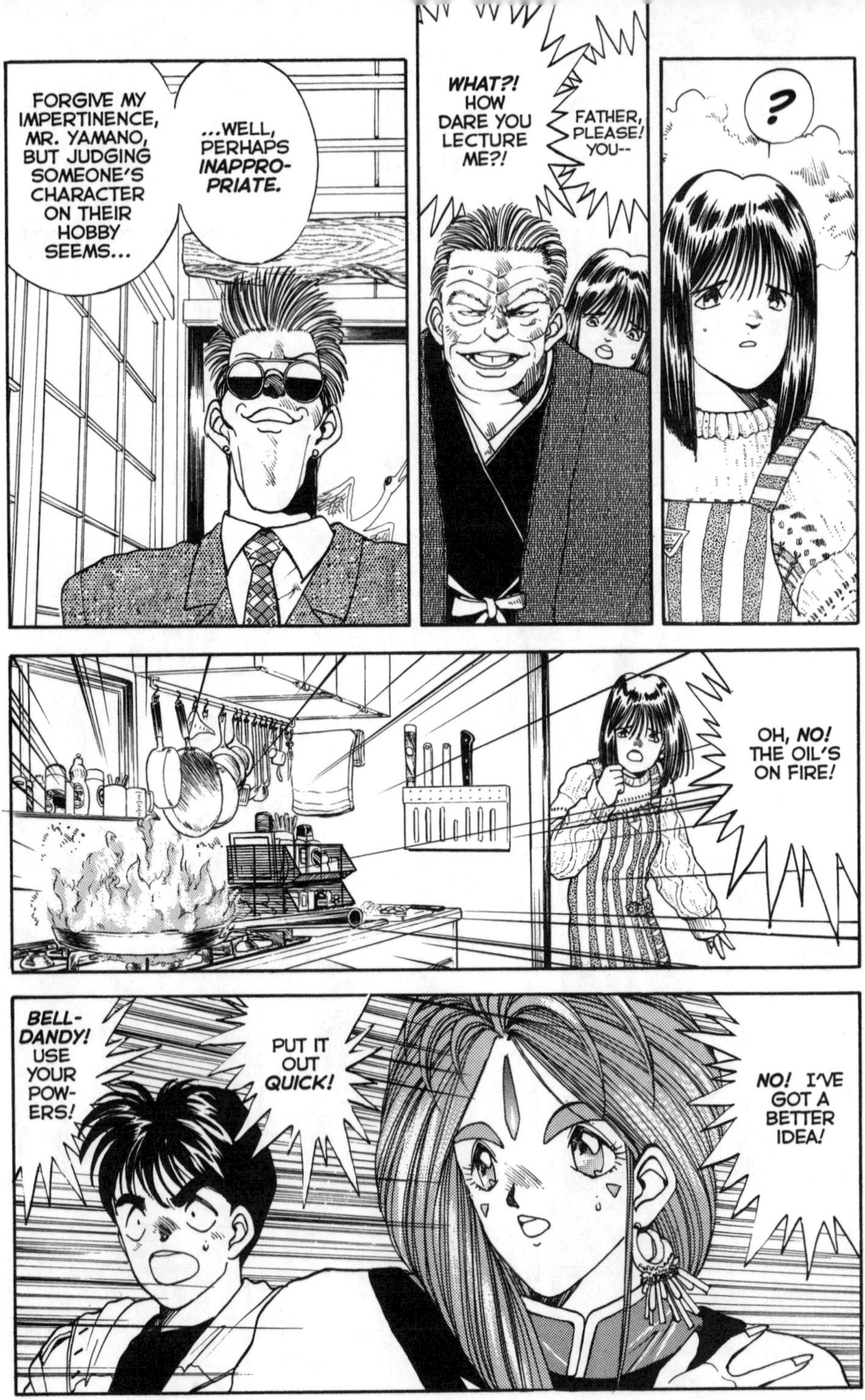

FORGIVE MY IMPERTINENCE, MR. YAMANO, BUT JUDGING SOMEONE'S CHARACTER ON THEIR HOBBY SEEMS...
...WELL, PERHAPS INAPPROPRIATE.
WHAT?! HOW DARE YOU LECTURE ME?!
FATHER, PLEASE! YOU--
?
OH, NO! THE OIL'S ON FIRE!
BELL-DANDY! USE YOUR POW-ERS!
PUT IT OUT QUICK!
NO! I'VE GOT A BETTER IDEA!

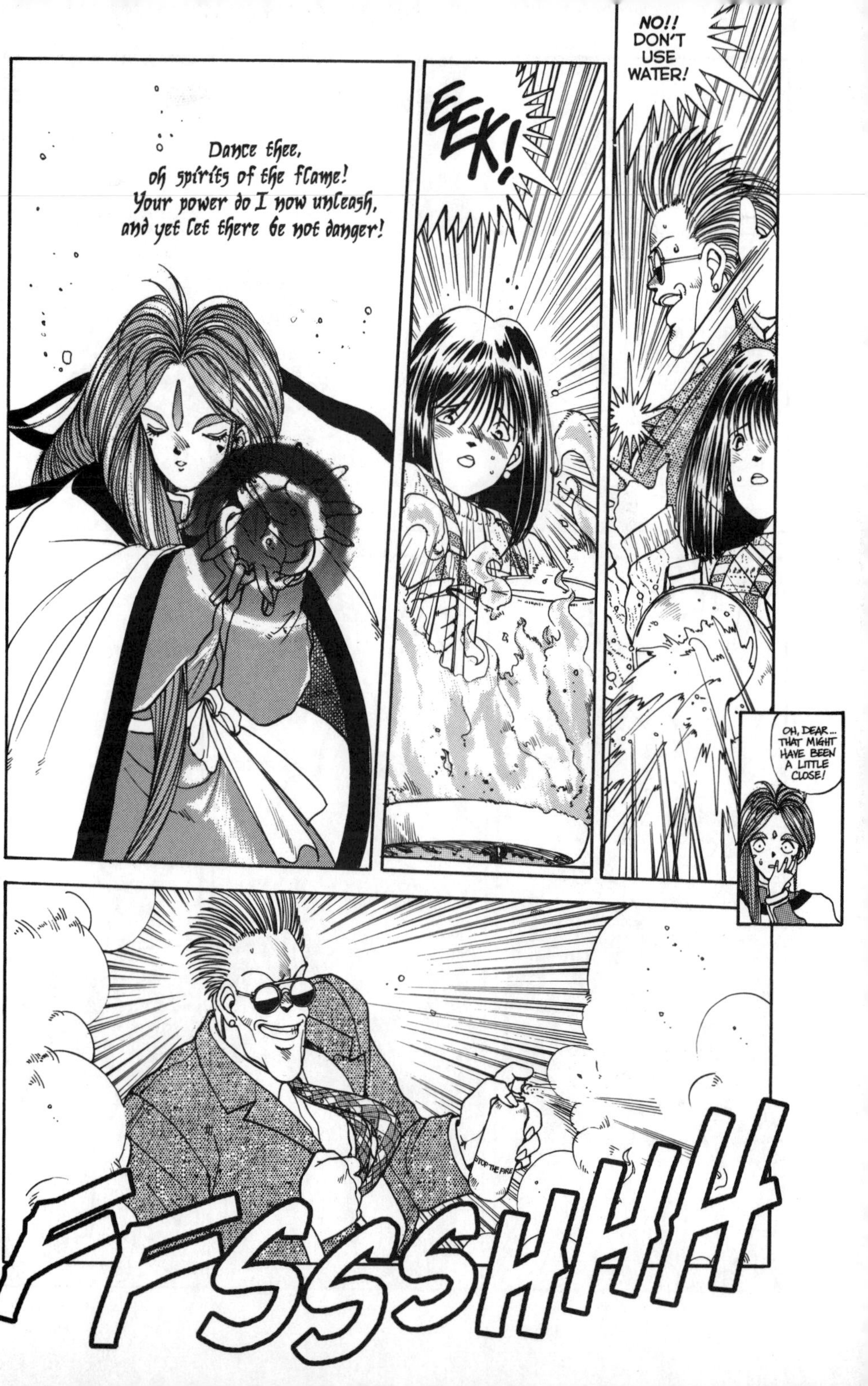
Dance thee, oh spirits of the flame! Your power do I now unleash, and yet let there be not danger!
EEEK!
NO!! DON'T USE WATER!
OH, DEAR... THAT MIGHT HAVE BEEN A LITTLE CLOSE!
STOP THE FIRE
FFSSSHHH

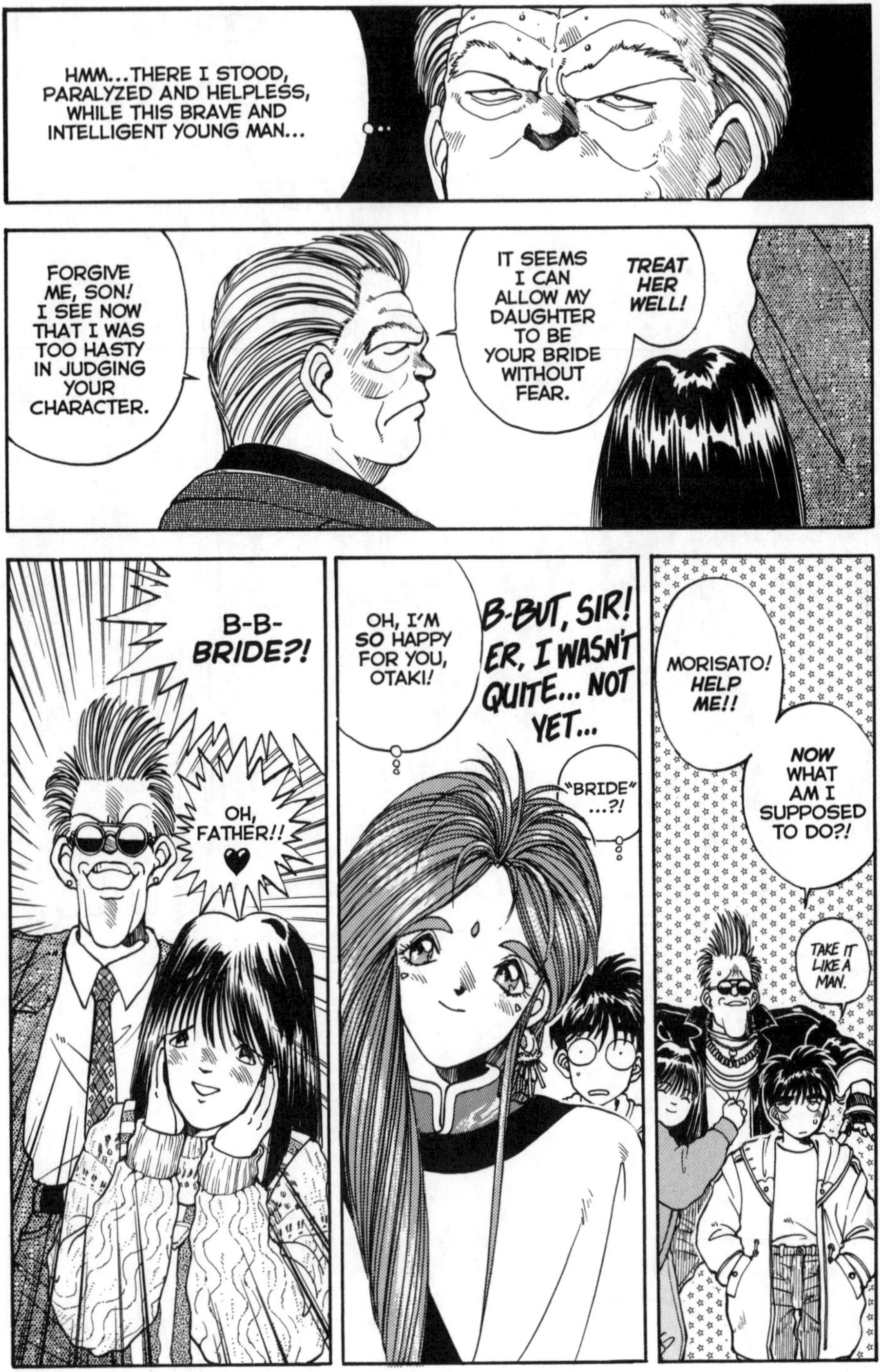
HMM...THERE I STOOD, PARALYZED AND HELPLESS, WHILE THIS BRAVE AND INTELLIGENT YOUNG MAN...
FORGIVE ME, SON! I SEE NOW THAT I WAS TOO HASTY IN JUDGING YOUR CHARACTER.
IT SEEMS I CAN ALLOW MY DAUGHTER TO BE YOUR BRIDE WITHOUT FEAR.
TREAT HER WELL!
B-B-BRIDE?!
OH, FATHER!!
OH, I'M SO HAPPY FOR YOU, OTAKI!
B-BUT, SIR! ER, I WASN'T QUITE... NOT YET...
"BRIDE" ...?!
MORISATO! HELP ME!!
NOW WHAT AM I SUPPOSED TO DO?!
TAKE IT LIKE A MAN.

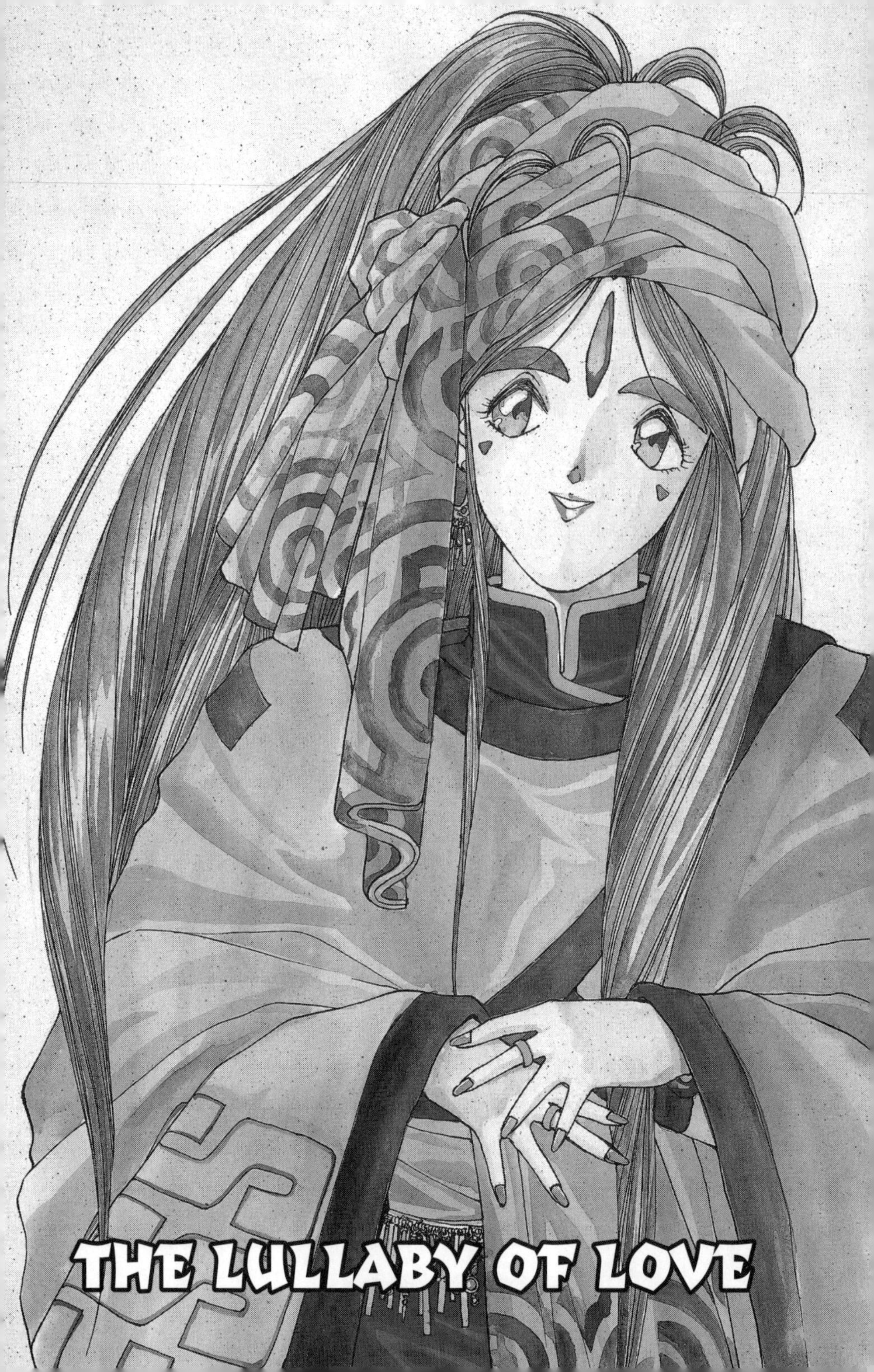
THE LULLABY OF LOVE

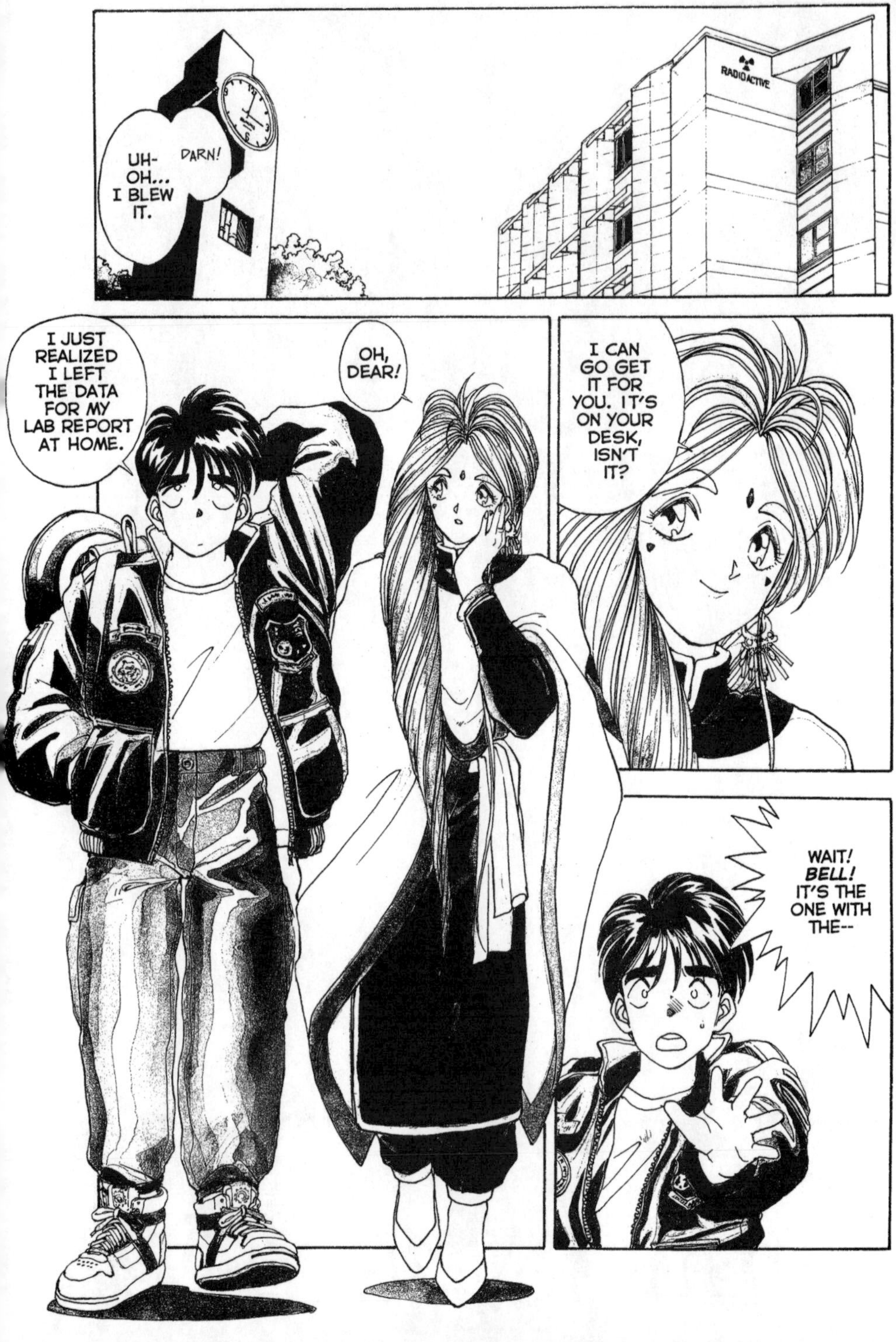
UH-OH... I BLEW IT.
DARN!
RADIO ACTIVE
I JUST REALIZED I LEFT THE DATA FOR MY LAB REPORT AT HOME.
OH, DEAR!
I CAN GO GET IT FOR YOU. IT'S ON YOUR DESK, ISN'T IT?
WAIT! *BELL!* IT'S THE ONE WITH THE--

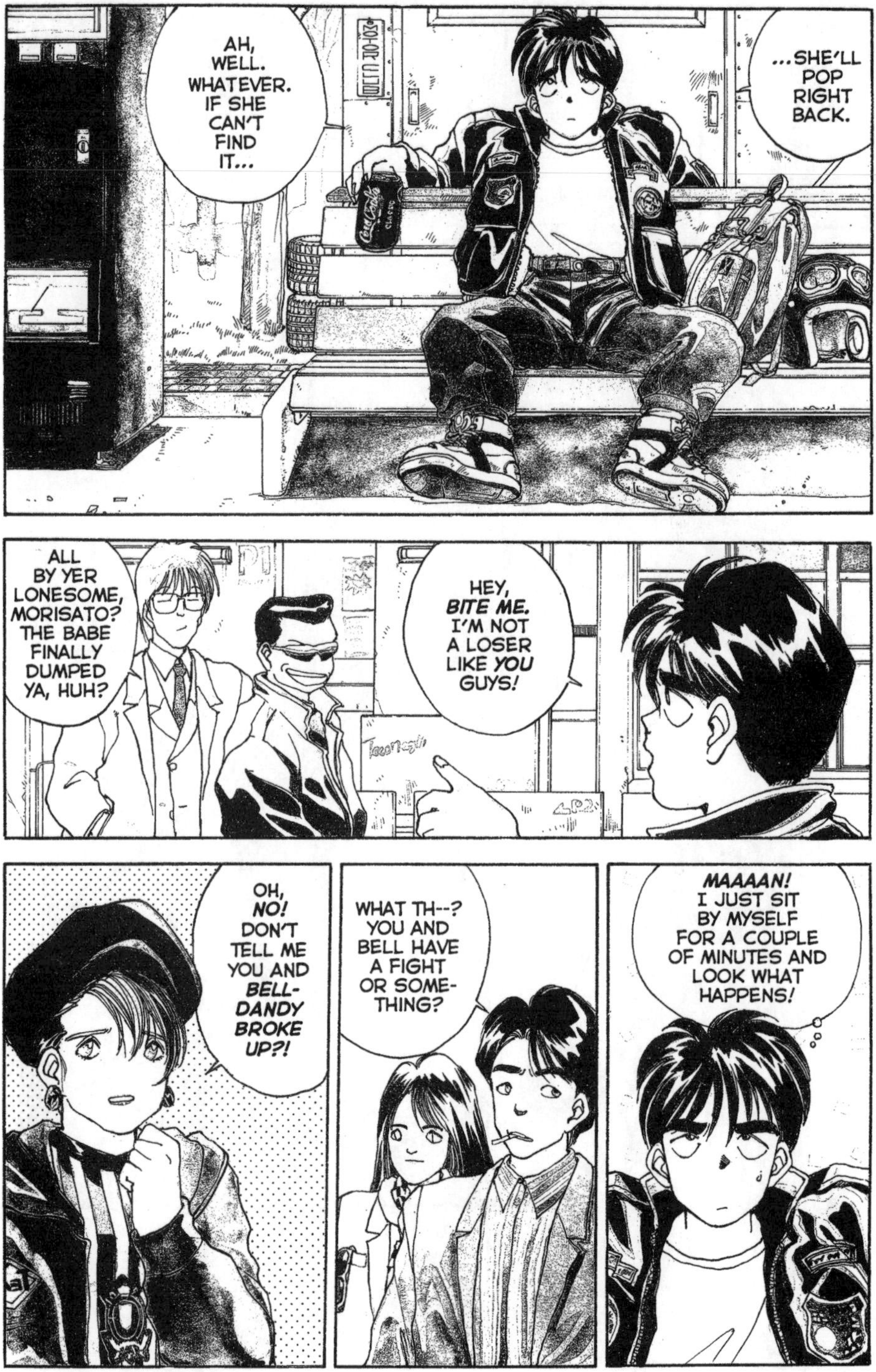
AH, WELL. WHATEVER. IF SHE CAN'T FIND IT...
...SHE'LL POP RIGHT BACK.
ALL BY YER LONESOME, MORISATO? THE BABE FINALLY DUMPED YA, HUH?
HEY, *BITE ME.* I'M NOT A LOSER LIKE *YOU* GUYS!
OH, *NO!* DON'T TELL ME YOU AND *BELL-DANDY BROKE UP?!*
WHAT TH--? YOU AND BELL HAVE A FIGHT OR SOME-THING?
MAAAAN! I JUST SIT BY MYSELF FOR A COUPLE OF MINUTES AND LOOK WHAT HAPPENS!

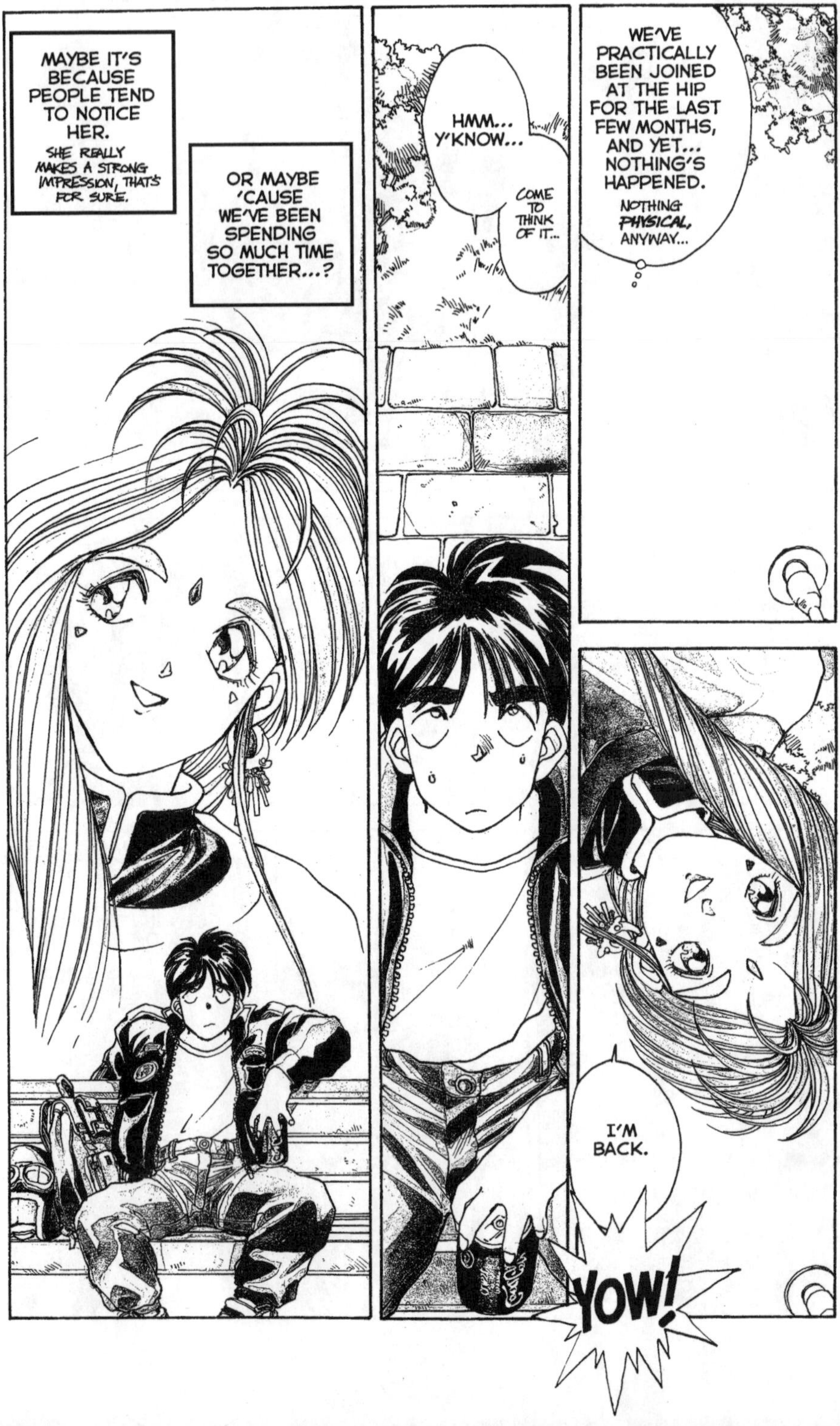
MAYBE IT'S BECAUSE PEOPLE TEND TO NOTICE HER.
SHE REALLY MAKES A STRONG IMPRESSION, THAT'S FOR SURE.
OR MAYBE 'CAUSE WE'VE BEEN SPENDING SO MUCH TIME TOGETHER...?
HMM... Y'KNOW...
COME TO THINK OF IT...
WE'VE PRACTICALLY BEEN JOINED AT THE HIP FOR THE LAST FEW MONTHS, AND YET... NOTHING'S HAPPENED.
NOTHING PHYSICAL, ANYWAY...
I'M BACK.
YOW!

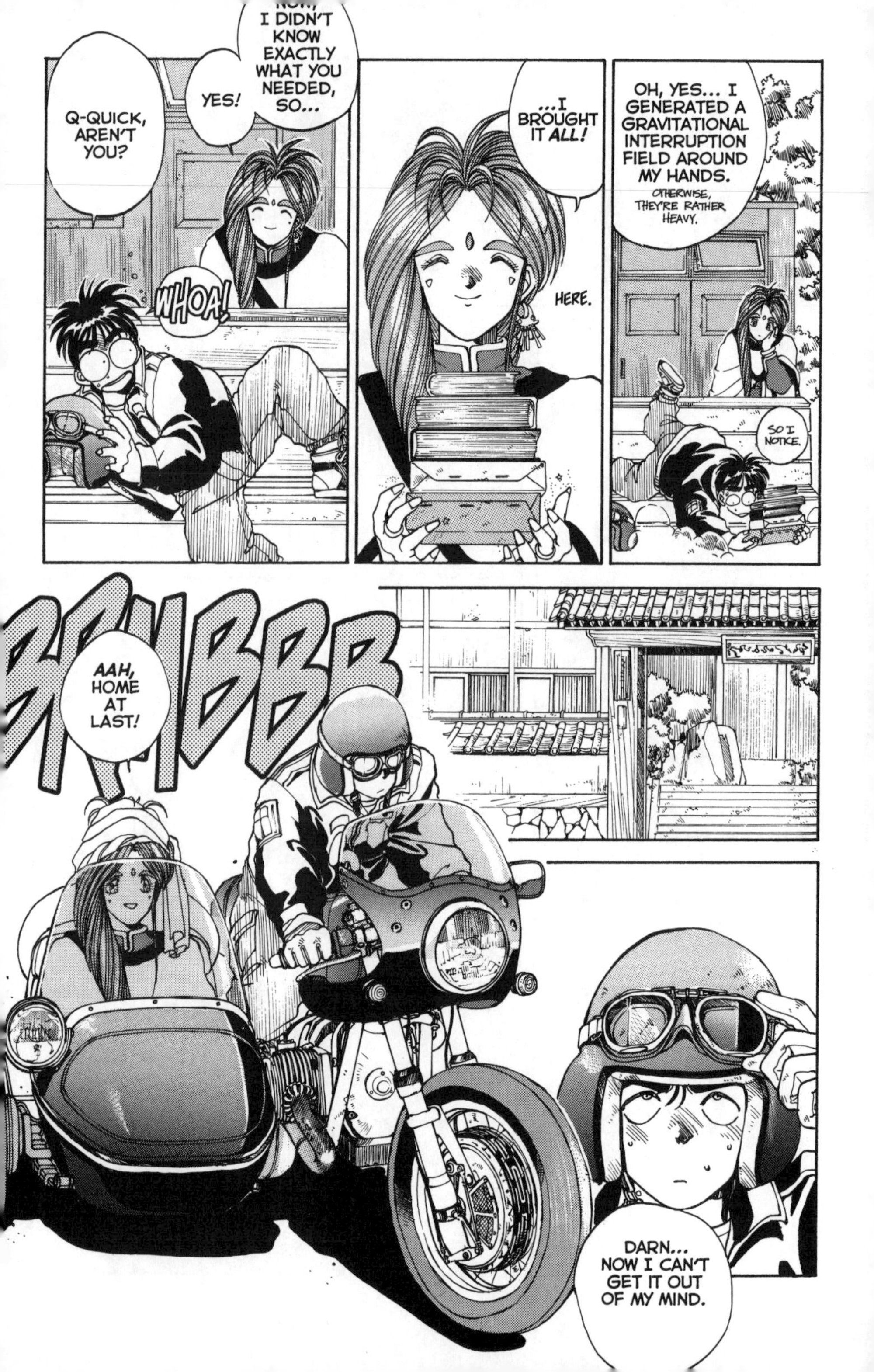
Q-QUICK, AREN'T YOU?
YES!
I DIDN'T KNOW EXACTLY WHAT YOU NEEDED, SO...
WHOA!
...I BROUGHT IT ALL!
HERE.
OH, YES... I GENERATED A GRAVITATIONAL INTERRUPTION FIELD AROUND MY HANDS.
OTHERWISE, THEY'RE RATHER HEAVY.
SO I NOTICE.
AAH, HOME AT LAST!
DARN... NOW I CAN'T GET IT OUT OF MY MIND.

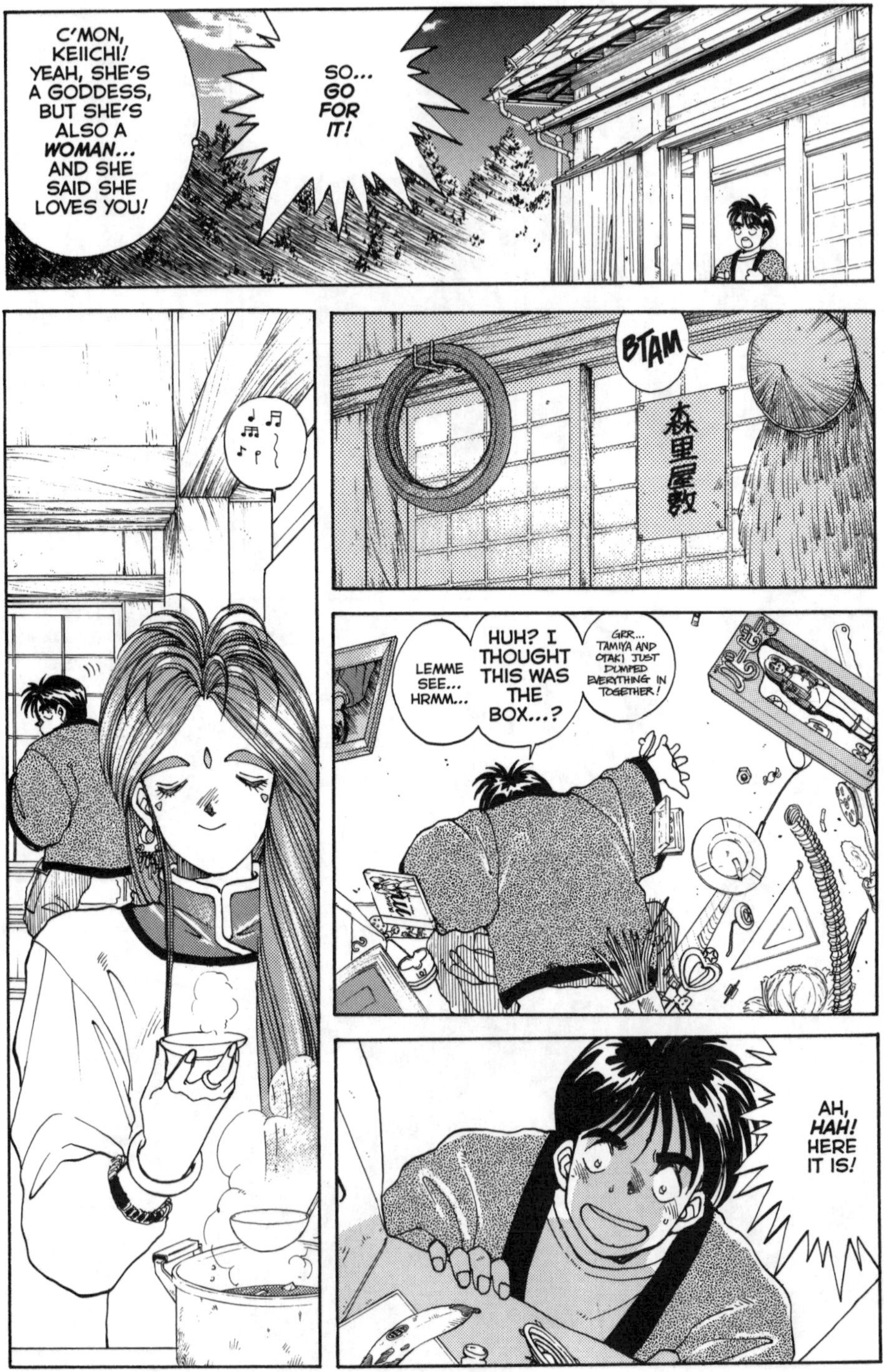
C'MON, KEIICHI! YEAH, SHE'S A GODDESS, BUT SHE'S ALSO A ***WOMAN...*** AND SHE SAID SHE LOVES YOU!
SO... GO FOR IT!
BTAM
LEMME SEE... HRMM...
HUH? I THOUGHT THIS WAS THE BOX...?
GRR... TAMIYA AND OTAKI JUST DUMPED EVERYTHING IN TOGETHER!
AH, ***HAH!*** HERE IT IS!

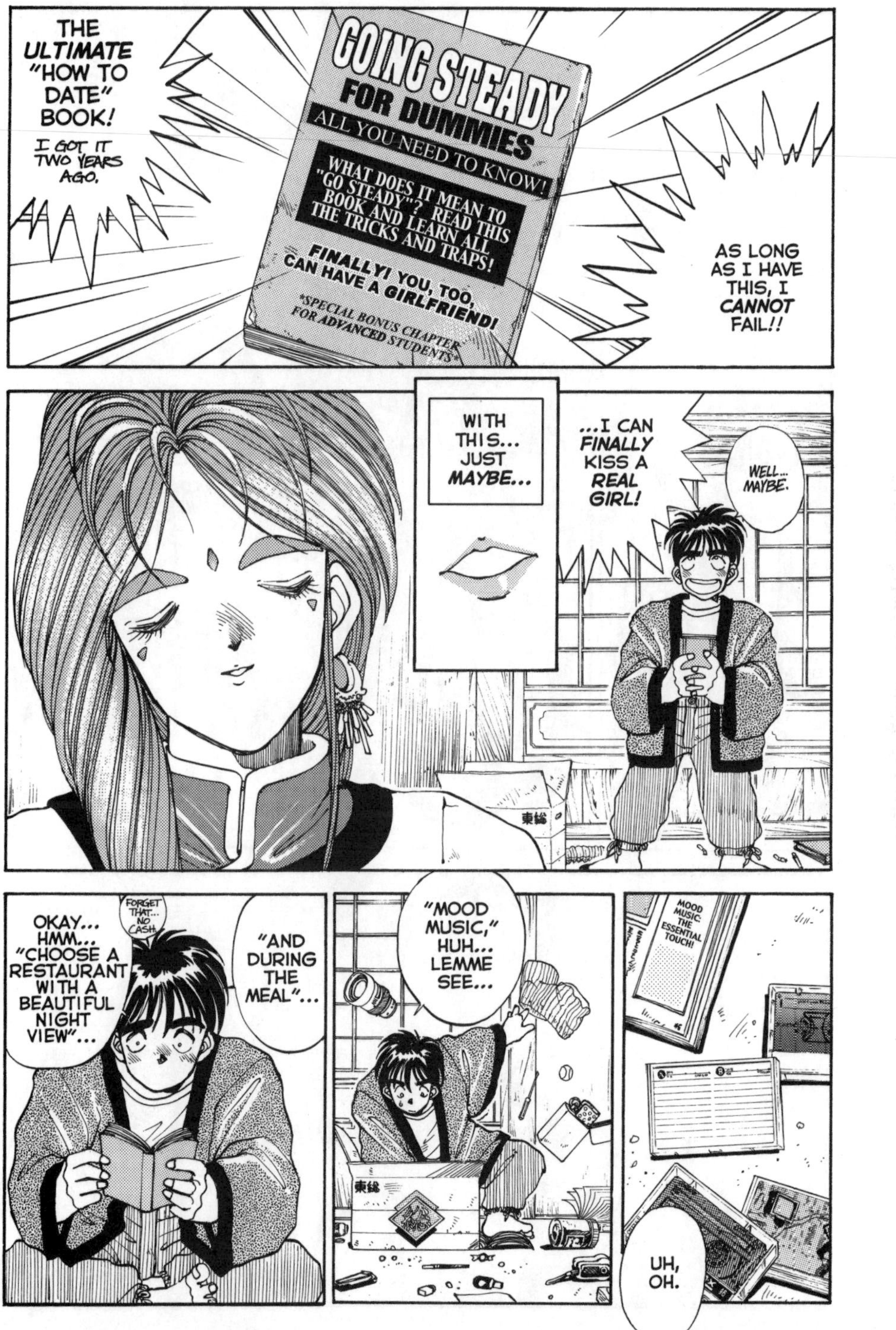

THE ULTIMATE "HOW TO DATE" BOOK!
I GOT IT TWO YEARS AGO.
GOING STEADY FOR DUMMIES
ALL YOU NEED TO KNOW!
WHAT DOES IT MEAN TO "GO STEADY"? READ THIS BOOK AND LEARN ALL THE TRICKS AND TRAPS!
FINALLY! YOU, TOO, CAN HAVE A GIRLFRIEND!
SPECIAL BONUS CHAPTER FOR ADVANCED STUDENTS
AS LONG AS I HAVE THIS, I CANNOT FAIL!!
WITH THIS... JUST MAYBE...
...I CAN FINALLY KISS A REAL GIRL!
WELL... MAYBE.
OKAY... HMM... "CHOOSE A RESTAURANT WITH A BEAUTIFUL NIGHT VIEW"...
FORGET THAT... NO CASH.
"AND DURING THE MEAL"...
"MOOD MUSIC," HUH... LEMME SEE...
MOOD MUSIC: THE ESSENTIAL TOUCH!
UH, OH.

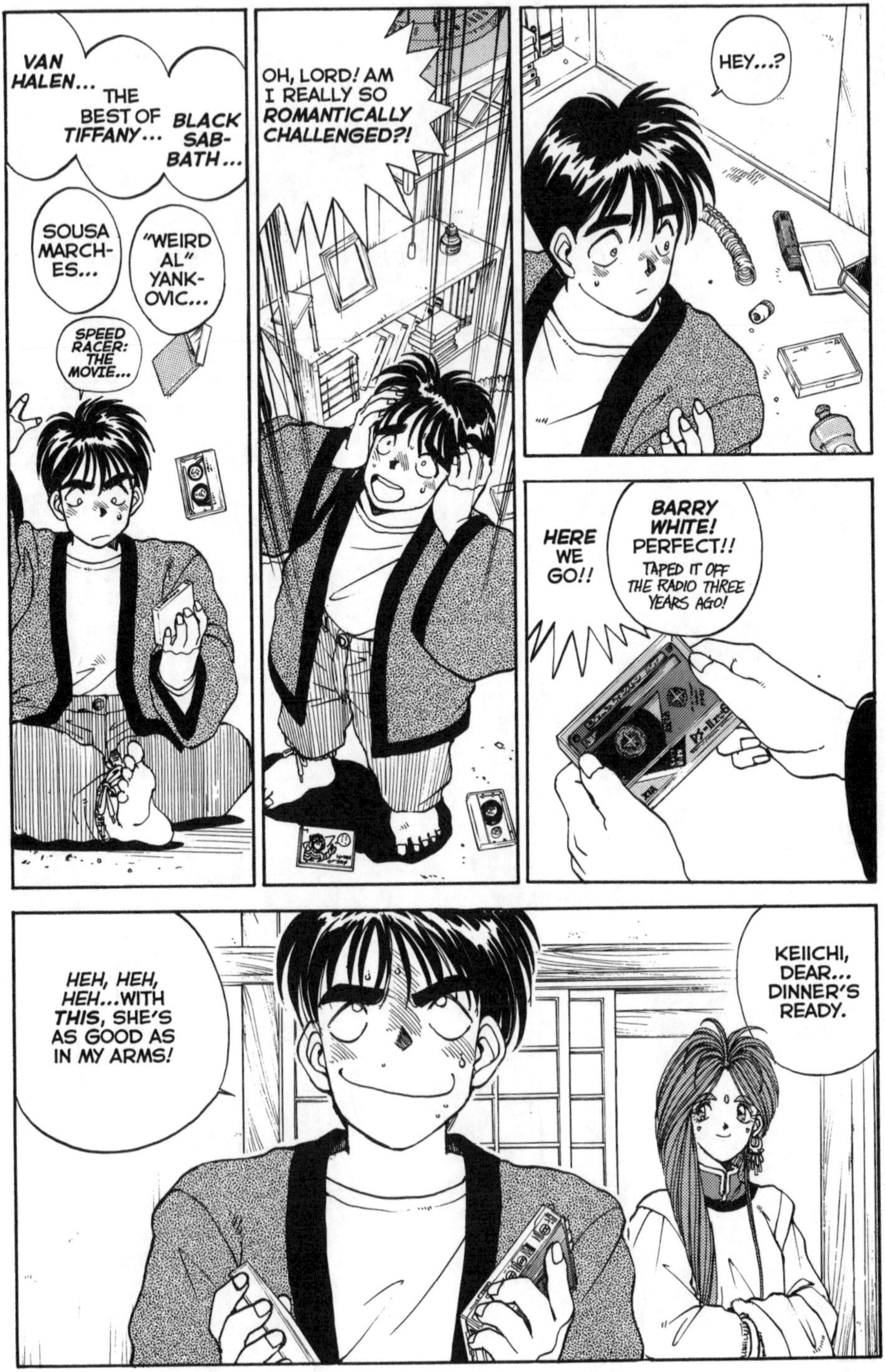
VAN HALEN...
THE BEST OF TIFFANY...
BLACK SAB-BATH...
SOUSA MARCH-ES...
"WEIRD AL" YANK-OVIC...
SPEED RACER: THE MOVIE...
OH, LORD! AM I REALLY SO ROMANTICALLY CHALLENGED?!
HEY...?
HERE WE GO!!
BARRY WHITE! PERFECT!!
TAPED IT OFF THE RADIO THREE YEARS AGO!
HEH, HEH, HEH...WITH THIS, SHE'S AS GOOD AS IN MY ARMS!
KEIICHI, DEAR... DINNER'S READY.

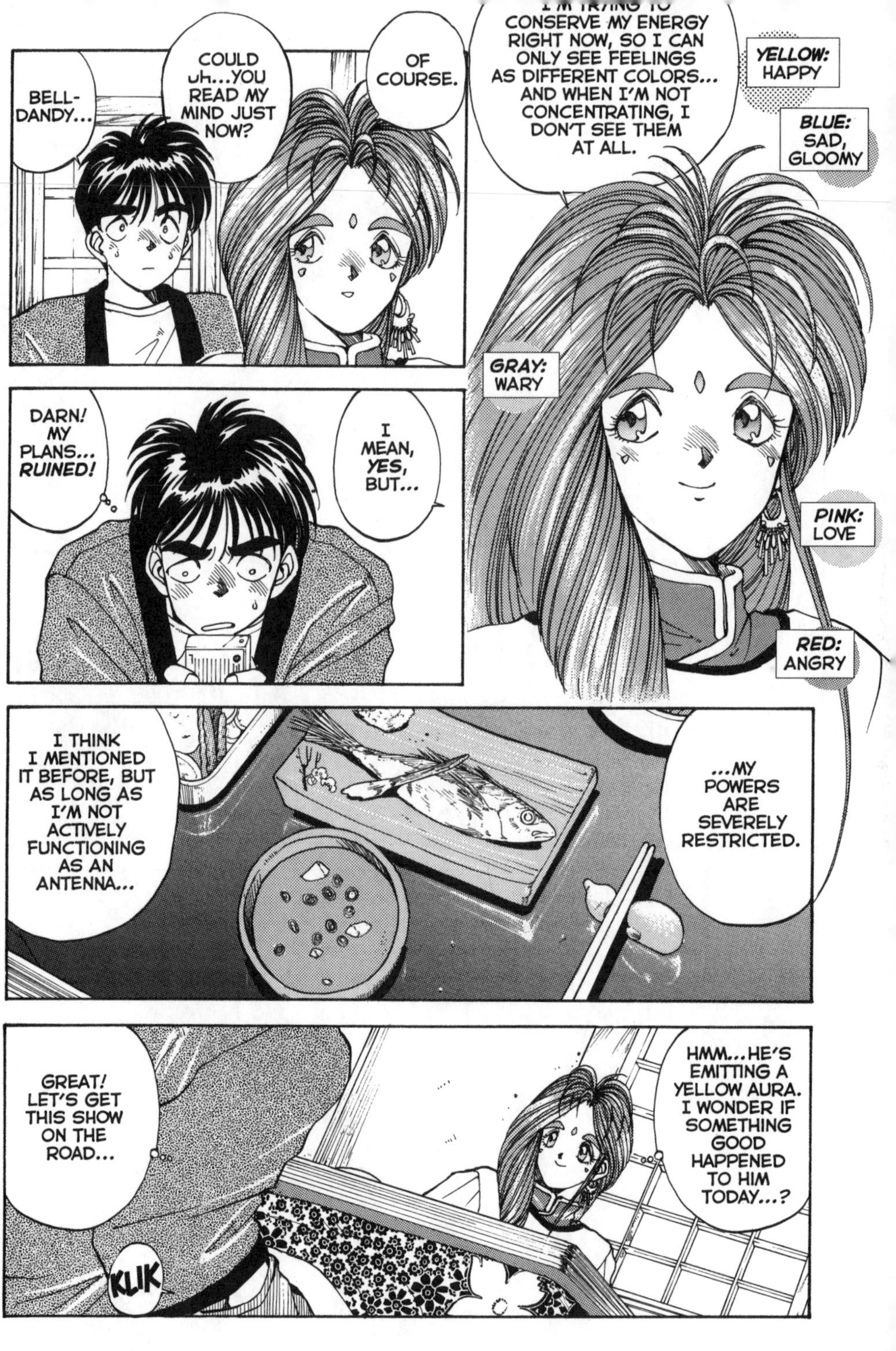
BELL-DANDY...
COULD uh...YOU READ MY MIND JUST NOW?
OF COURSE.
DARN! MY PLANS... *RUINED!*
I MEAN, *YES,* BUT...
I'M TRYING TO CONSERVE MY ENERGY RIGHT NOW, SO I CAN ONLY SEE FEELINGS AS DIFFERENT COLORS... AND WHEN I'M NOT CONCENTRATING, I DON'T SEE THEM AT ALL.
YELLOW: HAPPY
BLUE: SAD, GLOOMY
GRAY: WARY
PINK: LOVE
RED: ANGRY
I THINK I MENTIONED IT BEFORE, BUT AS LONG AS I'M NOT ACTIVELY FUNCTIONING AS AN ANTENNA...
...MY POWERS ARE SEVERELY RESTRICTED.
GREAT! LET'S GET THIS SHOW ON THE ROAD...
KLIK
HMM...HE'S EMITTING A YELLOW AURA. I WONDER IF SOMETHING GOOD HAPPENED TO HIM TODAY...?

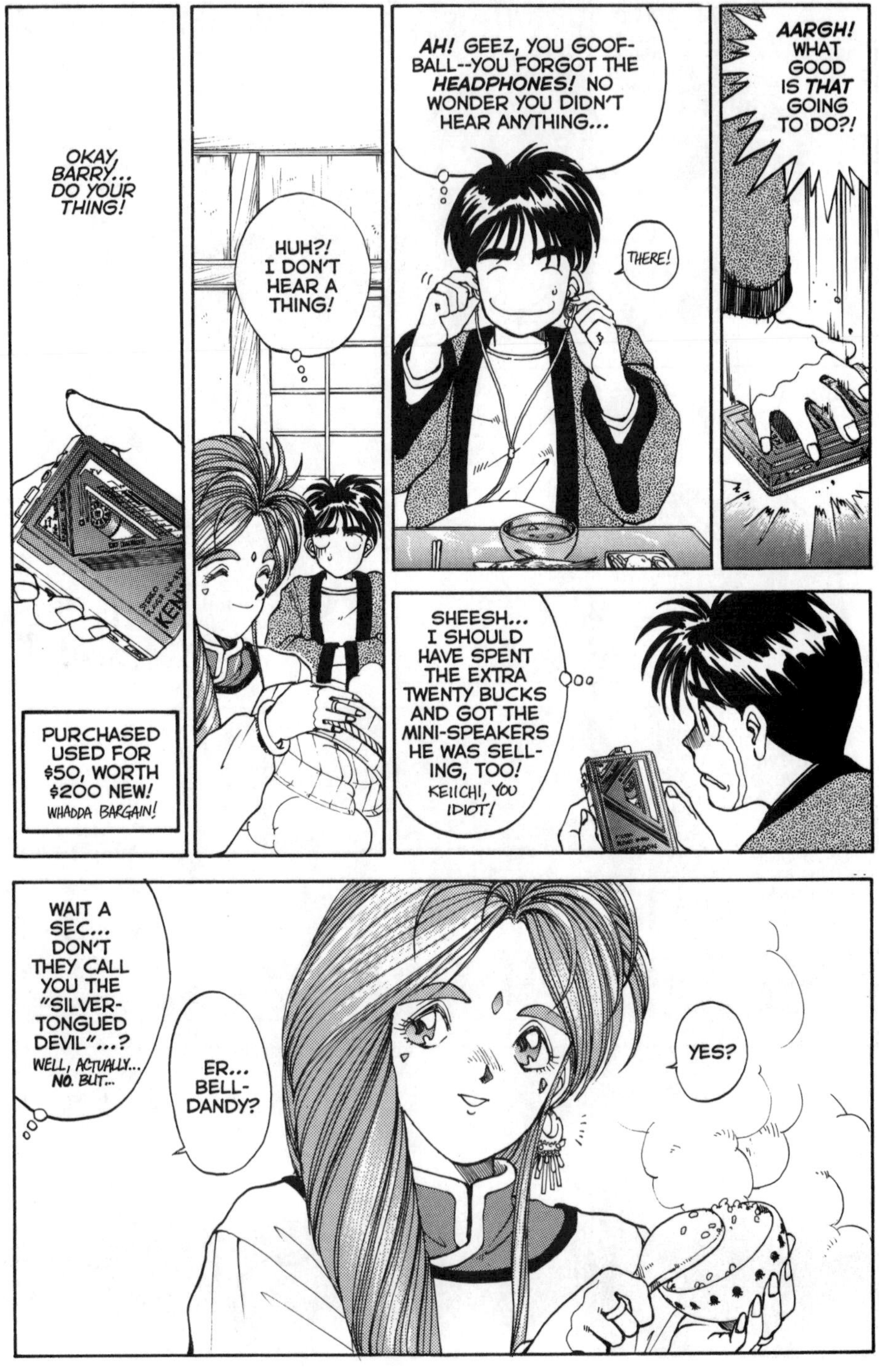
OKAY, BARRY... DO YOUR THING!
PURCHASED USED FOR $50, WORTH $200 NEW! WHADDA BARGAIN!
HUH?! I DON'T HEAR A THING!
AH! GEEZ, YOU GOOF-BALL--YOU FORGOT THE HEADPHONES! NO WONDER YOU DIDN'T HEAR ANYTHING...
THERE!
AARGH! WHAT GOOD IS THAT GOING TO DO?!
SHEESH... I SHOULD HAVE SPENT THE EXTRA TWENTY BUCKS AND GOT THE MINI-SPEAKERS HE WAS SELL-ING, TOO! KEIICHI, YOU IDIOT!
WAIT A SEC... DON'T THEY CALL YOU THE "SILVER-TONGUED DEVIL"...? WELL, ACTUALLY... NO. BUT...
ER... BELL-DANDY?
YES?

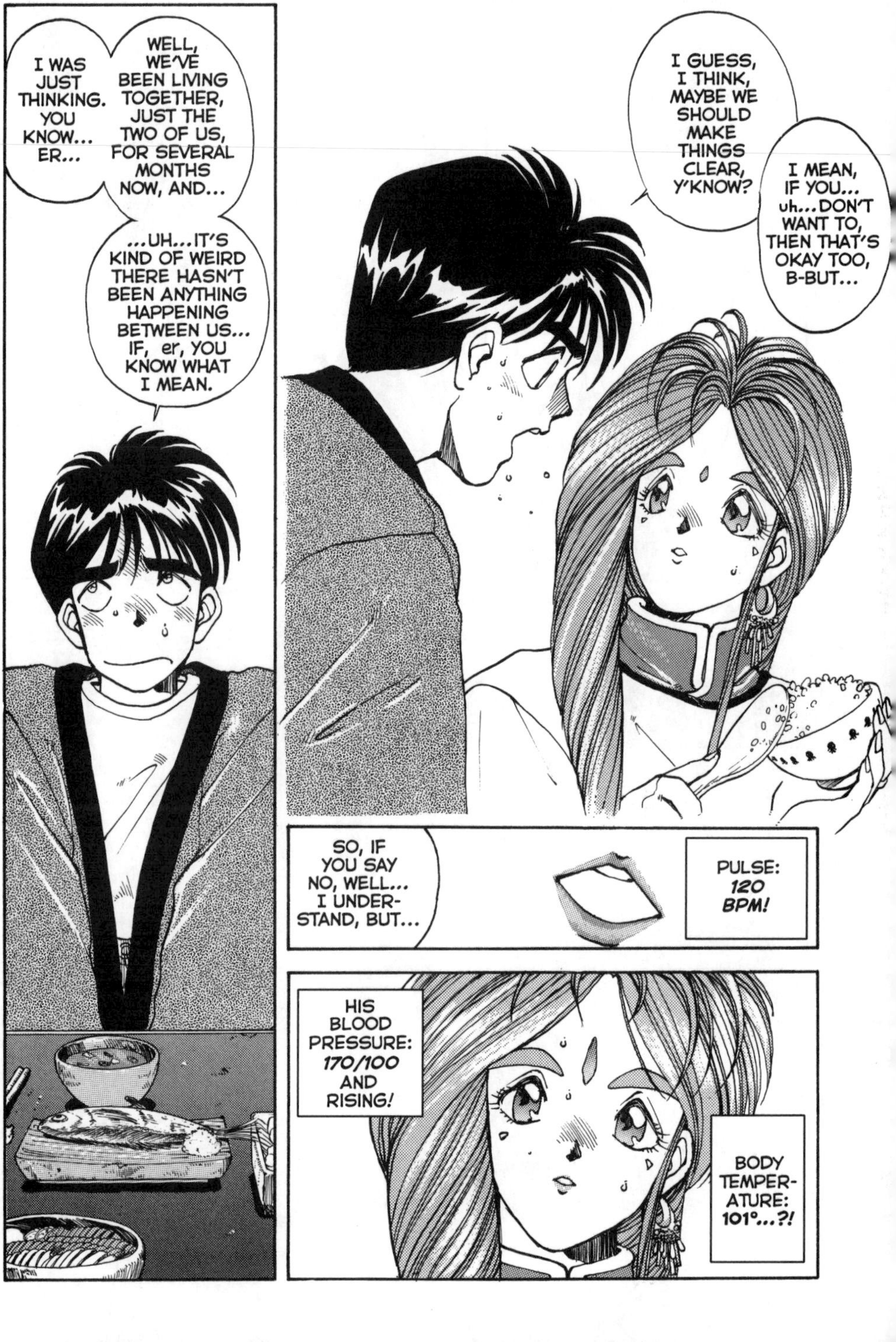
I WAS JUST THINKING. YOU KNOW... ER...
WELL, WE'VE BEEN LIVING TOGETHER, JUST THE TWO OF US, FOR SEVERAL MONTHS NOW, AND...
...UH...IT'S KIND OF WEIRD THERE HASN'T BEEN ANYTHING HAPPENING BETWEEN US... IF, er, YOU KNOW WHAT I MEAN.
I GUESS, I THINK, MAYBE WE SHOULD MAKE THINGS CLEAR, Y'KNOW?
I MEAN, IF YOU... uh...DON'T WANT TO, THEN THAT'S OKAY TOO, B-BUT...
SO, IF YOU SAY NO, WELL... I UNDER-STAND, BUT...
PULSE: *120 BPM!*
HIS BLOOD PRESSURE: *170/100* AND RISING!
BODY TEMPER-ATURE: 101°...?!

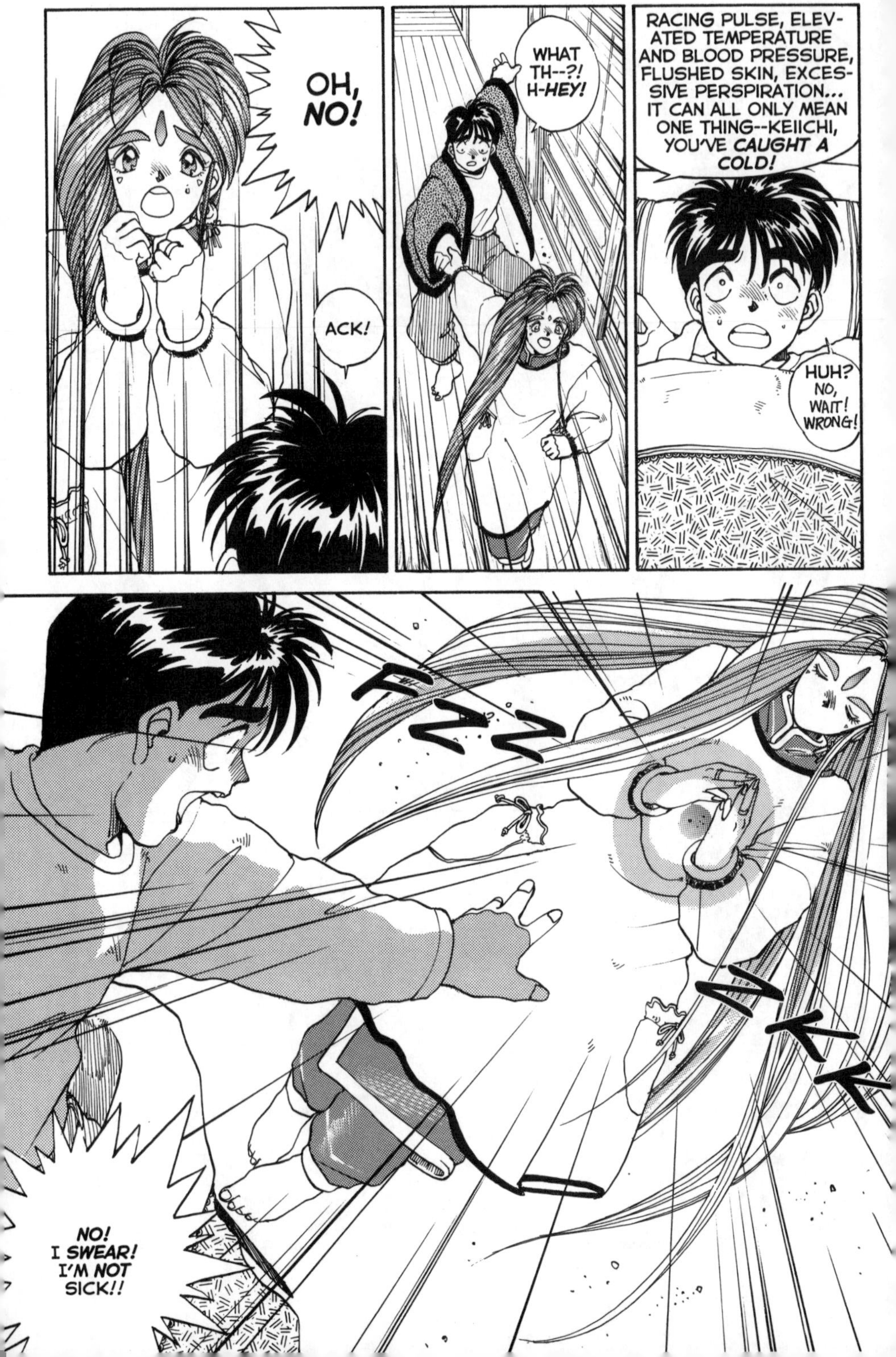
OH, NO!
ACK!
WHAT TH--?! H-HEY!
RACING PULSE, ELEVATED TEMPERATURE AND BLOOD PRESSURE, FLUSHED SKIN, EXCESSIVE PERSPIRATION... IT CAN ALL ONLY MEAN ONE THING--KEIICHI, YOU'VE CAUGHT A COLD!
HUH? NO, WAIT! WRONG!
FZZ
NO! I SWEAR! I'M NOT SICK!!
ZKKK

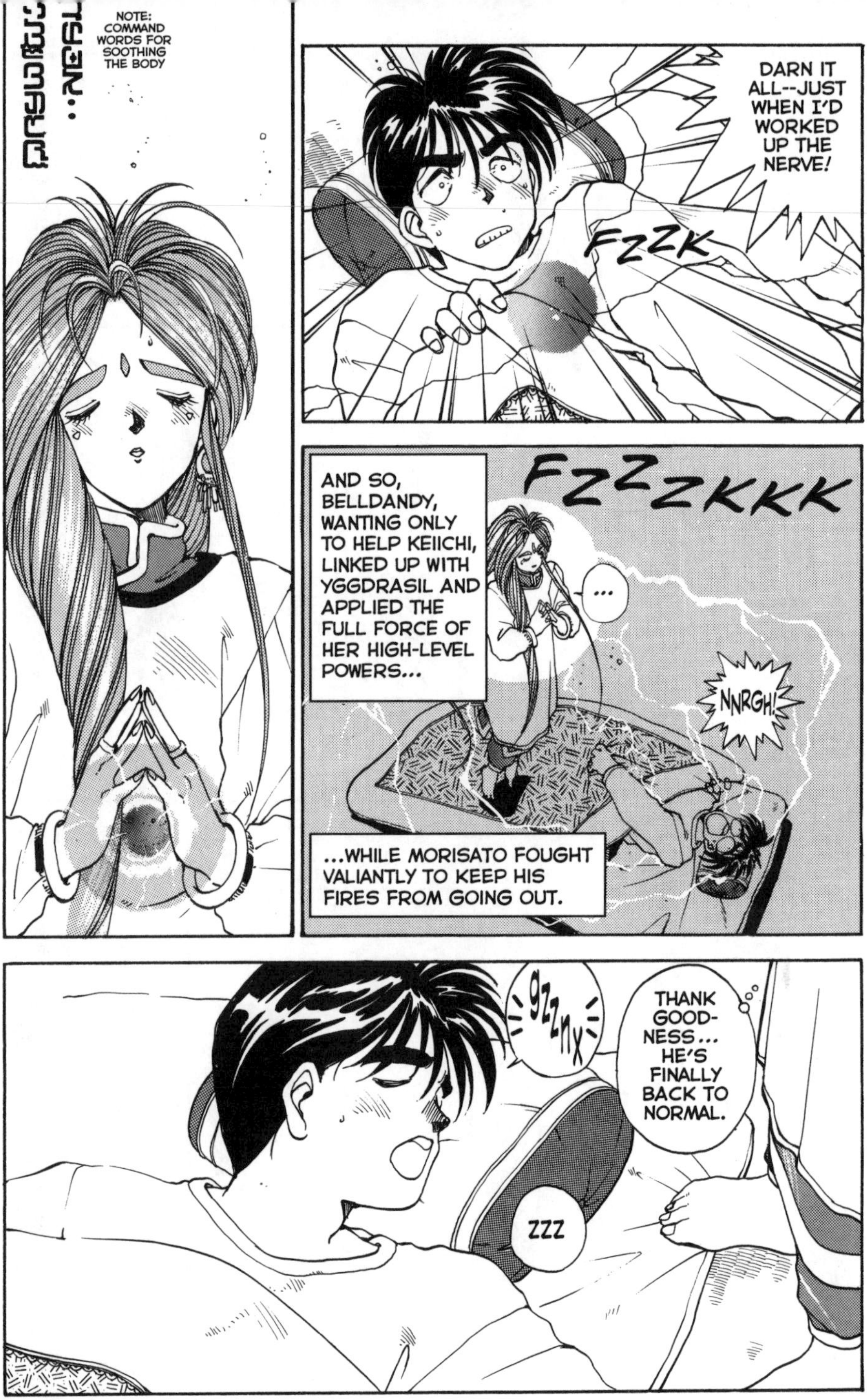
NOTE: COMMAND WORDS FOR SOOTHING THE BODY
DARN IT ALL--JUST WHEN I'D WORKED UP THE NERVE!
FZZK
AND SO, BELLDANDY, WANTING ONLY TO HELP KEIICHI, LINKED UP WITH YGGDRASIL AND APPLIED THE FULL FORCE OF HER HIGH-LEVEL POWERS...
FZZZKKK
...
NNRGH!
...WHILE MORISATO FOUGHT VALIANTLY TO KEEP HIS FIRES FROM GOING OUT.
GZZNX
THANK GOODNESS... HE'S FINALLY BACK TO NORMAL.
ZZZ

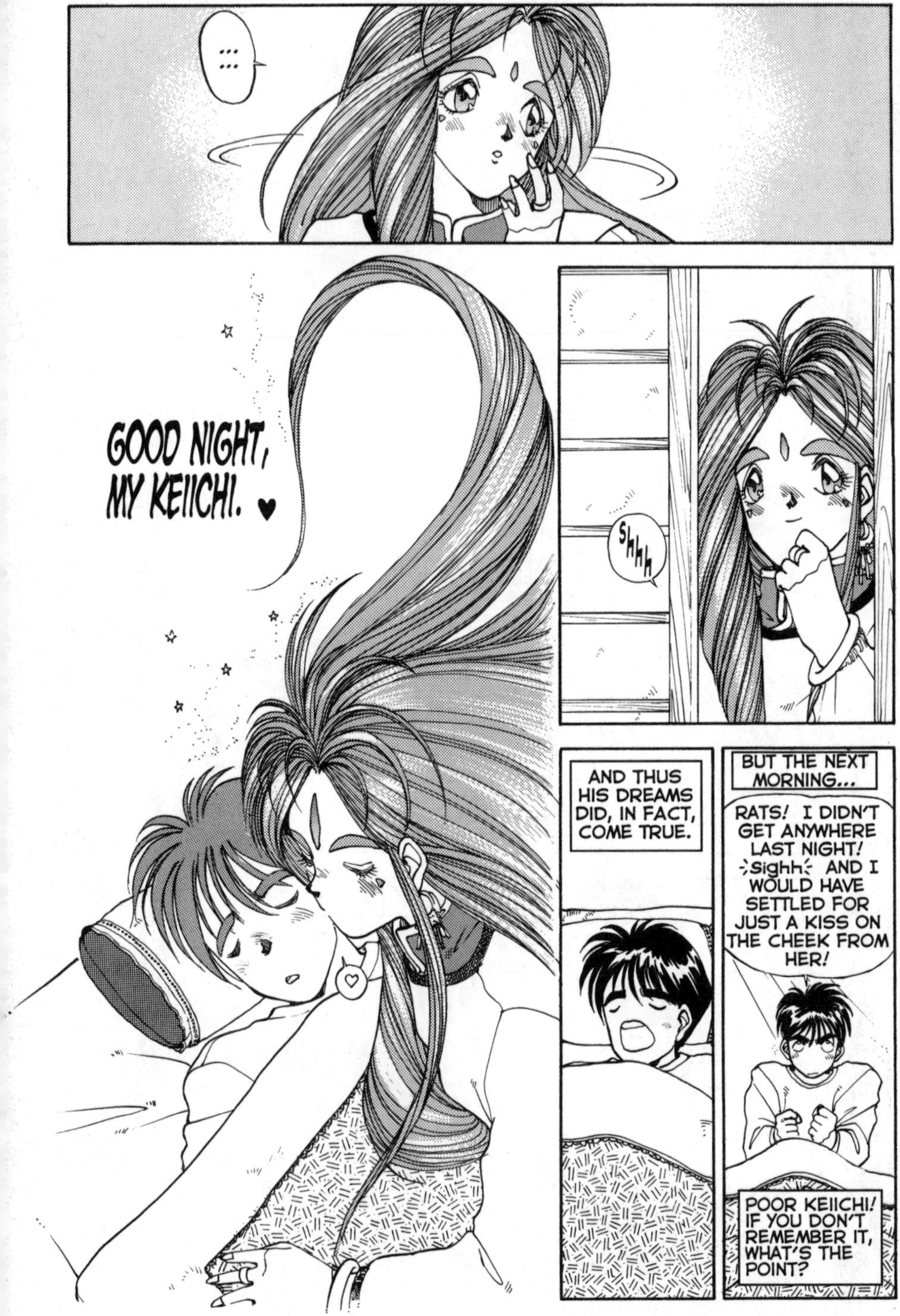

......
GOOD NIGHT, MY KEIICHI. ♥
Shhh
AND THUS HIS DREAMS DID, IN FACT, COME TRUE.
BUT THE NEXT MORNING...
RATS! I DIDN'T GET ANYWHERE LAST NIGHT! Sighh AND I WOULD HAVE SETTLED FOR JUST A KISS ON THE CHEEK FROM HER!
POOR KEIICHI! IF YOU DON'T REMEMBER IT, WHAT'S THE POINT?

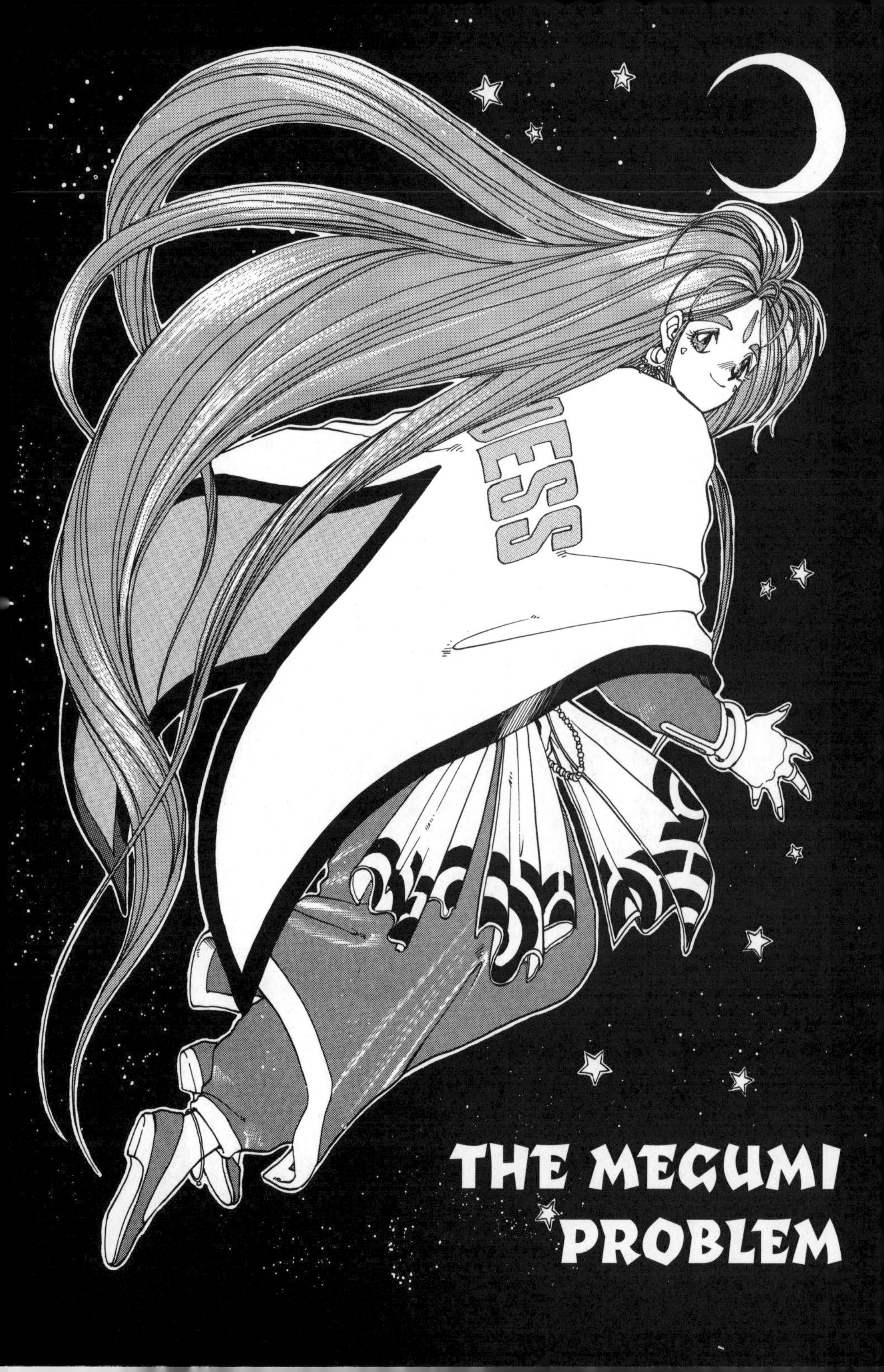

THE MEGUMI PROBLEM

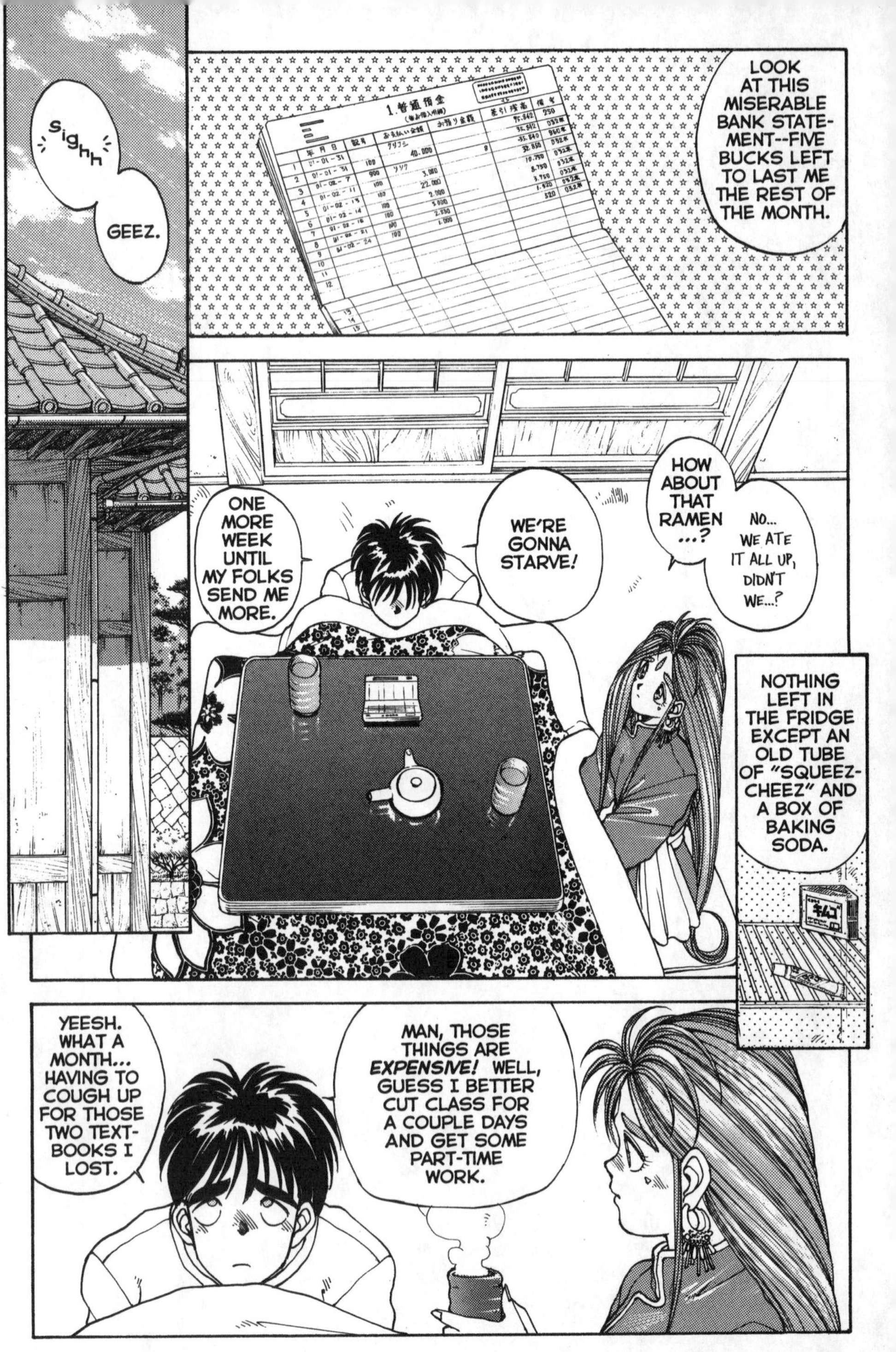
Sighh
GEEZ.
LOOK AT THIS MISERABLE BANK STATEMENT--FIVE BUCKS LEFT TO LAST ME THE REST OF THE MONTH.
1.普通預金
ONE MORE WEEK UNTIL MY FOLKS SEND ME MORE.
WE'RE GONNA STARVE!
HOW ABOUT THAT RAMEN...?
NO... WE ATE IT ALL UP, DIDN'T WE...?
NOTHING LEFT IN THE FRIDGE EXCEPT AN OLD TUBE OF "SQUEEZ-CHEEZ" AND A BOX OF BAKING SODA.
YEESH. WHAT A MONTH... HAVING TO COUGH UP FOR THOSE TWO TEXT-BOOKS I LOST.
MAN, THOSE THINGS ARE *EXPENSIVE!* WELL, GUESS I BETTER CUT CLASS FOR A COUPLE DAYS AND GET SOME PART-TIME WORK.

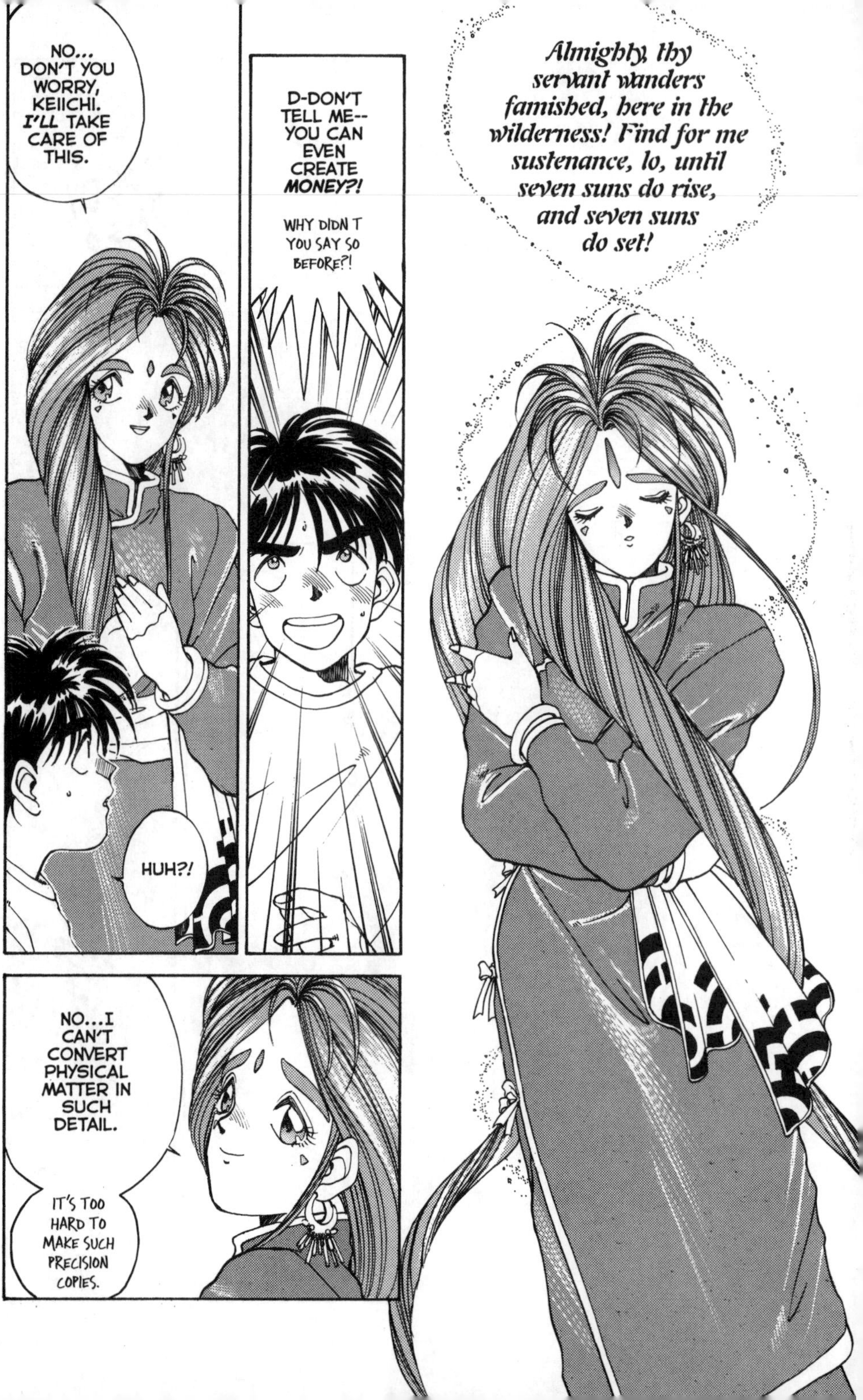
NO... DON'T YOU WORRY, KEIICHI. *I'LL* TAKE CARE OF THIS.
HUH?!
D-DON'T TELL ME-- YOU CAN EVEN CREATE *MONEY?!*
WHY DIDN T YOU SAY SO BEFORE?!
NO...I CAN'T CONVERT PHYSICAL MATTER IN SUCH DETAIL.
IT'S TOO HARD TO MAKE SUCH PRECISION COPIES.
Almighty, thy servant wanders famished, here in the wilderness! Find for me sustenance, lo, until seven suns do rise, and seven suns do set!

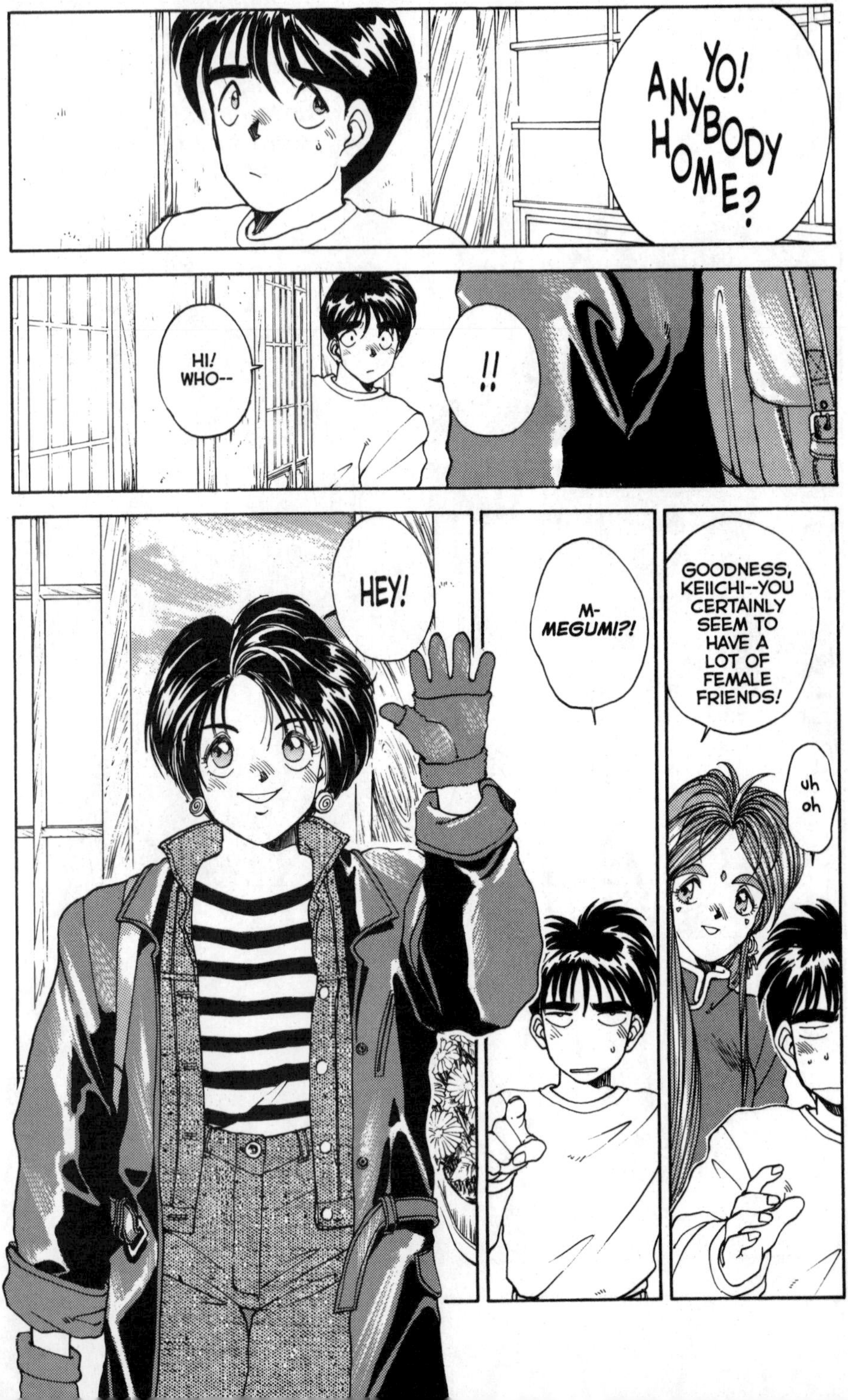
YO! ANYBODY HOME?
HI! WHO--
!!
HEY!
M-MEGUMI?!
GOODNESS, KEIICHI--YOU CERTAINLY SEEM TO HAVE A LOT OF FEMALE FRIENDS!
uh oh

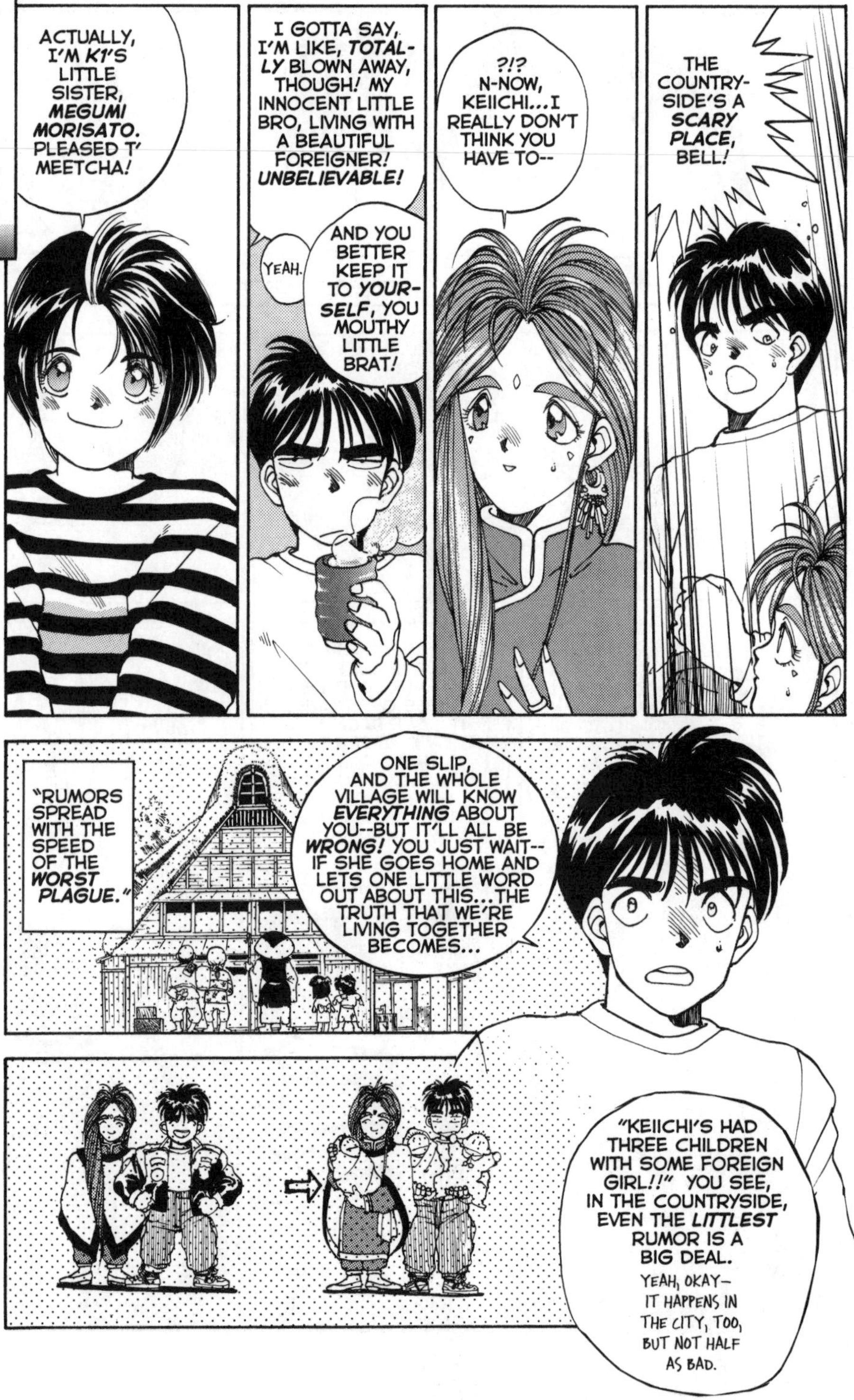
ACTUALLY, I'M K1'S LITTLE SISTER, MEGUMI MORISATO. PLEASED T' MEETCHA!
I GOTTA SAY, I'M LIKE, TOTALLY BLOWN AWAY, THOUGH! MY INNOCENT LITTLE BRO, LIVING WITH A BEAUTIFUL FOREIGNER! UNBELIEVABLE!
YEAH.
AND YOU BETTER KEEP IT TO YOURSELF, YOU MOUTHY LITTLE BRAT!
?!? N-NOW, KEIICHI...I REALLY DON'T THINK YOU HAVE TO--
THE COUNTRYSIDE'S A SCARY PLACE, BELL!
"RUMORS SPREAD WITH THE SPEED OF THE WORST PLAGUE."
ONE SLIP, AND THE WHOLE VILLAGE WILL KNOW EVERYTHING ABOUT YOU--BUT IT'LL ALL BE WRONG! YOU JUST WAIT--IF SHE GOES HOME AND LETS ONE LITTLE WORD OUT ABOUT THIS...THE TRUTH THAT WE'RE LIVING TOGETHER BECOMES...
"KEIICHI'S HAD THREE CHILDREN WITH SOME FOREIGN GIRL!!" YOU SEE, IN THE COUNTRYSIDE, EVEN THE LITTLEST RUMOR IS A BIG DEAL.
YEAH, OKAY— IT HAPPENS IN THE CITY, TOO, BUT NOT HALF AS BAD.

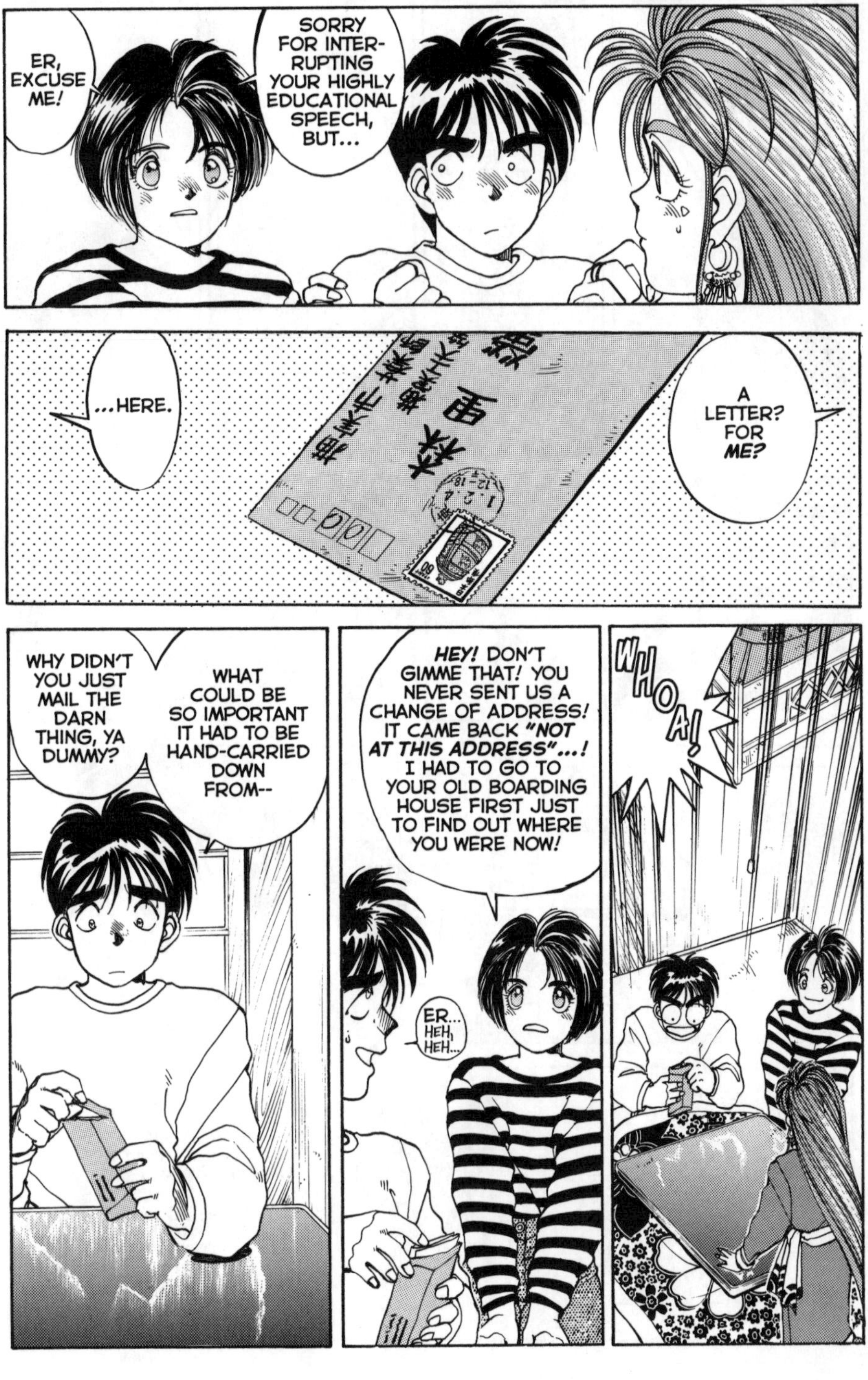
ER, EXCUSE ME!
SORRY FOR INTER-RUPTING YOUR HIGHLY EDUCATIONAL SPEECH, BUT...
...HERE.
A LETTER? FOR *ME?*
WHY DIDN'T YOU JUST MAIL THE DARN THING, YA DUMMY?
WHAT COULD BE SO IMPORTANT IT HAD TO BE HAND-CARRIED DOWN FROM--
HEY! DON'T GIMME THAT! YOU NEVER SENT US A CHANGE OF ADDRESS! IT CAME BACK *"NOT AT THIS ADDRESS"...!* I HAD TO GO TO YOUR OLD BOARDING HOUSE FIRST JUST TO FIND OUT WHERE YOU WERE NOW!
ER... HEH, HEH...
WHOA!

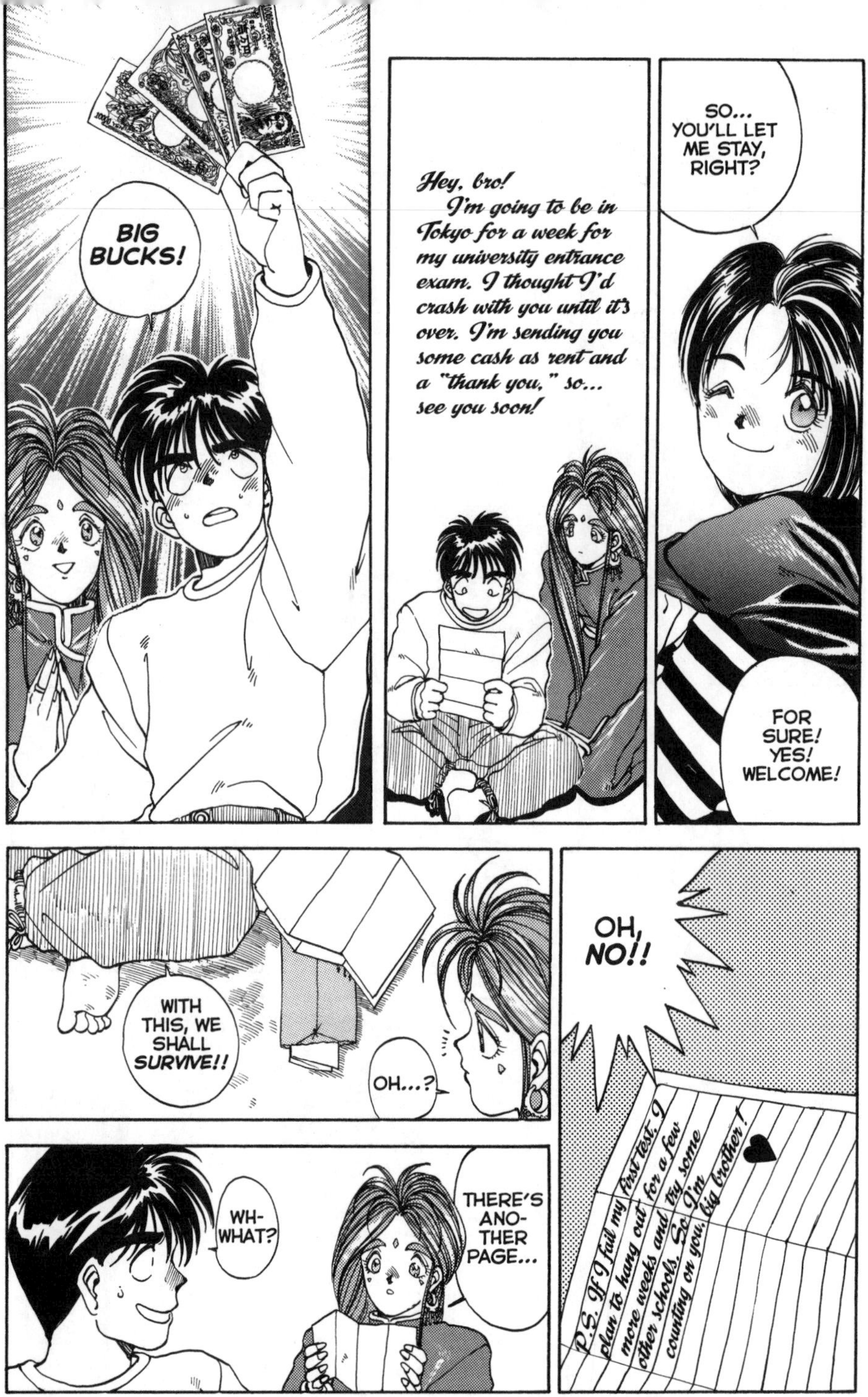
BIG BUCKS!
Hey, bro! I'm going to be in Tokyo for a week for my university entrance exam. I thought I'd crash with you until it's over. I'm sending you some cash as rent and a "thank you," so... see you soon!
SO... YOU'LL LET ME STAY, RIGHT?
FOR SURE! YES! WELCOME!
WITH THIS, WE SHALL SURVIVE!!
OH...?
WH-WHAT?
THERE'S ANOTHER PAGE...
OH, NO!!
P.S. If I fail my first test, I plan to hang out for a few more weeks and try some other schools. So I'm counting on you, big brother!

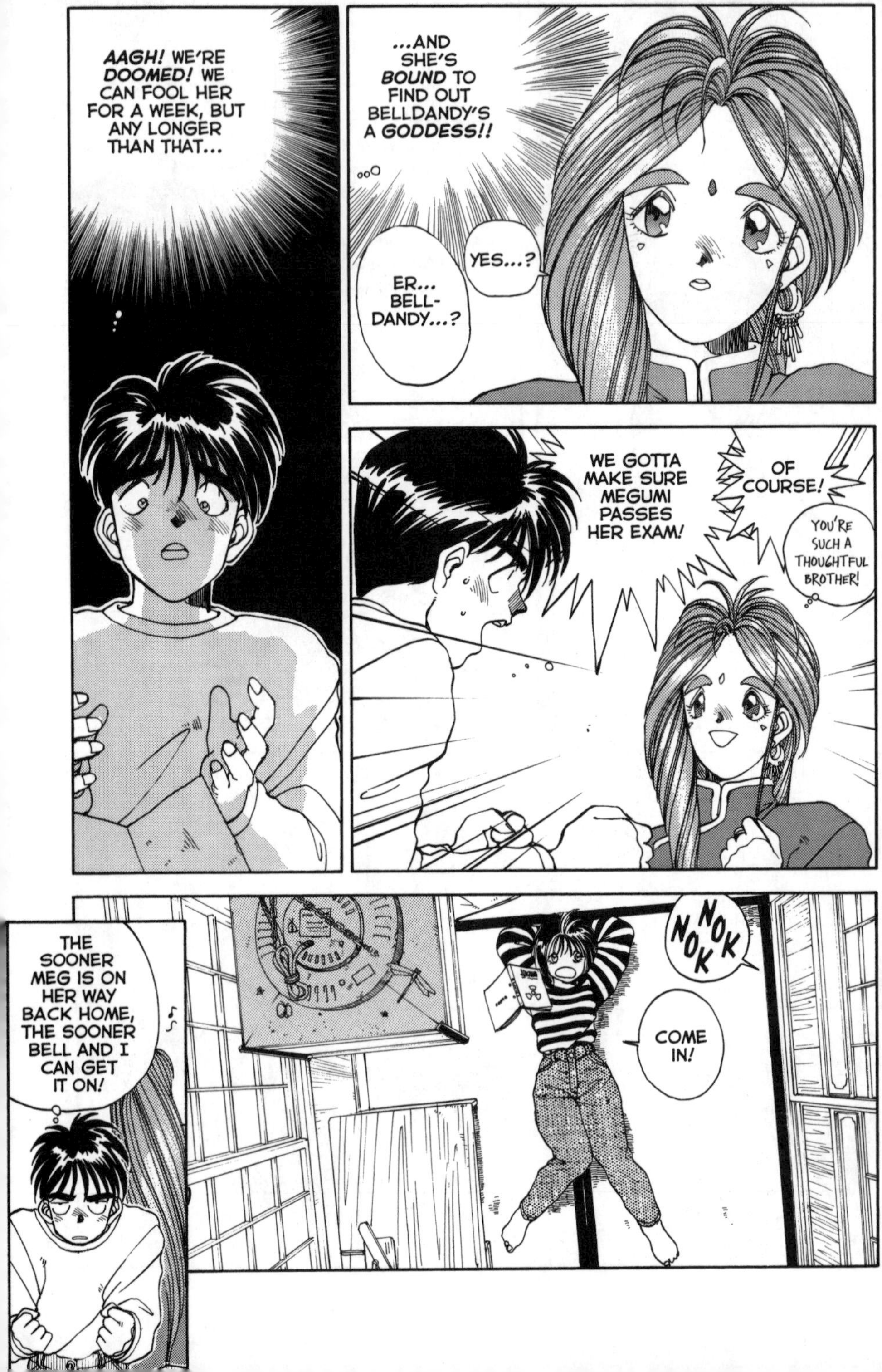
AAGH! WE'RE DOOMED! WE CAN FOOL HER FOR A WEEK, BUT ANY LONGER THAN THAT...
...AND SHE'S BOUND TO FIND OUT BELLDANDY'S A GODDESS!!
ER... BELL-DANDY...?
YES...?
WE GOTTA MAKE SURE MEGUMI PASSES HER EXAM!
OF COURSE!
YOU'RE SUCH A THOUGHTFUL BROTHER!
THE SOONER MEG IS ON HER WAY BACK HOME, THE SOONER BELL AND I CAN GET IT ON!
NOK NOK
COME IN!

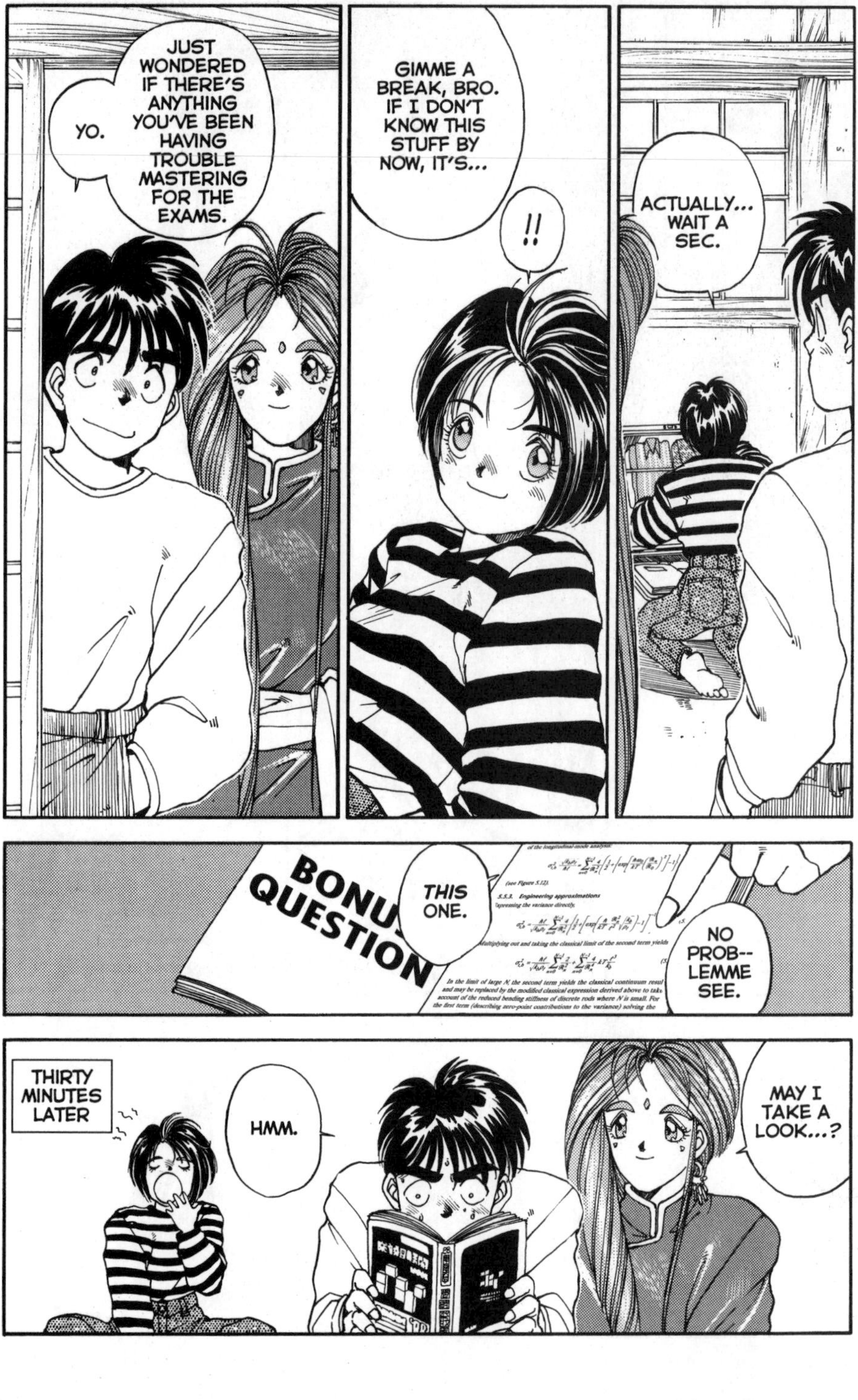
YO.
JUST WONDERED IF THERE'S ANYTHING YOU'VE BEEN HAVING TROUBLE MASTERING FOR THE EXAMS.
GIMME A BREAK, BRO. IF I DON'T KNOW THIS STUFF BY NOW, IT'S...
!!
ACTUALLY... WAIT A SEC.
BONU
QUESTION
THIS ONE.
NO PROB-- LEMME SEE.
THIRTY MINUTES LATER
HMM.
MAY I TAKE A LOOK...?

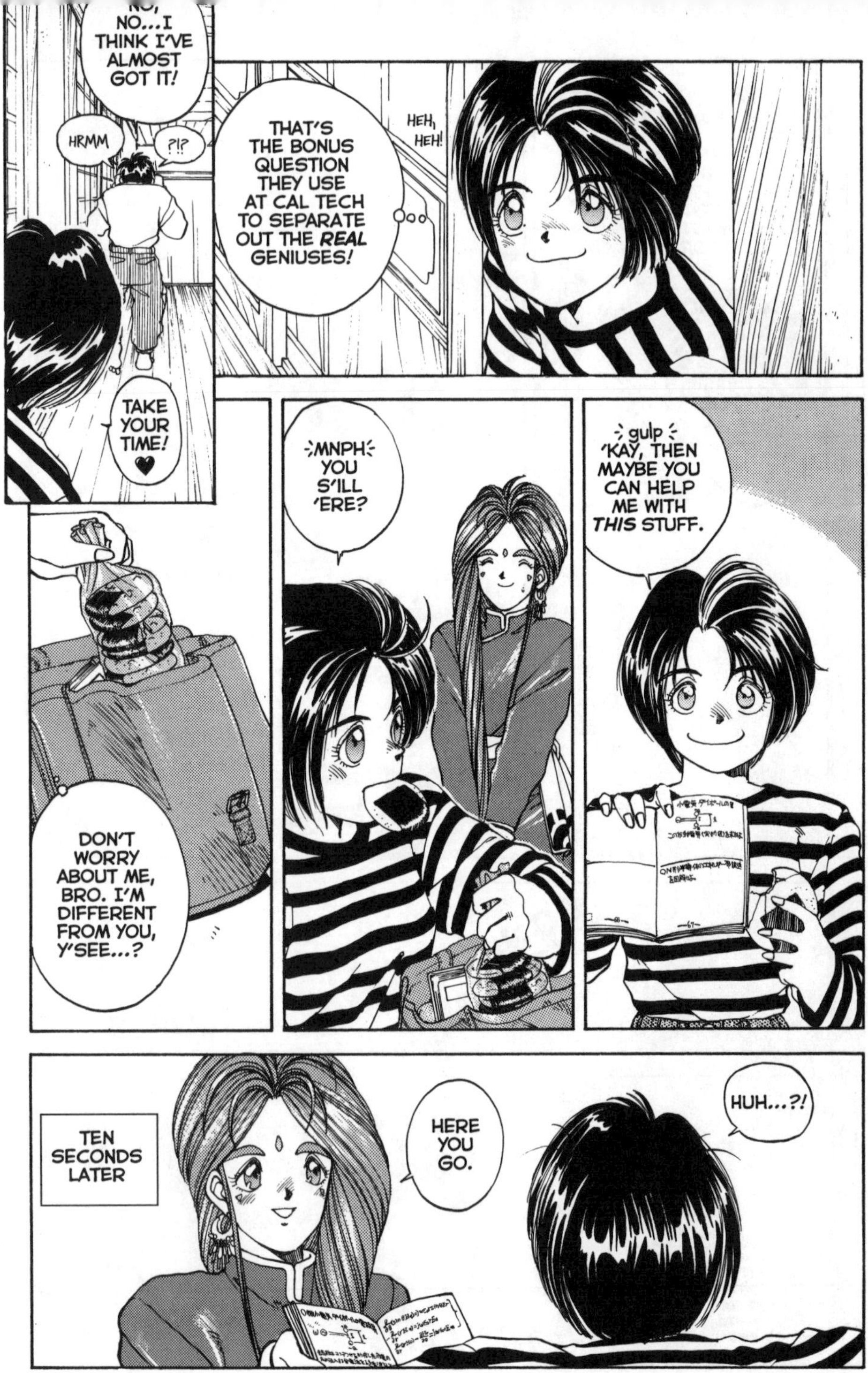
NO, NO...I THINK I'VE ALMOST GOT IT!
HRMM
?!?
TAKE YOUR TIME! ♥
THAT'S THE BONUS QUESTION THEY USE AT CAL TECH TO SEPARATE OUT THE *REAL* GENIUSES!
HEH, HEH!
DON'T WORRY ABOUT ME, BRO. I'M DIFFERENT FROM YOU, Y'SEE...?
MNPH YOU S'ILL 'ERE?
gulp 'KAY, THEN MAYBE YOU CAN HELP ME WITH *THIS* STUFF.
TEN SECONDS LATER
HERE YOU GO.
HUH...?!

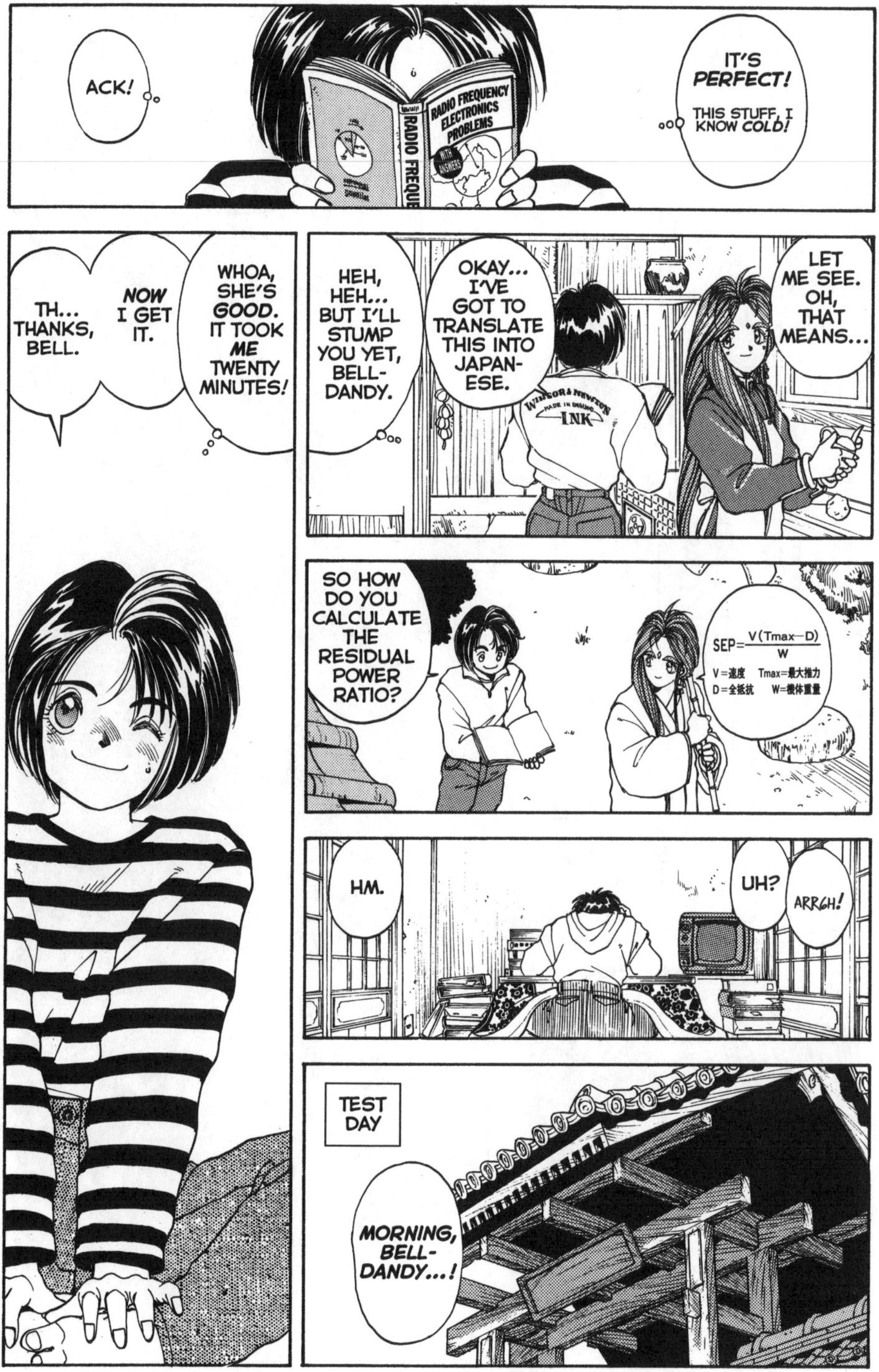
ACK!
RADIO FREQUENCY ELECTRONICS PROBLEMS
WITH ANSWERS
RADIO FREQUE
IT'S PERFECT!
THIS STUFF, I KNOW COLD!
TH... THANKS, BELL.
NOW I GET IT.
WHOA, SHE'S GOOD. IT TOOK ME TWENTY MINUTES!
HEH, HEH... BUT I'LL STUMP YOU YET, BELL-DANDY.
OKAY... I'VE GOT TO TRANSLATE THIS INTO JAPANESE.
WINSOR & NEWTON MADE IN ENGLAND INK
LET ME SEE. OH, THAT MEANS...
SO HOW DO YOU CALCULATE THE RESIDUAL POWER RATIO?
$SEP=\frac{V(T_{max}-D)}{W}$
V=速度 Tmax=最大推力
D=全抵抗 W=機体重量
HM.
UH?
ARRGH!
TEST DAY
MORNING, BELL-DANDY...!

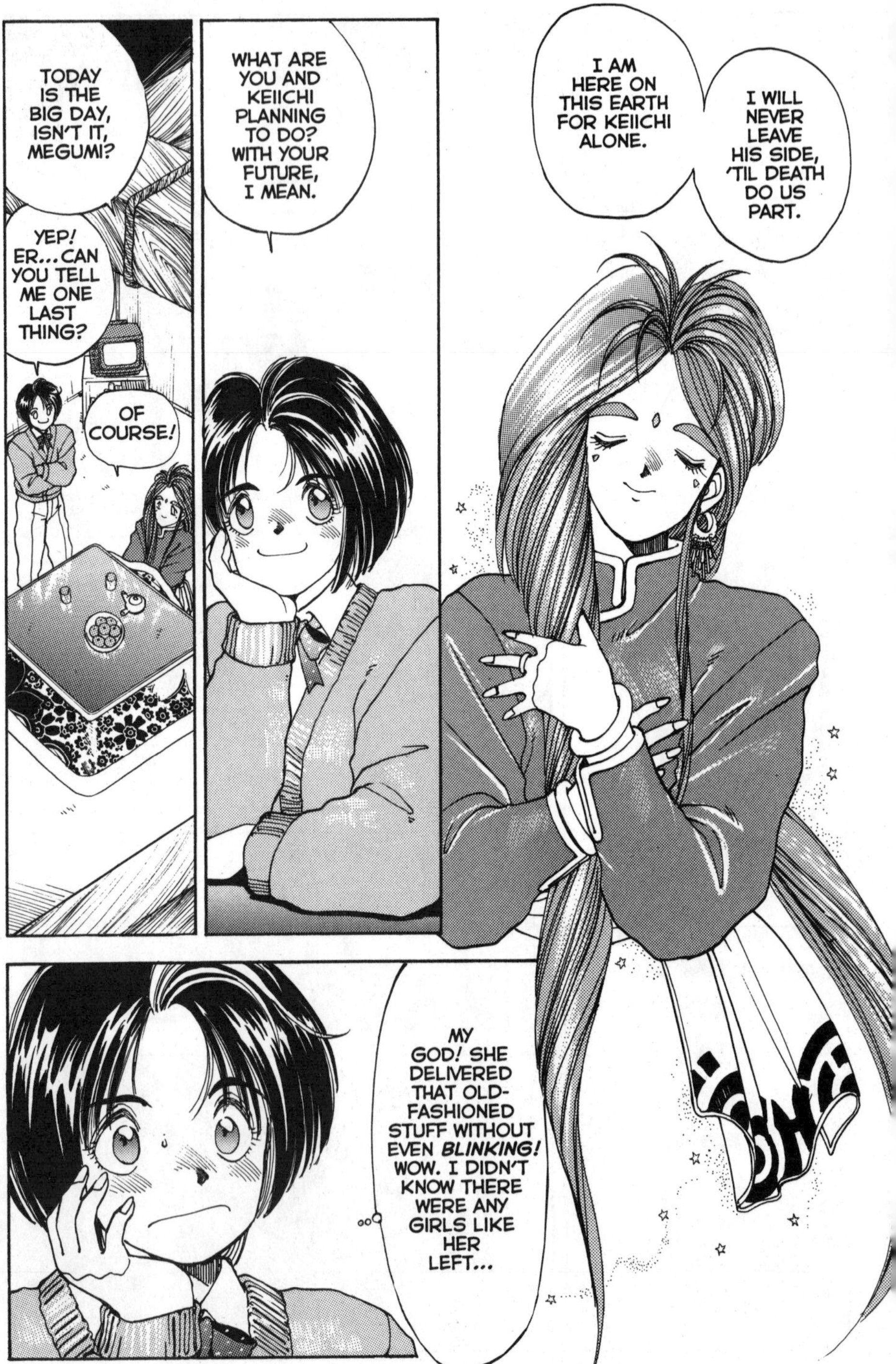
TODAY IS THE BIG DAY, ISN'T IT, MEGUMI?
YEP! ER...CAN YOU TELL ME ONE LAST THING?
OF COURSE!
WHAT ARE YOU AND KEIICHI PLANNING TO DO? WITH YOUR FUTURE, I MEAN.
I AM HERE ON THIS EARTH FOR KEIICHI ALONE.
I WILL NEVER LEAVE HIS SIDE, 'TIL DEATH DO US PART.
MY GOD! SHE DELIVERED THAT OLD-FASHIONED STUFF WITHOUT EVEN *BLINKING!* WOW. I DIDN'T KNOW THERE WERE ANY GIRLS LIKE HER LEFT...

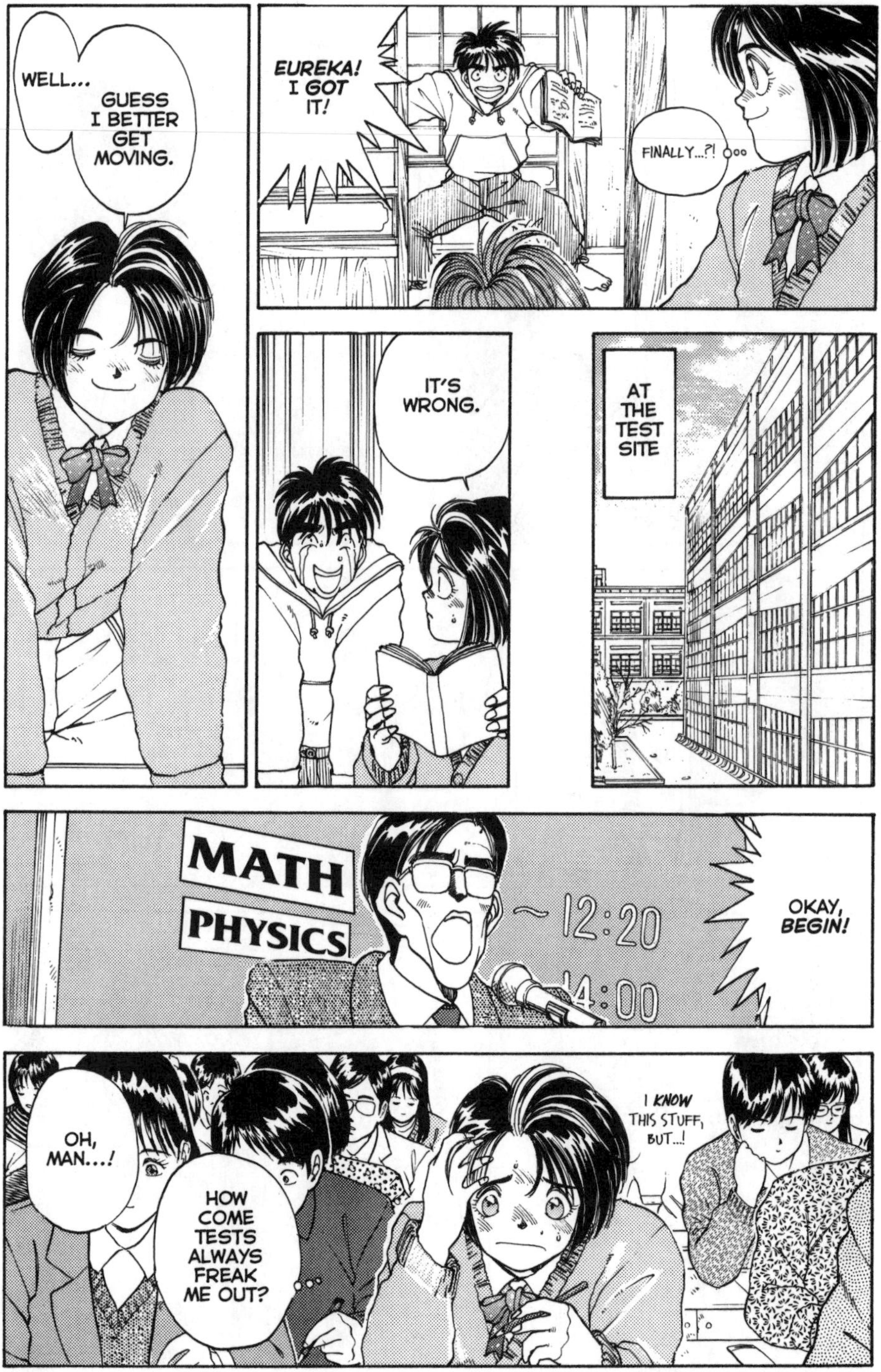
WELL... GUESS I BETTER GET MOVING.
EUREKA! I GOT IT!
FINALLY...?!
IT'S WRONG.
AT THE TEST SITE
MATH
PHYSICS
~12:20
14:00
OKAY, BEGIN!
OH, MAN...!
HOW COME TESTS ALWAYS FREAK ME OUT?
I KNOW THIS STUFF, BUT...!

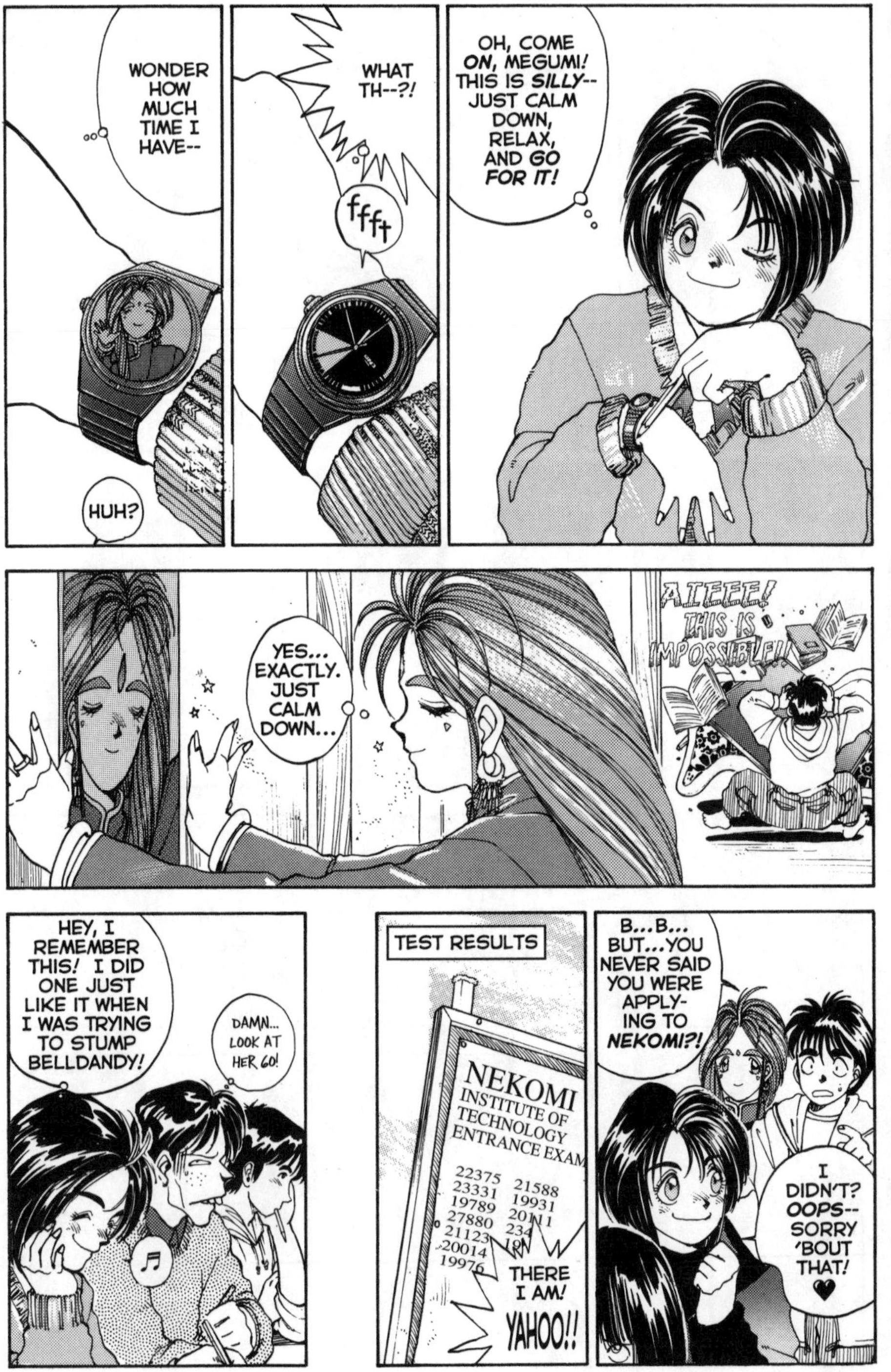
WONDER HOW MUCH TIME I HAVE--
HUH?
WHAT TH--?!
ffft
OH, COME ON, MEGUMI! THIS IS SILLY-- JUST CALM DOWN, RELAX, AND GO FOR IT!
YES... EXACTLY. JUST CALM DOWN...
AIEEE! THIS IS IMPOSSIBLE!!
HEY, I REMEMBER THIS! I DID ONE JUST LIKE IT WHEN I WAS TRYING TO STUMP BELLDANDY!
DAMN... LOOK AT HER GO!
TEST RESULTS
NEKOMI INSTITUTE OF TECHNOLOGY ENTRANCE EXAM
22375 23331 19789 27880 21123 20014 19976
21588 19931 20111
THERE I AM!
YAHOO!!
B...B... BUT...YOU NEVER SAID YOU WERE APPLYING TO NEKOMI?!
I DIDN'T? OOPS-- SORRY 'BOUT THAT!